Getting Started with Oracle Hyperion Planning 11

Design, configure, and implement a robust planning, budgeting, and forecasting solution for your organization using Oracle Hyperion Planning

Enti Sandeep Reddy

BIRMINGHAM - MUMBAI

Getting Started with Oracle Hyperion Planning 11

First published: September 2011

Production Reference: 1190911

Published by Packt Publishing Ltd.
Livery Place
35 Livery Street
Birmingham B3 2PB, UK.

ISBN 978-1-84968-138-4

www.packtpub.com

Cover Image by David Guettirrez (bilbaorocker@yahoo.co.uk)

Credits

Author
Enti Sandeep Reddy

Reviewers
Muhammed Jamshed Nawaz
Abhishek Sharma

Acquisition Editor
Amey Kanse

Development Editor
Amey Kanse

Technical Editors
Pooja Pandey
Aaron Rosario
Mohd. Sahil
Vanjeet D'souza
Conrad Sardinha

Copy Editor
Leonard D'Silva

Project Coordinators
Zainab Bagraswala
Vincila Colaco

Proofreader
Lesley Harrison

Indexers
Monica Ajmera
Rekha Nair

Graphics
Geetanjali Sawant

Production Coordinator
Arvindkumar Gupta

Cover Work
Arvindkumar Gupta

About the Author

Enti Sandeep Reddy, Consultant, is a recognized expert in the field of Oracle Enterprise Performance Management. He has been working on Hyperion products from version 7x onwards and is a certified Hyperion Consultant.

Reddy is a computer science engineer, holds a Masters Degree in Computer Science from International Institute of Information Technology, Pune, India.

He has helped numerous prospects making them realize the importance of Oracle Hyperion Solutions and supported some of the largest Oracle Hyperion Planning and Oracle Essbase implementations for several high-profile clients. He enjoys contributing to public forums and covering Oracle EPM through his site at www.hyperionconsultancy.com.

I would like to thank my parents (Enti Malla Reddy and Lakshmi Bai) and my brother E. Nanda Kishore Reddy, who taught me the very basics of life.

This book could never have been completed without the support and patience of my wife. Thank you Vaishnavi Sargod. Though, she knew naught of Hyperion, she has been more helpful than any co-author of a book, in terms of her encouragement and support. I would also like to remember my lovely in-laws, the Sargod family, especially the gracious Shyla Ravindra.

The staff at Packt Publication has done a spectacular job of getting this book to production. Amey Kanse organized the whole thing, Zainab and Vincila have been taking care of the deadlines and reminders and Pooja, helped with technical editions. Thanks to the entire team for enduring with the development of such a long book.

About the Reviewers

Abhishek Sharma is currently working as a Principal consultant in Oracle and has experience over 8 years in the field of Oracle Enterprise Performance Management. He has deployed Hyperion Planning solution acrossdifferent domains like IT, Manufacturing, Financeservices.

He loves reading and learning about the new things in Oracle BI space.

Muhammed Jamshaid Nawaz has over 6 years of proven track record of consulting and application development activities. He has a rich experience in the areas of Enterprise Performance Management, Business Process Management, and Enterprise Content Management with substantial knowledge of Oracle products including Hyperion Planning, Essbase, FDQM, OBIEE, BI Apps, and ODI. He holds certifications in various products including Hyperion Essbase and IBM Content Manager.

He worked as a Technical Consultant for over three years with IBM GBS Pakistan and is currently working as a Senior Consultant with Inplenion Business Consulting MEA based in Dubai, UAE.

Jamshaid actively participates in technology writing and reviewing activities. He has also co-authored an IBM Redbook, *Leading Practices for WebSphere Dynamic Process Edition V6.2* (http://www.redbooks.ibm.com/abstracts/SG247776.html)

www.PacktPub.com

Support files, eBooks, discount offers and more

You might want to visit www.PacktPub.com for support files and downloads related to your book.

Did you know that Packt offers eBook versions of every book published, with PDF and ePub files available? You can upgrade to the eBook version at www.PacktPub.com and as a print book customer, you are entitled to a discount on the eBook copy. Get in touch with us at service@packtpub.com for more details.

At www.PacktPub.com, you can also read a collection of free technical articles, sign up for a range of free newsletters and receive exclusive discounts and offers on Packt books and eBooks.

http://PacktLib.PacktPub.com

Do you need instant solutions to your IT questions? PacktLib is Packt's online digital book library. Here, you can access, read and search across Packt's entire library of books.

Why Subscribe?

- Fully searchable across every book published by Packt
- Copy and paste, print and bookmark content
- On demand and accessible via web browser

Free Access for Packt account holders

If you have an account with Packt at www.PacktPub.com, you can use this to access PacktLib today and view nine entirely free books. Simply use your login credentials for immediate access.

Instant Updates on New Packt Books

Get notified! Find out when new books are published by following @PacktEnterprise on Twitter, or the *Packt Enterprise* Facebook page.

Table of Contents

Preface

Oracle Hyperion Planning is one of the many products in the Oracle Enterprise Performance Management software suite, an industry-leading Business Intelligence software package. The primary focus of the Hyperion Planning product is to provide a planning, budgeting, and forecasting solution that helps you manage and coordinate all your business planning and budgeting needs.

This book is a practical guide to implementing a Hyperion Planning solution in your organization, which addresses all your planning, budgeting, and forecasting needs.

You will begin with the installation of Hyperion Planning and then design Planning applications as per some example user requirements. You will then learn how to create the planning objects. Next, the book moves on to explaining important concepts within Hyperion Planning such as data forms, task lists, business rule, validation rules, and workflows, with the help of many real-world examples to maximize your learning. Towards the end of the book, you will learn about user provisioning and access rights and budget process management.

What this book covers

Chapter 1, Getting Started with Oracle Hyperion Planning, covers the basic definitions of planning, budgeting, and forecasting. It discusses the importance of budget software and introduces Oracle Hyperion Planning. It also explains the process of Oracle Hyperion Planning application. Finally, it introduces Oracle Hyperion Planning architecture along with its connected products.

Chapter 2, Installation and Configuration, covers Oracle EPM architecture and deployment plans. It details us on how to install and configure Oracle Hyperion Planning and its complementing products.

Chapter 3, Introduction to Hyperion Planning Dimensions, introduces single-currency application and multi-currency applications. It also introduces the standard dimension of a typical Planning application.

Chapter 4, Creating an Oracle Hyperion Planning Application, depicts how we are going to create our first Planning application.

Chapter 5, Creating a Hyperion Planning Application (EPMA), teaches us how to add content to our site in the form of multimedia, listing/review apps, and so on.

Chapter 6, Settings, explains all the settings, which include dimension settings, performance settings, and evaluation order. It explores the area of Planning application design.

Chapter 7, Loading Metadata, introduces Planning Metadata and teaches how to load dimension and members, that is,metadata into a Planning application.

Chapter 8, Mastering Data Form, starts with introduction of the importance of data forms and explores into the areas of data form structure, its properties and finally explains the process of data form creation.

Chapter 9, Data Entry, explains the typical data entry operation involved in budgeting process and depicts all the options available to the end user or planner in a data form.

Chapter 10, Data Validation Rules, introduces the concept of validation rules and alter explains the process of validation rule creation. It also explains the importance and the relationship between company policies and validation rules.

Chapter 11, Security, explores the security aspect of the application. It explains user authentication, authorization and also helps in understanding data security and object security in Hyperion Planning application.

Chapter 12, Budget Process Management, introduces Budget workflow process and explains the planning unit hierarchy in detail.

Chapter 13, Mastering Budget Process Management, advances chapter demonstrates workflows of all three process management templates—free form, bottom up and distributed.

Chapter 14, Tasks List, talks all about task lists; it introduces and also explains the process of creating task lists in Planning application.

Chapter 15, Business Rules, explains different ways of calculating in Planning application. It introduces Business rules of Hyperion planning application and demonstrated the creation process as well.

Chapter 16, Advanced Business Rules, explores the advanced topics of Variables and runtime prompts of Business rules.

Who this book is for

If you want to successfully implement Oracle Hyperion Planning solutions, then this book is for you. Familiarity with Oracle Essbase and OLAP would be beneficial but is not essential.

While the book is intended for beginners, even experienced Planning developers and users will benefit from this book.

Conventions

In this book, you will find a number of styles of text that distinguish between different kinds of information. Here are some examples of these styles, and an explanation of their meaning.

Code words in text are shown as follows: "Create a folder DOWNLOAD_LOCATION."

New terms and **important words** are shown in bold. Words that you see on the screen, in menus or dialog boxes for example, appear in thetext like this: "Select **Yes To All** every time it pops the given window."

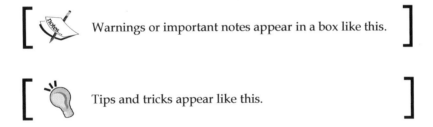

Warnings or important notes appear in a box like this.

Tips and tricks appear like this.

Reader feedback

Feedback from our readers is always welcome. Let us know what you think about this book—what you liked or may have disliked. Reader feedback is important for us to develop titles that you really get the most out of.

To send us general feedback, simply sendan e-mail to feedback@packtpub.com, and mention the book title viathe subject of your message.

If there is a book that you need and would like to see us publish, please send us a note in the **SUGGEST A TITLE** form on www.packtpub.com or e-mail suggest@packtpub.com.

If there is a topic that you have expertise in and you are interested in either writing or contributing to a book on, see our author guide on www.packtpub.com/authors.

Customer support

Now that you are the proud owner of a Packt book, we have a number of things to help you to get the most from your purchase.

Errata

Although we have taken every care to ensure the accuracy of our content, mistakes do happen. If you find a mistake in one of our books—maybe a mistake in the text or the code—we would be grateful if you would report this to us. By doing so, you can save other readers from frustration and help us improve subsequent versions of this book. If you find any errata, please report them by visiting http://www. packtpub.com/support, selecting your book, clicking on the **let us know** link, and entering the details of your errata. Once your errata are verified, your submission will be accepted and the errata will be uploaded on our website, or added to any list of existing errata, under the Errata section of that title. Any existing errata can be viewed by selecting your title from http://www.packtpub.com/support.

Piracy

Piracy of copyright material on the Internet is an ongoing problem across all media. At Packt, we take the protection of our copyright and licenses very seriously. If you come across any illegal copies of our works, in any form, on the Internet, please provide us with the location address or website name immediately so that we can pursue a remedy.

Please contact us at copyright@packtpub.comwith a link to the suspected pirated material.

We appreciate your help in protecting our authors, and our ability to bring you valuable content.

Questions

You can contact us at questions@packtpub.com if you are having a problem with any aspect of the book, and we will do our best to address it.

1
Getting Started with Oracle Hyperion Planning

He who fails to plan, plans to fail.

— Winston Churchill

Welcome!

In this first chapter, we will understand the basics of Oracle Hyperion Planning. In the process of understanding the basics of Oracle Hyperion Planning, we are going to introduce the gamut of complementing products for Oracle **Enterprise Performance Management (EPM)**. The chapter covers the following sections:

- **Planning, budgeting, and forecasting**: In this section, we'll understand the basic definitions of planning, budgeting and forecasting with an example.

- **Budget software and Oracle Hyperion Planning**: We'll understand the importance of budget software. We'll look into the current challenges faced in the budgeting process and how Oracle Hyperion Planning addresses them.

- **Oracle Hyperion Planning Architecture**: In this section, we'll learn about the components of Oracle Hyperion Planning architecture.

Planning, budgeting, and forecasting

Oracle Hyperion Planning is defined as a Web-based planning, budgeting, and forecasting software. We'll understand these three terms in this section with the help of some casual conversation between two gentlemen: John and Sam, given as follows:

John: Sam! Congratulations on your newly-bought apartment. How did you manage to buy it, considering it's a very expensive apartment worth 80,000 USD?

Sam: Thanks John. I have been saving money for some time to buy an apartment and managed to save 30,000 USD. The rest I got by taking out a home loan of 50,000 USD over a period of 15 years. I am pretty sure that apartment rates are going to increase in the near future.

John: That's good. But, how advisable is it, financially, to take such a huge home loan, considering you are going to re-pay a lot of money in the form of EMI's (Equated Monthly Installment to bank) every month? I hope, you don't end up paying more money to the bank.

Sam: Yes, you are right and that's the reason I am planning to repay the whole home loan amount in eight years rather than paying all 15 years and I forecast that the apartment price will appreciate from 80K USD to 100 K USD in three years. To save more money, I have started cutting down my personal expenses such as shopping, travel, and so on.

John: That's smart, so you have done all your planning already! Good luck.

This is a conversation that we might have heard or engaged in. The important observation from this conversation is that Sam has been 'planning'. Yes, the keyword is *planning*.

He planned and as per his plan, he saved money, and approached a bank for a home loan. He also planned to repay the loan amount quickly and he forecasts that his apartment price will appreciate by 20K USD in the duration of three years.

It would have not been possible for Sam to achieve his goal of buying an apartment without proper planning. If Sam has been living his life as if there is no tomorrow, then there is no plan and there is no prosperity too.

Therefore, individuals such as Sam plan and so do the corporate organizations. No organization is in the business with an objective to achieve nothing or make losses. The common goal is profit making that is generating more revenue. To achieve so, organizations plan.

Now, let us understand the definitions of planning, budgeting, and forecasting, and also understand the hidden, subtle differences between them.

Planning

The process of preparing for the future is planning. As a part of planning, Sam has to firstly set his goal. His goal was to purchase an apartment. To achieve it, Sam has to do initial research of his preferred location to buy an apartment, find out the market price, figure out the reputed builders, and many other such factors.

After rounding an apartment to buy, he'll start his financial plan to save and approach a bank for home loan. This is a simple plan. Now, let us try to relate the same to an organization.

Organizations initially set their goals or targets and plan accordingly. Hence, we define **planning** as the set of activities to achieve goal in preparing the future.

As a part of planning, generally, an organization has two types of plans:

- **Strategic planning**: A strategic plan includes the goals and objectives of an organization. It looks into its current business and aims by setting goals of what it wants to be in future. It includes a comprehensive strategic plan of how to achieve and it is at a very high level of an organization.

- **Operational planning**: This is a set of detailed guidelines or a detailed plan to be executed to achieve the strategic plan. This planning involves the granular details of setting the responsibilities of people, departments and divisions. Hence, it's rightly called 'operational'.

We'll learn more about these plan types from the Oracle Hyperion Planning application perspective in *Chapter 4, How to create an Oracle Hyperion Planning Application*.

Budgeting

We might have seen news papers printing in bold "*United states budget for fiscal year 2010...*" These are the budgets by the government of US, hence, it's defined as the 'government budget'. Likewise, organizations do budgeting, which is defined as a 'corporate budget', which is where our interest lies.

> **What is a budget?**
>
> **A budget** in an organization is a formal plan that may be short term (one year) or long term (three years or more) and it's aimed to control its operations and help the management in decision making process.

In short, budgeting in an organization is planning how to spend money or how to allocate money to different departments or divisions. In the previous example, Sam had initially set the goal of buying an apartment and made a plan, and as part of his planning, Sam budgetted to allocate more money to bank savings and less money to personal expenses such as travel.

Therefore, we can say that budgeting is a part of planning and without budgeting the planning cannot be successful in achieving the organizational or strategic goal.

Forecasting

Forecast is to predict the future. We need to realize the fact that planning deals with future as well.

We know that the future is always uncertain and we cannot make any planning in uncertainty. Therefore, we make few assumptions about the future, which is called **forecasting**. In our previous example, Sam assumes that the price of the apartment will increase in near future and his forecast is appreciation of his apartment's price from 80K USD to 100K USD.

We clearly see that forecast indicates the probable course of future events, whereas planning looks at actions in terms of what is to be done, how to do it, and when it should be done.

 Conclusively, forecasting acts as a prerequisite to planning and budgeting is a part of planning activity. These three activities are intertwined but yet they are different.

Budgeting software and Oracle Hyperion Planning

Currently, many organizations do planning, budgeting, and forecasting using spreadsheet programs such as Excel. This has been the case for many years. But, Excel spreadsheets have inherent disadvantages. The following are a few of the challenges that organizations face while performing planning, budgeting, and forecasting in Excel spreadsheets.

- **Time taken**: Working manually with Excel templates consumes more time.
- **Data integrity**: There is no centralized data storage and data lies in many Excel sheets. Hence, the information is prone to errors and is not very reliable.
- **Cost**: As it's a manually - driven process on Excel, the budgeting process needs many people to work on and it indirectly impacts the cost.

- **Scalability and adaptability**: Any organizational changes need to be captured right from the start in Excel, which is a very tedious, time consuming, and manually-driven activity.

Organizations have started to realize that Excel spreadsheets are not financial applications. In recent years, enterprise budget applications have started replacing spreadsheets, and Oracle Hyperion planning is one of the leading budgeting and planning applications in the market.

Oracle Hyperion Planning is defined by Oracle as a centralized, Web-based planning, budgeting, and forecasting solution that drives collaborative, integrated, event-based planning processes throughout the enterprise.

Here is the list of benefits that an organization would enjoy with Oracle Hyperion Planning:

- **Time taken**: The first and foremost benefit is that it eliminates the cumbersome Excel template maintenance and it shortens the planning cycle time.
- **Data integrity**: As data is stored in a centralized place and with the reliable security feature of Oracle Hyperion planning, integrity of data is upheld.
- **Cost**: It's a Web-based centralized application and does not need manual intervention, unlike Excel spreadsheets. Hence, the cost of maintenance comes down.
- **Scalability and adaptability**: Oracle Hyperion Planning is highly scalable and at the same time it does not impact the performance. Coming to adaptability, changes are incorporated into planning system with ease rather than starting from square one.

There are other benefits of Oracle Hyperion planning, listed as follows:

- The data entry, version control, process control, reporting and analysis is all done through a single interface in Oracle Hyperion Planning
- Powerful workflow and process management, as well as enhanced features for audit trials, task lists, e-mail notifications, and alerts
- Sophisticated reporting and analysis with drill down capabilities

However, the underlying planning and budgeting remains fundamentally unchanged but the software of Oracle Hyperion planning does it in a more reliable and efficient manner.

Oracle Hyperion Planning Architecture

In this section, we'll understand the following topics:

- **Oracle Planning Product Architecture**: We'll introduce and explore all the components of Oracle Hyperion Planning architecture

- **Oracle Hyperion Planning Process flow**: In this section, we'll learn how the components of Oracle Hyperion Planning communicate when an end user logs into a Planning application

- **Oracle Planning Solution Architecture**: In this section, we'll learn how additional products such as ODI, FDQM, and OBI are a part of a typical Oracle Hyperion Planning solution in an implementation

- **Oracle EPM**: We'll explore the basic idea of Oracle EPM and also learn where Oracle Hyperion Planning fits in the scheme of Oracle EPM products

Firstly, Oracle Hyperion Planning is always bundled with other Oracle Hyperion products that enhance its capabilities. When we buy the software from Oracle, it's available in three licensed packages. They are as follows:

- **Hyperion Planning Plus**: This is the most basic license package available. The list of products available in these packages is mentioned in the following table.

- **Hyperion Planning Suite**: This is a combination of Hyperion planning plus along with another product called 'Oracle Integrated Operational Planning'.

- **Hyperion Enterprise Planning suite**: As the name suggests, this package not only includes the basic products of Hyperion Planning Plus, but also has a lot of additional products such as Hyperion Workforce Planning and Hyperion Capital Asset Planning, as shown in the following table:

Hyperion Planning Plus	Hyperion Planning Suite	Hyperion Enterprise Planning Suite
Hyperion Planning	Hyperion Planning Plus	Hyperion Planning Plus
Hyperion Essbase	Oracle Integrated Operational Planning	Hyperion Workforce Planning
Hyperion Essbase Administration Services		Hyperion Capital Asset Planning
Oracle EPM Workspace		Oracle Integrated Operational Planning
Hyperion Business Rules		Oracle Integrated Margin Planning
Hyperion Calculation manager		Hyperion Profitability and Cost Management
Hyperion Shared Services		
Hyperion Financial Reporting		
Hyperion Web Analysis		
Oracle Data Integrator		
Hyperion Smart View		
Hyperion WebLogic		

As we see, there are many additional products mentioned in Hyperion Planning Suite and Hyperion Enterprise Planning Suite. They are as follows:

- **Oracle Integrated Operational Planning**: This is another module of Oracle Hyperion, which is aimed exclusively at Operational Planning.

- **Hyperion Workforce Planning**: This is a separately licensed module and as the name suggests it deals with the human resources of an organization. Hence, this module is handy in computing headcount salary and workforce-related expenses such as bonus, fringe benefits, overtime, and so on.

- **Hyperion Capital Asset Planning**: Organizations have assets such as real estate, equipment that cannot be converted into cash or revenue directly to the organization. These are defined as capital assets and Oracle Hyperion has a separate module to plan for capital assets and related expenses.

- **Oracle Integrated Margin Planning**: This is another specialized module that aids in understanding margins and Cost of Goods (COGS) of an organization.

- **Hyperion Profitability and Cost Management**: Profit for an organization depends on the cost spent. Hence, drivers of cost impact profitability and Oracle Hyperion has an offering in this space to provide insights with an objective to increase the profitability.

Oracle Hyperion Planning Product Architecture

Here, we'll understand the architecture of Hyperion Planning. This is a placeholder for detailed architecture. After we install and configure Oracle Hyperion Planning in the next chapter, *Installation and Configuration*, we would be better placed to understand all the components in detail about planning architecture. This architecture is divided into different tiers such as Client tier, Web Server, WebApp Server, Services tier, and Database tier. Hence, we'll revisit the architecture in the next chapter, where we will also cover the specifications in terms of supported operating systems, databases, application and web servers, memory and processor requirements in the *Compatibility* section in *Chapter 2*.

Broadly, Planning Product Architecture is divided into three layers, shown as follows:

- **Database Layer**
- **Application Layer**
- **Client Layer**

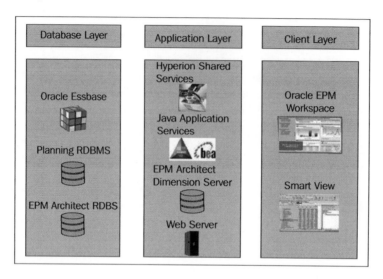

Database Layer

The database layer consists of databases both of relational and multidimensional in nature. Examples of relational databases are Oracle, SQL server, and so on (the complete list of compatible relational databases is covered in *Chapter 2, Installation and Configuration* under the section *Prerequisites*) and an example of a multidimensional database is Oracle Essbase.

- Relational Database (RDBMS)
- Oracle Essbase

Oracle Hyperion Planning is connected to both Oracle Essbase and Relational Database and in the following image, we can see the list of objects saved in RDBMS and Oracle Essbase separately:

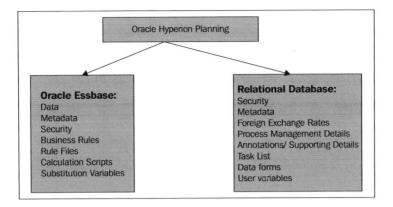

RDBMS

In the architecture diagram, we see both Hyperion Planning RDBMS and EPM Architect RDBMS. Oracle Hyperion Planning applications can be of two kinds— Classic and EPM architect—and both of these planning application types need a relational source. (We'll learn about Classic and EPM Architect Hyperion planning applications in *Chapter 4* and *Chapter 5*) Hence, to cater to both kinds of planning applications, we see Planning RDBMS and EPM Architect RDBMS in the previous architecture image.

This following information is saved in RDBMS of an Oracle Hyperion Planning application:

- **Security**: User privileges, system roles, and access rights of users/groups constitute security of Oracle Hyperion planning. The security of planning determines which user to access and what a user should access within a Planning application. Security is covered in depth in *Chapter 11, Security*.

- **Metadata**: Oracle Hyperion Planning application is made up of dimensions and dimensions have members. Dimension names, member names, properties of these members, and dimensions make metadata and it's stored both in Oracle Essbase and Relational source. More about planning metadata is covered in *Chapter 7, Metadata Load*.

- **Foreign exchange rates**: The rate at which one currency is converted to another is defined as exchange rate. A simple example is 47 INR (Indian Rupee) = 1 USD (United States Dollar), approximately. Organizations are no longer local; they are global and run their business in multiple countries and every country has different currency. It's becoming increasingly important for planning and budgeting application to handle the currency conversion on the fly. Oracle Hyperion Planning stores the exchange rates in the relational database and more about how Oracle Hyperion Planning application handles exchange rates can be learned in *Chapter 9, Data Entry*.

- **Process management details**: Process management is the review process of budgeting exercise in an organization. Every organization has a hierarchy and there is a defined approval process. The information includes who should promote to whom and who has the authority to finally approve. Process management has been covered in detail in *Chapter 12* and *Chapter 13*.

- **Annotations/supporting details**: Annotations are additional information and in Oracle Hyperion Planning application, we can add a document or add comments as a part of annotations to help planners in the process of planning budgeting, and forecasting.

  Supporting details are also additional information but it has in-built calculator and deals with members that are not a part of planning application dimensions.

  Annotations and supporting details are explored in detail in *Chapter 9, Data Entry*.

- **Data forms**: Data forms are Web-based spreadsheet such as grids for data entry by planners. The data form definitions are stored in a relational source, but the data that is entered into a data form is stored in Oracle Essbase. More about data forms is covered in *Chapter 8* and *Chapter 9*.

- **User variables**: User variables are created to limit the number of members displayed in a data form. A planner should see the members that are relevant to him. It hardly makes any sense for an HR planner to view members of sales team. More about user variables is covered in *Chapter 9, Data Entry*.

Oracle Essbase

Oracle Essbase is the most popular and powerful multi-dimensional online analytical processing server and Oracle Hyperion planning lies on the top of this engine. Oracle Hyperion planning essentially stores its data and consolidates in Oracle Essbase. Apart from storing the data, Oracle Hyperion Planning uses the business rules/ calculation scripts feature of Oracle Essbase.

As we see in the previous image, there is some information that is stored both in Oracle Essbase and its relational data source.

The following information is stored only in Oracle Essbase:

- **Data**: The data entered by end users or planners in planning application is stored in Oracle Essbase.

- **Calculation scripts/business rules**: In planning and budgeting, the typical calculations such as allocation computation, revenue calculation, expense calculation, balance sheet computation, and so on, can be achieved using business rules/calculation scripts. We'll learn how to write business rules in *Chapter 15* and *Chapter 16*.

- **Substitution variables**: One that takes the place of another is defined as substitute. We have dimension members such as month, year, and so on, in Oracle Hyperion Planning application. We can use substitution variables such as CurrentMonth, CurrentYear, which would refer to months and years. The substitution variables are very handy in data forms of Oracle Hyperion Planning application.

Application Layer

- Oracle Hyperion Shared Services
- Java Application Server
- EPM Architect Dimension Server
- Web Server

Oracle Hyperion Shared Services

Security of Oracle Hyperion Planning is the responsibility of Hyperion Shared Services. Hyperion Shared Services ensures the secure environment of not only Oracle Hyperion Planning but also of the whole Oracle EPM product suite. Hence, all Oracle EPM products, including Oracle Hyperion Planning rely on Hyperion Shared Services for User authentication and authorization. We can do the following security activities using Hyperion Shared Services.

- **User authentication and authorization**: Oracle Hyperion Shared Services obtains the identification credentials of a user such as user ID and password and validates these credentials against native directory of relational database or External User directories, which are corporate user identity management systems. Post authenticating, Oracle Hyperion Shared Services takes care of the user authorization too.

- **User directory configuration**: Oracle Hyperion Shared Services can be configured to external user directories such as Sun Java System Directory Server and Microsoft Active Directory, which are LDAP-based, for User Authentication.

- **User provisioning**: Oracle Shared Services provisions user and groups. Users of Oracle EPM products need to be provisioned with the roles specific to the roles of the product. For example, Oracle Hyperion Planning product has roles like Administrator, Provisioning manager, Planner, Interactive User and View User, and users are provisioned according to their usage and requirement.

More details of Hyperion Shared services can be found in *Chapter 11, Security.*

Java Application Server and Web Server

We understood that Oracle Hyperion Planning is a Web-based planning, budgeting, and forecasting application and users/planners can access the application on their browsers using a simple URL (that is an HTTP request).

A WebServer serves pages for viewing in a web browser. Hence, we need a WebServer that receives HTTP requests from users and sends out the result in response to the users upon processing the request by WebApp server.

After the WebServer receives a user's request, that is, a HTTP request, the subsequent responsibility is of Application server which serves the business logic to application programs. Therefore, J2EE Application server and a WebServer are a part of the architecture.

 Apache Tomcat and Apache Web Server have been respectively the default embedded Java container (J2EE App server) and embedded Web Server till recently. But in 11.1.2 version, Tomcat is no longer the default embedded J2EE server, it's replaced by WebLogic. Apache is no longer the default Web Server; it's replaced by Oracle HTTP Server.

The flow diagram of WebServer and AppServer is illustrated in the subsequent section of *Oracle Hyperion Planning Process Flow.*

EPM Architect Dimension Server

As said earlier that Planning application can be created in two ways – one way is Classic and the other way is using EPM architect. EPM Architect Dimension Server is applicable for Oracle Hyperion Planning applications, which are created using EPM Architect.

EPMA integrates the maintenance of Oracle Hyperion EPM products such as Hyperion Financial Management, Profitability and Cost Management, and Oracle Hyperion Planning.

We'll learn more of this in *Chapter 4, EPM Architecture.*

Client Layer

- Oracle EPM Workspace
- Smart View

Oracle EPM Workspace

Oracle EPM Workspace is the end-user web interface and is also termed as Zero foot print client, which lets a user access all Oracle EPM products including Oracle Hyperion Planning in a single portal.

Now, let us understand what is zero foot print and how Oracle EPM Workspace be rightly defined as zero foot print client.

As already mentioned, Planners/end users access Oracle Hyperion Planning either though Oracle Hyperion Planning web URL or they can access the same from Oracle EPM Workspace URL in browsers such as Internet Explorer or FireFox. Other browsers are not compatible with the current version (version 11.1.2). We'll look into the complete list of compatible browsers along with their versions in next chapter, *Installation and Configuration*.

Oracle Hyperion Planning is one of Oracle's many products. There are several other products; some are mentioned as follows:

- **Hyperion Financial Management**: This product is for financial consolidation.

- **Hyperion Performance Scorecard**: It's a Web-based scorecard solution offering from Oracle Hyperion where an organization can set its KPI's and monitor its performance.

- **ERP Integrator**: This is a new module of FDQM that helps in integration between ERP systems such as Oracle EBS to performance management applications such as Oracle Hyperion Planning and Oracle Hyperion Financial Management.

- **Oracle Business Intelligence**: This is an enterprise wide reporting solution that can make reports from all possible sources such as relational, multidimensional, and also, Oracle Hyperion Financial Management. It had a few reservations in making reports from multidimensional sources such as Oracle Essbase, but the latest release of 11g had ironed out all the issues of past, and now it's the mega star of all reporting products. And yes, we can create Oracle Hyperion Planning reports too.

- **Profitability and Cost Management**: Profit of an organization depends on money earned that is, Revenue and money spent (cost) and this product helps organizations understand their profitability.

- **Hyperion Web Analysis**: This is a reporting product of Oracle Hyperion which is known for interactive ad hoc analysis and it has ability to create reports from Oracle Hyperion Planning, Oracle Hyperion Financial Reporting and also from RDBMS, which makes it a very handy reporting product.

- **Hyperion Interactive Reporting**: This product creates very intuitive reports and it can talk to both relational and multidimensional sources to create reports. As it can communicate to multidimensional sources like Oracle Essbase, we can also use this reporting product to create reports from Oracle Hyperion Planning.

- **Hyperion Financial Reporting**: This reporting tool is known for its book quality financial reports and it has the ability to create reports from both relational and multidimensional sources. Hence, Oracle Hyperion Planning reports can be created using this tool.

All the above products can be accessed from one single web interface—Oracle EPM Workspace. We can work on all of these applications in terms of creating new applications, creating objects of a product or application, create web forms, and create reports; but its still a zero foot print client product.

The objective of a **zero foot print** product is the ability for the end user to work in his browser and not have the need to store the content of the applications on his system. In simple terms, a user is able to work or able to walk but his system will leave no foot prints of his walk (his work). Likewise, a planner works in his browser on his PC, using the Oracle Hyperion Planning application to enter data in the forms and others, but at the end there is no trace content from his planning application on his PC. Hence, we can rightly call Oracle EPM Workspace a zero foot print client component.

When Oracle Hyperion Planning application can be accessed from Planning Web, why is a planner/user recommended to access Oracle Hyperion Planning application from Oracle EPM Workspace?

Yes, a user can access Oracle Hyperion Planning application from Hyperion Planning Web using a URL which is different from the URL of Oracle EPM Workspace, but in most of the Oracle Hyperion implementations, we deploy more that just Oracle Hyperion Planning. Let us take an example of a client implementation, where we deployed Oracle Hyperion Planning, Oracle Hyperion Financial Management, and Oracle Business Intelligence as its reporting product. Now, end users would be more comfortable to access all these three application from a single portal rather than three different interface, and three different URL's. With Oracle EPM workspace, an end user is given one single URL and he will be able to access all three applications of Oracle Hyperion Planning, Oracle Financial Management and Oracle Business Intelligence reports from a single web interface of Oracle EPM Workspace.

Smart View

All the while, we have been saying that Oracle Hyperion Planning is a Web-based application, but we need to admit and agree the fact that the user community loves Microsoft Office and Oracle Hyperion cannot take away Office from users. Therefore, Oracle Hyperion has to offer EPM SmartView for Microsoft Office lovers.

SmartView provides integration with Microsoft Office with Oracle Hyperion Planning. It provides a Microsoft Office interface to Oracle EPM suite of products and Oracle Hyperion Planning is one of the Oracle EPM products.

Using SmartView, users can view, import, manipulate, distribute and even share data in Excel, Word, PowerPoint and Outlook.

For instance, planners can open the Planning application's data forms, enter data, adjust data and also calculate data in Excel interface using SmartView. Almost all the functionalities of the web based interface of Oracle Hyperion Planning can be accessed from Excel using Hyperion SmartView like tasklists, process management, annotations, data entry into the forms and others. It's also used to create ad-hoc reports in Excels.

Another important feature of Hyperion SmartView is that it lets a planner work both online and offline.

What is online and offline?

When a planner is connected to Planning server and works on Planning application, it's termed as online, this is usually the case when he is connected to his office network or is at workplace.

But, when the same planner is not connected to Planning server and sitting at an airport, he is still allowed to work on Planning application data forms in Excel using SmartView. Planners can perform operations such as entering data, adjusting data, and so on, and the changes made are synchronized back to the server when Planner connects to the server.

As a Planner is permitted to work even when he is not connected to the Planning server, its defined as 'Offline' and this offline feature is pretty useful to planners.

Oracle Hyperion Planning Process Flow

In this section, we'll understand the control flow among the various Hyperion Products when a user interacts with Oracle Hyperion Planning application.

Let us consider a simple scenario of a Planner entering Plan data into one of the data forms of an Oracle Hyperion Planning application.

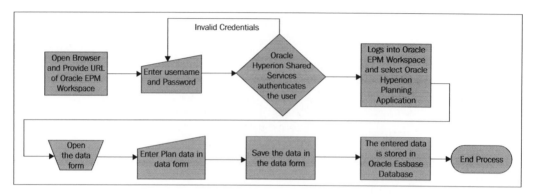

In the above image, a Planner firstly opens a browser and logs into Oracle EPM Workspace and then selects an Oracle Hyperion Planning application and enters data into a data form. The entered data is saved into Oracle Essbase. In this simple scenario, we mentioned Oracle EPM Workspace, Oracle Hyperion Shared Services, Oracle Hyperion Planning and Oracle Essbase.

The same flow helps us in understanding the communication between the Oracle Hyperion Planning components of Oracle EPM Workspace, Oracle Shared Services, Oracle Hyperion Planning, which is again connected to Relational Database and Oracle Essbase as shown in the following image.

Oracle EPM Workspace is the end user interface, and after a user provides their credentials, the user's details are authenticated using Oracle Shared Services, and the user is authorized to access the Oracle Hyperion Planning application.

Depending upon the operation performed in the Planning application, the information is stored or retrieved from a Relational source such as metadata or security information and/or from Oracle Essbase as shown in the following image:

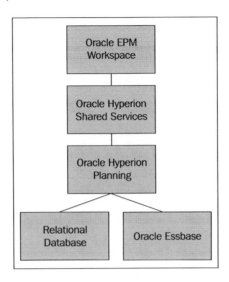

Now, we will understand the process flow including the Web Server and AppServer.

As we see in the following image, the flow is numbered. Firstly, a user logs into Oracle EPM Workspace to access Planning application. User needs to open a browser and provide the URL in Step 1, which is an HTTP request and Web Server handles all the HTTP request, as shown in the following image. Hence, Step 2 is WebServer receiving the request.

Oracle HTTP (default Web Server) server is the Web Server in our case. Web Server forwards the user request to Application Server in Step 3. Oracle WebLogic (default WebApp Server) is to do server side processing by providing business services to the client in Step 4.

In Step 5, Relational and Oracle Essbase databases are queried, Business Rules are run and the output of calculated data or retrieved data in a data form is sent back to the client-side browsers through the Web Server again from Step 6 through Step 10.

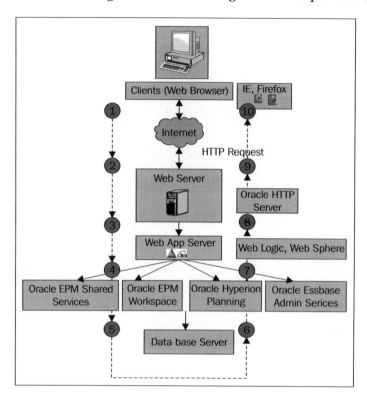

Oracle Hyperion Planning Solution Architecture

We'll learn briefly of a typical Oracle Hyperion Planning solution architecture, it would include additional products such as the following:

- **Oracle Data Integrator (ODI)**
- **Financial Data Quality Management (FDQM)**
- **Oracle Business Intelligence (OBI)**
- Hyperion Web Analysis
- Hyperion Financial Reporting

We'll learn how these products complement the solution of Oracle Hyperion Planning.

ODI and FDQM

We'll move from the left-hand side to the right-hand side in the architecture image given next. We see the source systems and ERP systems (which have transactional data) that are connected by Data Management products such as ODI (Oracle Data Integrator) and FDQM on the left-hand side.

ODI is useful in loading both metadata and data from ERP systems such as Oracle EBS or any other source system into Oracle Hyperion Planning applications.

Typically, the dimension members of Oracle Hyperion Planning application have the same naming convention as that of the **Chart of Accounts** (**COA**) of EBS. Hence, we can load the metadata with the help of ODI. Oracle EBS is not only needed to load metadata, but most importantly it is the source of actual data for Planning applications.

Let us explore this in more depth with an example. Consider that we are at the start of a fiscal year of 2011, which is from Jan to Dec. In the month of Jan, we had done Planning for the coming year of 2011 for all 12 months. Post completion of three months, that is the 1st quarter, the management needs to understand their performance in terms of where they actually stand against the plan. Hence, the actuals of the first three months are loaded and made available from the transactional systems such as EBS into the Oracle Hyperion Planning application, which will help us do a variance analysis between actuals and planned figures. Based on the analysis, management can alter the future plan for the rest of the year, if the acutals are not in line with the planned numbers. We will see in the next section that measuring and managing the performance against the goals is what Business Performance Management software like Oracle Hyperion Planning should do.

We'll understand more of actual vs plan later in this book.

We see FDQM and ODI in the architecture image shown next. We can load the data but the quality of loaded data is more important and these days it has become a business issue which is paving the way for products like FDQM (Financial Data Quality Management).

FDQM with the framework of ODI (Oracle Data Integrator) along with ERP I (ERP integrator) adapter has the ability to integrate Hyperion planning with ERP systems/ transactional systems such as Oracle EBS or PeopleSoft. With the help of this kind of integration, a planner now can drill back to the transactional systems such as Oracle EBS from a web form of Planning application.

We'll understand more about the metadata load and data load in *Chapter 7, Metadata Load* and *Chapter 8, Data Load*.

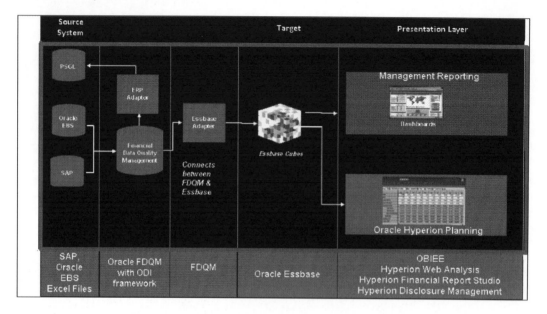

OBI (Oracle Business Intelligence) and Hyperion Reporting Products

OBIEE 11g is the latest offering from Oracle and this new release has the ability to make reports from Oracle Hyperion Planning/Oracle Essbase flawlessly. There are many other reporting products such as Hyperion Web Analysis, Hyperion financial Reporting, and so on that can also be used to create reports out of Oracle Hyperion Planning applications depending upon the reporting requirements.

We see Oracle Hyperion Planning is in the presentation layer as it's the web interface to the end users/planners. We see Oracle Essbase connected to Oracle Hyperion Planning in the above architecture.

Therefore, apart from the products bundled within Oracle Hyperion Planning, there are other products that complement the solution of Oracle Hyperion Planning in an enterprise.

Oracle EPM

These days the buzzword is EPM and in the Oracle world it's Oracle **Enterprise Performance Management (EPM)**. Oracle Hyperion planning is one of the products of Oracle EPM. Now, let us first understand what EPM means and then learn how Oracle Hyperion planning is related to this buzz about EPM.

EPM is synonymous with Business performance management and it's defined as a set of management and analytic processes that are aided by technology to enable businesses to define strategic goals and then measure and manage performance against those goals.

To make the definition simpler we can say that an organization would have its goals and management would like to periodically measure the performance to check how close to or how far from those goals they are. Financial planning is the core business performance management process and Oracle Hyperion Planning is the technology that fits the bill. Hence, Oracle Hyperion planning is a part of Oracle EPM.

Let us take a look at the Oracle EPM architecture and spot the presence of Oracle Hyperion Planning in it.

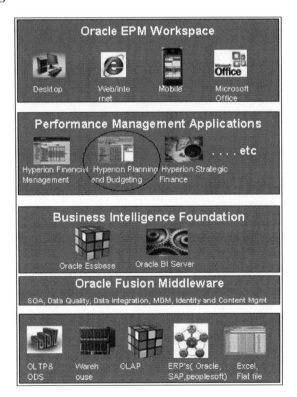

We'll move from top to bottom, starting with 'EPM workspace'. EPM workspace is a web based portal to access all Oracle Hyperion products along with Oracle Business Intelligence and it sits on the top of Performance Management Applications.

Next is the layer of 'Performance Management Applications'. We see Oracle Hyperion Planning highlighted and rounded to signify that it resides here. Other products that are a part of 'Performance Management Applications 'layer are Hyperion Financial Management, Hyperion Strategic Finance, Hyperion Scorecard, and Hyperion Profitability and Cost Management.

The next layer is 'Oracle Business Intelligence Foundation'. Oracle Essbase, BI server are included in this layer. BI server is the core engine for Oracle Business Intelligence (or OBI). We have already learned that Oracle Essbase would be the backend and foundation for Oracle Hyperion Planning applications.

The bottom layer is Oracle Fusion Middleware which connects to all the possible data sources of an enterprise as we see in the above image.

We'll continue with the architecture of Oracle EPM in the next chapter explaining at a granular level before we start installation of Oracle Hyperion Planning software.

Summary

In this first and very basic chapter on Oracle Hyperion Planning, we started by understanding the basic terms—planning, budgeting, and forecasting. Later we discussed the importance of budget software and the learned the currently faced challenges, then we introduced Oracle Hyperion Planning as one of the leading budgeting software applications and learned how it addresses the challenges.

Next, we learned about the architecture of Oracle Hyperion Planning and explored the connected products such as Oracle EPM Workspace, Oracle Essbase, Oracle Smart View, and Oracle Shared Services.

We also understood the process flow of Oracle Hyperion Planning application with the help of a simple scenario of a planner entering data into a data form.

Later, we learned about the architecture of a typical Oracle Hyperion Planning solution in an enterprise, where we introduced products such as Oracle Data Integrator (ODI), Oracle FDQM, and Oracle Business Intelligence as a reporting platform and understood how well these products complement in a typical implementation.

Finally, we understood EPM (Enterprise Performance Management) and also learned about the role of Oracle Hyperion Planning in the context of oracle EPM solution.

In the next chapter, we'll install and configure Oracle Hyperion Planning software.

Installation and Configuration

2

Before beginning, prepare carefully

— *Marcus Tullius Cicero*

In *Chapter 1*, we familiarized ourselves with the architecture of Oracle Hyperion Planning and in this chapter; we will install and configure Planning software.

Take a look at the following conversation between a client and a Hyperion consultant:

Client: *We were impressed by the demo of Oracle Hyperion Planning and we have decided to go with it and have already bought the license from Oracle. Now tell me what's next.*

Hyperion Consultant: *The next step is to finalize the hardware and then start the installation of Oracle Hyperion Planning.*

Client: *Ok, but Oracle has not sent me any software media - we have no CD or DVD.*

Hyperion Consultant: *We can download the software from the Oracle E-delivery website, which is now called as Software delivery cloud. That's not a problem. First, finalize the hardware in terms of number of servers so that my team can start the download and then install the software.*

This chapter is divided into the following sections:

- **Oracle EPM architecture and deployment**: In this section, we will revisit EPM architecture and explore it in a tier-wise fashion, which will help us in understanding the different Oracle recommended deployment plans.
- **Prerequisites**: In this section, we will look into few prerequisites that need to be taken care of before we kick-start the installation process.

- **System requirement check**: This is an important section that provides information regarding supported platforms for Oracle EPM installation in terms of operating systems, relational databases, web browsers, and more.

- **Preparing the installation files**: In this section, we will learn where to download the software from and what files are to be downloaded. At the end of this section, we should have the installation media ready.

- **Installation of the software**: In this section, we will learn how to install Oracle EPM Products along with Oracle Hyperion Planning in a step-by-step manner.

- **Configuration**: In this section, we will learn the sequence of Configuration and learn how to configure the installed Oracle EPM Products.

- **EPM Services**: We will learn about the start up sequence of Oracle EPM Services in this section.

- **Validate and Verify**: In this last section, we will learn how to validate the installation and also verify by accessing all the system products of Oracle EPM along with Oracle Hyperion Planning.

As we work through the install process, we will get a better understanding of the relationship between the complementing products such as Hyperion Shared Services, Oracle EPM Workspace, and Oracle Essbase with Oracle Hyperion Planning. At the end of the chapter, we will have not only installed Oracle Hyperion Planning software successfully on our systems, but also have a better understanding of the Planning architecture.

This is a long chapter and it's expected that the reader install the software as we go through the chapter.

Let's hope for a smooth ride ahead and that we reach the finish line with a successfully installed and configured Oracle Hyperion Planning system.

Oracle EPM Architecture and deployment

In this section, we will learn about the four tier architecture of Oracle EPM and will understand the deployment strategies as well.

Oracle EPM Architecture is divided into four tiers and they are as follows:

- **Web and WebApp tier**: This tier comprises all the Oracle EPM System Products that would require Web Server and WebApp Server. In our case, it is Oracle HTTP Server and Oracle WebLogic respectively.

- **Client tier**: This tier is for the end user or Planner, who will be accessing Planning application on their PCs. Therefore, this tier comprises the products that must be installed on the end user's system to access Planning application.

- **Database tier**: This is the relational database tier. In our case, it is Oracle. There are other supported databases as well, which we will cover in section *System requirement check* section.

- **Services tier**: This tier includes two servers. One for Oracle Essbase and one for a few other services, as shown in the following image:

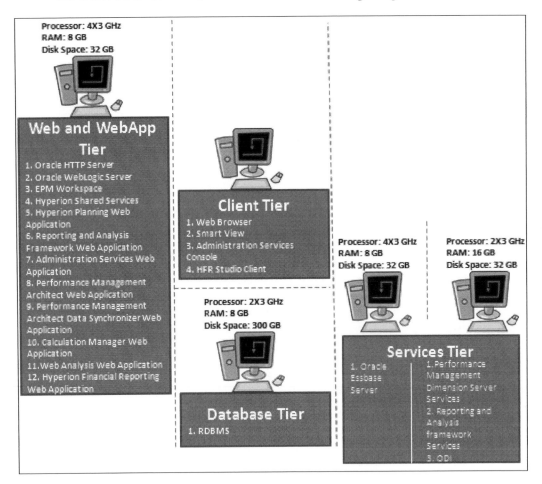

The memory, processor, and disk space requirements mentioned in the previous image are the minimum configurations recommended by Oracle with an assumption of 100 users and with 35% concurrency.

We can see a total of five servers used in the deployment architecture image. We need to note that it's not mandatory to use this number of servers or systems. It's a reference deployment plan which would be useful for reference.

> Depending on the size of the Oracle Hyperion Planning implementation, the hardware requirements will vary. It usually varies from development environment to production environment. The reason being that in a development environment, only a few developers and implementation teams would be working; whereas in the production environment, planners would be accessing it organization-wide.

One of the first steps in the implementation of Oracle Hyperion Planning project is to plan the deployment. The deployment would change when the number of users increases. For example, if the number of users is around 500, then the deployment plan changes, as illustrated in the following image:

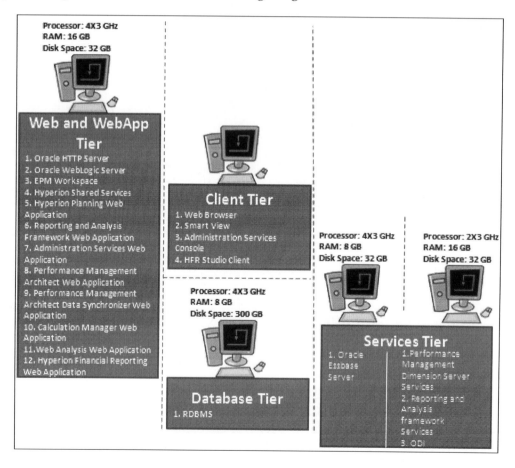

These are two different deployment plans where the user count is 100 and 500 respectively. Now, we cannot replicate the same in our book. We will install all the components in one single machine, which we define as **single machine deployment**. But, remember, this single machine installation is strictly for tutorial purposes and is not recommended for any production deployment.

What is the basis upon which we divided the products or components on different servers? Why not install Oracle Essbase server on the same machine where we have installed EPM Workspace and Hyperion Planning?

The logic behind this kind of division is components such as Oracle EPM Workspace, Hyperion Planning, EPMA, Essbase Administration Services need both the Web Server (that is Oracle HTTP Server) and also the WebApp Server (Oracle WebLogic). Therefore, it's recommended to install all products that have common dependencies on one server.

Let us take the example of Oracle Hyperion Planning. We understood in the previous chapter the importance of Web Server and WebApp Server and we have also learned that Oracle EPM Workspace is the common end user interface to access multiple applications, and Oracle Hyperion Planning is one of them.

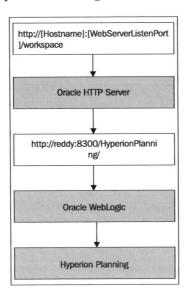

An end user or planner accesses Oracle EPM Workspace, then the request is passed through Oracle HTTP Server to the App server (that is, WebLogic) and then to the application of Oracle Hyperion Planning. Nevertheless, the same Planning application can operate in isolation and can be accessed by the provided URL, or can be accessed from Oracle EPM Workspace.

The moral of the story is that Oracle Hyperion Planning would require both App server and Web server, and components such as Hyperion Shared Services, Administration Services, and so on would also require both App server and Web Server. The same logic holds true that these sub modules do operate and can be accessed individually or can be brought together with the help of one single interface, that is Oracle EPM Workspace.

Therefore, in the deployment plan, we have shown all the modules or components that require both WebApp Server and Web Server in one machine or server and the tier is rightly named the **Web and WebApp tier**. Coming to the other machines or tiers, RDBMS is on a separate machine ,which needs no Web Server and WebApp Server, and likewise, even Oracle Hyperion Essbase doesn't need either of them.

We pretty well understand the logical bifurcation of the machines or servers. Now, let us complicate situation. What if, if we want to install Hyperion Shared Services on Machine 1, EPMA on Machine 2, Workspace on Machine 3, and Hyperion Planning, Oracle Essbase and Administration Services on Machine 4. It would look like the following image:

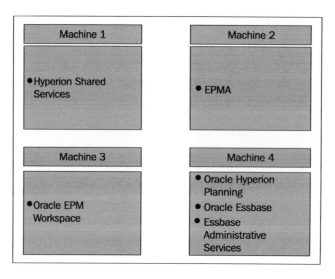

In this situation, we don't have a clear bifurcation of the Web and WebApp tier, Database tier, and Services tier. They are all mixed. The question here is how do we plan the deployment?

In these kinds of scenarios, we need to first realize that all the Machines from 1 to 4 would require WebServer and WebApp Server because of the products in them (Oracle Hyperion Shared Services, EPMA, Oracle EPM Workspace, Oracle Hyperion Planning, and Essbase Administration Services) would require.

Therefore, we need to install Web Server and WebApp Server on all the machines.

Considering these kinds of situation, Oracle has done a smart thing. When we install Hyperion Foundation Services, which we do on all the servers or machines, the system installs both WebServer and WebApp Server (Oracle HTTP Server and Oracle WebLogic).

We will install Hyperion Shared Services on Machine 1 and then we will have to install Oracle WebLogic on the same machine. Likewise, we need to install Oracle WebLogic on Machine 2, 3, and 4 as well because all the components; such as EPMA, Workspace, Hyperion Planning and Administration Services will require WebApp Server i.e. Oracle WebLogic.

 The installation Sequence of the products on different machines or servers is not important and can be done in any order but we need to be careful of the Configuration sequence of these products.

Prerequisites

After we have decided the deployment plan in terms of the number of servers, we will look at the prerequisites before we check the system requirements.

There are four important prerequisites:

- **Web Server preparation**: We learned the role of Web Server in *Chapter 1* and we need to ensure that Web Server is installed as per the deployment plan. The default Web Server is Oracle HTTP Server.

 Microsoft **Internet Information Services (IIS)** is a prerequisite for Performance Management Architect Service. Out of the components we are installing for Hyperion Planning, the only component that needs IIS .NET is EPMA Dimension Server. Nevertheless, EPMA is out of the scope of this book.

- **WebApp Server preparation**: We have learned that there are a few products of Oracle EPM, along with Hyperion Planning, that would need WebApp Server and we need to install WebLogic on the servers or machines in accordance with our deployment plan.

> When the client purchases Oracle Hyperion Planning, Oracle provides a limited usage license of Oracle WebLogic for Oracle EPM products.

- **Database preparation**: As per the architecture, we need RDBMS and we can either install Oracle Database, Microsoft SQL Server or even IBM DB2. We will look at the complete list of supported databases in the *System requirement check* section.

  We need to note that the installation and configuration of Oracle EPM products are two different activities.

> We need a relational database set up before the commencement of configuration. Hence, we can install RDBMS before we start configuring installed Oracle EPM products. It's common to install RDBMS before even starting the installation of Oracle EPM products, though we don't use RDBMS during Oracle EPM Product installation.

- **Web browser preparation**: The supported browsers are Internet Explorer and Firefox. The following are the options that need to be enabled for smoother access of Oracle EPM applications on the browsers:
  - Enable JavaScript
  - Enable cookies
  - Allow pop-up windows

System requirement check

In this section, we will learn how to select the right platform for Oracle Hyperion Planning.

There is a Support Matrix reference document which has information about the compatible Operating Systems, JDK Versions, RDBMS, WebServer, and WebApp Server.

Where can we get this Support Matrix Reference Copy?

We can find it at the following address:

```
http://www.oracle.com/technetwork/middleware/bi-foundation/oracle-
hyperion-epm-system-certific-131801.xls
```

> It's important to work on a compatible platform. A few brave people might tell us of their success stories of installing on incompatible operating systems such as XP, with a smile. Let's not make that mistake; stick to supported operating systems if you want to have a lasting smile. Also, Oracle will not provide any support if the software is not installed on supported operating systems.
>
> Oracle Hyperion 11.1.2 is the only version that is compatible with Windows 2008 operating system.

Preparing installation files

In this section, we will learn about the Oracle EPM Software download. For this software download, we have two simple questions—where do we download the media/software from and what files do we download for Oracle Hyperion Planning?

We will learn the answers in the following sections:

- Software download
- Oracle Hyperion Planning download files
- Installation media preparation

Software download

The media/software can be downloaded from Oracle E-Delivery website or Oracle Software download center.

The following are the links to Oracle E-Delivery and Oracle Software download center respectively:

- `http://edelivery.oracle.com/`
- `http://www.oracle.com/technetwork/middleware/epm/downloads/index.html`

One can download the software from either of the mentioned links. If we are downloading from Oracle E -Delivery website, we need to select the appropriate **Product Pack** and **Platform**.

In the following image, we have selected **Oracle Enterprise Performance Management System** as the **Product Pack**. In our case, the system is 32 bit. Hence, we select **Microsoft Windows (32 bit)**.

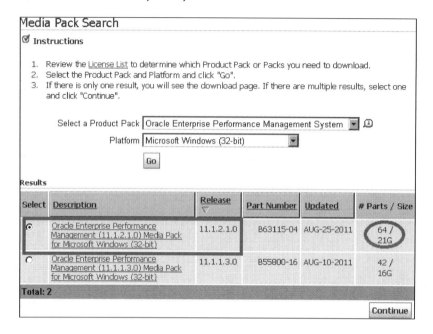

In recent implementations, clients would like to make use of the 64-bit hardware advantage and procure 64-bit servers. If this is the case, then you need to download 64-bit software and select the appropriate platform.

It's also important to note that 32-bit software can work on 64-bit hardware, but the opposite is not true.

We can see that currently there are two release in the version of 11.1.2.1.0 and 11.1.1.3.0. The 11.1.2.1.0 is the latest and we are going to download and work with it.

Every new release always comes with its own inherent bugs and issues. It's evident that as sub versions of a release increase, the stability of the release also increases. An example would be 11.1.1.1, 11.1.1.2, and 11.1.1.3. Of course, the latter version would be more stable. The latest version is 11.1.2 and it won't be a surprise if Oracle comes up with another version such as 11.1.2.1.1.

We observer that there are a total of 64 files that are related to the whole Oracle EPM software. We need to know the relevant download files for Oracle Hyperion Planning and we will learn that in the next section.

Oracle Hyperion Planning download files

We have already learned that the software can be downloaded either from Oracle E-Delivery or Oracle Software download center.

Oracle Software download center

If we are downloading from Oracle Software download center, we see the list of software files of all the Hyperion products, as shown in the following image.

Reserving ourselves to Hyperion Planning, we need to download all the files that are ticked in the following image:

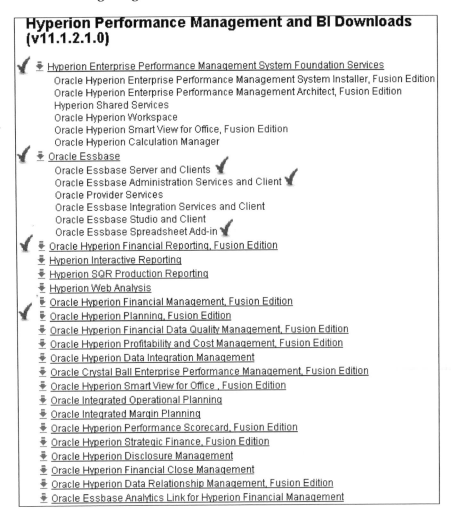

Oracle E-Delivery

If we are downloading from the Oracle E-Delivery site, then we need to download the following files with the mentioned specific part numbers.

 Wait! What is a part number?

In Oracle E-Delivery site, every file of the media/software has a unique ID; this ID can be understood as part number.

Therefore, files of different versions would have different part numbers.

The following table lists the files to be downloaded from Oracle E-Delivery. The part numbers are strictly for version 11.1.2.1.

Hyperion Product Pack	Part Number
Oracle Hyperion EPM System Release 11.1.2.0.0 - Start Here: Installation Documents and Readmes – English	V23952-01
Oracle Hyperion Enterprise Performance Management System Installer, Fusion Edition Release 11.1.2.0.0 for Microsoft Windows (32-bit)	V20650-01
Hyperion Enterprise Performance Management System Foundation Services Release 11.1.2.0.0 for Microsoft Windows (32-bit) Part 1 of 4	V20799-01
Hyperion Enterprise Performance Management System Foundation Services Release 11.1.2.0.0 for Microsoft Windows (32-bit) Part 2 of 4	V20800-01
Hyperion Enterprise Performance Management System Foundation Services Release 11.1.2.0.0 for Microsoft Windows (32-bit) Part 3 of 4	V20801-01
Hyperion Enterprise Performance Management System Foundation Services Release 11.1.2.0.0 Part 4 of 4	V20802-01
Oracle Hyperion Calculation Manager Release 11.1.2.0.0	V20779-01
Oracle Hyperion Enterprise Performance Management Architect, Fusion Edition Release 11.1.2.0.0	V20782-01
Oracle Essbase Release 11.1.2.0.0 Part 1 of 2	V20783-01
Oracle Essbase Release 11.1.2.0.0 Part 2 of 2 for Microsoft Windows (32-bit)	V20790-01
Oracle Essbase Clients Release 11.1.2.0.0 for Microsoft Windows	V20792-01
Oracle Essbase Spreadsheet Add-in Release 11.1.2.0.0 for Microsoft Windows	V20791-01
Oracle Hyperion Financial Reporting, Fusion Edition Release 11.1.2.0.0	V20798-01
Oracle Hyperion Enterprise Performance Management Reporting and Analysis Core Components Release 11.1.2.0.0	V20841-01
Hyperion Web Analysis Release 11.1.2.0.0	V20851-01
Oracle Hyperion Planning, Fusion Edition Release 11.1.2.0.0	V20832-01
Oracle Hyperion Smart View for Office, Fusion Edition Release 11.1.2.0.0 for Microsoft Windows	V20842-01

Oracle recommends downloading the software (in ZIP file format) to a common install directly and preferably a network shared drive. Also, it's better to download the software directly to the server where it is going to be installed on.

Preparing installation media

After downloading all the required files we have little work to do before we hit the installation executable. Let us do it in steps.

1. Create a folder called DOWNLOAD_LOCATION.

2. Now, unzip all the files(the files that we downloaded in the *Software download* section) into the DOWNLOAD_LOCATION folder.

3. While we are carrying out the unzip process, we will get frequent messages, as shown in the following image:

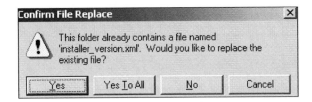

4. Select **Yes To All** every time the window pops up.

After we have unzipped all the files, our DOWNLOAD_LOCATION folder will look like the following image:

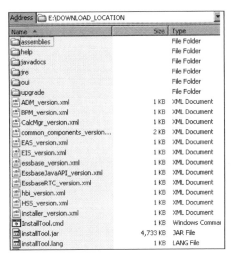

Installation of Oracle Hyperion Planning

Installation of Version 11 is different from its precursors. Along with simplifying the installation, the process for upgrades, and the application of patches has also been simplified to a great extent. Anyone familiar with the earlier version 9 knows how complicated the installation and patching process was.

Oracle, after it bought Hyperion, aims to standardize the installation and patching process. Thanks Oracle.

Double-click on the `InstallTool.cmd` file. This will commence the installation process. As we will see, it checks a few pre-requisites such as assemblies and environment variables. Post checking for all pre-requisites, it will launch the installation tool. We can see the same message in the following image:

Next, in the **Select a language** window, select **English**. We can take a look at what other languages it supports, just out of curiosity.

As we can see, the whole installation process is divided into the following steps:

1. **Welcome**: In this first step, the installer checks for a few prerequisites.

2. **Destination**: Here, we select the drive location where we intend to install Oracle Hyperion.

3. **Installation Type**: In this section, we select the type; whether to upgrade, to newly install, or to reinstall.

4. **Product Selection**: This gives us the option to select the products which we intend to install out of the whole suite. We do this by checking and unchecking the relevant products in the list.

5. **Confirmation**: This shows the list of products which need to be installed, which depends on the Product selections we made in the previous step.

6. **Progress**: As the installation activity progresses, we can see the progress percentage count up. Finally, if the install completes successfully, a success message will appear.

7. **Summary**: Once the installer has finished, it shows the list of all the products and their status. In this section, we will see the message 'Installation successful'.

Welcome

In this first step, the installer checks the operating system. It also checks the availability of memory and whether the user who is installing has admin privileges.

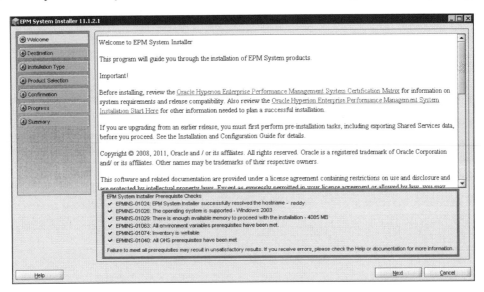

The checkmarks highlighted in this image indicate that our system meets the criteria.

Destination

Select the drive name onto which we intend to install Oracle Hyperion Planning. As it's a new installation, the system lets us edit/browse to the location of Hyperion home. If it is not a new installation and Oracle Hyperion is already installed, we cannot change the location of Hyperion Home.

Click on **Next**.

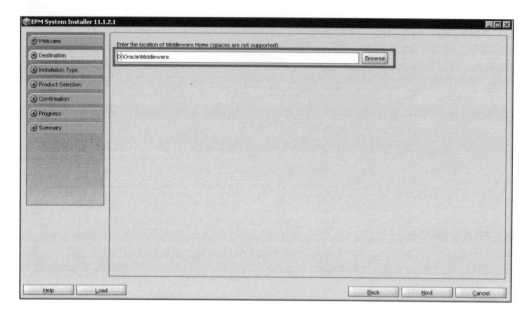

Installation type

Here, we will discuss about the available options. As we can see, new installation is the only possible option and the other options are grayed out. There are a few reasons for this:

- **New installation**: When we are installing for the first time, this is the apt option (like in our case).

- **Re-install this release**: If we would like to reinstall the same products of Hyperion, we should select this option. When any of the installed products of Oracle EPM System are not working and need to be repaired, we can perform a reinstall. When we reinstall, we also need to reconfigure.

[When we are re-installing any product, we need to ensure that all the Oracle EPM services are stopped.]

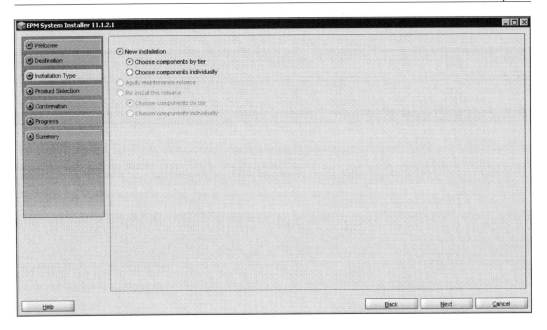

- **Apply maintenance release**: Oracle Hyperion does come up with maintenance releases. For example, if we already had version 11.1.1.1 installed and we intend to apply maintenance release of 11.1.1.3, we would opt for this. In these scenarios, this is option handy.

Product selection

There are two ways of selecting products as we see in the following image.

We can see that few products such as **Financial Close, Disclosure Management, Financial Management, Strategic Finance**, and a few others are grayed out. The reason for this is that we have downloaded only related files of foundation, Oracle Essbase and Oracle Hyperion Planning. We did not download the files of other products. It's as simple as that.

If we don't want to view these unavailable products (HFM, Strategic Finance), there is a **Hide Unavailable Products** option, as we can see in the above image.

We can choose new installation either 'by tier' or 'by components' individually. We can selected either of these and proceed. The difference is a matter of display format as we can see in the following images.

By tier

We can view three tiers:

- Client tier
- Web application tier
- Services tier

We can recollect that these are the tiers by which we divided Oracle EPM Architecture and now we should be able to co-relate. In a typical installation, where multiple servers are involved in distributed environment, we would use this option of 'by tier'. For example, we are deploying Oracle EPM Products in two tiers (that is two machine deployment), we can make one server as Web Appl tier and the other one for Services. To achieve installation of products based on tiers, we can check all the products under Web Appl when we are installing the software on first machine and we will check all products under Services when we are installing the software on the second machine,which is the Services Server. This way, this option of 'by tier' is useful when we have multi-tier deployment.

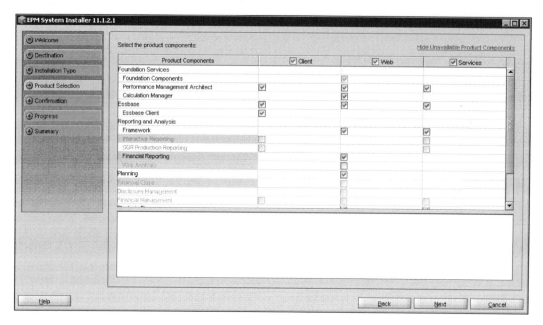

But in our case, it is single tier and single machine deployment.

 The EPM system installer automatically selects all the available products for installation as we have downloaded the installation assemblies for the components needed for Hyperion Planning.

By components/products

By components/products shows the list of products ready to be installed as shown in the following image and this options suits single machine deployment, as we have not divided our deployment into different tiers.

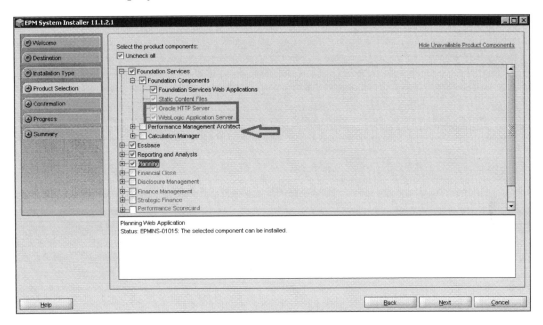

We have been stating that installation of Foundation takes care of Web Server and WebApp Server installation and now we can witness the same; both Oracle HTTP Server and WebLogic are installed and as we can see in the earlier image.

We have unchecked both **Performance Management Architect** and **Calculation Manager**, as it is out of the scope of the book.

Confirmation

This section gives the list of products to be installed.

We can view the products and their **Install Type** is **Install**. We can also view any **Status** messages. As we have not initiated the installation, there is no status message as of now, as shown in the following image:

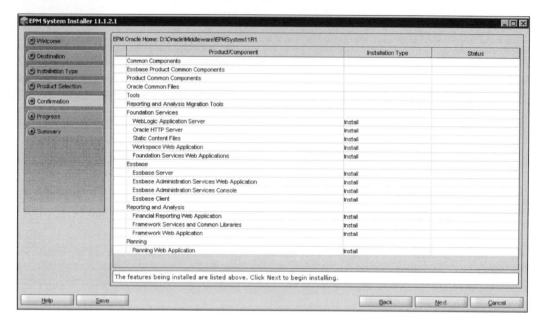

Click on **Next.**

Progress

As the installation progresses successfully, it places a green tick against every component whose installation gets completed. We need to wait patiently wait till all the components are installed successfully.

We can view the status of the installed products in the following image:

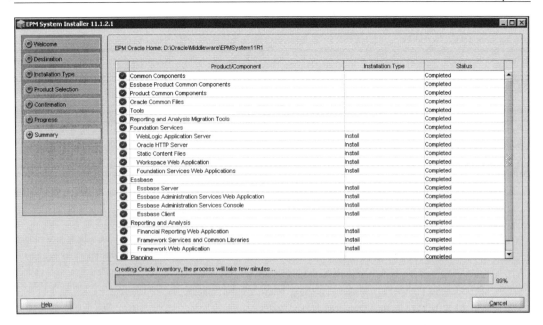

Summary

After all products are successfully installed, we get **Successful Installation** message as shown in the following image. All selected products are ticked in green and their status is **Completed**.

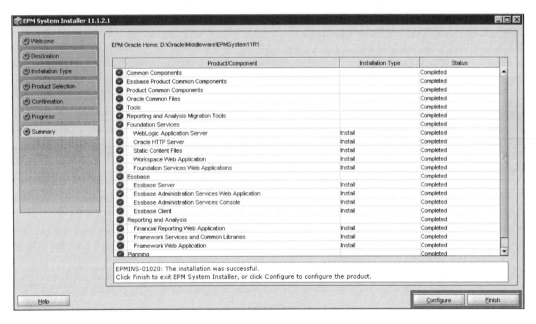

This is the happy ending of the installation of Oracle Hyperion Planning and other Oracle EPM Products.

We can view the options of 'Configure' and 'Finish' in the following image.

If we are not tired after the installation, then we can continue with configuration by clicking on **Configure**; else finish it by clicking on **Finish** and we shall start configuration after a while; maybe after a coffee.

Installation on multi-machine deployment

Installation of Oracle EPM on multiple machines in a distributed environment is made easy with the help of **EPM System Installer**. There are a few important considerations when we are installing in distributed environment. They are as follows:

- Installation of Oracle EPM products can follow any sequence, but we need to strictly follow a recommended order of configuration of the products.
- When we install different products of Oracle EPM on multiple machines in distributed environment, we need to ensure that Oracle EPM home is / Oracle/Middleware on all the machines consistently.
- We have already learned that all the web application products of Oracle EPM are typically installed on one machine, where we will be administering WebLogic Server.

Configuration

In this section, we will learn the following:

- Database preparation
- Configuring Oracle EPM in a single machine
- Configuring of Oracle EPM
- Configuration of Oracle EPM in a multi-machine distributed environment

Database preparation

We shall discuss the following:

- Oracle database creation
- Oracle database schema creation

Before we start configuring Oracle EPM products, we need to install an RDBMS. The popular RDBMS vendors such as Oracle Database, Microsoft SQL Server, and IBM DB2 are all supported RDBMS.

For more information of the version and compatibility of the RDBMS, refer to the *System Requirement* section. In our case, assume that we have installed Oracle database.

Each Oracle EPM System product would require to be configured with database. We can use one single database for all the products to configure at a time or we can use different databases for each product. In our case, we will create an Oracle database and multiple schemas for each product of Oracle EPM System.

We will create an Oracle database with the name 'HYP' and will create multiple schemas in the next section to cater to each product of Oracle EPM to be configured.

Oracle schemas creation

We will create separate schemas for each Oracle EPM product. In the following table, we can view the list of products, their respective schema names and also the recommended Oracle sizing details:

Oracle EPM System Product	Schema Name	Size
Oracle Hyperion Shared Services.	HYPSS	100 MB
EAS.	HYPEAS	32 MB
Oracle Hyperion Planning.	HYPPLAN	100 MB
Oracle EPM Workspace.	HYPWS	100 MB
Reporting and Analysis	HYPRA	250 MB

 We need to note that the schemas or users in the Oracle database need to have the following roles and privileges of Create Session, Create View, and Resource.

In a production environment, we would have a separate database server and we would create Oracle Database and schemas in it. We need to note the information of Server Name, Database name. This information will be used later in the configuration.

Configuring Oracle EPM in single machine

We have already learned that Oracle Hyperion Planning makes use of several other Hyperion Products such as Essbase, Shared services, Calculation Manager, Performance management architect, EAS (Essbase administration services), and Oracle EPM Workspace.

When all the products are installed on a single machine, EPM System Configuration will configure automatically in the correct order.

Configuring Oracle EPM products

The following section explains the configuration of Oracle EPM products.

Sequence of configuration

We are going to start Oracle EPM product configuration and in the process of configuration, we will need the database schemas, which we should have already created.

 We can configure all the products of Oracle EPM with one single schema, but it's not recommended. We will use separate schema for each product.

As we are going to configure each product with separate schema, the sequence of configuration is very important. We are going to configure in the following order:

- Hyperion Foundation
- Essbase
- Planning
- Reporting and Analysis
- Hyperion Workspace

We need to note that 'Enterprise Performance Management Architect' is out of the scope of this book and we will not be configuring both EPMA and Calculation Manager.

How do we start configuration?

Navigate and select **EPM System Configurator** to initiate configuration.

All Programs | Oracle EPM | Foundation Services | EPM System Configurator

It will lead to a screen, where we see the 'icon type'. Icon type suggests that the status of the configuration—**Pending, Configured**, and **Configuration Failed**. It also gives the list of installed products that can be selected for configuration. We see the icon type as **Pending** for all the products as we have yet to configure.

We see the main products to be configured are as follows:

- Hyperion Foundation
- Essbase
- Planning
- Reporting and Analysis

 Hyperion Foundation is the first and foremost product category to be configured. We also need to note that 'Configure Web Server' under 'Hyperion Foundation' should be the last to be configured

Common tasks of Oracle EPM product configuration

Typically, a product of Oracle EPM has the following tasks as a part of the configuration process:

1. Register with Shared services: This step registers the product with Hyperion Shared Services so that the User Authentication and Authorization of the product can be managed from shared services.

2. Shared Services provides authentication and authorization services to all Hyperion products. It provides a centralized interface for managing authorization to all Hyperion products. This centralized approach enables us to define a user only once and grant him access to multiple Hyperion Applications. Hence, products like EAS (Essbase administration services), Essbase, Panning and Workspace need to register with shared services.

3. Configure database: Every products links to relational source. This step configures the database with the product.

4. Deploy to App Server: This step deploys the product to application server. An example of an application server is WebLogic.

We will understand these three common tasks better once we start the configuration process.

Configuring Hyperion Foundation

After we launch the EPM Configurator, we need to provide the Oracle EPM Instance information as shown in the following image:

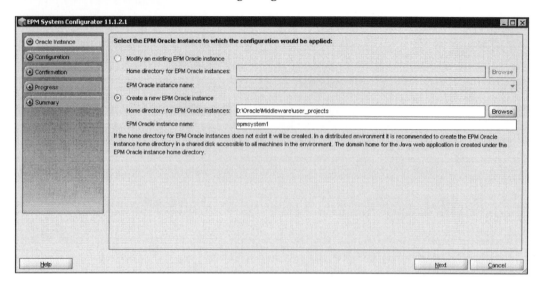

We will first configure Hyperion Shared Services, where **Hyperion Foundation**, **Common Settings**, **Configure Database**, and **Configure Oracle Configuration Manager** are automatically selected. We will select **Deploy to Application Server**, and also need to ensure that **Configure Web Server** is not ticked in the following image:

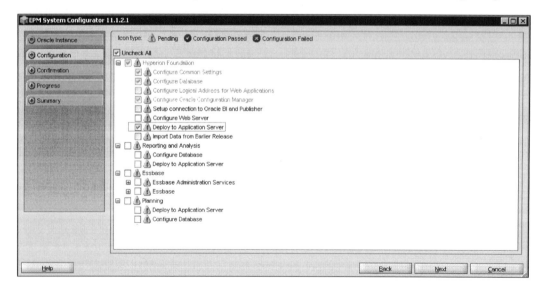

Click on **Next** to provide the database schema details of HYPSS, which we created for Hyperion Shared Services product.

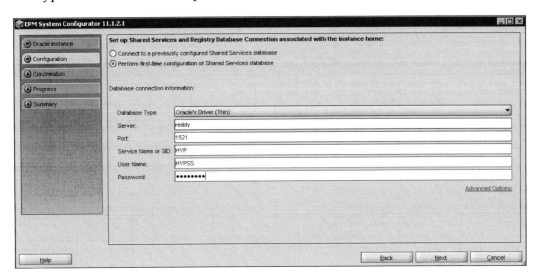

We see two interesting options: **Connect to a previously configured Shared Services database** and **Perform 1st-ime configuration of Shared Services database**. We are configuring for the first time and we have selected the option of 'Perform 1st time configuration'. We need to remember this step as we are going to re visit under the section "Configuring Oracle EPM in distributed environment".

We provide the following information in the previous image:

- **Database Type**: It's Oracle, in our case.
- **Server**: This is the server where we have installed Oracle (that is, the database server). It is a single machine installation for us; hence it has the same server name as the server where we installed Hyperion Planning.
- **Port**: As we select Oracle as the database type, the appropriate port number is automatically selected, which is 1521, if it's Microsoft SQL server then the port number is 1433, and if it's IBM DB2, then 50000 is the default port number.

 We need to ensure that the database instance is configured to these default port numbers. If they are configured to any other port number other than default, then we need to use the configured port number.

- **Service Name or SID**, **Username**, and **Password**: Provide appropriate service name, schema name (this is for username), and password
- Click on **Next**.

- By default, **Create Windows Services for configured components** is checked. This step creates Windows services for products and they start automatically. After successful configuration, we can view services as Windows services (**All programs | Run | services.msc**).

- Enable SSL for web application: If we want to enable SSL (Secured Socket Layer), which is more secure way of communication and its generally used in Production Environment. When SSL is enabled, the URL's start with HTTPS

- **Mail server (SMPT) Setup**: Some of the Hyperion products provide the facility of sending information such as reports, alerts via emails to users. For these features to work, we need to provide an SMTP Mail Server. Hyperion Planning also provided email notification to uses through Workflows and Task lists.

- **User Name** and **Password**: These credentials are only required if an SMTP server is configured.

- **Admin Email**: Here, provide the SMTP administrator's e-mail ID to send notifications to him. It's required only when we are configuring with SMTP.

  We'll go with the defaults as we are not configuring SSL or SMTP mail server. Click on **Next**.

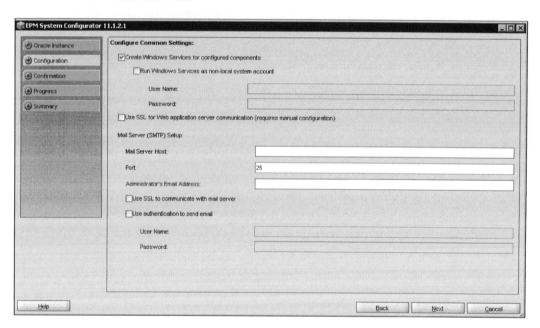

- It leads to the following window of **Common Settings**. We have learned by now that installation of Oracle WebLogic has been taken care when we had installed Hyperion Foundation Services. Here, in this configuration step, we can either use the default domain created in WebLogic or create a new domain. We will create a new domain as shown.

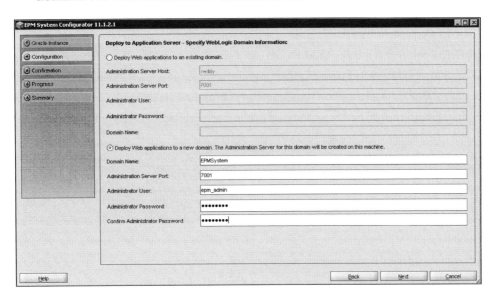

We will give a domain name and also provide a user name and password as shown in the previous image. Click on **Next**.

- Next, we see the port number of Hyperion Shared Services for Oracle WebLogic deployment:

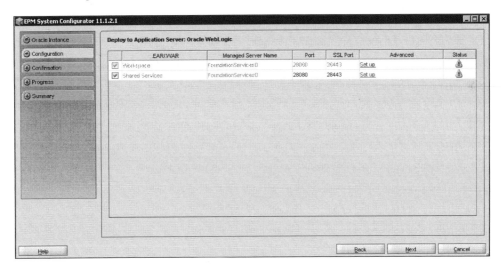

We will accept the default port number. We should take care to note these port numbers and ensure that there is no conflict

After selecting 'Next', it will ask us to provide an e-mail address. It is for registering Oracle configuration manager. This would help us in getting updates regarding any security issue or bugs as far as the Hyperion product is concerned. For tutorial purpose, we can neglect it and move ahead by clicking on 'Next'. It will give you a pop up that " You will be remained uninformed of critical security issues" as shown in the image below. We are OK with it, but we need to ensure that we will provide this information ,when we are deploying the product on a client side.

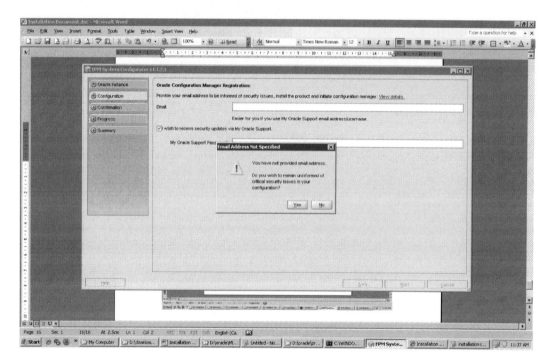

Click on **Next** and set the password for Hyperion Shared Services. We will set it to 'password'.

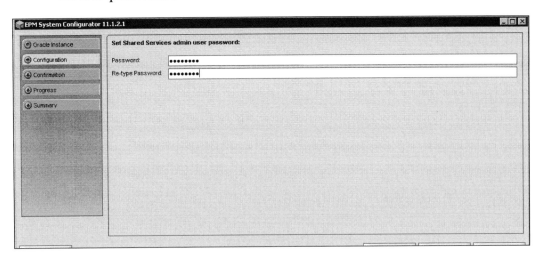

- EPM Configurator confirms the list of activities to be performed under Hyperion Foundation Configuration.

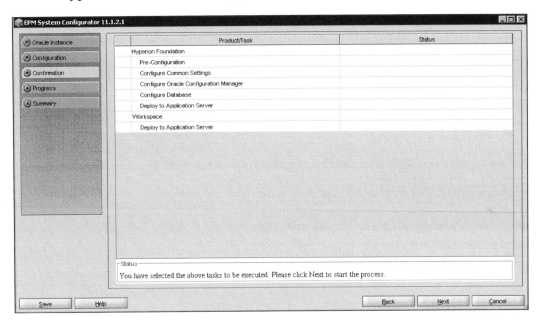

Click on **Next**.

- After a while the configuration will complete. This is the end of Hyperion Shared Services Configuration, as shown in the following image:

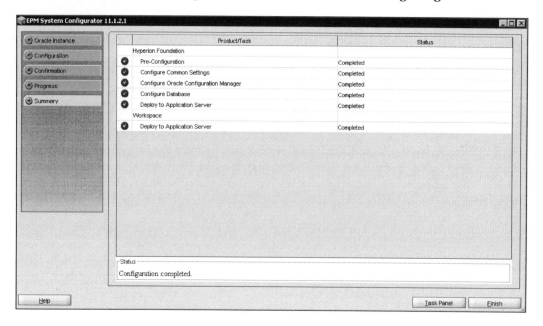

Configuring Essbase

In the configuration of Essbase, we first will configure Essbase and then will configure Essbase Administration Services.

Essbase Configuration

Select **Essbase Custom Configuration**, as shown in the following screenshot, to configure Essbase Server. We have already learned that Essbase Server does not need to be deployed with WebApplication Server and need not be configured with any Oracle Schema. Hence, we will not see any deployment of this product with Oracle WebLogic, and also, no database configuration.

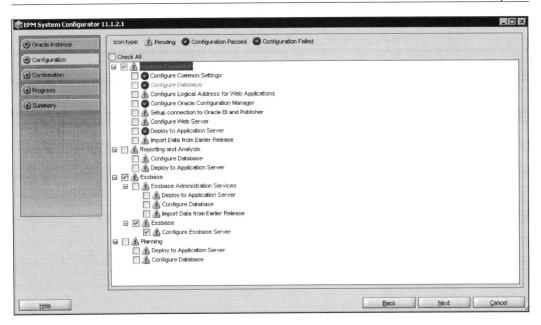

Here, we need to provide Essbase Server Configuration information. We need to pay close attention to the port numbers, as shown in the following image:

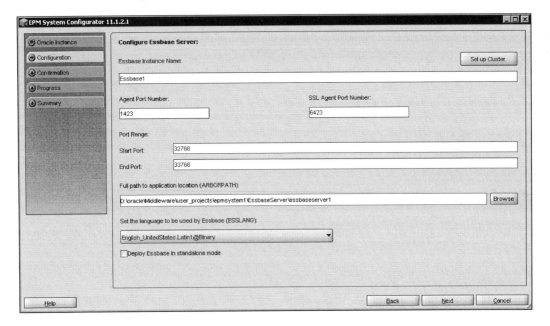

We will stick with the default settings:

- **Agent Port Number**: This is the port number that Essbase server uses to communicate with the client requests. It is 1423 by default.

- **Port Range**: This is the range used by Essbase server applications.

- **Full path to application location (ARBOPATH)**: This is the location of Essbase applications.

> **What is ARBOPATH?**
>
> This brings old memories. **Arbor** was the company that first shipped Essbase software. Later, Hyperion merged with Arbor. In a way, it's good. At least, it brings old memories, as said.

- **Set the language to be used by Essbase (ESSLANG)**: Let it be **English**. There are other international languages that can be selected for the interface.

  Don't check **Deploy Essbase in standalone mode**.

> What is standalone mode for? In some cases, a few assignments require only to work on Essbase software and they don't want to manage user authentication and Authorization using Hyperion Shared Services. The standalone mode is useful in those cases. It's usually the case with test environments.

- Click on **Next** and configure Oracle Essbase Server. We can see in the configured activities that Essbase product is configured with Shared Services, but there is no WebApp deployment step.

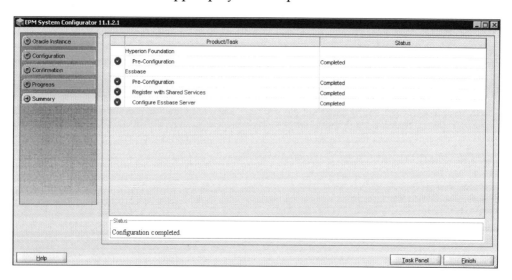

This marks the end of Oracle Essbase configuration. We will look into the configuration of Essbase Administration Services in next section.

Essbase Administration Services Configuration

In this section, we will first register EAS product with Shared Services, configure with the database, and finally deploy to Application Server (that is WebLogic).

Select the following as shown in the below image:

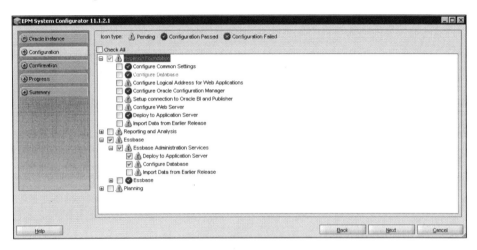

Click on **Next** to provide configuration details. We are not using any previously used database schema. Hence, we have selected **Perform 1st-time configuration,** as shown in the following image.

We will provide the details of the schema "HYPEAS" that we created earlier for EAS.

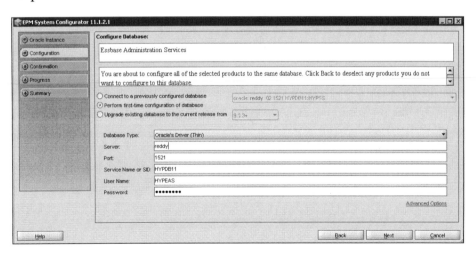

Click on **Next,** and in this window, we will select **Deploy web application to an existing domain** that is EPMSystem and go ahead by selecting **Next** as shown in image below:

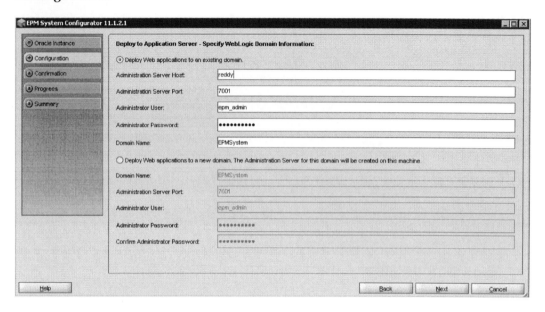

Click on **Next** to view the Application Server port details.

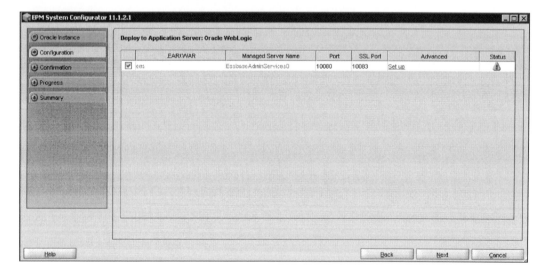

Finally, click on **Next** and configure EAS with the usual steps of registering with Shared Services, Database Configuration, and Web Application Server deployment.

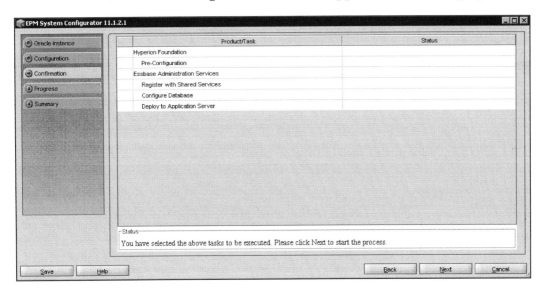

This is the end of Essbase configuration.

Configuring Hyperion Planning

Even for Hyperion Planning Product configuration, the steps remains the same. We will select configure product, configure database, and finally deploy to application server as shown in the following image:

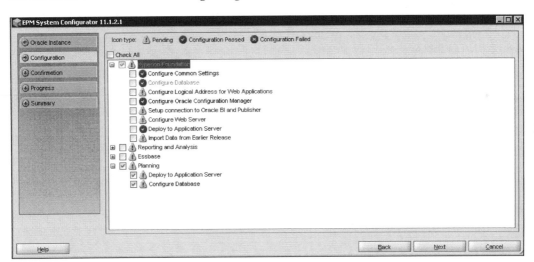

Click on **Next** to provide the database configuration details. Here, we provide the details of the schema HYPPLAN, which we created for Hyperion Planning Product earlier.

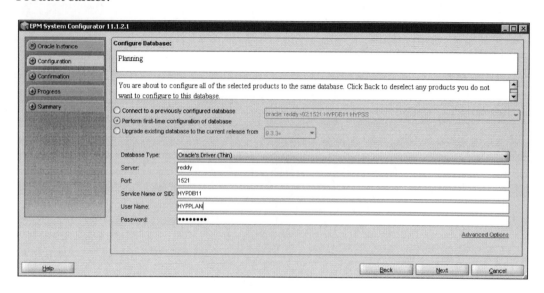

Click **Next** and here we will need to select **Deploy web application to an existing domain**, that is EPMSystem and go ahead by selecting **Next** as shown in the image below:

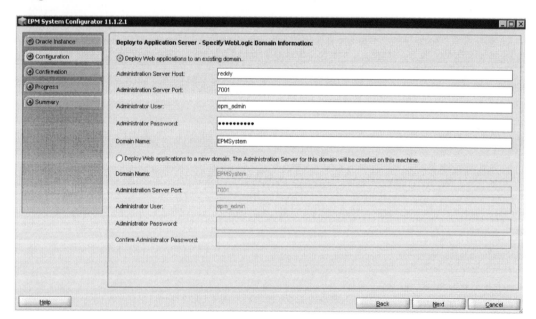

Click on **Next** to view the port number of 8300 for WebLogic Deployment. Hence, we can access Planning application directly from the URL.

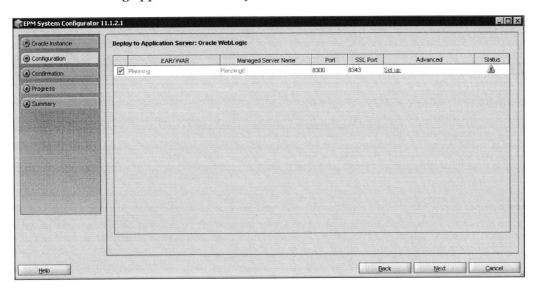

Click on **Next** to configure Hyperion Planning and we can view the completed status of the same:

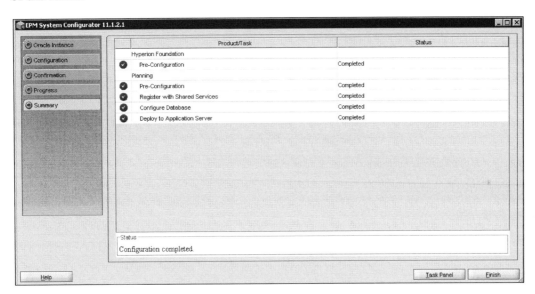

This is the end of Hyperion Planning Product Configuration. Click on the **Task Panel** button.

Now, we need to recap that we have configured individual products starting from Hyperion Foundation, where we configured the Oracle Hyperion Shared Services product followed by Oracle Essbase Server, and then EAS (Essbase Administration services). We have also configured Oracle Hyperion Planning.

Now, we are yet to configure Reporting and Analysis, and Oracle EPM Workspace.

Configuring Reporting and Analysis

The configuration of Reporting and Analysis is responsible for product configurations such as Web Analysis, Hyperion Financial Reporting. These are the reporting tools that are capable of creating Hyperion Planning Reports and we have installed them as well.

Select the activities under **Reporting and Analysis**, as shown in the following image:

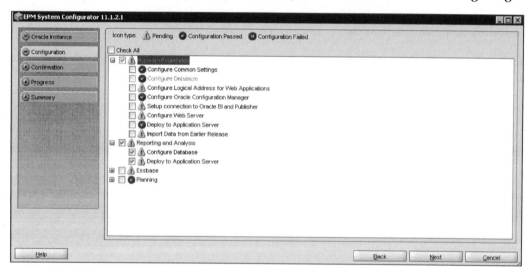

Click on **Next** to provide database configuration details. Here, we will give the details of Oracle Schema "HYPRA' created for Reporting and Analysis product configuration.

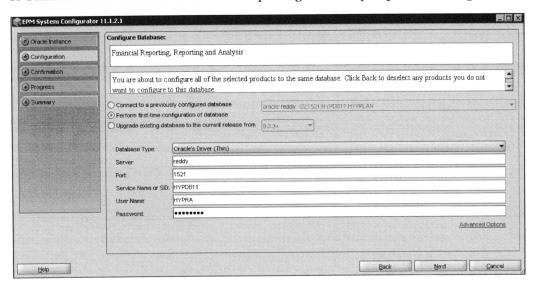

Click on **Next**.

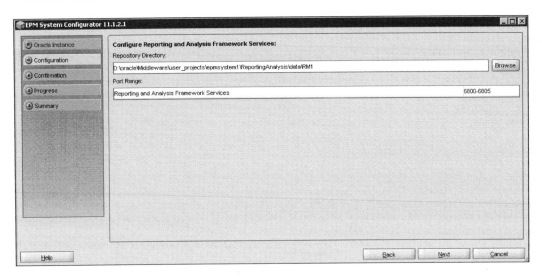

In the next step, we can view the port information and the list of products to be deployed to Oracle WebLogic.

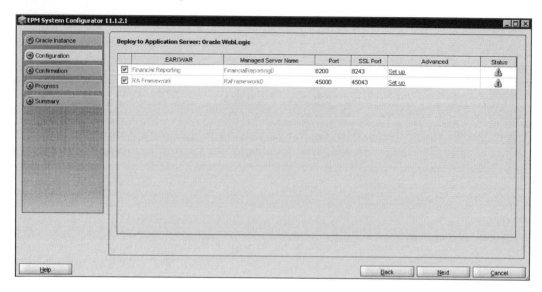

Click on **Next** and configure Reporting and Analysis, which includes Shared Services registration, configure database, and finally deployment to Application Server (that is WebLogic).

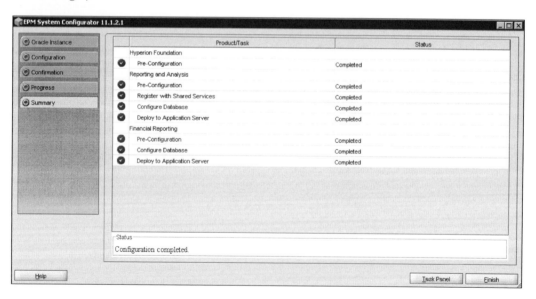

This is the end of Reporting and Analysis configuration. Click on **Task Panel** to get back to the home page of **Configuration**.

Configuring Oracle EPM Workspace

This is the last step in the configuration of Oracle EPM. We will select **Configure Web Server**, as shown in the following image. We can also see that all other products—Hyperion Foundation, Essbase, Planning, and Reporting and Analysis—are configured successfully and therefore we see green ticks against them.

So far we have deployed the products of Shared Services, EAS, Planning and Reporting products such as Web Analysis to WebApp Server Oracle WebLogic. To make all of these products to be accessible from a single end user interface of Oracle EPM Workspace, we need to configure all the products with Web Server—Oracle HTTP Server—as shown in the following image:

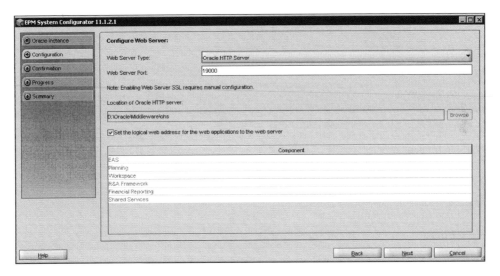

We can also view the list of products in the previous image, which are configured with Web Server.

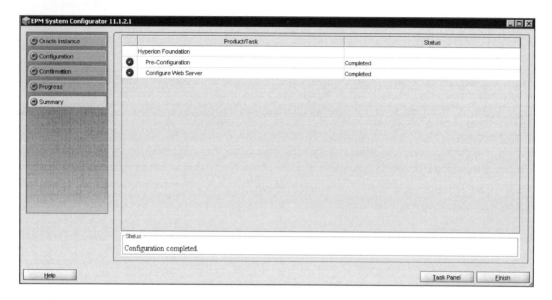

Configuring Oracle EPM Products in distributed environment

We will explore the configuration in distributed environment with an example. Imagine that there are three machines—Machine A, Machine B, and Machine C—and we have installed Oracle EPM System Products, as shown in the following image:

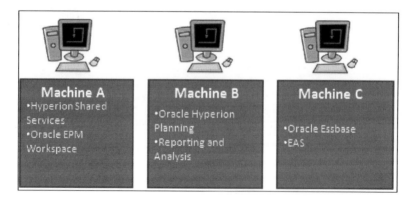

The following is the sequence of Oracle EPM Configuration.

1. Firstly, we will configure Hyperion Shared Services on Machine A. As per the recommended sequence, Shared Services is first followed by Essbase, EAS, Planning, Reporting and Analysis, and finally Workspace.

2. We need to recall that products such as Oracle Hyperion Planning, Reporting and Analysis, Oracle EPM Workspace, and EAS need to be registered with Shared Services. We will run EPM Configurator on Machine C because Essbase has to be configured before Oracle Hyperion Planning.

    When we run the EPM Configurator on Machine C, the first task is to configure with previously configured Shared Services on Machine A, as shown in the following image.

    We use the option of **Connect to a previously configured Shared Services Database**.

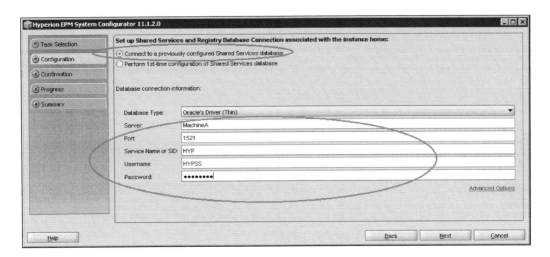

    This is how we configure all the products of Oracle EPM System with Hyperion Shared Services to maintain one single interface to authorize and authenticate users across the applications of different products.

    After registering with Hyperion Shared Services, other configuration tasks like Database configuration and Deployment to WebApp Server follow in the usual fashion.

3. We will run EPM Configurator on Machine B, where we will register again with the previously configured Shared Services and configure the Hyperion Planning and Reporting and Analysis products.

4. Finally, we will configure the Web Server for Oracle EPM Workspace.

Oracle EPM Services

Oracle EPM Installer creates Windows services of the products and we will learn the recommended order of starting these services and also learn how to start the services in this section.

Starting Oracle EPM Services

This is one of the more confusing areas to most of the Planning developers. As such, we will explore this in greater depth.

There is a script called `start.bat` which is available at `MIDDLEWARE_HOME/user_projects/epmsystem1/bin`. Starting this script will start all the Oracle EPM Services installed on the machine. The script also takes care of the correct order.

We can also start the services from **Start** menu.

Start | Programs | Oracle EPM System | Foundation Services | Start EPM System

Likewise, a single stop script is also available to stop all the Oracle EPM Services and it's available at the same locations, where we have start script.

Recommended order of starting services

The following is the start up order that provides information about the products and their Windows service names as well.

- Relational database.
- User directories (external user directories such as MSAD, which we generally configure with Hyperion Shared Services in implementations). Need to ensure that the configured User directories are started.
- Foundation Services includes both Hyperion Shared Services and EPM Workspace.
- Reporting and Analysis Framework.
- Web server.

The remaining services can be started in any order. They are as follows:

- Essbase server
- Administration Services Application server
- Web Analysis Application server
- Planning Application server
- Hyperion RMI registry

The following table lists the Services order along with the Windows service names:

Services	Windows Display Name	Service Name/Path
Foundation Services Managed Server Application Server	Hyperion Foundation Services - Managed Server Application Server	HyS9Foundation Services
Hyperion Reporting and Analysis Framework - Agent Service	Hyperion Reporting and Analysis Framework	HyS9RaFrameworkAgent
Reporting and Analysis Framework Application Server	Hyperion Reporting and Analysis Framework – Web Application	HyS9RaFramework
Web Server	Oracle Process Manager(EPM_epmsystem1)	-
Essbase Server	Essbase Server	Start->Programs->Oracle EPM System-> Essbase -> Essbase Server -> Start Essbase
Administration Services Server	Hyperion Administration Services- Web Application	Hys9eas
Financial Reporting Services	Hyperion Financial Reporting - Print Service	FRPrintService
Financial Reporting Application Server	Hyperion Financial Reporting – Web Application	HyS9FRReports
Web Analysis Application Server	Hyperion Web Analysis- Web Application	HyS9WebAnalysis
Planning Application Server	Hyperion Planning –Web Application	HyS9Planning
Financial Management Services	Hyperion RMI Registry	Hyperion RMI Registry

We need to note that the timing between starting each service is important. For example, when starting Shared Services, it is important to provide a delay before the next service is started to ensure Shared Services is fully started. If the delay is not provided, the applications will not work properly.

Validation and verification of Oracle EPM Products

After all the hard work of installing and configuration, in this section, we are at the last step where we will validate and verify our installation.

Validation of Oracle EPM Products

We can validate the installation with the help of **EPM System Diagnostics**. We have to run EPM System Diagnostics on each machine of deployment and the system generates an HTML report.

This web report is like a report card at the end, which gives information of the status whether the configuration of a component completed successfully or not. If any of the tasks fail, it's painted in red, else it's displayed in comforting green. It provides more information about the task and the test description as well.

How can we launch Oracle EPM System Diagnostics?

Navigate to MIDDLEWARE_HOME/user_projects/epmsystem1/bin, double-click on

validate.bat.

We can also launch the same from **Start** menu. **Programs | Oracle EPM System | Foundation Services | empsystem1 | EPM System Diagnostics**. It takes a while and then shows the web report.

Verification of Oracle EPM Products

We will verify the installed products by logging into the products. The following image lists the products and their URLs:

Product Name	URL
Hyperion Shared Services	http://[Hostname]:[WebServerListenPort]/interop/
	http://reddy:28080/interop/
EPM Workspace	http://[Hostname]:[WebServerListenPort]/workspace/
	http://reddy:19000/workspace/
Administration Services	http://[Hostname]:[WebServerListenPort]/easconsole/console.html
	http://reddy:1423/easconsole/console.html
Oracle Hyperion Planning Application Wizard	http://[Hostname]:[WebServerListenPort]/HyperionPlanning/AppWizard.jsp
	http://reddy:8300/HyperionPlanning/AppWizard.jsp

In this image, we can also view the URLs of the products with the default port numbers and on the machine's host name 'reddy'. We will set the credentials to the username 'admin' and password as 'password'.

Summary

We started the chapter with Oracle EPM Architecture in tiers—Client, Web and WebApp, and Database and Services. These tiers helped us in understanding and deciding the deployment plan. We have also looked into two of the Oracle-recommended deployment strategies, which would be very handy when we propose to a client.

We understood the prerequisites even before we initiated the software download. We have also learned how and what to download for Oracle Hyperion Planning. We spoke of Support Matrix reference guide, which will be useful in determining the right platform for Oracle Hyperion Planning implementations.

We have understood installation and configuration of Oracle Hyperion Planning and its complementing products such as Oracle Essbase, Hyperion Shared Services, EAS, Reporting and Analysis and Oracle EPM Workspace. We talked about the configuration when multiple machines are involved in a distributed environment. We also learned the correct order in which to start Oracle EPM windows services.

Before we concluded the chapter, we validated and verified that the installation worked by logging in to all the products.

3

Introduction to Hyperion Planning Dimensions

First master the fundementals

— Larry Bird

We successfully installed Planning software in the previous chapter. Before we start Planning Application creation, we will learn the very basics of Planning Dimensions in this chapter.

Let us take a look at a likely conversation between a lazy client and a hardworking Oracle Hyperion consultant:

Client: *How are you guys progressing on the installation front?*

Hyperion consultant: *We have successfully installed and tested the configuration.*

Client: *Now, what's next?*

Hyperion consultant: *We need to understand the as is or current process of your organization so we can design the Planning solution accordingly. We would request you put us in touch with the gentleman who can help us in understand the Planning and budgeting of your company and who can also help us arrange interviews with the correct teams or departments as a part of the user interviews.*

Client: *Okay, that sounds good. I'll talk to Mr. XYZ to get in touch with you and he can help you with the understanding of our current processes and also help you with user interviews as a part of requirement gathering.*

Hyperion consultant: *Thanks. So, we'll understand the requirement to finalize the dimensional Structure and later we'll create the Planning application accordingly.*

From this conversation, it is evident that the Planning Application is made up of Dimensions and we will introduce them in this chapter, in the following sections:

- Hyperion Planning Dimensions
  - Accounts
  - Year and period
  - Scenario
  - Version
  - Entity
  - HSP_Rates
  - Currency

- Dense or Sparse

Hyperion Planning Dimensions

Technically, **dimensions** are the basic foundation of a Planning Application;, it's like a skeleton to the body of a Planning Application.

Dimensions are composed of members and are the place holders of the stored and calculated numbers in the cube.

All the dimensions together are generally referred to as an **Outline**, which basically means the whole structure of the Planning Application or Planning Cube.

There are two types of Hyperion Planning applications:

- Multicurrency Planning application
- Single currency Planning application

Every Planning application has a set of Standard Dimensions and these dimensions vary from multicurrency Planning application to single currency Planning application.

What is the difference between multicurrency and single currency?

Multicurrency, as the name suggests, is the Planning Application that caters to the requirement of Planning, which is spread across different countries with different currencies. Typically, with effect of globalization, most companies operate in different countries with different currencies. Therefore, our Planning application needs to have many currencies or multi-currencies; hence, the name 'multicurrency'.

Coming to the dimension of these Planning Applications, there are additional two dimensions—Currency and HSP_RATES in a multicurrency planning application which are not present in single currency application. These two dimensions are responsible for currency conversion using exchange rates, which we will be explored in *Chapter 10*.

Now, we can list the standard dimensions in both Planning Applications. The Standard Dimensions List is shown in the following image:

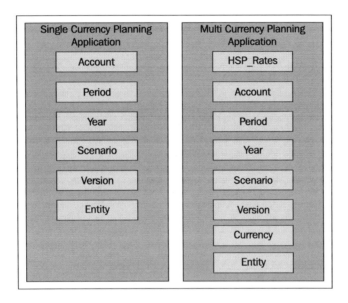

The same dimensions list can be seen in the following image showing the outlines of a multi currency and a single currency application in the Essbase Administration Services Console.

The following screenshot showing **Essbase Administration Services (EAS)** View of Planning Application gives the outlines of both single currency and multicurrency.

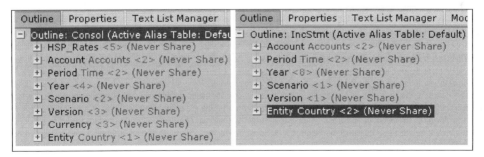

> The standard dimensions are the mandatory dimensions for any Planning Application. Nevertheless, a Planning Application may have additional dimension that are called as **custom dimensions** or **user-defined dimension**, which are in addition to the standard dimensions.
>
> Note: There can be maximum 13 custom dimensions in a planning application.

Why are all these standard dimensions required for each and every Planning Application?

Planning Application stores data in an Essbase Cube. Essbase is a multidimensional database. It is structured around the concept of dimensions. Dimensions are meant to categorize data values. Data is accessed and stored via a cube intersection consisting of a member from each of the dimension in an application.

We have already said that dimensions are meant to categorize data values.

Let's assume an example of a fictitious company XYZ. XYZ operates in India, Europe, and USA. XYZ wants to track revenue earned and cost incurred at different locations on monthly basis. Along with the actual revenue/cost numbers for each location, XYZ wants to track the budgeted revenue/cost numbers as well, so that the management can carry out variance analysis.

If we analyze the requirement of XYZ Enterprises, we can easily infer that XYZ wants to categorize its data based on following criterion:

- Revenue/expense accounts
- Month and year
- Location
- Actual/budget numbers

Each of the criterion mentioned here is used for categorizing data values that represent a dimension. We will explore each of the generic dimensions in more detail in the following sections.

Account Dimension

This is one of the standard dimensions. All KPI's, measures, metrics, drivers, which we are going to decide and design as a part of Planning Application are all part of Account dimension.

The examples such as Revenue/Expense, which we mentioned as the Planning requirement of XYZ fictitious company, are Account Dimension members.

As mentioned, all the measures such as profit, loss, expenses such as IT expense, rent expense, HR expense, and so on form the Account Dimension Members. We will learn about the important of Account Dimension and how to design it as per the requirement in *Chapter 7, Metadata Load*.

Within Account dimension, there are many hierarchies and aggregations happening, as per the design.

Let's explore this through an example. Imagine a hierarchy of 'Gross Margin'. It would be computed as total revenue subtracted with total cost incurred.

Gross Margin = Total Revenue - Total Cost.

Here, we see the Account dimension members Gross Margin, Total Revenue, Total Costs, Sales, Others, Purchases, Other Costs.

You can see the Account Dimension View in Planning Application and EAS Console in the following figure:

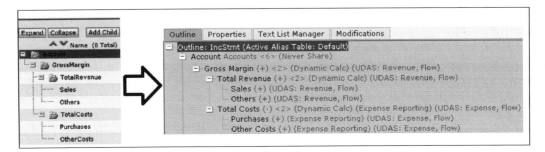

Year and Period dimension:

These two dimensions are also standard dimensions. They both represent time. Year, as the name suggests represents fiscal year.

Period would have time periods such as half years, quarters, or months, and has information of different calendar distribution of weeks such as 445, 454, or even.

> Generally, members of a dimension can be renamed but Year dimension members cannot be renamed once they are created. Nevertheless, we can add alias names to the members of year dimension; if not; rename the members.
>
> The other dimension, whose members cannot be renamed, is "Currency".

The Year and Period dimension View in Planning Application and EAS Console can be seen in the following figure:

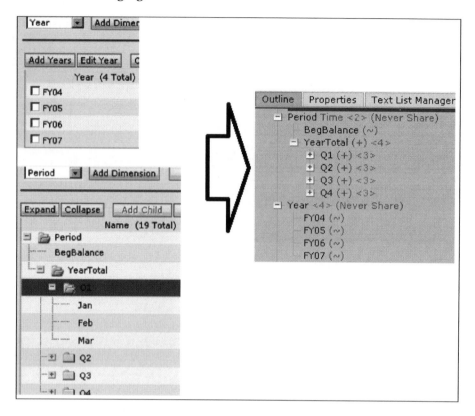

Scenario Dimension

This dimension is very broad categorization of data in a Planning Application.

The following are some of the examples of Scenario Dimension members:

- Budget
- Actual
- Forecast

The Budget scenario would reflect the Budget or Plan numbers entered by Planners or Users as a part of the Organization's budgeting activity. Whereas the actual scenario will contain the actual numbers extracted from Transactional Systems like ERP's.

We will understand in depth of these scenario members and how to design, in *Chapter 7, Metadata Load*. But for now, we first 'Plan' and then check our plan against actuals to see where we stand. Hence, actuals and plan numbers are important to measure the performance of an Organization.

Scenario dimension has one important Property of 'Time span'. For every Scenario Dimension member, we define the time span. The time span includes a starting year, ending year, staring period, and ending period.

These properties are used to enable the scenario for user input for a range of months and years based on the time span properties. Also, data entry and calculation can only be done during the time span.

For example, most organizations create a budget for 12 months (January through December) of the next calendar year. For enabling input to all months throughout the next calendar year, start year, and end year properties will be set equal to the budget year, and the start month and end month properties will be set to January and December respectively.

Time span properties can be set to equal different values for each of the scenario members based on requirements.

Scenario comes very handy in cases where an organization has different plans. Different plans are one year planss and long term plans, such as five-year plan.

In the following figure, you can see Scenario Dimension Members:

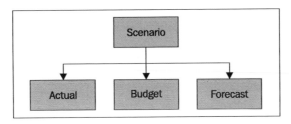

The following figure shows Scenario Dimension View in Planning Application and EAS Console:

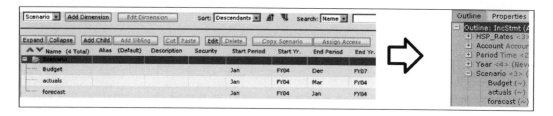

Version Dimension

Version Dimension is used to enable the **versioning** functionality for the Planning applications. As Planning, Budgeting, and Forecasting are usually iterative processes with several intermediate milestones, business users might be interested in creating versions during the process lifetime.

Additionally Version Dimension also provide options for controlling the way users input data through the user of different types of Version Dimension Members.

Two types of members can be created in the Version Dimension, they are as follows:

- Standard bottom up
- Standard target

These version types are covered in detail from design perspective in *Chapter 7, Metadata Load*.

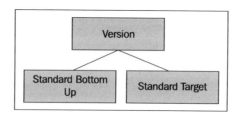

One can enter data only at level zero or base level members in **Standard Bottom Up**. In standard target, data entry is possible at any level in the hierarchy. This is the main difference between these two.

Let's explore this in more depth through a simple example. Imagine the company Apple is planning and it has a product, iPAD, to be sold in a city Chicago and it has to be sold in schools, offices and residential places in this city. First, we set a target for the product to be sold in Chicago. The target is 100 sales. Now, schools contribute 25, office 50, and residential 25, these are base level values entered, which is our bottom up. This way, the targets set are achieved with bottom budgeting.

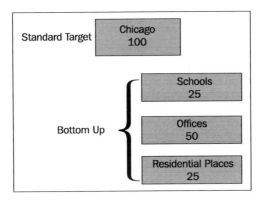

Bottom up facilitates bottom up budgeting/forecasting. In case of a bottom up budget/forecast users input data for level 0 members and the numbers for the parent members are automatically calculated based on the hierarchy and aggregation property. For example, in bottom up budgeting the expenses are provided for each of cost center and the total expenses at region/business level are automatically calculated based on the numbers provided for the base level cost centers.

The target version facilitates top down budgeting. In top down budgeting/ forecasting, users input numbers at parent levels such as expenses for the entire region and those numbers are allocated to base levels, to each cost center, based on the actual numbers.

Some companies also use a combination of top down and bottom up budgeting, target version also facilitates in such scenarios as the user can input at any level in the hierarchy.

For iterative planning, version dimension is the key. We can have versions such as draft1, draft2, and so on.

You can see Version Dimension View in Planning Application and EAS Console in the following image:

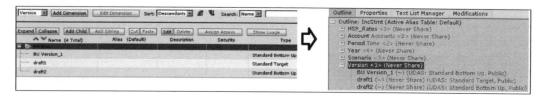

Entity Dimension

This is one of the Standard dimensions.

It's the key dimension that defines business organization hierarchy, workflow, and entity responsibilities in an organization.

Members such as cost centers and profit centers are arranged in a hierarchy based on the way the budget process flows through the organization. We will learn more of it in the *Chapter 12* and *Chapter 13* to understand how budget flow is related to entity dimension and its hierarchies design.

The dimension typically includes geographical regions, departments, Business units and other member's basis the way budget flow happens in an organization. Each entity will be tagged with its specific currency with result that data entry for a country or location will be known for its currency automatically.

Coming to our fictious Manufacturing Company XYZ, we mentioned that Planning involved Revenue/Cost numbers for locations. Here, locations are the members of Entity Dimension.

In the following image, you can see Entity Dimension view in Planning Application and EAS Console:

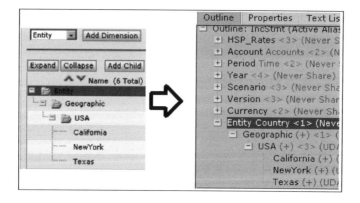

HSP_RATES Dimension

This is a multi currency Planning Application Dimension.

Members of the **HSP_Rates** Dimension can be divided into two types based on the data they hold:

- Input members.
- Currency rate members.

It comprises of **HSP_InputValue**, **HSP_InputCurrency** members, as shown in the following image HSP_Rates Dimension view in EAS Console:

For example, if an application has three currencies— the American Dollar USD, Indian Rupee INR, and UK Pound—we would have three corresponding members, such as:

- **HSP_Rate_USD**
- **HSP_Rate_EUR**
- **HSP_Rate_INR**

This is shown in the previous image.

What is the use of input members?

When a planner enters data in USD, let's say a Planner entered 10 USD in a data form, then the value of 10 is stored in **HSP_InputValue** and the currency code USD (in this case) is stored in **HSP_InputCurrency**.

Coming to the currency rate members such as **HSP_Rate_USD**, **HSP_Rate_EUR**, and so on, they store exchange rate values. We will cover exchange rates in more in detail in *Chapter 10*. Note that we cannot see **HSP_Rates** dimension in the planning application, it's a system generated dimension and it is visible only in the Essbase outline through EAS Console.

Currency Dimension

This is again a multi currency Planning Application specific dimension. We understand that organizations plan in different currencies.

As mentioned earlier, our fictitious XYZ manufacturing company operates in three countries—India, USA, and Europe. Hence, the Planning Application should be flexible and cater to the needs of Planners from all three countries so that they can plan in their respective own currencies.

As the name suggests, this dimension has all the currencies that we select as per the Planning Application requirement.

The following image shows Currency Dimension View in Planning Application and EAS Console:

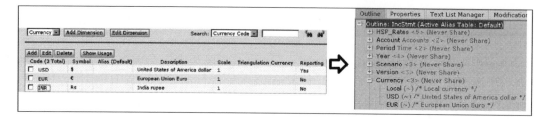

More of currency conversion with Practical examples will be covered in *Chapter 10*.

Dense and Sparse

It's an Essbase concept in which, every dimension labelled either **Dense** or **Sparse**. As Planning Application created an Outline in Essbase, we need to know what is the default labelling of these standard dimensions.

The definition of Dense or Sparse impacts the performance of the cubes and determines the design of the cube. We know that an Essbase cube is made up of dimensions and at granular level; it is made up of all data blocks. Therefore, data blocks make a cube in a way similar to how bricks make up a house.

It is important to know the list of all Standard Planning Application Dimensions and their respective default Dimension Label.

You can see the Dimension and its default Label in the following image:

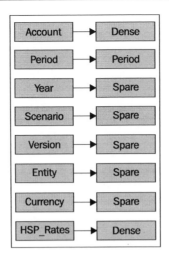

 We can add additional dimension to the existing
Standard Set of Planning Dimension, which are called as
Custom Dimensions. They are Sparse by default.

We can change the label of a dimension from Sparse to Dense or vice versa,
depending on the performance of the cube or application.

Summary

In this chapter, we have introduced and defined the basic dimension of a
Planning Application.

We have learned that there are two kinds of planning applications — multi currency
application and single currency application. We have also understood the differences
between them, not only in terms of dimensions, but also their business requirements.

We have introduced every standard dimensions starting from Accounts dimension
to Currency dimension. We have seen the how these dimension look in both
Planning Application and in EAS Console.

This chapter's objective is to introduce Planning Dimensions and we will learn more
about them in subsequent chapters.

In the next chapter, we'll learn how to create our first Oracle Hyperion Planning
Application.

4
Creating an Oracle Hyperion Planning Application - the Classic Way

A patient man has great understanding, but a quick-tempered man displays folly.

— Biblical proverb

In the previous chapter, *Hyperion Planning Dimensions*, we introduced the dimensions of a typical Planning Application, which will pave way in creating our first Planning application in this chapter. By the end of the chapter, we will have our first Sample Planning application standing tall and smiling.

Take a look at a possible conversation between Oracle Hyperion Planning guru (such as John Goodwin) and an Oracle Hyperion Planning beginner.

Planning beginner: *I have installed Planning Dimensions, and learned the basics. I feel confident enough to create Planning Application now. Do you have any suggestions for me right now, Mr. Planning Guru?*

Planning guru: *Yes, I do. I would suggest you create a sample Planning Application, explore it, and after that try to create a Planning Application based on a user's requirements.*

Planning beginner: *What's the point in creating a Sample Application? I am confident that I can directly create an application based on a user's requirements now.*

Planning guru: *No, you are absolutely wrong; be patient. Creating a sample application is not as easy as you think and it gives a whole lot of information in terms of application creation, and also helps one to understand the sequence of steps involved in Planning Application creation. You can later create a Planning Application based on a user's requirements, but now stick to making a sample application. There is no point in running into issues when you create your own application. Making a sample application is a good cushion to allow you the freedom to make errors.*

Planning beginner: *As you say Mr. Guru. Let me explore creating a sample Planning Application for now.*

In this chapter, we are going to create a Sample Planning Application and in the later chapters, we will create applications based on specific user requirements.

In essence, a Hyperion Planning application can be created in two ways:

- First, the classic way of creating an application, which is covered in this chapter.

- Second, we can use Performance management architecture to create a Planning application, which will be covered in next chapter, *Chapter 5, Creating a Planning Application Using EPMA*.

There is a lot of action and practical work in this chapter, unlike the previous chapter, which was just theory.

A classic application is the old-fashioned way of creating a Planning application. It is a standalone application and the maintenance of structure, dimensions and data exchange is not integrated with other applications created with Planning, HFM, Essbase or HPCM. By using EPMA the Planning application will be integrated with other applications and the whole environment of multiple applications is easier to maintain.

So, if you just want to create a separate Planning application, just do it the classic way. If you are going to create in a multi-application environment such as Hyperion Planning, HFM Application, and Essbase Application, then use the EPMA way.

In this chapter, we'll learn the following with an objective to create our first Sample Planning application.

- **Hyperion Planning application creation process**: This section gives the over view of the Planning Application creation process.

- **Pre-requisites of a Planning application**: In this section, we'll learn the prerequisites required before we can start creating Planning application.

- **Data source creation**: In this section, well discuss the very first step of creating a relational data source for the Planning application.
- **Application creation**:
  - ○ **Calendar settings**: In this section, we'll learn how to set up the Calendar, which includes the starting fiscal year, month, and also total number of years
  - ○ **Currency settings**: In this section, we'll learn how to make a Planning application multi currency or single currency and also set the default currency for the application
  - ○ **Plan Type settings**: In this section, we'll learn how to create more than one plan type and also understand the importance of multiple Plan types
- **Planning Application registration**: After Hyperion Planning application is created, it has to be registered with Oracle Shared Services and in this section, we'll learn how to register it and also understand the significance of registering a Planning Application to Oracle Shared Services.
- **Deployment of a Planning application to Oracle Essbase**: The Planning application stores data in Oracle Essbase cube. We'll learn how to create an Oracle Essbase database for the Planning Application in this section.
- **Sample Planning application initialization**: Hyperion Planning comes with a bundled sample application and we need to initialize this. We'll learn how to initialize it in this section.

Planning Application creation process

The section explains the complete process overview of a typical Hyperion Planning application creation. The following steps are in sequence and the order is important:

1. **Application creation**: This is the very fist step to create a Planning application. We'll create the data source database (Relational repository DB) for the Planning application and then we will start the Planning application creation process. We will also ensure that all the pre-requisites are met as a part of this step.

2. **Dimensional structure**: As we start creating Planning application, we need to set the Currencies, Calendar, and Plan type.

   Currencies and Calendar settings would help in creation of standard Planning dimensions of period, year, and currency. Coming to the other standard dimensions such as entity, account, year, period, scenario, and version, we need to load metadata. Loading metadata means adding members and their properties to the dimensions of a Planning application. How to load metadata will be covered in *Chapter 7, Metadata Load*.

Therefore, we set the following as a part of the Dimension Structure:

- ° Currencies
- ° Calendar
- ° Plan type
- ° Scenarios and versions.
- ° User access: Once we have finalized the dimension structure, we are good to go with user and group security access. Here, we need to consider security in Planning, based on the user privileges. This is covered in detail in *Chapter 9, User provisioning and access rights*.

3. **Data form creation**: In this section, we create data forms resembling the budget templates of an organization. *Chapter 10, Data forms* elaborates on data forms. We will create task lists and learn more about them in *Chapter 14, Task Lists*.

4. **Business rules**: Post data form creation, we create business rules. Business rules are the one which have the absolute analytical ability. The common calculations such as allocation computation, revenue calculation, expense calculation, balance sheet computation, and so on, can be achieved using business rules. *Chapter 11* and *Chapter 12* enlighten us about business rules. We need to note that not all calculations must happen through business rules, some may occur through member formulas in Planning outlines as well. We will explore the member formulas option in later chapters.

5. **Review and approval process**: Finally, after form creation and business rules, we incorporate the review and approval process of budgeting within our Planning application. We will learn about the review and approval process in detail in *Chapter 14, Planning Process*.

The following figure gives a high-level overview of the steps involved in any Planning application creation. It all starts with application creation, and then finalizing the dimension structure, where we build all the dimensions and their hierarchies with the help of metadata loading process. Once the dimension structure is finalized, we go ahead with setting the security. Next is the very important activity of data forms creation followed by business rules. Finally, we look into the review and approval process.

The overview of the planning application creation process is shown in the following image:

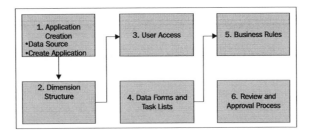

Prerequisites

A Hyperion Planning Application has its arms attached to a relational data source and Essbase cube. So we need to create a Relational Database Source for a Planning Application before we initiate the process of creating the Planning Application.

First things first, we need to create a relational source. As Oracle is our RDBMS, we'll create a schema/user by name 'PandB' and give the appropriate privileges of DBA. If we are not sure of how to create a schema within Oracle and give the privileges of DBA, shout out loud for a DBA. We must get one in a company and they'll take care of it. Or, you could Google it and decide that it's easier to do that than wait for a database administrator.

Creation of Oracle schema

We will be creating multiple Oracle schemas as a part of this book. Hence, we will learn the steps of creating an Oracle schema.

1. Go to **All Programs | Oracle Home | Application Development | SQL Plus** as shown in the following image:

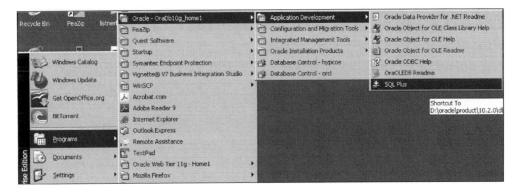

2. It opens the SQL Editor, as shown in the following image:

```
SQL*Plus: Release 10.2.0.1.0 - Production on Tue Mar 1 14:39:08 2011

Copyright (c) 1982, 2005, Oracle.  All rights reserved.


Connected to:
Oracle Database 10g Enterprise Edition Release 10.2.0.1.0 - Production
With the Partitioning, OLAP and Data Mining options

SQL> |
```

3. Type the following to create a user/schema with the name 'PandB' and the password of 'password'.

```
SQL*Plus: Release 10.2.0.1.0 - Production on Tue Mar 1 14:39:08 2011

Copyright (c) 1982, 2005, Oracle.  All rights reserved.


Connected to:
Oracle Database 10g Enterprise Edition Release 10.2.0.1.0 - Production
With the Partitioning, OLAP and Data Mining options
SQL> create user panb identified by password;

User created.

SQL> grant dba,connect, resource to panb;

Grant succeeded.

SQL> commit;

Commit complete.
```

 The user/scheme needs to have DBA privileges/DBO role. If it is Oracle, it's DBA and if it is MS SQL server, it's DBO.

Hyperion planning-related services

Ensure that all the services of Hyperion Planning are up and running. For the list of services and the order that the services ought to be started in, refer to *Chapter 2, Installation and Configuration*, where we discussed those topics.

Security

If we ask ourselves whether every user can create a Planning application, the answer would be no. It can't be the case, that way every user will create their own Planning Applications and start toying with the product until it's buried.

 We need to assign "Application creator" and "Dimension editor" roles for a user to create a Planning application.

We'll cover in detail all the available roles and what they are meant to do in *Chapter 8, Security*.

In our case, we are going to use 'admin' as the user, who already has these provisions. To cross verify whether the user 'admin' has the roles of 'Application Creator' and 'Dimension Editor'. Let's login into Shared Services

1. Log in to Shared Services, its URL is `http://hostname:280280/interop/index.jsp`.

2. Use **admin** as the user and **password** as the password to log into the Shared Services console.

3. Navigate the **User Directories | Native directories | Double click on users**, as rounded in the following image then provide **admin** for **User Filter** and click on **Search** as shown:

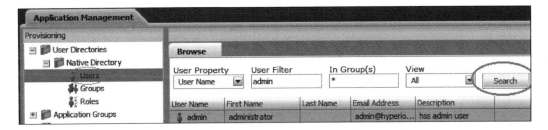

5. Right-click on the user **admin** and go to **Provision**, as shown in the following screenshot of Shared Services user provisioning:

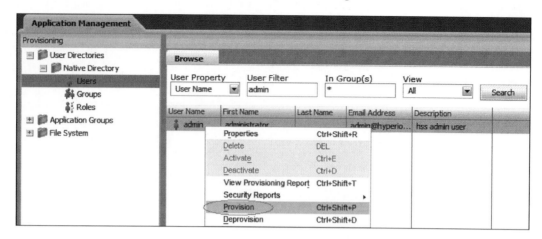

Expand **Shared Services** under **Selected Roles**. As we could see, the admin user is already an **Administrator** along with having the needed **Dimension Editor** and **Application Creator** roles assigned to him. He is kind of a big daddy already and therefore can create a Planning application.

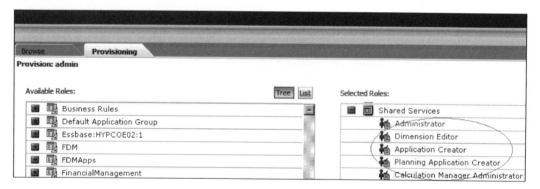

 The user who needs to create a Planning application needs to have Application Creator roles. We need the additional role of **Dimension Editor** as the same user going to create dimensions. These two roles — **Application Creator** and **Dimension Editor** — are the roles of **Shared Services**.

Application group creation

Application groups are the place holders for the applications which we create. Its intent within Shared Services is to organize registered applications and make Shared Services aware of applications for user/group provisioning. If an application is not registered with Shared Services, it cannot assign users or groups to it.

The created Applications might be Essbase application, Planning application or even HFM, which is in the suite of Oracle Enterprise performance management.

To simplify, application groups are like folders, we can have a folder named 'Planning' which is exclusively meant only for Planning applications i.e. a new application group with the name 'Planning'. So we can create a new folder, that is a new application group with the name 'Planning' and select Planning as the application group for each Planning Application.

How to create an application group?

1. Log in to **Shared Services**. We know the URL and credentials, which is

   ```
   http://hostname:280280/interop/index.jsp.
   ```

2. After we log in, we can see **Application Groups**. Right-click on it. We'll get the option of creating a new folder.

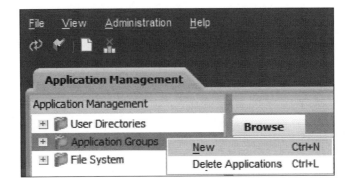

3. Go ahead and create a new folder and name it `Planning`, as shown in the below image, and finally select **Finish**.

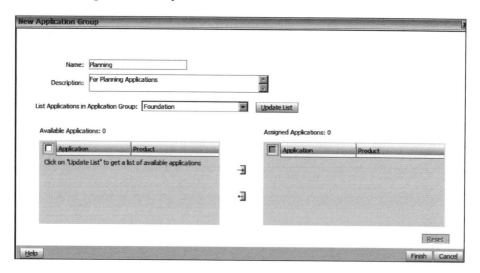

Before we go to the next section of *Data source creation*, we will quickly do a recap of the *Prerequisites* section.

- We have created an Oracle schema by name "PandB" with DBA role

- We checked that all the related services of Hyperion Planning are up and running.

- We ensured that the user who is going to create the Planning application needs has the appropriate roles of Application Creator and Dimension editor in Shared Services

- Finally, we created an Application group called `Planning`, which we will use in the Planning application creation process

Data source creation

In this section, we'll create a data source for our Hyperion Planning application. Every single Planning application needs a separate and individual relational database/schema. Planning applications cannot share databases/schemas and we cannot reuse the Planning system database (whose name is 'HYPPLAN', and which we used to configure the Planning product in *Chapter 2*) that we used when Planning was installed and configured. It is important to note that we cannot have a same relational source for two different Planning applications. In this section, we'll create a data source with the name 'PandB', which will be used in the next step of application creation.

Every new Planning application would need a new data source (that is an Oracle schema/user in case of oracle database or a new Database if MS SQL Server is the RDBMS).

Step 1: Logging in to Classic Application Wizard

How do we create data source?

We have the Hyperion Planning application wizard. As the name suggests it's not magical, but it is smart enough to manage data sources of Hyperion Planning applications. We can create, delete, and edit data sources, and also manage (create, delete, and edit) Planning applications. Hence, this wizard is capable of managing the data sources and also Planning applications.

The wizard has other names such as the Classic Application Wizard and Planning administrator. Now, we know when some one uses these terms, what exactly it means. We know that Workspace is the single door entry to all the products. We can access the Hyperion Planning Application Wizard through the Oracle EPM Workspace too.

Firstly, we can access the Planning application wizard directly with the following URL:

```
http://hostname:8300/HyperionPlanning/AppWizard.jsp
```

Or else, we can access it through the workspace. The workspace URL is `http://hostname:19000/workspace/index.jsp`.

After logging in to the Workspace, navigate to access the **Planning Administrator | Application Wizard | Classic Administrator**:

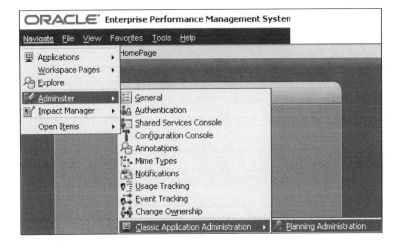

Step 2: Manage data source

If we are directly logging in to the Application wizard, we can use 'admin' and 'password' as credential set, the same credentials hold true for logging in to the Workspace. After logging in to the Application wizard, we will see the following options

- **Create**: This helps to create a new Planning application, before that we need to create data source for the Planning application.

- **Delete**: This is used to delete an existing Planning application. We use this option to say 'bye bye' to an application, that is, to delete an application.

- **Register**: After an application is created, we register the Planning application to the Shared Services. This option will help us in re-registering the Planning application with the Shared Services.

    The main page of Classic Application Wizard is shown in the next screenshot:

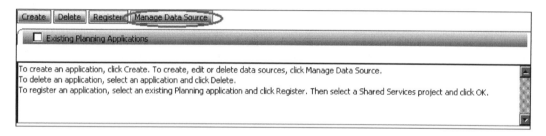

Step 3: Create the data source

If we read this section carefully, we will soon learn that we need to select **Manage Data Source,** as that's the very first activity to be done before we can start creating Planning application.

Click on the **Manage Data Source** button on the Classic Application Wizard main page Select **Manage data source**, as shown in the previous image. This provides us with the following information:

- **Data Source Name, Application Name**, and **Application Description**: This part of the window gives you information about the Planning application's name and its corresponding relation data source name and also the description of the Planning application. The description and the name of the application are provided while we create an application. As we have not created any Planning applications, we see no applications.

- **Cancel**: If we observe carefully towards the bottom right-hand side, we see option of **Cancel**, which will take us back to the home page of 'Application Wizard'.

- **Create Application**: Let's use common sense; we need data source for a Planning application to start creating. So once we are ready with the relational data source, we should be able to create a Planning application. Hence, we select this option after we get the source name in the window provided.

The mentioned points are reflected in the next image. Select **Create Data Source** to create one.

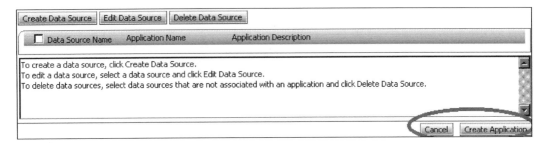

Step 4: Relational database information

Create Data Source' leads you to the window where we need to provide the following information for creating a data source:

- Data source name: Here, we have named the data source name as PandB. It's the required field. This is the name given to the data source, it's the same name given to the name of the relational data source created in the section *Creation of Oracle Schema*.

- Data source description: This is an optional field; we can give any meaningful description. We can skip this as well.

- Select database platform: Here, we need to select the database type.

  Examples of database types are Oracle, Microsoft SQL Server, and IBM DB2. Yes, for us, it's IBM DB2.

 No sooner the companies acquire any other product, their labeling changes immediately. DB2 is now called IBM DB2. Hyperion is now called Oracle Hyperion.

Okay, let's get back. In our case, we select Oracle database as repository.

There are mainly two divisions in the following image — **Application Database** and **Essbase Server**, as highlighted. Under **Application Database**, we need to be careful in giving the right information. In our environment, we have installed our Oracle database on the same system. The host name of the machine is 'reddy-676311e2b'.

> In Production environment, we generally have a different machine/ system/server as database server. We need to give information about the database server/system under 'Application database'.

- **Server**: This is the host name of the server, where the database is installed. In our case, its oracle database

- **Port**: You may need to change the port number from default depending on how the relational database is deployed in the organization. Else, as we select the database type, the port number is picked automatically. For Oracle its 1521, for Microsoft SQL server its 1433 and for IBM DB2 its 50000 by default.

> Ports have to be changed only if the reader is using non-standard ports.

- **Database**: We provide a name for the Oracle database. By now, we should have created an Oracle Database by the name 'orcl' and an Oracle schema/ user by the name 'PandB'.

- **User**: This is the schema/user that we should have created as a part of our Pre requisites. We can recall that we had created a user/schema by the name 'PandB' then. We are using the same schema here.

- **Password**: This is the password of the schema/User, which we mentioned in the previous step, that is password of the user 'PandB', which is 'password'.

After providing all the information, we can test ourselves. Click on **Validate Database Connection**. If all is well, we will get the message shown in the following screenshot which shows the relational database information for our planning application, saying that **The database connection was successful**.

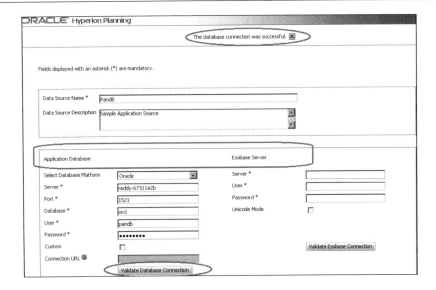

Step 5: Essbase information

Likewise, we need to provide information for the Essbase server. In our case, we had installed everything on one server. Hence, we see the same server name. Provide 'admin' and 'password' as the credentials and click on **Validate Essbase Connection**.

If the Essbase server is running, communication channels are good enough and we have provided correct information about the Essbase server, we will get a message stating **Essbase Connection was successful**, as shown in the following screenshot showing the Essbase information for our Planning application:

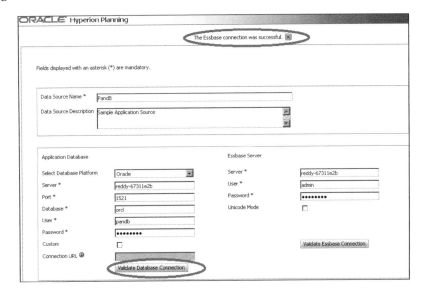

In production environments, we would have distributed environment. Let's hypothetically assume a three server setup. First is the Application server, where we had installed Hyperion Planning. Second is the Essbase server. Third is the Database server, where we had installed the Oracle database.

For the Application database, we'll give the information of the third server (server 3), whereas for the Essbase server information, we should give the information of the second server (server 2).

Now, we should be able to co-relate how Planning as an application has its connections both to relational source and also Essbase. Remember the two arms of a Planning application, which we mentioned earlier.

We see the option of Finish below, click that and now the data source with the name 'PandB' should get created. If the source is created successfully, we should get the following message, as shown in the following screenshot:

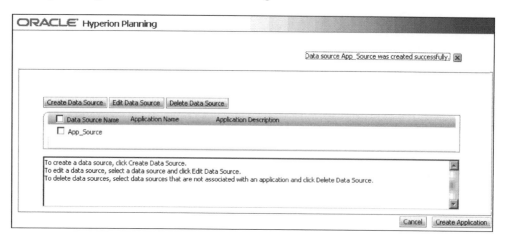

We see the newly created source **PandB**. This is the end of 'Data source creation'.

In the next section, we'll start creating a Planning Application using the data source 'PandB.

Creating a Planning application

In this section, we are going to create our first Planning Application using the same data source of 'PandB', which we created in the earlier section on *Data source creation*.

As a part of creating an application, we need to first provide the following information:

- General information
- Calendar
- Currency
- Plan type

Resuming from where we had left off in the previous section, that is, Classic Planning Administration Wizard, after the **PandB** source is listed, as shown in the following image, we need to select the source name **PandB** by clicking on it and then selecting the option of **Create Application**, which we would see towards the bottom right-hand side.

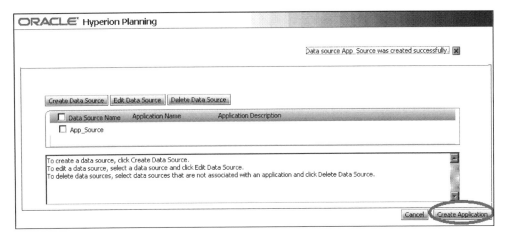

 We need to first select the source name, before we go ahead with application creation.

General information

In the very first tab of **Select**, we need to provide the following information:

- **Data Source**: It's a drop down, where we need to select the Relational data source. In our case, we had already created a data source by name 'PandB, which we should be able see. As it's the only data source we had created so far, we see only one and it is selected by default.

- **Application**: Here, we can use our own creativity to name our first Planning application. We'll stick to the same name as **PandB**. Hence, the data source name and application name is will both be **PandB**.

- **Application Description**: As it's understood, it's the description of the Planning Application. We can use any description we wish. Let's make it a meaningful one - for example, **Sample Application**.

- **Shared Services Project**: We know by now that **Shared Services** is used for user management and we will use the Application Group 'Planning' created as a part of pre requisite earlier. This step will register the Planning Application 'PandB' with Shared Services

Why do we need to register with Shared Services?

We need to use **Shared Services** for user provisioning. We need to create users and provide them with a role to access Planning application, we do it all within Shared Services. So, let's respect the old man **Shared Services**.

- **Instance**: Leave this set to the default. We have not created any instance. The default Planning instance is created as a part of Planning Configuration using EPM Configuration after installation.

- **Calculation Module**: In a Planning application, we need to incorporate the logic for allocation computation, revenue calculation, expense calculation, balance sheet computation, and so on. We employ either calculation manager or business rules for that. These are simple calculation scripts that we write to take care of the business logic. Calculation manager is a new addition to EPM architecture. Let's stick to the old one, business rules. We'll learn more about calculation manager in the next *Chapter 6, Creating an application using EPMA*.

The Classic application supports both Calculation Manager and Business Rules, while EPMA Planning application only supports Calculation Manager.

We do see that the option **Sample Application**, its smartly sitting in the bottom. This option will be helpful in creating a sample Planning application. We are going to use this option later. But for now, let us not select this option. Upon enabling this option, we won't be able to edit the other tabs of **Calendar, Plan Types**. So, let us be patient and come back to this option to check it later.

The screenshot shows the general information as shown next:

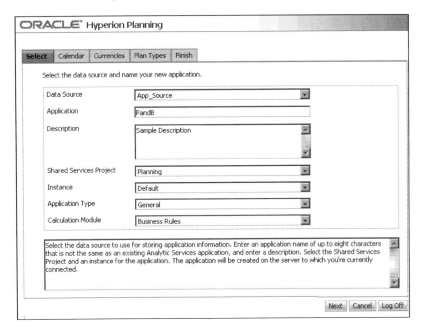

Select **Next** to go the next tab of **Calendar**.

Calendar

The **Calendar** tab is responsible for two standard dimensions; they are Year and Period. Year dimension would have the Fiscal Years and Period dimension would have the base time periods. Examples of period are quarters, months, and even days.

As we can see in the image below, the 'Base time Period' is responsible for 'Period' dimension. We could see the following options:

- **12 months**: This is the most commonly used period. Selecting this option creates both quarters and months (12) in the Period dimension. As planning and budgeting activity of a typical organization would involve both quarters and months. This is the most prevalently used.

- **Quarters**: By selecting this option, our Period dimension will have only quarters: such as Quarter1, Quarter 2, and so on, without month members.

- **Custom**: To cater to more varied requirements, we can customize the periods further by selecting **Weeks** or **Daily**. Hence 'Custom' gives us the freedom to select either **Weeks** or **Daily**.

  When you select 'Custom', you need to select two options as per the requirement

  ○ Prefix: We need to either type 'Week' or 'Day' here.

  ○ Periods per year: How many weeks or days can be determined by what number is given here. This field determines how many custom members need to be created for a single calendar year. For example if we are creating weekly base time periods, the periods per year will be set equal to 52 as there are approximately 52 weeks in an year.

These two are not editable unless we select the **Custom** option.

The following screenshot shows how the Period dimension would vary depending on the 'Base time period' selection.

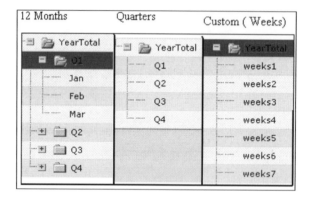

 Period dimension is created in a manner that months roll up to quarters, and quarters roll up to years.

What would be the criteria to choose of the options of 'Base time period'?

The answer to this depends on the Planning and budget activity of the organization for which we are implementing. If an organization's Planning is interested in data down to the weekly level; i.e. interested in doing weekly Planning and Budgeting, then we would create weekly base time periods using the Custom Base Time Period option. Nevertheless, 12 months is the most common choice.

On the right-hand side of the following image, we have to enter information for starting fiscal year, month, and also the total number of years. This information will determine our Year dimension.

We also need to provide information on weekly distribution; we see the available options—Even distribution, 4-4-5 weekly distribution, 4-5-4 weekly distribution, and 5-4-4 weekly distribution.

What are these weekly distributions?

Let's answer by taking 5-4-4 weekly distribution as an example. This means that the first month of a quarter has five weeks, the second month has four weeks as does the third month. The same pattern of five weeks for the first month, and four weeks for second and third months would repeat for the rest of the quarters too. By default, quarterly numbers are spread evenly over the month, when you want to spread the numbers using the 445 method, you have to tell the application here that you are going to use it and make specific settings on specific accounts (mostly balance sheet accounts). So, if you choose even distribution here, you cannot use the 445 distribution any more.

It also benefits the weekly distribution in terms of allocating numbers entered at summary time periods to base time periods. For example, if the user enters a number at Q1 and weekly distribution is set equal to 5-4-4 than the system will automatically allocate the number to the base months based on the assumption that Jan has five weeks, Feb has four, and Mar has four weeks. Jan will get a major share whereas Feb and Mar will get an equal share of the amount entered for the summary time period Q1.

The total number of years is also important, which directly reflects how many years of plan the organization would prefer or number of years whose data the Planning Application will hold.

 Total number of years can be changed by adding more years even after application creation. It should be noted that Start Year can never be changed after application creation.

The following screenshot shows the Calendar tab of Planning Application Creation:

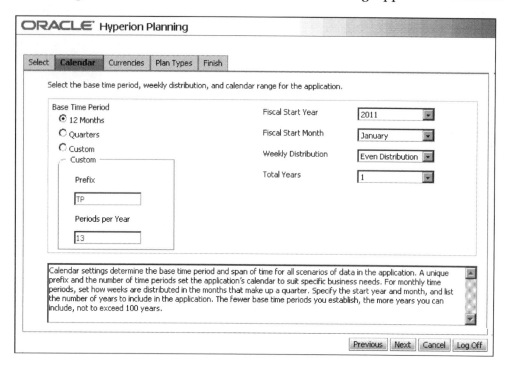

Make no changes in this **Calendar** tab. **Select Next** to see the **Currencies** tab.

Currencies

In this section, we are going to set the default currency and we will decide if the Planning Application is going to support multiple currencies and select the options appropriately.

In which case do we use 'support multiple currencies'?

Suppose an organization is spread across different countries, say in the US, UK, and India. As a part of our Planning and Budgeting activity, planners from these countries need to enter data. Indian planners prefer to enter plan data in INR, US planners enter in USD, and likewise, planners from the UK would prefer to enter the numbers in GBP. In this case, the entities can be understood as India, UK, and USA. Though the data is entered in different currencies, the management would be interested to see the financial reports in a single currency. If the organization is headquartered in the UK, then the financial report has to be in GBP and for that INR and USD need to be converted to GBP. The currency conversion happens with the help of the exchange rate.

In the previous example, as the financial reports are needed to be reported in GBP, we define GBP as the 'Reporting Currency'. More about the reporting currency and related concepts will be explored in *Chapter 9, Data Entry*.

Hence, if the requirement involves multiple currencies, we need to create an Application that supports 'multiple currencies'.

Default Currency: This is the default currency for the entire Planning application. There might be many entities such as the UK, US, and India, and these entities have their own respective currencies. But, the entire Planning application has a currency, which is defined as default currency. The **Default Application Currency** establishes the first Reporting Currency for the Planning Application in which all entities local currency will be converted. Support multiple currencies: 'Yes' or 'No' will determine, if our Planning application supports multiple currencies.

 In a multi currency application, it creates two additional Standard Dimensions—Currency and HSP_Rates. The creation of these dimensions depends on us selecting the option to Support multiple currencies.

The following screenshot shows the Currencies tab in Planning Application Creation:

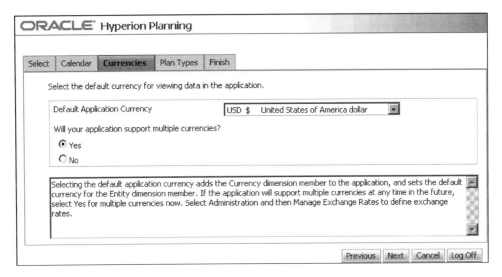

 The settings of default currency and 'Support multiple currencies' cannot be revoked after application creation. We need to think carefully before making a selection.

Click on **Next**.

Plan types

In this section, we will introduce plan types and understand the significance of multiple Plan types.

What is a Plan type? A **plan type** is a kind of a Planning model; technically, it's an Essbase cube. Let try to understand this in more detail. By now, we have stated many times that every Planning application is connected to an Essbase database or cube.

Each Hyperion Application creates a corresponding Essbase Application. For each of the selected plan types an Essbase database is created. The names of the Essbase Application and databases are the same as those of Hyperion Planning Application and plan types.

When we create a Planning Application, we select and name the plan types to be created as part of the application.

We can have as many as three plan types in an application in addition to the plan types required for the separately licensed Planning modules. If we opt to select three plan types then we will ultimately be creating three Essbase databases.

For example, if we have a Planning application named 'Plan1' with three plan types Incstmt, BalSheet, and Revenue, we'll see how it looks in Essbase console (EAS) and also in the application creation tab of 'Plan Type'.

In the following image , on the left-hand side is the plan type selection, while we create a Planning application and on right-hand side , we can see the Essbase databases by the same names of plan type in Outline Editor of EAS console.

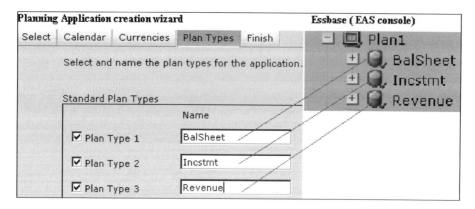

Therefore a plan type is nothing but an Essbase database of an Essbase application.

We'll visit plan types in this chapter under the section *Plan type settings*. Now, let us get back to dimension structure.

Why do we need many plan types, isn't one plan type sufficient?

It depends on the requirement for planning and budgeting of the organization. Separate Planning models in a single application can be incorporated with the help of multiple plan types. Different Planning types mean different Planning models, for example our requirement demands our separate 'Revenue' and 'Expense' models, and then we need two plan types.

Creating multiple plan types in a single application provides benefit of lower user/group security administration and lower metadata maintenance effort.

Once the plan types are created, they cannot be changed. Even if we need one more plan type in the later course of time, it cannot be made. Therefore, we need to be very careful while we select the plan types. We need to keep the changing requirements in mind; we may select two plan types even if we need only one.

Maximum three plan types can be customized; additional two plan types may be added if Workforce and Capex are initialized for the app.

It's also important to know that data can be shared between plan types and also members of Accounts, entities, and so on. Dimensions are associated with plan types. Similarly, some of the members might be associated with both the Plan types, ABC and XYZ. In such scenarios, one of the plan types needs to set as the source plan type for the account member. We'll see about how to associate and other settings in *Chapter 6, Settings*.

As shown in the following screenshot, there are three plan types, and we can tick them to select, or uncheck them to deselect. The name of the plan type can be given accordingly.

The names of the plan types can be changed by the users but they must follow the standard Essbase naming conventions of no more than eight characters with no spaces or special characters.

The following screenshot shows the **Plan Types** tab of Planning Application Creation:

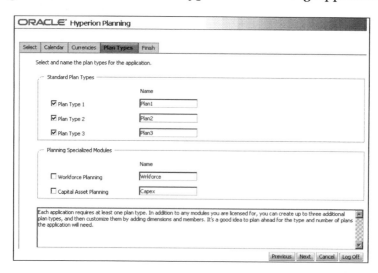

As we are going to create a sample Planning application, no need to edit or select anything in this tab. Now, select the very first tab **Select**, where we had firstly given the name of application and its description.

Taking a closer look, we'll realize that the name of the application and description are lost, let's provide it again as we had already discussed in the section *General information*. This time we need to carefully select **Sample Application**, calmly lying at the bottom. Tick it as shown in the following screenshot:

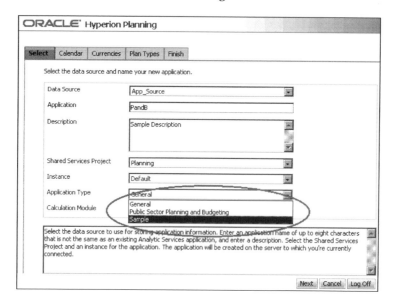

And then click on **Next**. As we have selected **Sample**, the control does not navigate to the next tab, **Calendar**; rather, it jumps to the last section **Finish**. As we have selected sample application, it assumes the settings of **Calendar**, **Currency**, and also **Plan type**. Now we know why we did not select Sample Application initially. It is because then we can learn and explore about the other tabs. You can see that the information within **Calendar**, **Currency**, and **Plan Type** is grayed out. It appears to be warning us—no entry.

In next section, we'll lean about the last tab, **Finish**.

Finish

To err is human, that's why the Oracle Hyperion Planning product has been built in a manner that gives us a second chance to correct mistakes before the application starts getting created. In this section, it displays the whole list of settings and selections, which we had done by providing information in the tabs **Select**, **Currency**, **Calendar**, and **Plan Types**.

It provides information that the Planning application name is **PandB** and its data source name is also 'PandB'. Description of the Planning application is **Sample Application** and its **Shared Services** project is **Planning**. We need to remember that we created the application folder `Planning` in **Shared Services** under the **General information** section. 'Business Rules' is the calculation mode for the application. This is all the information that we provided in the **Select** tab of the application creation screen.

January 2010 is the starting date of our Planning application. The total number of years of our Planning application is four. This information has been provided in the tab **Calendar**.

USD is the default currency of our application and it's a multi currency application with only one plan type; whose name is 'consol'.

 We need to remember that we have ticked **Sample Application**. By the virtue of this selection, system had done the settings of **Calendar**, **Currency**, and **Plan Type**. In real-life business scenarios, when we create a new application for a client, we don't select **Sample Application**; rather we provide the appropriate settings, as per the requirement.

The following shows the **Finish** tab of Planning Application Creation:

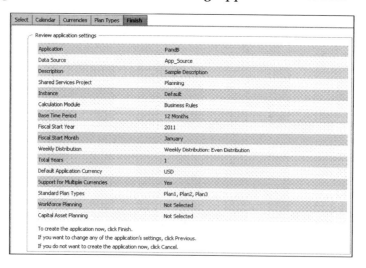

After reviewing all the settings, select **Finish**, this will initiate the Planning application creation process and it will bore us with an hourglass for a while and then rewards us with a note of congratulations. It should display the text **You have successfully created a new Planning application**.

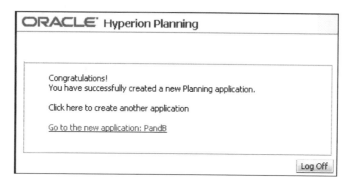

Now, let's move out of the wizard's world. Select **Log off**, which should be hiding right at the bottom. When it prompts a message **Do you want to end the session**, select **Yes**. This will lead to the home page of Hyperion Planning page.

We have successfully created our first Planning application, so let's move ahead by logging into **PandB** Application for the first time.

Sample Planning Application initialization

In the previous section, we successfully created the PandB Planning Application. In this section, we'll initialize our Sample application.

What is initialization of a sample application?

When we create an application, it does not create any data forms, task lists, member formulas, or Business Rules by default. We need to create them explicitly and we'll learn how create data form, task lists, business rules in the later course of the book. For the benefit of training, Hyperion Planning is bundled with a Sample Application with a few default Data forms, task lists, and other artifacts. The Initialization activity presents these pre-made artifacts and makes them available.

 Initialization of a Sample Applications is strictly for tutorial purposes. We would never do this in a real-life implementation. This activity of initialization has to be bypassed if we are creating any real-life Planning Application based on a user requirement application

Step 1

Access PandB Planning Application by logging into either Hyperion Planning URL or Oracle EMP Workspace

Planning URL: `http://hostname:8300/HyperionPlanning/LogOn.jsp`

Oracle EPM Workspace URL: `http://hostname:19000/workspace/index.jsp`

Using Planning URL

We need to provide appropriate credentials of admin (username: admin, password: password). Here, we do have a drop down for **Application**. As of now, we have created only one Planning application, so we see only 'PandB'. If there are many Planning applications, we need to also select the Planning application into which we intend to log in.

Select PandB and click on **Login** to get into the Planning Application.

Using Oracle EPM Workspace URL

We can alternatively access Planning Application through Oracle EPM Workspace

How can we access a Planning Application from Oracle EPM Workspace?

After we log into Oracle EPM Workspace, we see an option **Navigation**. Navigate to the following path:

Navigate | Applications | Planning | PandB, as shown in the following image.

There is also an option of **Refresh**, in case Planning applications are not updated. If we created a new Planning Application after we logged into Workspace, we cannot see the updated list of Planning Applications. We need to use the **Refresh** button to fetch the updated list of Planning Applications.

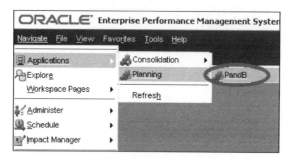

 It is recommended to access Planning Application through Oracle EPM Workspace

Step 2

After we log in, we see on left-hand side that there are no forms. It looks like an empty desert. Go to **Administration | Initialization | Initialize Sample Application** as shown in the following image:

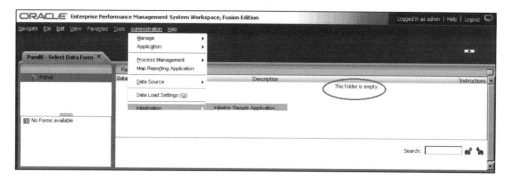

This will start initializing the Sample Application. It takes a while; in the mean time, getting some coffee is not a bad idea.

Finally, a message stating that the **Sample Application has been initialized** appears, as shown in the following image. Until we get this message, we should not do anything; we can sip on that coffee though.

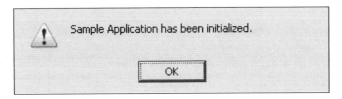

Now, we can view a few data forms which were not there before initialization.

The following image shows data forms of Sample Planning application:

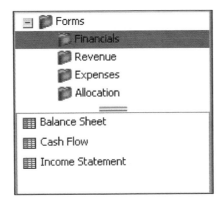

This is the end of initialization of Sample Planning Application and before we move on to the next section of creation the Database of Planning Application, we need to remember that this section is strictly meant for tutorial purposes, to work and get hands-on experience on the sample application, which is bundled along with the software. We don't do this in any of the real-time implementations.

Registration of Planning Application

When we had first logged into Application wizard, we had seen an option of registering an application. Registering an application involves registering it with Shared Services, this way user management of the Planning application can be managed from Shared Services.

The Application Wizard's main screen is shown in the following screenshot:

As a part of our Planning application creation, under the section **General information,** that is under the tab **Select,** we had already provided information about Shared Services project. If we don't remember, go back to the *General information* section. During that step the application 'PandB' has been registered with Shared Services. To reconfirm, we'll try to see the application in 'Shared Services'.

Follow these steps:

1. Log in into Shared Services. We can directly log in to share services using its URL or from the workspace as shown in the following screenshot:

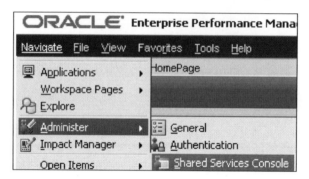

2. After we log in, on left-hand side we see **User Directories** and **Application Groups**. Expand **Application Groups,** we will find **Planning,** Expand **Planning** to check whether the application 'PandB' is under it or not.

3. Now, navigate **User Directories | Native Directory | Users**. Select **Users**.

4. There is a property **User** filters. Type **admin** in the space and click on **Search**.

5. Now, right-click on the username **admin** and select **Provision**. It leads to a new window, where under **Available Roles,** we could see **Planning** and also **PandB** application under it.

This is to verify that the Planning Application that we created, that is, **PandB** is registered with **Shared Services**.

Hence, we can conclude that registration was done as a part of the 'Application creation' process already. If we wish to re-register, we can do so by selecting the application name and clicking on **Register**. Otherwise, there is no need to do anything, the application has already been registered.

We get the option of **Register** in the very first page of Application wizard, as shown next:

Upon selecting the application 'PandB' and selecting **Register Application**, we will get the list of **Shared Services** projects. We need to recall that we had already created `Planning` folder in **Shared Services**.

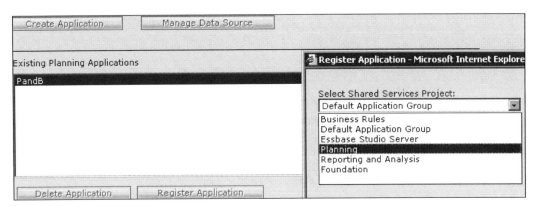

In cases where we create another Shared Services project, we can re-register using this option. Else, for us, there is no need to do anything as PandB is already registered.

Database creation

The Hyperion Planning Application creates a Hyperion Essbase application. To confirm the same, we can log in the EAS console and check the list of Essbase applications, we should see an application by name 'PandB' now expand it and check the database as shown in the image below. To our surprise, we see no Essbase database within the PandB Essbase application.

In this section we'll create a Planning database, which will create the Essbase database with an outline.

Acess the PandB Planning Application either through Workspace or Hyperion Planning web and navigate as

Administrator | Application | Create Database, as shown in the following image:

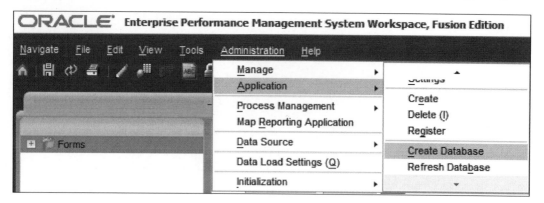

We see two options—**Create Database** and **Refresh Database**. Select **Create Database**, which will lead to a new window, as shown below:

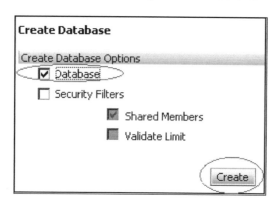

- **Database**: When we create a new Planning Application, we need to create a Database for the first time, so this selection will create the Essbase database as well. After the database has been created, whenever we make any structural changes to the Planning application such as adding new members to a dimension or changing the properties of any members of a dimension, and so on, we need to refresh the database using the option of **Refresh Database**. We will use this option extensively in the later chapters.

- **Security Filters**: In Planning application, it's very important to set up security. When we set up security access, the information is stored in Relational database. Now, imagine a scenario where we have a reporting tool such as **HFR (Hyperion Financial Reporting)** or **WA (Hyperion Web Analysis)** and we intend to create reports directly from these reporting tools by accessing data of a Planning Application, which is stored in Essbase database.

  Access information is stored in Relational database, but the Reporting tools would access data directly from Essbase cube. In these situations it's important to push security filters from relational source to Essbase. This will create a `Essbase.sec` file, which is used by Hyperion Essbase for user authorization.

 Security Filters need to be created / refreshed each time there is any change in the outline or access rights assigned to the outline.

We create for the first time, and as gradual changes can be captured by updating the security filters.

- **Validate limit**: Essbase limits the maximum size of each row in the `Essbase.sec` file to 64KB. `Essbase.sec` file containing rows with size greater than 64KB won't function properly with Essbase. Hyperion Planning provides an option to validate this limit at the time of security file creation / refresh, enabling you identify and resolve issues in security filters before pushing them to Essbase.

We'll learn more about the security filters in *Chapter 9, User provisioning and access rights*.

As we are going to create database for the first time, we'll check the **Database** and then select **Create**, as shown in the previous image. The system gives us a warning. It instructs us to be careful, warns us that this is a dangerous activity, and recommends that we make a backup.

 In real life business scenarios, it's recommended that we export the data from Essbase before creating or refreshing the database because the data could be erased on a refresh depending on the dimension changes. But in our case, it is not significant for the initial create action but is important later for Refresh actions.

So, we'll proceed by selecting **Create**.

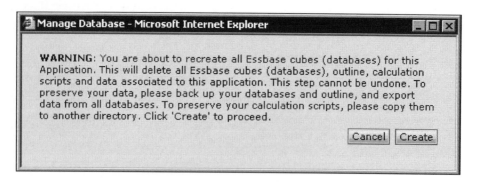

 In real life business scenarios / Production Environments, it's very important to take a complete backup before refreshing the database.

When the database is being refreshed, if an end user or Planner tries to access the Planning Application, a message **Cannot Process your** request is shown because the application is being refreshed.

We'll be disappointed to see status as 'Failed' and there are few errors as shown in the image below. Let's pay close attention and pull out the members that are mentioned in the error message. The error message clearly says that there is an error with member formula with member name. This is a good hint to debug. We know that there is some problem with the members formula and are also aware of the list of members which have a problem.

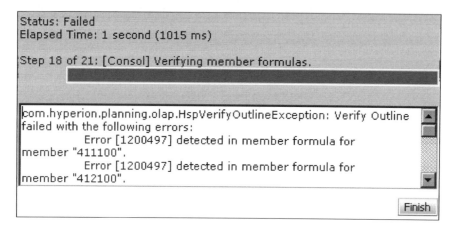

Click on **Finish**.

This is not a generic issue which one would face while creating a database for the first time. It is important note that this only occurred because it is the Sample application. As we have initialized sample application, it had created member formulas which are the wrong ones. In real time, we are any ways not going to initialize the sample application. Hence, this error will not come.

Let us not blame Oracle by making a mistake of packing a sample application which has errors. It's a wonderful opportunity to learn how to correct these member formulas and then refresh the database. Our objective is to make the status 'Success' rather than 'Fail'.

Lets get into debugging mode by rolling our sleeves up and solving this in steps:

1. First list down all the members which have member formula error. This information can be pulled from the 'database create fail message' window. There are nine members, starting from 411100. This list of members will be used in the later points.

2. These are all account dimension members; we'll go the Account dimension and hunt for these members.

3. After we login into Planning Application, Go to.

    Administration | Manage | Dimensions.

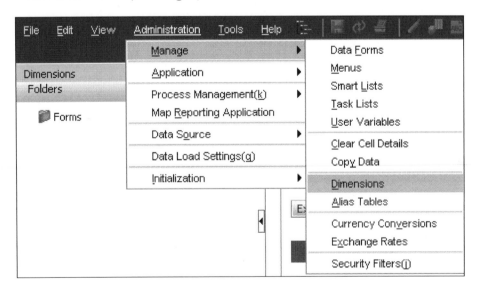

4. In this window, we see a drop down of all dimensions under **Dimension** tab. If **Account** is not the selected dimension, select Account dimension. Now, type the member which we have found to have member formula problem. For ex: 411100 as shown in the following screenshot and click on the search image as shown:

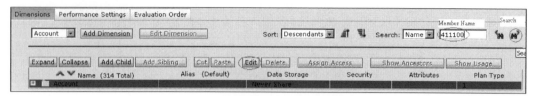

5. The system will search for the member and highlight the member which we had searched for. Now, as the member is already highlighted, click on 'edit' (the edit option is visible in the above image).

6. After selecting 'Edit', a new window opens up, which has 3 tabs. The last tab is 'member formula'. As we take a closer look at the formula, we see FY09 (highlighted) in the below image. Now, we need to recall that the sample application which we created has totally 4 years and its starting year and month are January 2010. Hence, FY09 is out of question and it's not a member in our 'Year' dimension. Refer to the section titled 'Finish' which was the last step in our Planning application creation.

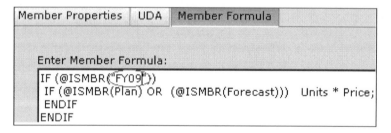

7. Now, go to the Year dimension drop down. In Year dimension, we see its members fro FY10 to FY14. Therefore, FY09 is not a part of this sample application, but few of the member formulas are using FY09, this is exactly the reason Database creation was failing. FY09 needs to be replaced with some other year, which is a part of our Year dimension. We'll replace it with FY10, as this is the existing year in our application. Hopefully the next Planning version will be devoid of this mess.

8. Now, click on 'Validate member formula', it'll throw an error stating that 'The entered member formula is invalid'.

9. Change FY09 to FY10, and click on 'Validate member formula' again ,this time it should say that 'Member formula is valid'

10. Select **OK** and select **Save**.

11. Repeat the same steps from step 3 for all the members, which have stated that they had problem with member formulas and we'll observe a common pattern that all of these member formulas have with FY09. Replace it with FY10. Post the changes, validate, and save. There are 9 members which needs this correction.

The errors and debugging which we have done are strictly for educational purpose. We might not even get the same errors in other versions of Hyperion Planning.

In a real life implementation, we are not going to use sample application. This way, we are not going to initialize an application. Therefore, we won't face these errors.

In most of the real life business scenarios, we actually have to load the metadata first before we create the database. We might be loading more metadata and refreshing the database later on. Metadata loading is the process in which we add members and also set their properties of Planning dimensions.

We can add members or change member properties later too. Every time we make these structural changes, we need to ensure that the database is refreshed.

Now, let's refresh the database, navigate to:

Administration | Application | Refresh Database.

This time, we are not going to create a database, we are going to refresh a database.

If a Planning Database contains data and we go on to recreate it, all data will be lost. This doesn't happen in the case of a Database refresh.

As usual, after we select **Refresh**, it will give you a warning. Click on **Refresh** to proceed. This time it should go through and finally should give us the below image which indicates that the status is **Succeeded**.

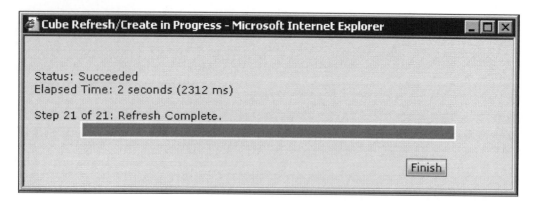

We have successfully created a flawless database. Now, we can open to EAS console and check if system had actually create an Essbase application by name **PandB**, we can see it created 'PandB' Essbase application and also its database whose name is **Consol**, which was our plan type. Double click on outline in the EAS console, we could see the dimensions too as shown in the following image.

The following screenshot shows the EAS console:

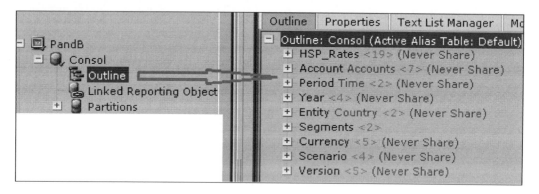

Summary

In this chapter, we learned all the steps involved in the creation of a typical Planning Application. We started with understanding the overview of the steps involved in a Planning Application creation. We had taken care of few pre requisites before we started Application Creation. We first created Data source required for Planning Application and then started the Planning Application Creation.

We learned about Planning Application Wizard in the process. Post creation of Planning Application, we initialized the Sample Planning Application Initialization of sample application (Which is only for tutorial purpose, and has no relevance when it comes to any Planning application based on User requirement or any real time implementation).

We relooked at the relationship between Essbase Application and Planning Application. We also learned how to create an Essbase database and its importance. In next chapter, we'll create a Planning application using EPMA (Enterprise Performance Management Architect).

5
Creating a Hyperion Planning Application (EPMA)

Change is inevitable but growth is optional

— John C. Maxwell

Let us take a look at a possible conversation between two Hyperion Planning Consultants. One is a senior consultant and the other once is a novice.

Consultant1: *I have been working on Hyperion Planning for a long time from version 4 to 9. How about you?*

Consultant2: *I started working with it recently and currently am working on version 11 and I find EPMA to be very good. It's a new way of managing and administering applications.*

Consultant1: *Yes. Yes, I know, it was there in version 9 as well. But, it had inherent problems and I never found a reason to look into it as am happy with the Classic Wizard.*

Consultant2: *Yes. indeed it's true that there were a few issues in the earlier versions. But in version 11, it is stable and believe me, the features and functionality are good and it's the future.*

EPMA Stands for **Enterprise Performance Management Architect**. It's a new way of managing application where EPMA helps in building and maintaining Hyperion Financial Applications/Hyperion Performance Management Applications (HFM, HP, Essbase, and so on) in one single user interface. Though there were many issues with EPM architect in version 9x, version 11 has offered a stable performance management architect. Now, things have changed. We can opt to grow by choosing EPM architect.

As mentioned earlier, an Hyperion Planning Application can be created in two ways. One is by using old way and its rightly termed as Classic and the other way is by using Performance Management Architect. EPMA is the new hero on the block, as EPMA is a single interface to manage different Performance Management Products. In the previous chapter, we saw how to create a Planning Application using Classic strokes. In this chapter, we'll create a Planning application using the modern EPMA.

Note: It is important to note that this chapter serves as an introductory chapter of EPMA and details of EPMA are beyond the scope of the book. Readers would be recommended to skip this chapter, and visit it only when they will be learning EPM architecture.

The chapter is divided into the following sections:

- Why EPMA
- EPMA Modules: We'll introduce the six modules of EPMA, which are:
  - Dimension Library
  - Application Library
  - Calculation manager
  - Data Synchronization
  - Application Upgrades
  - Library Job console
- Planning application creation process flow
- The prerequisites of a Planning application
- Application creation
- Deployment

Why EPMA

Before we start understanding these modules, we have to question ourselves.

Why do we need Performance Management Architect, which has so many confusing modules? Can't we just be happy with Classic Application Administration alone?

Oracle Hyperion version 11 is called 'Fusion Edition'. The Oracle Hyperion Products Suite includes various products such as Oracle Hyperion financial Management, Oracle Hyperion Planning, and Oracle Essbase and also to name a few recent additions Oracle Hyperion Profitability and Cost Management.

Different products have different interfaces and different ways of managing applications. It would be great to have a single common interface which can manage different applications in terms of creating, managing and even deploying. This wish is answered in the form of 'Performance Management Architect' by Oracle god. EPMA is closely integrated with all Performance Management products and now, we can rightly call the Oracle Hyperion Version 11 the 'Fusion edition'.

EPMA modules

There are six EPMA modules and understanding these modules will help us in sub sequent section of 'Application Creation Process'.

By the way, where can one access or see these modules?

After we log into Oracle EPM Workspace, we can view the modules. Let us not be too naïve by asking *how do we log into workspace*, we know by now that the workspace URL is `http://hostname:19000/workspace/index.jsp`.

We'll navigate to administer, as shown in the following image, we can see the mentioned six modules:

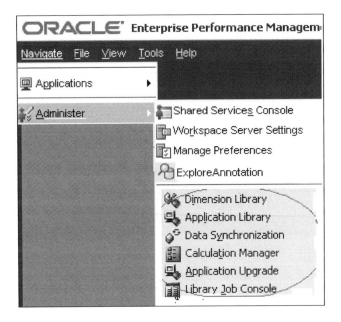

We'll start with the Dimension Library module.

Dimension Library

Applications have dimensions, which are the basic building blocks. We need to note that EPMA is not a luxury of only Hyperion Planning application. He is an architect who serves all of his clients of Oracle Hyperion Performance Management applications such as Hyperion Planning, Hyperion financial management, and so on.

Dimension Library is a centralized location from which you can manage dimensions and dimension properties. It includes features such as adding, deleting, and modifying dimension members/member properties. Hence, it's termed the **Dimension Library**; in short, it's the library of dimensions.

 Dimension library does not have a preset list of dimensions by the virtue of installation. We need to either import dimensions or create dimensions within the library.

The following are some uses of Dimension Library:

- First and foremost, its usage is to manage dimensions from a central location. Catering to many Performance Management Applications
- Secondly, we can add/delete/modify members and dimensions
- The final usage is to set properties of both dimensions and members of an application

Select **Dimension Library** from the list of modules. We can do that by navigating as shown:

Navigate | Administer | Dimension Library

As we haven't imported dimensions, nor created an application, we see no dimensions in the **Shared Library** nor do we see any Planning application.

But typically, it would look as shown in the following image.

The window is divided into three sections—**Shared Library**, **Application**, and **Properties**.

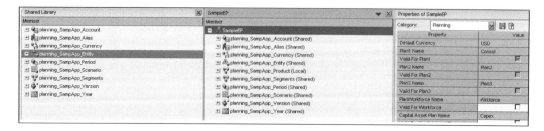

We had created a Planning Application in the previous chapter, so why don't we see that application here in Dimension Library?

Though EPMA and Hyperion Planning seem to be good friends, they are not the thickest of friends. The Planning Applications, which were created using 'Classic Wizard', are not visible through EPM architect. Hence, we don't see the Classic Planning Application.

Shared Library is the library of dimensions, which is meant to be shared by Performance Management Applications. Here dimensions are categorized into two kinds, as discussed here:

- **Local**: These dimensions are created within an application. A dimension can be created in Application View by dragging a dimension from Shared Library to the Application View. It can be defined as a local dimension; it need not mandatorily be a shared dimension only. In short, these dimensions are specific only to an Application.

- **Shared**: These are the dimensions that are shared in nature and available to all the applications. Even after plucking from the basket of 'Shared library' into a Planning application, they carry their 'shared' nature. These shared dimensions can be considered to be confirmed dimensions in the data warehousing perspective.

The main difference between a local dimension and a shared dimension is that in case of a shared dimension any changes made to a dimension in the Shared Library will automatically get impacted and inherited to all the applications in which the shared dimension is present.

For example, there is a Planning Application and HFM Application. Both of these applications have a common dimension 'Entity', which is a shared dimension.

Now, any change made to this dimension-'Entity' in 'shared library' would automatically bring the same change to the 'Entity' dimension within an application in which it's present. Therefore, the dimensional changes would impact both the Planning Application and HFM Application, as 'Entity' is a shared dimension.

Whereas, if the Entity Dimension has been a local dimension in both HFM and Hyperion Planning Application, any changes made to the Entity dimension in Hyperion Planning Application would have no impact on the Entity Dimension in the HFM Application as they are not 'shared' in nature.

An **Application** is also called an **application view**. This is the middle section in 'Dimension Library'. Created Performance Management Applications can be viewed here. Also, the application that is selected to edit from the 'Application Library' can be managed over here. We can see the application node right at the top along with its dimensions and members in the following image showing application view:

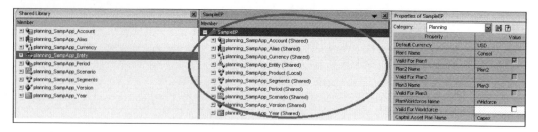

We can see in the previous image that a few dimensions are shared and a few are local. The Account dimension is shared, whereas the Product dimension is local.

Properties is the rightmost section. It is a context-sensitive section that updates based on the selection in the shared library or application view. This section provides information of the properties of members/dimensions and application. These are the properties of an application view, that is, properties of an Application. Hence, when we select a dimension in application view of an application, the properties of that specific dimension are shown in this section. For example, if we select a dimension in application view, we see the properties of the selected dimension and can edit the properties too.

In the 'Application View' screenshot, we can see three sections. Here, the application's name is **SampEP**. The rightmost section is the **Properties** section. As the application SampEP node is selected in the Application View, we see **Properties of SampEP** and it displays all the properties of the SampEP application.

Application Library

There is one more library— the application library. This is the module that is actually responsible for creation of a Planning application. This is not only responsible for Planning application creation, it also lets us create other Performance Management applications.

This library enables us to manage all Performance Management applications, which includes creating, editing, and deploying applications.

It displays all the applications that are created using EPM architect. It does not show any application that was not created using EPMA.

The uses of the Application library module are listed as follows:

- Creating an application
- Duplicating an application
- Deleting an application
- Opening an application
- Validating and deploying an application
- Re-registering an application with shared services
- Synchronizing between applications

As a part of Planning application creation, we'll learn about validating and deploying applications in the later sections of the chapter.

Calculation manager

In planning and budgeting, the typical calculations, such as allocation computation, revenue calculation, expense calculation, balance sheet computation and so on, can be achieved using business rules.

We can create business rules for Planning either in this Web-based calculation manager or in EAS (Essbase Administration Services) console.

 It is important to note that for a Planning Application created using EPMA, only calculation manager can create business rules.

Calculation manager offers an ease of writing rules or scripts, not only for Hyperion Planning but also for other Performance Management Applications such as HFM, Essbase, Hyperion Planning, and others, in a single, Web-based interface.

Data synchronization

We have learned by now that applications such as Hyperion Planning, Essbase application, Hyperion financial management, and others, can be created using EPM architect. Now, this data synchronization is an effective way of synching data between EPM applications. It can also synchronize between EPMA applications and interface tables/external sources.

We can demonstrate data synchronization with an example. For a typical Planning implementation, there is an important concept of actual versus budget or variance analysis. We know that at the beginning of the fiscal year, we plan for the future. Let us understand that we plan to generate 1000K USD revenue by selling 50 units of a product. Over a period of time, we would like to know where our plan stands by understanding how close the actual numbers are to our planned numbers. After three months, that is one quarter, we realize that we have actually generated 800K USD by selling 40 units of a product and we generated lesser revenue than we had planned - there is a difference of 200K USD. Here, in this example, 1000K USD is the planned number and 800K USD is the actual number and the analysis of actual versus budget will help us to understand our performance.

Hyperion Financial Management Applications have 'actuals' data and we know that in the Planning application, we enter planned numbers. Now, we need to load the actuals data from the HFM application to Planning application so that we can compare the actual figures versus the plan. In this scenario, we can use data synchronization to load the data from the source HFM to the target destination of our Hyperion Panning application.

It's a pretty simple interface in which we select type, source, and destination, as shown following image:

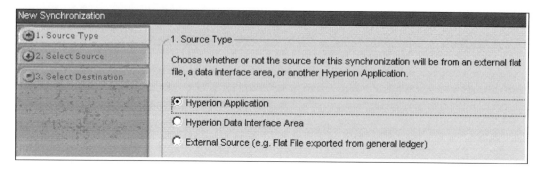

Application upgrade

If we want to upgrade the Planning applications from a previous release, this is the option to use. Also, if we already have a classic Planning application and if we want to take advantage of functionalities such as data synchronization, ease of managing all EPM applications in a single interface, then we can upgrade it to EPM application.

The steps involved are seen on the left-hand side of the following image. The application summary lists the available applications that are upgradeable. Next is the selection of applications and finally, we'll get to know the summary if the application has been successfully upgraded.

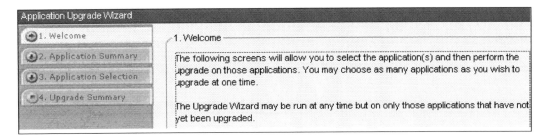

Library job console

This is a single console that gives us all the information about what is happening in the EPMA world. In the below image we can see the activity description, what kind of an activity is that and at what time it has happened. It can answer all the questions that Sherlock Homes could possibly think of.

It basically keeps track of all the jobs and reports their status and percentage completion. Here examples of jobs would be application validation, application deployment, and so on. The following screenshot shows library job console:

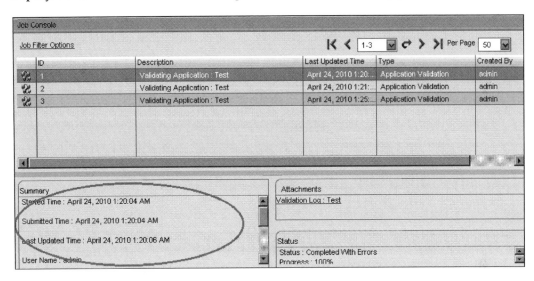

In the given example, in the above image, we have validated an application by the name **Test** Hence, its job **Type** is **Application Validation**.

We can see the **Summary**, which provides more information of when the activity had started, when it was last updated, and also, who submitted/initiated the job. Along with the summary, we can view the logs under **Attachments** and also its **Status** in terms of percentage of completion.

Planning Application creation process

In this section, we will learn the complete process of a typical Hyperion Planning application's creation. The following steps are in sequence and the order is important:

- **Import metadata**: The very first step in a Planning application creation is to import metadata. We can import metadata either through a flat file or we can even import metadata directly from an external data source using 'Interface Tables'. In this chapter, we'll use a flat file that is already bundled with the Planning software for tutorial purpose. Remember that we had learned about importing Metadata with the help of 'Dimension Library' module.

- **Application creation**: This is the step where we actually start creating an application. This process can be broken into three major activities. These three activities are elaborately discussed in the later part of this chapter.

  - ◦ **Application type**: In this section, we provide the very basic information of the Planning application name, its plan type information, currency information, and calendar information to start with.

  - ◦ **Dimension selection**: After the basic information is provided, the section deals with the dimensions that needs to be provided for the Planning application.

  - ◦ **Application settings**: In this last step, we set/edit the properties of application/dimensions/members.

  Along with these three activities, we need to validate and deploy as the final steps in application creation. These are described as follows:

  - ◦ **Validate**: Before we create our Planning application, it's wise to validate our settings. This step takes the information that we have provided into account and checks if it's right. This step is necessary before deployment.

  - ◦ **Deployment**: This is the step that actually creates Planning application and exports the Planning application from EPM architecture to Planning product that is EPMA deploys the Planning application to the Planning server based on the application specific metadata created. We need to note that at the time of 'Deployment', the application is again validated for errors and if it contains any errors, the deployment fails.

- **User access**: Once we have finalized the dimension structure, we are good to go with user and group security access. Here, we take care of the security part in Planning based on the user privileges. This is covered in detail in the *Chapter 9, User Provisioning and Access Rights*.

- **Data form creation**: In this section, we create data forms resembling the Budget templates of an organization. *Chapter 10, Data Forms*, talks all about data forms.

- **Business rules**: Post data form creation, we create business rules. Business rules are rules which have absolute analytical ability. Common calculations such allocation computation, revenue calculation, expense calculation, balance sheet computation, and so on, can be achieved using business rules. *Chapter 11* and *Chapter 12* teach us all about business rules.

- **Review and approval process**: Finally, after form creation, business rules, and task lists, we incorporate the review and approval process of budgeting within our Planning application. We learn about the review and approval process in detail in *Chapter 14, Planning Process*.

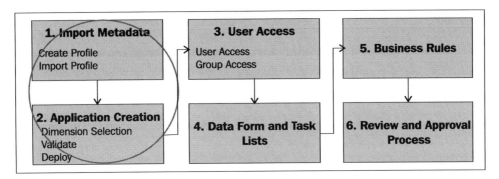

Observing carefully the image, the first two steps differ from the Classic Planning application creation process flow and that's exactly what we are going to cover in this chapter. We can refer back to *Chapter 4, Create Planning Application Classic*, in the *Planning application creation process*, section.

Prerequisites

A Hyperion Planning application needs a relational source. Hence, we need to create a relational source for a Planning Application before we initiate the process of creating Planning application.

We'll create an Oracle schema by the name of "epma" and provide DBA/DBO privileges to the schema.

Ensure that all the services of Hyperion are up and running. If any of the services are not started, refer to *Chapter 2, Installation and Configuration*, where we discussed the order in which the services ought to be started.

For a user to create a Planning application using EPM architecture, he needs to be provisioned with the roles of 'Application creator' and also 'Dimension Editor'. These are roles provisioned in 'Shared services'. We have already learned how to provision in shared services in previous *Chapter 4*.

The prerequisites are more or less the same as we discussed in *Chapter 4* in the section called *Prerequisites*. It's worth going back to previous chapter to glance at it.

Application creation

As a part of Planning Application creation, the first step is to create a dimension and its members, that is load metadata.

We achieve that by creating an import profile and then we will use this import profile to import dimensions from flat file or interface tables.

We have to first import the profile that is create metadata and then start creating an application. Therefore, it can be broken into two parts:

- Import profile
- Application Creation

Import profile

Before we start the creation of an application, the primary task is to load dimensions into the shared library. This way, when we create a brand new application and it can use the imported dimensions of the shared library.

The idea of having dimensions in shared library is to have set of dimensions in the common repository and use them in applications such as HFM; Hyperion Planning, and others, when need them.

How do you load dimensions?

We can load dimensions using import profiles. We can also manually create a dimension and its members in the shared library. But, it's not a practical approach. Just imagine an Accounts dimension; it could have hundreds of members.

 In a typical implementation, it's not possible to create a dimension and add its members manually. Technically, it can be done. But it's not pragmatic, considering there could be hundreds to members to a dimension. Manual addition will turn into a nightmare.

We create an import profile file, which has information on all dimensions, members, and their properties.

We have a sample import profile file bundled with the software. We'll use that for the purpose of this tutorial. What is the point in reinventing the wheel?

The sample import profile is located in `D:\Oracle\Middleware\EPMSystem11R1\products\Planning\bin\sampleapp` as shown in the following image:

The name of the import file is `SampApp Source Flat File.ads`.

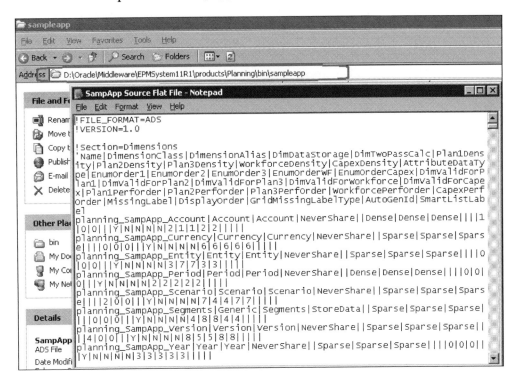

Steps to create and import a profile file

Profile creation: In this step, we use the file `SampApp Source Flat File.ads`. Open the Dimension Library module. We don't have any import profile file, we are going to create one now.

1. Now, go to **File | Import | Create Profile**.

2. Here, we have to provide information for the following fields:

    ◦ **Profile Name**: Recommend to give a relevant name

○ **Import Type**: We can import metadata either through flat file or Interface tables. In our case, we are using a flat file `SampApp Source Flat File.ads`.

○ **Description**: This is an optional field. Give the description of the profile.

○ **Application**: By default this is set to **Shared Library**, it means that the dimensions will be imported into shared library. Dimensions can be imported directly to Planning application, but as we have not created any EPM Planning application, we can only see **Shared Library** as of now. Else, we could see the list of EPMA application along with 'Shared Library'.

○ **File Name**: In this field, we'll upload the file `SampApp Source Flat File.ads`. Click on **Upload** and then browse for the file and then select **Upload**. Select **OK**.

 This import file is used as the sample file based on which the import profile is created. Later on, the same import profile can be used to import all Import Files containing the same sections/dimensions as this file. Members, hierarchies, and their properties can change from one import file to another.

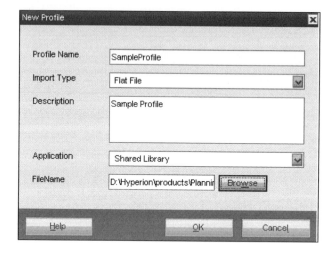

3. **File Properties**: This will open a new window, where we need to fill in details of the File properties.

   ○ **Column Delimiter**: The delimiter selection depends on the delimiter used in the .ads file. If we look at our `SampApp Source Flat File.ads` file, it's evident that 'Pipeline' is the delimiter. Select 'pipeline 'as the delimiter as shown in the image below.

   ○ Deselect **Remove Double Quotes**. We might have member formulas where double quotes are used. Hence, deselect this option.

   ○ Deselect **Remove White space**.

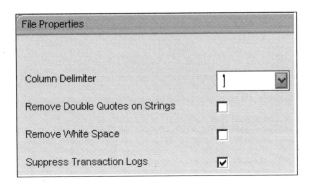

   ○ Click on **Next**.

4. **Map Dimensions**: In this section we are mapping dimensions from the flat file `Source Flat File.ads` file to the Shared library of Dimension library.

   ○ Select the option **Create dimensions for the non-mapped for the non-mapped dimensions with the source dimension name**, as shown in the following image. Let's elaborate. We have dimensions that are not yet mapped in the flat file `Source Flat File.ads`. Selecting the option makes the names of the dimensions same as it is in the flat file into shared library. Else, it's also permissible to type in the names of our choice in the second column **Shared library**. Nevertheless, this option becomes very handy when we are importing a dimension for the first time, which does not exist already in the Shared Library and we would wish to have the dimension the same names as it is in the source file.

- ○ **Select all Merge as shared**: In cases where a dimension in the flat file is already present in the shared library and we would like to merge it. The option does the same.

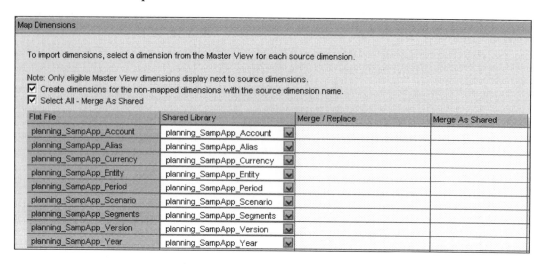

- ○ Click on **Next**.

5. We'll get a pop up informing us that the profile has been created successfully and asking us if we would like to execute the profile. We have waited long enough for this. Select **Yes**, as shown in the following image:

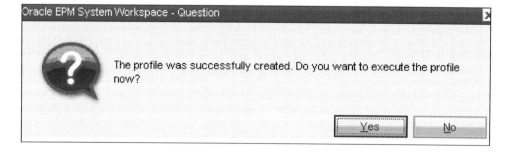

As the profile execution happens, we get one more pop up of the job task, as shown in the following screenshot. We have to get used to this, as every job/ task execution within EPM architect results in this pop up that will take us to the doorstep of a library, that is the library job console.

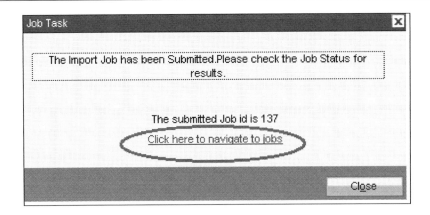

6. We select **Click here to navigate to jobs** to see the job console and the status of this activity, as shown in the previous image.

7. Job console gives information under **Description** that **SampleProfile** is being imported to **Master**. Here, **Master** means 'Master view', which is nothing but common Dimension Library and provides a log file that can be viewed by selecting Import Results under **Attachments**. In the following image, we can see the status of completion in percentage. Read out **Summary**; it has detailed information about the time, user, and the details of the activity as well.

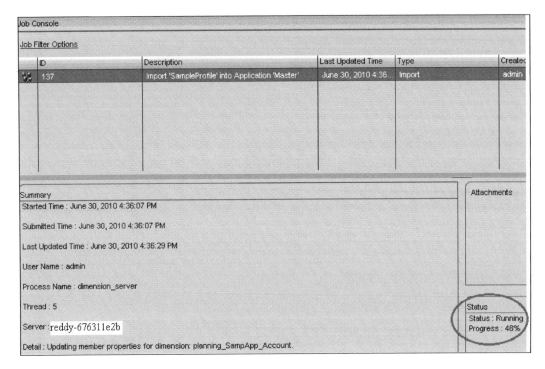

8. Now, we know how handy the job console is.

9. Oracle EPM Workspace is very user friendly and it has all tabs within it. So when you open library job console, it opens a new tab. After this, if we open 'Dimension Library' and want to get back to library job console, there's no need to do any complex navigation such as **Navigate | Administer | Dimension Library**, simply select the **Library Job Console** tab.

10. Go back to Dimension Library and we should see the newly imported dimensions in shared library, as shown in the following image. We should wait for a while for the import job to complete, which is when we see the status of the job changes to complete.

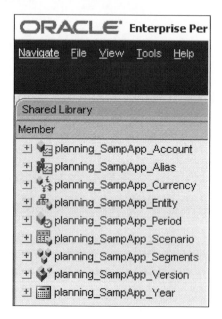

Now, we have successfully imported nine dimensions and we are ready to create an application of Planning, which can make use of these dimensions. In next section, we'll learn how to create Planning application using EPM architect.

Application creation

The concepts of Plan type, Default currency, multiple currencies, and so on, were explained in the previous chapter. In this chapter, let us not duplicate our effort by re-explaining. It's recommended to refer to *Chapter 4* for any conceptual clarity of the above mentioned terms.

With that disclaimer, let's proceed.

Let's do it in steps:

1. Navigate to **File | New | Application**, as shown:

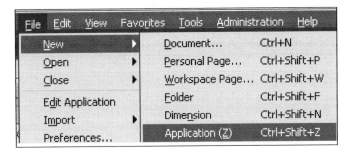

2. It will lead to a wizard, where we are going to create a Planning application by providing details in three tabs. The three tabs are:

    ○ **Application Type**: In this section, we'll provide the basic information of the Planning application name, plan type information, currency information and calendar information. This is the very basic information any Planning application would need before the dimensions for the application are selected

    ○ **Dimension Selection**: In this section, we'll select the required dimensions and can create new dimensions too.

    ○ **Application Settings**: In this section, we can modify the application settings and we'll see how to do that in detail.

Application type:

Application wizard opens and the first tab of the wizard is **Application Type**. We provide the following information in this section as we can view in the following image.

- **Name**: Here, give the name of the Planning application. Underscores and special characters are not allowed in application names. If you try to use one, the system will not let you proceed. In our example, the application name is 'EPMapp'.

- **Type**: As it been told million times that EPM architect is not the luxury of only Hyperion Planning, it serves the needs of other Hyperion products too. In this 'type' drop down, we can see the applications which can be created examples are Essbase, Planning, and HFM, and so on. Our interest lies in Hyperion Planning, hence, select 'Planning'

- **Description**: Provide an appropriate description. This field is optional.

- **Create Blank Application**: We can create a blank Planning application without adding dimensions and settings its properties.

  What is the advantage of creating a blank application?

  Creating a **blank application** is a manually driven process. In this process, we first create a blank application and later create dimension within the **Application View** section of **Dimension Library** by dragging the dimensions from 'shared library' or create dimensions local to the application inside the **Application View**. Dimensions can be either dragged as shared or local dimensions into the **Application View**. After making dimensions available, we need to activate the dimension associations and set the properties. This is very different from what the application wizard offers, where we map dimensions and set properties which will create a Planning application.

  We had already imported the dimension and we are not going to create a blank application. Hence don't select the option of **Create Blank Application**.

- **Auto Create Local Dimensions**: We know by now that the concept of local dimension and shared dimension. Selecting this option creates the standard dimensions such as entity, account, scenario, and so on, which are local in nature with the names of entity, account, scenario, and others. The same name is followed. Also, we can add custom dimensions if needed to add to the existing standard dimensions.

  For tutorial purposes, we had already imported the dimensions from the flat file. So, let's use these dimensions in shared library. Therefore, there is no need to select this option.

- **Plan Type**: We have already talked about Plan Types, please refer to the section called 'Plan type' in the previous Chapter 4 'How to create a Planning application' for reference and conceptual clarity. We'll create one plan type. Hence, let only one plan type be ticked and name the plan type 'Consol' as shown.

- **Default Currency**: Tick 'multiple currency' and also check if the default currency is USD.

- For **Calendar** settings, let the default settings of **Base Time Period**, **Fiscal Start Month**, and **Weekly Distribution** be the same.

  - ○ **Create New Local Period Dimension**: We had already imported the 'Period' dimension and we don't need to have a local period dimension in our case. Hence, let us not select this option.

  - ○ **Create New Local Year Dimension**: On the same lines, we don't need a local Year dimension. We'll use the Year dimension which we had imported by the virtue of import profile. Hence, don't select this option too.

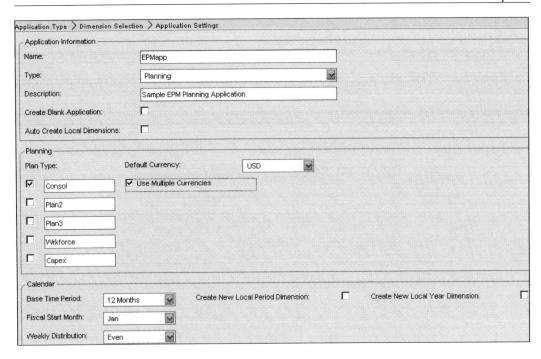

Click on **Next** to proceed to the next section.

Dimension Selection

In this section, we'll add dimensions to the Planning application. We need to recall that every Planning application needs to have standard dimensions—**Entity**, **Version**, **Scenario**, **Account**, **Year**, and **Period** for a single currency application. If it's a multi-currency application, we need to have an additional 'Currency' dimension.

As we see in the following image, the dimensions are already seen as "new" in the second column. These dimensions are seen as against the type of dimensions they are.

For example, 'PlanningSampApp_Entity' is the new dimension that is going to be added to the Planning application, whose dimension type is 'Entity'. This is the meaning of the very first row.

If there are multiple dimensions of the same type in the shared library, the user has to manually map to one of the available dimensions. For example, if there is more than one Entity dimension in the Shared Library than in the Dimension Selection step of the Application Creation Wizard, then the Entity dimension will not be automatically mapped, the user will have to do it manually. In our case, there is only one dimension for each of the standard dimension types and they are the dimensions that we want to use for our application, therefore we don't have to perform any manual mapping.

If we pay close attention to the 'Shared library' of Dimension Library, we see nine dimensions. Apart from the standard dimensions for multi-currency Planning application, there is a custom dimension **planning_SampApp_Segments.** We would like to have this custom dimension as a part of our Planning application. Hence, we'll select the **planning_SampApp_Segments** from the drop down of the custom dimensions as shown in the following image:

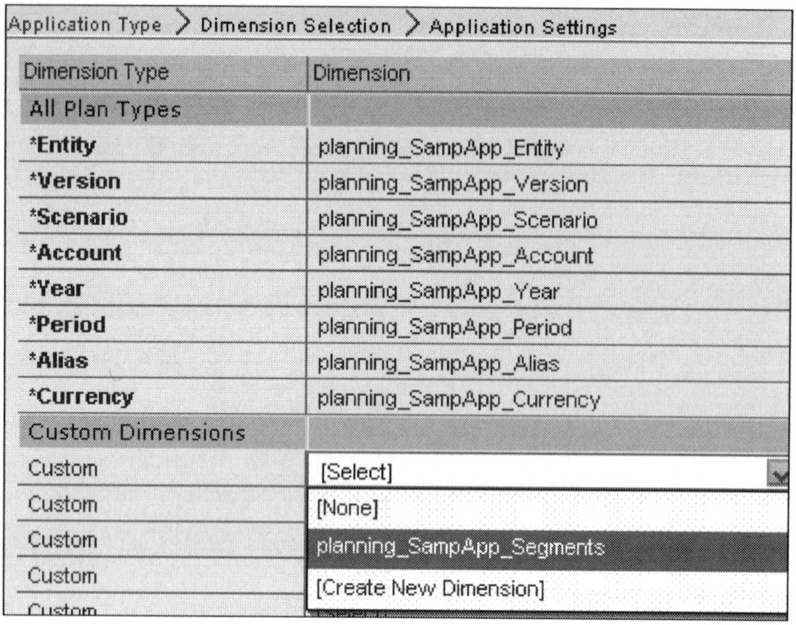

Application Type > Dimension Selection > Application Settings	
Dimension Type	Dimension
All Plan Types	
*Entity	planning_SampApp_Entity
*Version	planning_SampApp_Version
*Scenario	planning_SampApp_Scenario
*Account	planning_SampApp_Account
*Year	planning_SampApp_Year
*Period	planning_SampApp_Period
*Alias	planning_SampApp_Alias
*Currency	planning_SampApp_Currency
Custom Dimensions	
Custom	[Select]
Custom	[None]
Custom	planning_SampApp_Segments
Custom	[Create New Dimension]
Custom	

Click **Next**.

Application Settings

In this section, we can edit the application properties. As we see on left-hand side the application name 'EPMapp'. We can expand to check the dimensions that we intended to add to it. Towards its right, we see the properties window. This window gives information of what we had provided earlier in terms of default currency, Plan name, Date format, and so on, as shown in the following screenshot.

Let's go down and pay attention to a message **Press the Validate button to validate your application**. There is also an option to **Deploy when finished**. We'll not deploy as we finish this step. We'll deploy separately from the application library. It's not as though that's a better way of deploying, but the idea is to show how we can deploy from application library.

For now we'll click on **Validate**, as shown in the following screenshot:

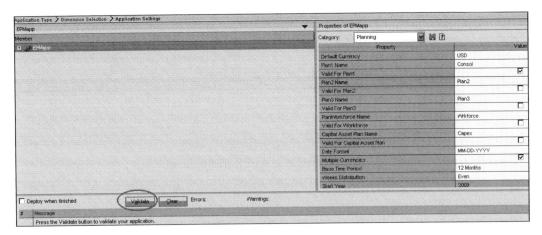

If our application is flawless, we should get 0 errors and 0 warnings as shown next:

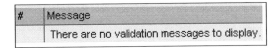

There are no validation messages to display means, no errors or warnings. We need to ensure that the count of errors and warning is zero for an error free application.

 We can validate an application from the application library also.

What happens during validation?

Validation is a very important activity that checks for the following before we deploy an application:

- Start Year definition check
- Year dimension members check
- Whether start month is defined or not
- Whether default alias table is defined or not
- Whether default currency is defined or not
- Whether all the standard dimensions are present or not

- Whether the base time periods and weekly distribution has been defined or not
- Whether the Min one Plan type, which is needed, is present
- Checks Scenario to Year/Period Associations
- Checks for duplication in Member Names/Aliases

Click on **Finish**. This will open the dimension library and this time we can see the new Planning application EPMapp, as shown in the following screenshot. We need to recall that 'dimension library' has three sections:

- **Shared library**: we can see with the list of dimensions that were imported from flat file.

- **Application view**: Planning application 'EPMapp' is seen now. We can expand it to see its dimensions, which are shared dimensions. We have not created any local dimensions for this application.

- **Properties**: These are the properties of the application' EPMapp' as we see in the following screenshot that as the Application node is selected in the **Application View**, the **Properties** section displays all Application properties accordingly.

  It's no more empty. If we can recall, it was all empty when we first opened the module of 'Dimension Library'.

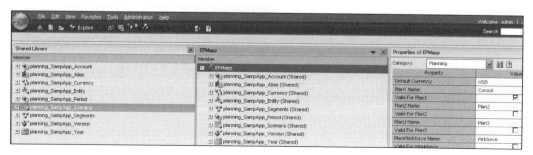

Deployment

After validation, the next task is to **deploy** the application. All the while during the application creation process, we have defined dimensions and set properties and even validated the Planning Application. The actual application creation takes place only when we deploy an application. We know that Planning application has its arms connected to both Essbase and relational source; we have not connected nor provided any information of Essbase and relational data source so far. We'll do that in the application library module as we progress with 'Deployment'.

We need to validate before deployment. Hence, even though we try to deploy an application, EPMA does perform an automatic validation before the beginning of the deployment.

When we are using EPMA for creating Hyperion Planning we are actually defining the metadata required for creating the Planning application, not the application itself. As a part of the deployment process, EPMA uses this metadata to create a Hyperion Planning Application on the Hyperion Planning instance.

We deploy an application using Application library module:

1. Go to **Application Library**. We should see the new application **EPMapp**.

2. Right-click on the application, we see option of both **Validate**, **Deploy**.

3. We had already **Validated**, now we should select **Deploy** to initiate deployment as shown in the following image:

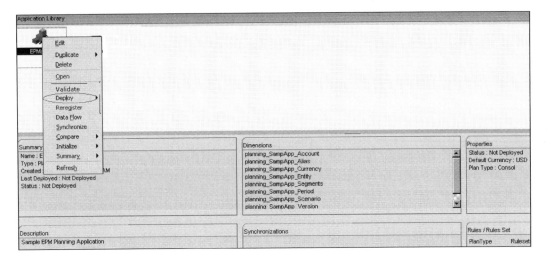

- We see the options of **Deploying Application, Deploying Rules,** and **Deploying All**. Taking a closer look, we can see that only **Validate Application** is not grayed unlike other two options. We have not written any rules (i.e. business rules in calculation manager) so far to deploy. Hence, select **Deploy Application**.

- It leads to the screen (shown the next screenshot), where we provide information about the following:

  ○ **Application Name**: We had already provided application name. Hence, we see the same name here in this field.

- ○ **Description**: We had already provided this information while creating the application.

- ○ **Instance name**: Let's stick to the default.

- ○ **Web Server**: We had installed all the components into one machine. Hence, the same old machine host name is reflected in this field

- ○ **Application Server**: Leave this set to the default.

- ○ **Shared Services Project**: From the drop down, select 'Planning'. We need to recall that we had created a folder in 'shared services' in chapter 4 under section 'General Information'.

- ○ **Data Source**: Here we go. This is the filed, where we provide information of both the relational data source and Essbase. We had done a similar activity in the section *Database creation* in *Chapter 4*.

As we see, we had not created a source, though we had created an Oracle schema by name 'EPM' in section *Prerequisites* of this chapter earlier. Select **Create Data Source** to create a source.

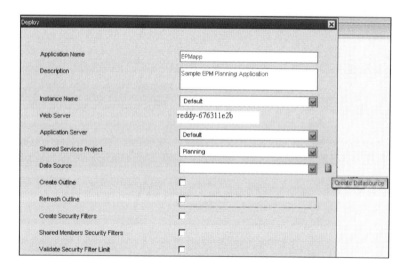

After we select **Create Data Source**, it opens another window.

From here, it's a kind of déjà vu experience as we have done these steps in *Chapter 3*, when we had created our first Planning Application. We provide both relational data source information and Essbase information in this section.

This wizard has four sections as we can see on the left-hand side, they are as follows:

- Data source details
- Database details
- Essbase server details
- Summary

Data source details

We provide information about the **Data Source Name**, **Data Source Description**, and **Product**. The **Product** is already set to **Planning,** as shown in the following image:

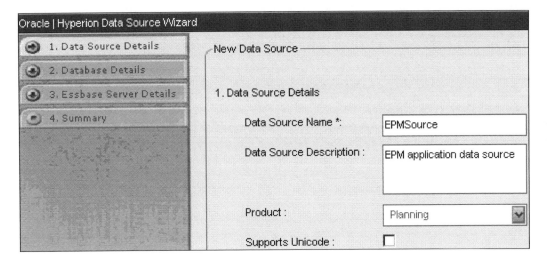

Click **Next**.

Database details

In this section, as the name suggests we provide information about the database. In our case, its an Oracle relational database.

- **Database Type**: This can be Oracle, SQL server, or DB2. We have Oracle as our database.

- **Server**: The server where the Oracle database has been installed.

- **Port**: As we know by now, the default port number for the Oracle database is 1521. It's selected by default.

- **Database**: This is the database name of Oracle. It's HYPCOE in our case.

- **Username**: This is the name of the schema or user which we have created. The user creation was mentioned in *Prerequisites* section. The schema 'epma' has been created and we mention the same.

- **Password**: This is the password of the schema/user.

Finally, after providing all the information, we'll test, as we always do. Select **Test Connection**. If the information is right, we should get a message saying **Connection Successful**.

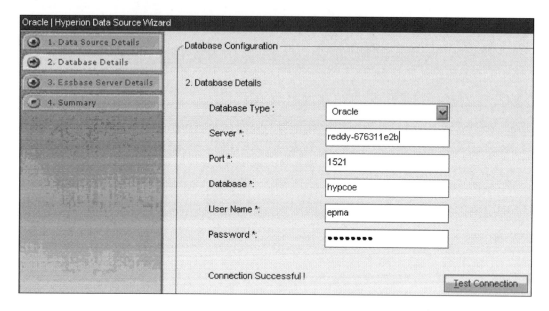

Click on **Next** to move to next section of Essbase.

Essbase Server details

In this section, we will provide the Essbase server details.

- **Essbase Server**: It's the hostname of server/system where Essbase is installed
- **Essbase Username**: The same old superhero, 'admin'
- **Essbase Password**: Needless to say, it is 'password', all in lowercase

We'll test this connection too. We cannot go wrong with this. After getting a success message, select **Next**:

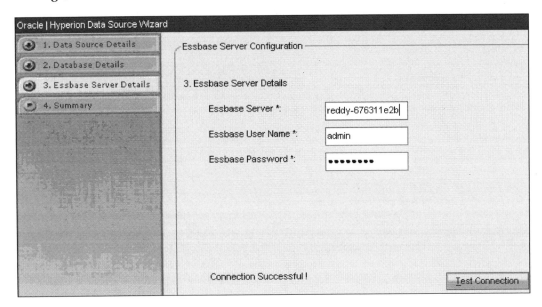

Summary

Finally, the **Summary** is a sweet success message following the data source creation.

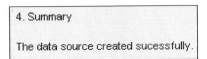

Now, select **Finish** getting back to where we had left. Now, we see the newly created data source 'EPMSource' as shown in the following image:

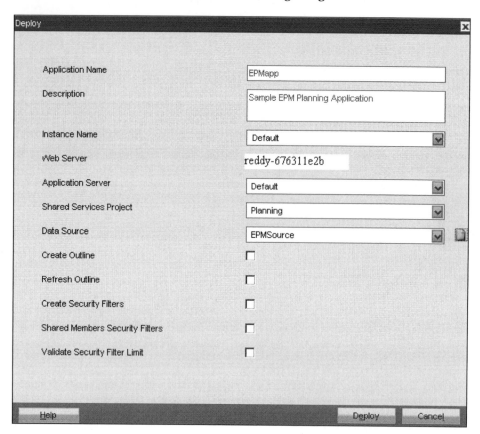

Here we will look at a few more options, such as Create outline, Refresh outline, Create security filters, and so on. These are exactly the same fields which we had discussed in *Chapter 4* under section *Database creation*. Refer to that section. We also need to note that in the previous chapter, we saw the above shown options from the 'Administration' Menu after we logged into the Planning Application, but here we have these options on the EPMA 'Deployment Interface' only.

Let us not create outline while we deploy; the objective is to create a Planning application first. Therefore, without ticking other options, click on **deploy**.

As we know status of every job can only be viewed in the 'Library job console', the deployment activity begins and gives us the below shown pop up. We had seen this kind of pop ups which take us to the library job console.

We'll do the same. Click on **click here to navigate the job**.

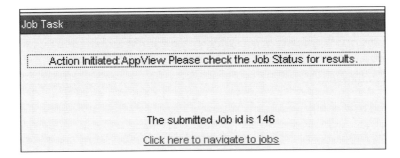

We have already seen the Library job console, it opens and gives information about the deployment activity. It gives information in 'description' that the application **EPMapp** is being deployed and it also gives information about the type of job **PlanningAppDeploy**, it means deployment of Planning application.

It also provides more information under 'summary'.

We need to pay attention to **Status**; this shows the percentage of completion. Deployment is complete only when the status progress is **100** %.

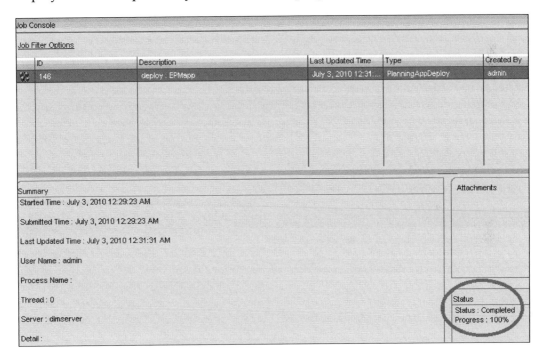

This marks the end of EPM Application creation of 'EPMapp'.

Now, we can log in to Planning web or the Workspace to log in to the Planning application EPMapp. Hopefully, we can all remember the Planning web URL and Workspace URL. I am sure we are smart enough to have added them to our browser's favorites list by now.

We have successfully created a Planning application using EPMA. We need to recall that after we create a Planning application, we log in to the application and then create its database. Refer to the section about *Database creation* in *Chapter 4*. Even for the application EPMapp, we need to follow the same process to create its database.

We are not creating the database of Planning application EPMapp as it's the same process which we had done in the previous chapter in the section 'database creation'

Before we end this chapter, let us reiterate the point that EPMA in Version 11 is more stable than the previous implementation in version 9. A few of the challenges in version 9 were as follows:

- Deploying an application
- Adding shared members
- To deal with huge number of dimension and members
- Load dimension using interface tables

Summary

In this chapter, we have learned the basic modules of EPMA and have understood the over all process of creating a Planning Application using EPMA.

We have also learned the differences between EPMA and Classic and now we should be able to understand when to use Classic Wizard and EPMA. As said earlier, this chapter is an introductory chapter of EPMA.

In the next chapter, we'll learn about the settings of dimensions/members and also of a typical Hyperion Planning application. The next chapter is one of the most important chapters of the book, which will help designing an application in real life situations.

6
Settings

Learn as you go and don't be afraid to question the status quo

— *Albert Einstein*

In the previous chapters, we learned how to create a Planning application. In this chapter, we'll make use of the already-created Planning application 'PandB' to take our understanding to the next level by learning about settings. This chapter will guide us in learning the dimension settings and will help us in making decisions in terms of which setting to pick, based on the user's requirements. This chapter will immensely help you while designing a Hyperion Planning application based on user requirements.

Before we get into the chapter, let us take a look at a possible conversation between a Hyperion support analyst and a Hyperion Solution architect:

> **Hyperion Support analyst**: *I have been involved with support and maintenance of Hyperion Planning for many years and I look into support issues based on the tickets raised.*

> **Hyperion Solution architect**: *That's good. What are the areas that you have been working on?*

> **Hyperion Support analyst**: *I look into almost all the areas of Hyperion Planning. I can create data forms, task lists, work flows, and so on. I am responsible for administration as well, which includes regular backups and restoration.*

> **Hyperion Solution architect**: *How about designing an application? Can you design a new Planning application based on user requirements and understanding the current challenges of a customer's budgeting process?*

> **Hyperion Support analyst**: *I have always worked on Planning applications that were already created. I am not sure how to design a Planning application. Although I can create individual objects within Planning application, I would not know the rationale behind the creation.*

> **Hyperion Solution architect**: *Yes, I understand that most support/ administrators would know the ins and outs of the product, but they lack the knowledge that would help in designing a Planning application.*

The following topics are going to be covered in this chapter:

- **Dimension settings**: In this section, we'll learn about all the settings and properties of the standard dimensions. So far, we created an application with its dimension. This section provides in depth information about the dimensions.

- **Dimensions**: This section individual dimension settings covering all standard dimensions starting with Accounts dimension.

- **Performance settings**: In this section, we'll see the settings that will improve the performance of Hyperion Planning application.

- **Evaluation order**: In this section, we'll see how the data types of different dimensions respond in conjunction with forms.

It's important to understand all of the settings discussed in this chapter and it's even more important to co-relate every single setting with real life Planning applications, as if we are designing an application from the implementation perspective. This chapter may not be as entertaining as the other chapters, but it's very important to understand and at the same time, we might need to refer to other chapters and re-read some sections to get better conceptual clarity. Therefore, let's put our thought process in the implementation mode and kick off the chapter.

We'll start with dimension settings, in which we'll discuss settings of all dimensions (both **standard** and **custom**), though with bias towards accounts dimension, as it's the most important and complex dimension to design. In the process of learning the dimension settings, we'll cover account types and a few basics such as aggregation and storage.

Next, we'll spend some time on performance settings and evaluation order. After that, we'll be exhausted enough to grab some coffee. Now that we have spoken enough of how the chapter is structured, we shall start with dimension settings.

Dimension settings

There's no need to list all the standard dimensions, as we should know them in our sleep by now. For convenience, it is listed again:

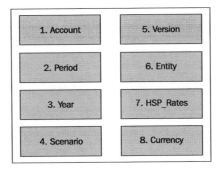

In *Chapter 3, Hyperion Planning Dimensions,* we already learned the basics of dimensions and their usages. In this section, we are going to re-visit the dimensions to learn more granular details about them in terms of their properties and settings and how would one make a choice between the available options given a situation/ requirement. We'll make use of our friend that is Planning application 'PandB' all throughout this chapter.

Log in to the Oracle EPM Workspace and navigate to the Planning application 'PandB'. After we have opened the required Planning application, go to the properties of the dimensions.

We can go to properties of a Planning dimension after we had logged in to:

Administration | Manage | Dimensions as shown; this will show us the Planning **Dimensions** page.

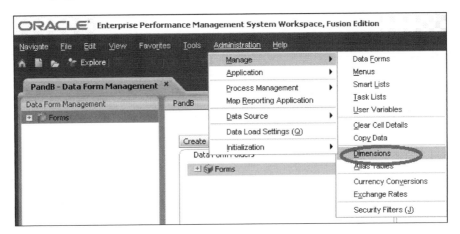

It opens the home page of Hyperion Planning dimension and we can see the three tabs highlighted in red as shown in the following image:

Those three tabs are **Dimensions**, **Performance Settings**, and **Evaluation Order**. This section focuses on the very first tab **Dimensions** and we'll learn about the other two in the later part of this chapter.

Dimensions

In the **Dimension** home page of the Planning application, we can see the following options:

- List of dimensions
- Add Dimension
- Sort
- Search

List of dimensions

We see the dimension **Account**. We can also see the drop down showing the list of all dimensions defined in the Planning application 'PandB'. They are **Account, Currency, Entity, Period, Scenario, Segments, Version,** and **Year**, as shown:

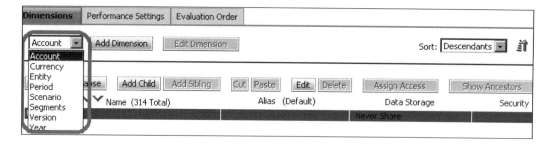

Adding a dimension

By the virtue of the sample Planning application **PandB**, we already have the standard eight dimensions.

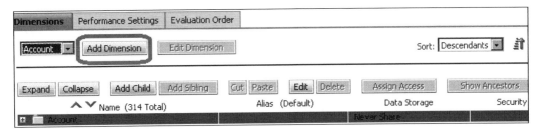

Though it is a multi currency Planning application, we don't see the HSP_Rates dimension in the list of displayed standard dimension in drop down list of dimensions. It is important to note that HSP_Rates is not visible in the Planning application, but it is visible in the Essbase Administration Console.

If we have a blank Planning application, which is a typical real life situation, we can create individual dimensions by using the option **Add Dimension.** For the sample **PandB** Planning application as well, we can still add dimensions, but that would be additional custom dimensions, as all standard dimensions are created already.

Why do we need an additional custom dimension?

Every organization has its own way of budgeting. We cannot have a pre-packaged Planning application that will suit the needs of all the organizations, as the budgeting would differ from one organization to the other. Hence, there is a facility to customize a Planning application to suit to the needs and requirements of an organization's budgeting process. Nevertheless, there are a few standard dimensions, which would be common to the budgeting models of all organizations.

Custom dimensions will help the application in providing further split to the budgeted numbers of revenue or cost (for example, budget revenue per product per customer).

For example, a typical IT company would be interested in doing its budgeting at the project level. But, we don't have projects as a predefined standard dimension in our Planning application. Therefore, we should create custom dimension called project.

We need to remember that every structural change has to be followed by the database refresh. Therefore, when we add a member, change the properties of dimensions/members or even add new dimension the database will undergo a refresh, that is, outline restructure.

We cannot have two standard dimensions of the same kind, this means that we cannot have two account dimensions, two entity dimensions, two version dimensions, or two currency dimensions. Though we can have multiple custom dimensions.

Sorting the dimensions

This is the option to arrange dimension members either in ascending or descending order. We need to pay close attention towards the right-hand side of **Descendants** and **children**; there are two icons — ![asc] for sorting in ascending order and ![desc] for sorting in descending order.

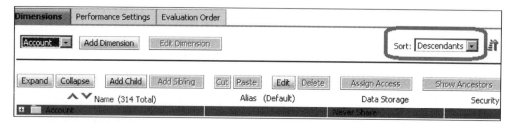

What is the difference between 'children' and 'descendants'?

For a particular member ABC, children are the list of members who are immediately below the member ABC in the defined hierarchy, and descendants would be the members who are not only immediately below ABC, but also the members who are below ABC in the hierarchy. Let us try to understand with an example:

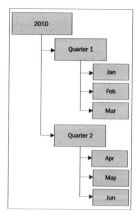

For **Quarter1**, the children are **Jan**, **Feb**, and **March**. For **2010**, the children are **Quarter1** and **Quarter2**, whereas for the same **2010** member, the descendants are **Quarter1**, **Jan**, **Feb**, **March**, **Quarter2**, **April**, **May**, and **June**.

Another example would be: Prince William and Henry are the children of Prince Charles, whereas Prince Charles along with William and Henry are the descendants of Prince Philip. Don't ask who all these princes are!

Searching for a member in the dimension

To search a member in a dimension within any of its hierarchies, we use the **Search** option. We can search either by the name of the member or its alias name. If we are not sure whether the search key word is **Name** or **Alias**, then we can use **Both**. This is very handy; we'll realize its importance as we start working on the application.

We can see search up the hierarchy with [icon] and search down the hierarchy with [icon] as shown in the following image:

Next, we'll move on to individual dimensions. We will start with the Account dimension.

Account Dimension

This is the most important and complex dimension of all the dimensions of a Hyperion Planning application. The Account dimension of PandB application gives us lot of information. The following sections will cover all about Account dimension:

- **Hierarchies**: We will see the typical hierarchies of an Account dimension in this section and understand their functional meaning.

- **Dimension page options**: These are the common options that are available on the home page of Dimensions.

- **Account Types**: This section talks about the account types which are applicable for the 'Account' dimension. It's important to understand account types before we design the 'Account' dimension.

- **Basics of Dimensions**: A few basic concepts of 'Storage' and 'Aggregation' will be covered in this section. These are applicable to all dimensions.

- **Account Dimension Member Properties**: This last section of the 'Accounts' dimension explains all the settings of a member of an Account dimension.

Hierarchies

Let us spend some time understanding the hierarchies at a high level. It's not a given that every Planning designer would create the hierarchies and its content in the same fashion. The objective of learning more of these hierarchies is to get a feel for how a designer would think while implementing them.

The primary hierarchies of the Account dimension of this PandB application are as follows:

- Statistics
- Income statement
- Balance sheet
- Cash flow

The account dimension hierarchies are shown in the following image:

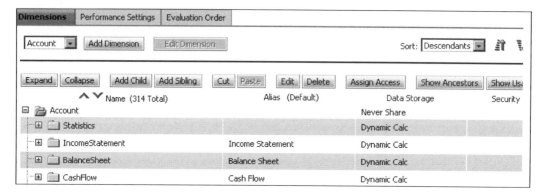

Let us start from the first hierarchy statistics.

Statistics

All through the Oracle Hyperion educational websites and in the world of Hyperion Planning presentations, we often hear that Hyperion Planning is a driver-based Planning product. Let us try to understand what a driver is.

Let us take an example of an IT organization. A typical organization would need a few supporting departments such as a general administration department, an HR department, and so on. We'll consider only the general administration department for now. General administration includes indirect costs such as rent, utilities, and others.

This general administration department caters to the needs of multiple divisions of the IT organization. For simplicity's sake, let us say that the IT organization is broadly divided in two divisions and they are BPO and KPO. The general administration department serves both these divisions.

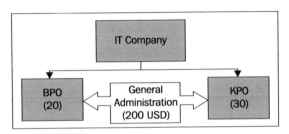

There are 20 employees in BPO and 30 employees in KPO. We need to understand that the cost incurred by the general administration department is, in a way, the cost for serving these two divisions. Now, if we need to know which division is using how much, we need to think of a driver that can be useful to make that calculation. Let us assume that 200 USD is the total cost of the general administration department. Now, management would definitely be interested in knowing how much out of 200 USD is spent in serving BPO and how much for KPO, individually.

If we take headcount as a driver that is, 20 employees in BPO and 30 employees in KPO, we can clearly conclude that there are total 50 employees and the total cost is 200 USD; hence the cost per employee is 4 USD. Therefore, for BPO, 4 USD * 20, that is, 80 USD of the total 200 USD were spent by the general administration department for the BPO division. Likewise, 4 USD * 30, that is 120 USD was used for the KPO division.

In this example, we have introduced a driver **headcount**.

While we interview users as one of the initial activities in any Planning implementation, we compile all the needed drivers and collate them under a hierarchy called **statistics**.

 There is no definite rule of thumb for designing hierarchies; it depends only on the business case and the budget model and will vary client to client.

Income statement

The next hierarchy that we see in the account dimension hierarchies screenshot is **IncomeStatement**.

Income statement is one of the basic and mandatory financial reports of any organization. In simple language, it gives information of what has been sold in a period of time and how much cost has been incurred, and along with that, what was the expense in the same period of time, and finally its tells you how much profit you made. Big bosses of every organization would be interested in knowing the health of their organization and they can find this out by looking at the P&L statement or the income statement.

 Now, we know that organizations need to look at income statement reports and we understand that there is a need to plan and budget expenses and revenues.

To generate an income statement, we need to create hierarchies and members in a way that we can represent all the components of the P&L statement, that is, all types of expenses and revenues.

Expand the **IncomeStatement** hierarchy of **Account** dimension, and you will see **Net Profit**. Now, try to correlate the whole hierarchical structures within **IncomeStatement** that result in **Net profit** and that is what exactly an organization would need at the end of the day; that is what we call the *bottom line* in the finance world.

Balance sheet

The next hierarchy in account dimension hierarchies screenshot is **BalanceSheet**. This is another mandatory financial report for any organization. It gives us a snapshot of the company on any particular day. It should reflect assets (what we have), liabilities (what we owe), and equity (worth).

If we have to make an equation, it would be the following:

Equity = assets − liabilities and it can be rewritten as **assets = liabilities + equity**.

For more information on these terms, either search for them using Google or read any basic financial reports book. Again, we would design the hierarchies and members in a manner such that balance sheet financial reports can be generated. When we expand the view the high level hierarchies of **BalanceSheet**, we see **TotalAssets** and **TotalLiabilities** and **Equity**.

Cash flow

The last hierarchy in account dimension hierarchies screenshot is **CashFlow**. It's another important financial report that gives information of the movement of cash over a period of time. In simple language, it gives information of how much cash was there at the beginning of the period and how much cash has been received and spent in the same period. Finally, if we have to equate, we could do it as follows:

Cash on hand at the end of a period = Cash on hand at the beginning of the period + Cash received in the same period – cash spent in the period.

We again design our hierarchies in a manner to suit to the needs of this report. In the course of chapter, we'll learn about aggregation, with the help of which, we can achieve additions and subtraction, which we see in the above equation.

We discussed hierarchies to get a feel of Account dimension. Again, it's the prerogative of the Planning application designer how he wants to design hierarchies and its members. There is no definite thumb rule.

Dimension page options

Now, let us look at the application and learn a few of the available options of Account dimension. When we are on the Planning dimensions page, we see the following options, as shown next:

Most of the options are self-explanatory:

- **Expand**: A hierarchy that has children or descendants and can be expanded by selecting the hierarchy member. Click on **Expand**. Try to do it after you select **IncomeStatement**; we can see that it expands and shows you the members under it.

- **Collapse**: This is exactly the opposite of the expand option. Select **IncomeStatement** and click on **Collapse**. It shows only the **IncomeStatement** closing out its members.

- **Add Child**: To add a child member to a member in a dimension, we opt for this. It is important to know that the new member is added as the last children of the selected member.

- **Add Sibling**: To add a sibling to a member, we select this option.

 We have seen that we can add a dimension and here, we see that we can add children to them too. We need to know that a typical Planning application implementation cannot have all of its dimensions and members created manually with these options. As the count of members for Account and Entity dimensions are many in number, we load metadata, which does the same job of dimension and member creation.

- **Cut** and **Paste**: We can even cut a member and paste it from one position in the hierarchy to the other using these options.

- **Edit**: This is a very important button, which leads to the properties of a member. To edit/look at the properties of any member, we need to select the member and click on **Edit**. It opens a new window with appropriate and available properties of that member.

- **Delete**: This is the easiest of all to understand. It's an option to delete members, but we need to remember that when we delete a member, it's a structural change and to reflect the change, we need to refresh the database. We cannot afford to forget that.

 We need to refresh a database even if the position of a member is changed or one of the Essbase specific properties is changed or a new member is added. If we specify it only under Delete it will make readers think that the database refresh is only required when a member is changed.

- **Assign Access**: In the Planning application, we can set security to the user even at an individual member level. Imagine Entity dimension to have members USA, UK, and others. We would like to have UK planners to access UK-related Planning data and USA planners to access USA-related Planning data, and at the same time we don't want UK planners to view US entity related information and vice versa. To achieve this, we need to have security set for the members of USA and UK groups. We provide a set of users to access 'UK' and an other set of USA Planning users to access USA entity members. More about security is covered in *Chapter 9, User Security Provisioning and Access Rights*.

- **Show Usage**: This is an interesting option, which provides information on where the selected Dimension member is being used. It will list the Data forms, Task lists, and other artifacts in which the member is being used.

  Let us elaborate. Expand hierarchy of **IncomeStatement** and you will see member name **300000** with alias name **Net Income**. Select the member and click on **Show Usage**. It should show the list of data forms where this member is being used. Therefore, it will show **IncomeStatement** data form, as shown in the following image. This means that the member **300000** is being used in the data form **IncomeStatement**.

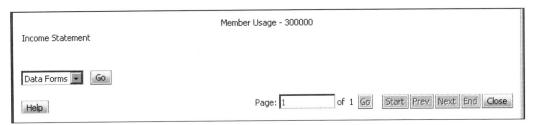

Account types

Every member of the accounts dimension has to be defined as one of the account types mentioned as follows. While we design a Planning application and create the account dimension, we need to assign these account types to all the members based on the nature of the members. In this section, we'll see how can one decide which member is of what account type. The understanding of the business is more important when we take a call on defining the account type, rather than any technical understanding. Even if we have not done MBA finance from best of B schools, it's easy to label an account type. We are sure and smart enough to know what is an expense account member or revenue account member and likewise the other account types. If we still doubt ourselves, let us prove ourselves wrong by exploring these definitions in more detail.

The available account types are:

- Expense
- Revenue
- Asset
- Liability
- Equity
- Saved assumption

Let us see all the account types in more detail.

Expense and revenue

An **expense** is something that makes a hole in your pocket and **revenue** is something that puts money into our wallets. This is not a financial book for us to give the definitions in financial terms; so please bear with us if you are a finance guru. We define these terms to help a non-finance guy understand, as these are basic terms that are useful while designing Account dimension in a Planning application.

Before that, we need to recap our knowledge on income statement and balance sheet. This will help us in understanding account types better. Let us take a look at a sample income statement:

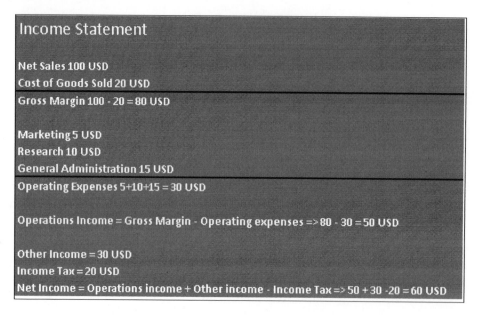

Let us read and try to understand it from top to bottom. First, it starts with the top line which is always *revenue* or *sales*. Next, we see **COGS (Cost Of Goods Sold)**. This is the cost incurred during the process of making goods or products. For example, for a manufacturing company, COGS would be the cost of making the product. Next is the gross margin, which is a simple subtraction of COGS from 'net sales'. So far, so good.

Now, we have more expenses, that is *Marketing*, *Research*, and *General Administration*. These are all the departments or functions that a company will have, but they don't generate revenue. For example, Research is a cost and it takes money from the company. These are generally called under the category SG&A. If you're more interested in getting into details of SG&A, try Yahoo! search for a change this time. Why should Google always profit? Yes, we have arrived at 'Operating expenses' so far.

We can see Operations income calculated. Finally, we have net income, this is called 'bottom line'. We might have used 'bottom line' in our day to day life without knowing the financial meaning of it though. The objective of this knowledge is not to start working on the financial reports but to understand account types. Let us not bury ourselves too much into accounting basics. Let us come out of it.

Hence, it's clear that we have 'expenses' and 'revenue' in our income statement. Now, if we have to categorize income statement items between 'revenue' and 'expense', it should not be a difficult task.

To quote a few, *Net Sales* and *Other income* are of *Revenue* type. Whereas 'COGS', marketing, research, and income tax are of 'expense' account type. We should get a feel of Planning implementation by now as we are able to label account dimension members as 'revenue' and 'expense'.

When we design an Account dimension and its members, most of the **IncomeStatement** members are either 'revenue' or 'expense'.

Now let us look at the PandB application and its members of the Account dimension. We need to note that the **IncomeStatement**, **BalanceSheet**, and **CashFlow** are the three main hierarchies. First, we'll look at the member properties of the **IncomeStatement** hierarchy. Expand the hierarchy as shown in the following image:

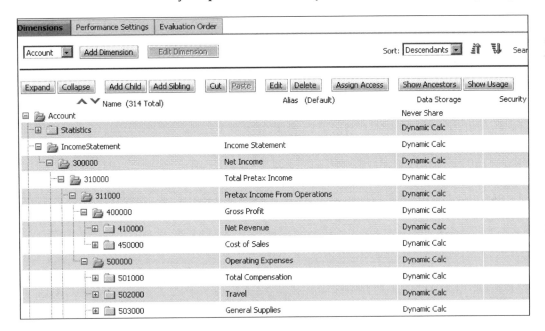

Now, we will see the account type of the members of **IncomeStatement** hierarchy. There are so many members in this hierarchy that it's impossible to check the member property of each and every individual member.

Select **Gross Profit** and click the **Edit** option. It opens a new window and we are only interested in **Account Type** as of now. Other properties will be visited in the later sections of the chapter. The value for the **Account Type** property is **Revenue**, as we can see in the following image:

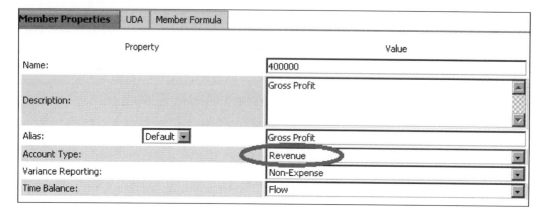

With our understanding of revenue and expense, we can check the **Account Type** property for the other members—travel and general supplies. From the name, we can make out that there are travel expense and general supplies expense and of course their account type would be **Expense**. We can also take a look at the **Account Type** of other members as well.

Assets, liabilities, and equity

We have spoken of balance sheet and we'll take a look at a sample balance sheet, which is very simple.

Assets are something that we have; it includes cash, buildings, inventory, and so on. Simply put, these assets have monetary value. Liabilities are a monetary obligation. If we are running a company, we have to pay salaries to employees, and we might need to pay a loan amount to the bank (if we have taken out a loan). All these constitute liabilities.

 Equity is the subtraction of liabilities from assets.

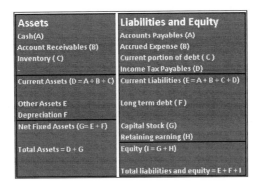

Assets	Liabilities and Equity
Cash(A)	Accounts Payables (A)
Account Receivables (B)	Accrued Expense (B)
Inventory (C)	Current portion of debt (C)
	Income Tax Payables (D)
Current Assets (D = A + B + C)	Current Liabilities (E = A + B + C + D)
Other Assets E	Long term debt (F)
Depreciation F	
Net Fixed Assets (G= E + F)	Capital Stock (G)
	Retaining earning (H)
Total Assets = D + G	Equity (I = G + H)
	Total liabilities and equity = E + F + I

We won't get into the intricate details, the important information is that we can see that the **Assets** part is on the left-hand side and **Liablitlities and Equity** is on the right hand side.

If we have to label Cash, then Accounts Payables as one of the account types; it's easy for us to make them assets type and liabilities type respectively.

Let us quickly look at the hierarchy of our very own PandB Planning application. It's very obvious that the members of BalanceSheet cannot be of account type— revenue and expense—because balance sheet comprises assets, liabilities, and equity. We'll expand the **BalanceSheet** hierarchy and check the account type of the member properties of the few of them. We can see that the hierarchies are themselves designed in a manner that assets, liabilities and equity are of separate and individual hierarchies and the members under them that belong to them would be of either assets, liabilities, or equity type.

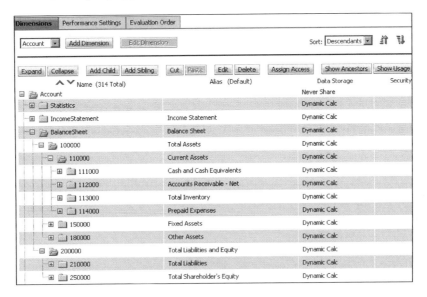

Check the member properties of **Account Receivables**, **Total Inventory**, and **Cash and Cash Equivalents**. By the virtue of their business sense, we know they are all assets.

Now, we can also check the member properties of of members under **Total Liabilities** and **Total Shareholder's Equity** as shown in the previous screenshot. There are, of course, liability and equity account type respectively. The grouping has been done smartly already and when we are designing account dimension while implementing, it's always better to group this way. Again, it's not a rule of thumb, but we can see that it makes life easier and much simpler.

Saved assumption

All the drivers and ratios can be ganged into hierarchies. All of these members have the account type of 'saved assumption'.

Let us understand with an example, there is a member **BonusPerHead**, it's a member of **Statistics** hierarchy. We'll ask ourselves a few simple questions:

- Is **BonusPerHead** revenue?
- Is **BonusPerHead** an expense?
- Is **BonusPerHead** an asset?
- Is **BonusPerHead** a liability?
- Is **BonusPerHead** equity?

For all the questions, which we had asked in soliloquy, the answer is simple plain NO. It's a driver and that's what makes it a 'saved assumption'.

Incidentally, we see the same nature of the member of another hierarchy 'Ratios'. We should spend some time in looking at the member properties of few of the members of 'Statistics' and 'Ratios'. We'll get bored soon as every member is of the 'Saved Assumption' account type, but at least, we'll understand the Account Type 'Saved Assumption' at the end.

Basics

In this *Basics* section, we'll learn two concepts, and they are as follows:

- Aggregation: This section covers all the aggregation options available, such as adding, subtracting, multiplying and so on, and how they determine the data roll up behavior.
- Storage: This section talks about the nature of data whether it is stored or calculated upon user retrieval. It has got more variants, which we'll see.

Aggregation

Refer to the earlier screenshots showing sample the income statement and balance sheet respectively.

Let us understand the significance of aggregation with an example; we have seen the basic outline of **IncomeStatement**. It starts with Revenue/Net Sales, followed by expense items, which are COGS (Cost of Goods sold). It's important to select the right aggregation option for the member as this determines how the members roll up and aggregate.

To calculate gross income, we can use simple mathematics, as follows:

Gross Income = Net Sales – COGS

Here, we understand that COGS has to be subtracted from Net Sales to arrive at Gross Income. As we understand the logic of Gross Income, we know to subtract. Now to make the Planning application understand and do subtraction is the responsibility of aggregation options.

In the previous example, we would make aggregate option of + for Net sales, and – for COGS.

Hence, when gross income has to be calculated, it does some simple math to calculate Net Sales – COGS.

Now, let us look back into our application **PandB** and its **Account** dimension members. Expand the **IncomeStatement** hierarchy.

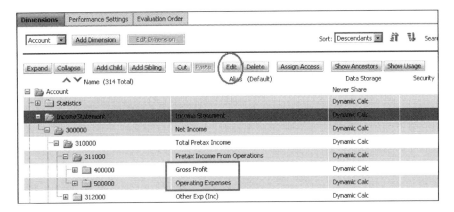

Here in the previous image, check out the member property of both **Gross Profit** and **Operating Expenses**. Before that we need to understand that **Operating Expenses** has to be subtracted from **Gross Profit** to arrive at the **Total Pretax Income** from operations. With that knowledge, we can conclude that aggregation of + (addition) would be for **Gross Profit** and, subtraction from **Operating Expenses** and we would see the same in their respective member properties.

Where do we see the aggregation option of a member?

We need to first select the members and then select **Edit** option. It opens a new window as shown in the following image and the field to the right-hand side **Plan Type** field is aggregation option as rounded.

If we select the **Gross Profit** member and look into its properties by selecting **Edit** options; it would appear as shown next.

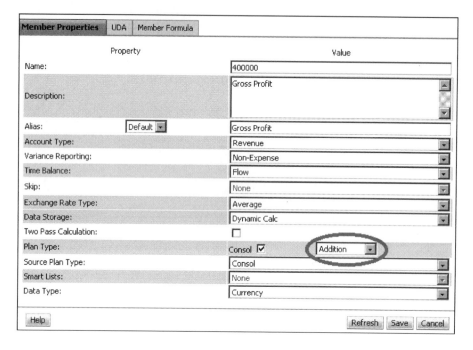

There are other aggregation options such as multiplication, division, percentage, and ignore. Multiplication and division are self explanatory. The percentage aggregation type is used when we want to see the data in percentage format. For example, if we enter 0.7, it'll multiply by 100 and show it as 70 % in the forms.

There is another aggregation option called ignore. A member that has property set to ignore does not participate in aggregation/calculation. For example, we have a parent **A** and its children—**B, C,** and **D**—as shown in the following screenshot:

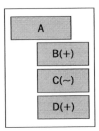

Effectively, **A** = **B** + **D**, and **C** would not participate (as this property is ignored).

From an implementation perspective, this is very important, as aggregation leads to the right data. If we end up setting the wrong aggregation options; for example, if we add both revenue and expenses for income statement, then we know that we are showing a dubious profit number to a company—though the boss might be happy for a moment—but we know that's a blunder. We need to be careful as these aggregation settings impact the figures and numbers that are going to be in the financial reports that will be distributed across the organization.

Storage

To understand the storage options available, we need to recall what we learned about the basics of dense and sparse in *Chapter 3, Introduction to Hyperion Planning Dimensions*; please refer to that.

The storage options have two objectives:

- Save the disk space
- Optimize the performance

Let us see how we can achieve this with the available options.

Where can we see the Storage properties/settings for a Dimension member?

Select the Dimension members and select **Edit** option, it leads to a new window, the member properties window. For demonstration purposes, let us select **Gross Profit** member and look into its properties, as shown in the following screenshot. We can see the **Storage** options as circled in the following image:

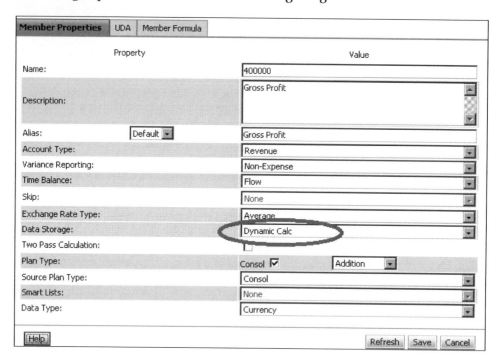

The following are the data storage options:

- StoreData
- DynamicCalcAndStore
- Dynamic Calc
- ShareData
- NeverShare
- LabelOnly
- StoreData

This is the default storage setting and with this option, data values are stored. As the data values are stored, of course it will eat the disk space. But at the same time, data values for the member with this storage setting have better performance, as the values are already stored and it just needs to pull them out to throw into a report.

 StoreData provides better retrieval performance.

In Planning and Budgeting, data entry is the most common activity. You can learn about data entry in *Chapter 9*, *Data Entry*.

 All the members, where data entry is expected is always set as StoreData.

Let us look back to our sample **PandB** application. Look at the **Account** dimension, go to its level 0 members (level 0 member are the members that do not have any children) straightaway, as shown in the following image. We see the member highlighted as **Store**.

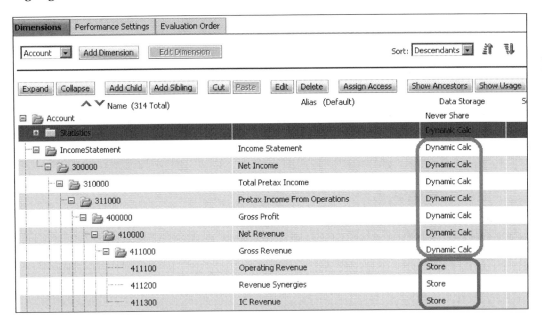

We can drill down and look at the level 0 members of other hierarchies of account dimension to reconfirm the same idea.

DynamicCalcAndStore

This setting does not store data values, unlike StoreData, until a user retrieves the data for the first time. Upon first time, the member value is calculated based on the aggregation operator or the member formula whichever applies and is stored and all the subsequent retrievals are done in the manner of the 'store data' as data values now are stored. Its dynamic nature is only until a user retrieves the information for the first time.

Therefore, until it's retrieved for the first time, it does not consume disk space but after it has been retrieved it stores the values and thereby consumes space.

We don't generally use this in typical implementations because it's recommended to be used by sparse dimension member with a very complex member formula or a sparse member that is retrieved very frequently.

DynamicCalcAndStore members cannot take user inputs and so it cannot be used for data entry.

Dynamic Calc

This is the most used storage setting for account dimension members. This setting never stores data; the member with Dynamic Calc setting retrieves data every time a user requests. It does not store data, unlike the StoreData or DynamicCalcAndStore.

Because of its 'no storage' nature , it has the huge benefit of saving disk space, but at the same time it would take more time to retrieve as it does not store any data value and retrieves data for every single user request.

While designing hierarchies, we should not use Dynamic Calc for the members where planners are expected to enter data because data values are not saved even when a user/planner enters data for a member with Dynamic Calc setting does not store.

Its very prevalent to set the parent level dense dimensions with Dynamic Calc setting.

Let us look at the PandB application and its account dimension. The image under StoreData has few members circled, which are of Dynamic Calc and all of these members are the parents of their own little world of hierarchies and all the level 0 as we see, rounded in red are of store type.

This setting needs to be avoided, when the dimension is sparse.

ShareData

ShareData required when we need alternate roll ups.

Wait, what is an alternate roll up?

There are scenarios where users will want to analyze the same data from multiple perspectives. For example, sales data needs to be analyzed location, business and department wise. This means that there is a need to aggregate the same data along multiple hierarchies. In this case the hierarchies would location wise, business wise and department wise in the Entity Dimension. The first hierarchy is designated as the main hierarchy.

The rest of the hierarchies are called alternate rollups and members from the main hierarchy are used as shared members in the alternate hierarchies/rollups.

Data is entered/calculated only once in the main hierarchy and shared along all the alternate rollups.

It can be better understood with an example, but for this demonstration, open the outline of the Essbase application Sample_U in EAS console (if you're wondering where this Essbase application came from, don't. We did not create it; it's the default application that comes with the software package) and its database Basic, as shown in the following image.

The following screenshot shows Product dimension of Sample_U Essbase application:

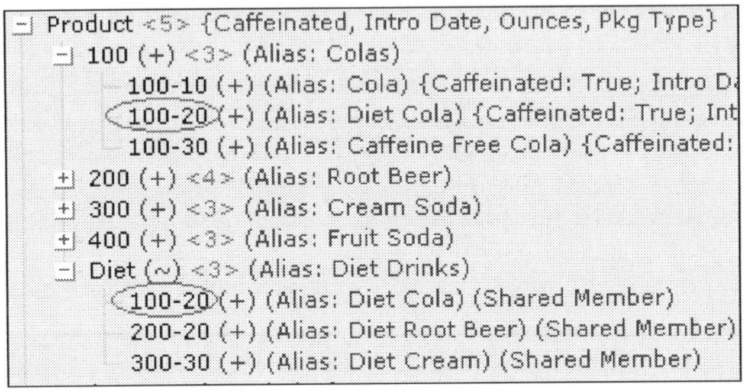

As we see **100-20** is reflected under two hierarchies, that's why it's rightly termed **alternate roll up**. Functional understanding is that **100-20**, that is **Diet Cola**, needs to roll up to **100 (Colas)**, and at the same time, the same **100-20**, that is **Diet Cola**, also needs to roll up to **Diet (Diet Drinks)**. Hence, the same member **100-20** is in two hierarchies to address the functional requirement. Though it appears twice at two places, it's actually stored only under **100** and not under **Diet**. This way, the data values are stored only once and with the help of pointer, which the shared member has, it retrieves the data.

In these kinds of situations, use **Share**.

NeverShare

When a parent has a single child, you use **NeverShare** for the parent. Here, we need to introduce the concept of *Implicit Sharing*. If the parent and its child members are tagged as store data and there is only a single child which aggregates to the parent than in this scenario Essbase rather than storing a separate value for the parent member points the parent to the same value stored for the child. This is referred to as Implicit Sharing.

The NeverShare storage property can be used on the parent member for overriding implicit sharing.

LabelOnly

These are for the namesake. They neither have the ability to store data nor is any data associated with them. It's more or less for navigational convenience. There are a few members that do not need to be aggregated and at the same time no need to store any data. For example, in our **Account** dimension of **PandB** application, we have the hierarchy **Statistics**, which are all drivers collated. There are a few payroll-related drivers and a few revenue-related drivers. It does not make any sense to aggregate their children as they are drivers, as shown.

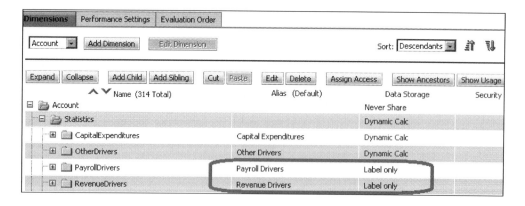

As we can see PayrollDrivers and RevenueDrivers are label only, they don't need to have any aggregated value because it does not make any logical sense by adding drivers such as **Bonus %** and **Bonus Type**.

For these kinds of hierarchies, we set them as 'label' only. We don't set any members of income statement or balance sheet as label only, as we need them to have an aggregated value and it has been designed very carefully to store the data.

Account Dimension member properties

In this section, we'll learn all the property features of an Account dimension member. Select any account dimension member and select **Edit**. It opens a new window of the member properties. We select the **IncomeStatement** member, which is an Account dimension member for tutorial purposes and see its properties as shown in the following image:

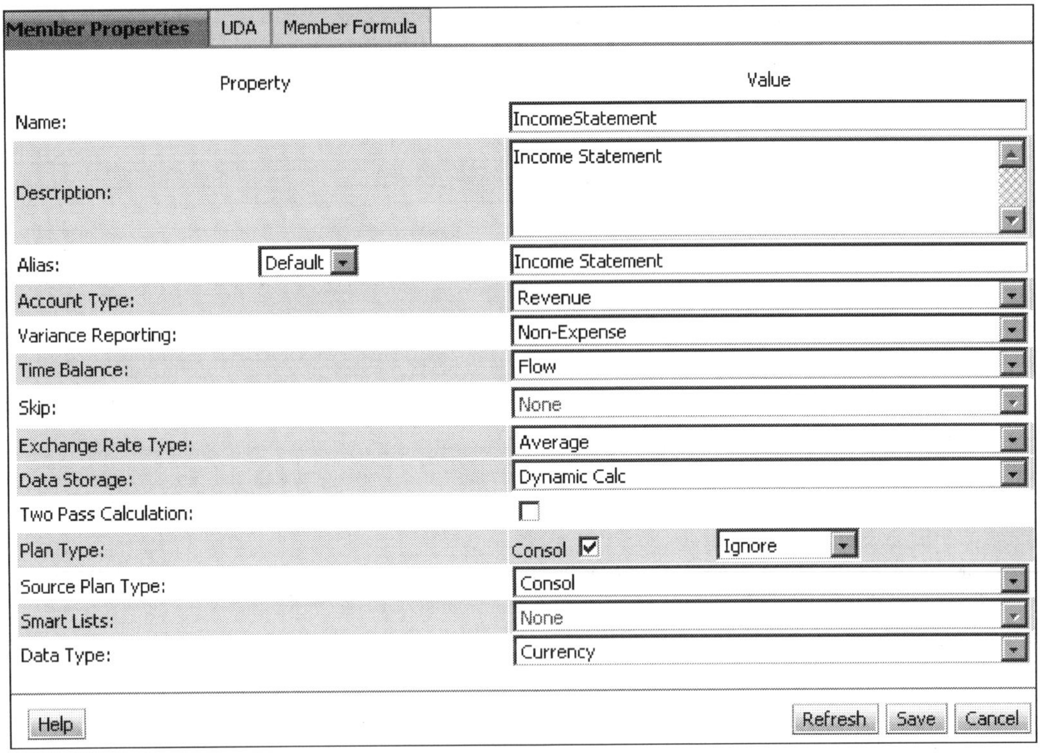

Member Properties	UDA	Member Formula	

Property	Value
Name:	IncomeStatement
Description:	Income Statement
Alias: Default	Income Statement
Account Type:	Revenue
Variance Reporting:	Non-Expense
Time Balance:	Flow
Skip:	None
Exchange Rate Type:	Average
Data Storage:	Dynamic Calc
Two Pass Calculation:	☐
Plan Type:	Consol ☑ Ignore
Source Plan Type:	Consol
Smart Lists:	None
Data Type:	Currency

Help	Refresh	Save	Cancel

- **Name**: This is the name of the member.

- **Description**: It's an optional field where we can provide the description of a member.

- **Alias**: This is again an optional field. This is nothing but another name. As we saw for member 300000, the alias is 'Net Income', which is the alternate name and more meaningful to our users. When we make reports, we can make use of the alias name as well.

- **Account Type**: We have already learned about account types. This is a drop down from which we can select the account type on the basis of the meaning of the account dimension member. Refer back to the previous section called 'account type' for any further information on it.

- **Variance Reporting**: This field is automatically selected on the basis of the selection of account type. Though we can edit and change the settings, but as account type is selected, the default variance reporting that is, either **Expense** or **Non-Expense** is selected.

- As we know that based on the account type selection, settings of time balance are selected and we need to know that even **Variance Reporting** field is also set by the virtue of the 'account type' selection.

There are only two options in this field—**Expense** and **Non-Expense.** Now we know that there are six account types and one of the account types is **Expense**.

 Therefore, apart from account type **Expense**, for all other account types, the default selection of variance reporting is **Non-Expense**.

Variance analysis in simple terms is the comparison between actuals and budget. Let us consider a simple example, we thought that in the month of December we would spend 2000 USD, but eventually when we have completed the month of December, we realized that we actually had spent 2500 USD. Here, to relate, 2000 USD was the budgeted expense and 2500 USD is the actual expense. Now, every organization would need to know this variance for better control.

Now, let us co-relate actuals and budget with **Expense** and **Non-Expense.** When we set a account member as expense, the actual amount is subtracted from the budget amount for the variance and similarly, when we set it as a **Non-Expense**, the budget amount is subtracted from actual amount for the variance.

This is designed to handle the difference between variance reporting of expense and non-expense accounts.

For expense accounts if the actual number is greater than the budgeted number, this is a negative sign for the company.

Whereas if for revenue accounts, the actual numbers are greater than the budgeted numbers, this is a positive sign for the company.

Tagging accounts for variance reporting automatically switches the sign of the variance based on the variance reporting tag when the @VAR and @VARPER functions are used for variance.

- **Time Balance**: This is an important property which will determine the nature of aggregation. The default settings are set based on the **Account Type** selection again. For example, for the account dimension member, when we select the account type **Expense**, the **Time Balance** property is set to **Flow** by default.

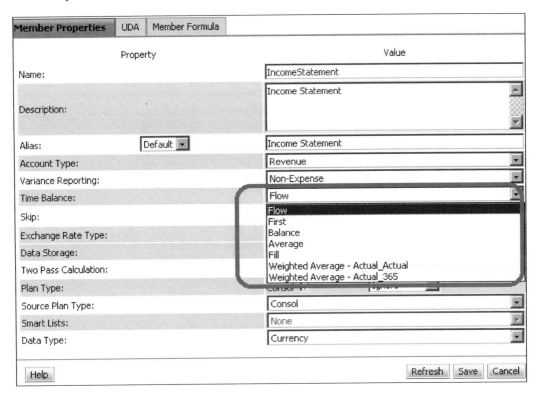

We'll learn about the available options of time balance with an example:

  ° **Flow**: This is the simplest option; it aggregates or sums up of all the values to the parent. It would add Jan, Feb and March to Quarter1.

  ° **First**: This uses the beginning data value of Jan to Quarter 1.

  ° **Balance**: This is opposite to First, it uses the ending value that is of March to Quarter1.

  ° **Average**: This option averages the data values that is the average of Jan, Feb and March. (Jan + Feb + March)/ 3.

  ° **Weighted Average - Actual_Actual**: This setting assumes that the year is a leap year with February having 29 days and Quarter 1 would have 91 days in total (Jan = 31 days, Feb= 29 days and March=31 days).

  ° The Quarter 1 value is calculated by first multiplying the monthly values with the no of days of the month and the sum all the values post multiplication and divide by the total number of days of the quarter. If we look at the below table, we should be able to co-relate.

- **Weighted Average-Actual_365**: This setting does not assume the year is a leap year, Hence, Feb would have 28 days only. With this single difference we would have total no of days in Quarter 1 as 90 (Jan =31, Feb = 28 and March = 31). The Quarter 1 values are calculated by first multiplying the monthly values with the number of days of the month and then summing all the values post multiplication and dividing by the total number of days in the quarter. The only difference is the number of days in Feb.

This is how the data is spread depending on the time balance property. Now, let us make a table that explains all the time balance properties.

Time Balance Property	Jan	Feb	March	Quarter 1
First	20	30	40	20
Balance	20	30	40	40
Flow	20	30	40	90
Average	20	30	40	30
Weighted Average _Average	20	30	40	30
Weighted Average _Actual _Actual	20	30	40	30

Time Balance is covered in detail *Chapter 9, Data Entry*.

- **Skip**: This setting will help in handling the missing values and zeroes in short. As we can see, there are four possible options for **Skip** property.

 The **Skip** property is applicable only for the account members whose time balance property is first, balance, or average. For 'flow', this skip property is not applicable.

Remember that with the help of these settings, we'll instruct what to skip:

  ◦ **None**: Nothing to skip. Hence, while calculation or aggregation both zeroes and #missing values are considered. It is important to note that zeroes and missing are not the same. missing means absence of numbers, while zeroes signify the number 0.

  ◦ **Missing**: Selecting this option means that you want to skip #missing values. Therefore, #missing values are excluded while calculating any parent.

  ◦ **Zero**: This is the same as the 'Missing' setting; the difference here is that it skips zeroes, rather than #missing values. Hence, Zeroes are skipped but #missing values are included.

  ◦ **Missing and Zeros**: Both zeroes and #missing need to be skipped in this case while calculating the parent.

- **Exchange Rate Type**: This is applicable only to multi currency Planning applications. Exchange rates are covered in *Chapter 9, Data Forms*.

- **Data Storage**: We already learned in the previous sections of the chapter about the storage options available. As we can see, the **Dynamic Calc** is the storage property for this member.

- **Two-Pass Calculation**: This is covered in detail in *Chapter 11, Getting Started with Business Rules*.

- **Plan type**: We learned about plan types in *Chapter 3, Introduction to Hyperion Planning Dimensions*. In our sample application PandB, we have only one plan type, called consol. Imagine an application with three plan types. Say they are income statement, balance sheet, and revenue. Let us repeat, we have hypothetically three plan types. Now, our accounts dimension would have a whole list of members that are related to balance sheet, income statement, and even revenue related that is three different Essbase outlines in three different Essbase databases. Now, it makes a lot of sense to separate these members based on their nature. We can assign all the balance sheet related members to 'BalanceSheet' plan type and assign all income statement related members to 'IncomeStatement' plan type, likewise, we do the same for revenue related account members to be assigned to the 'Revenue' plan type.

We need to recall that if we have three data types, it means we would have three database cubes under one Essbase application and we would have three Essbase database outlines.

In our case, we have only one plan type, hence it's selected by default, else we get all the available data types and we need to select them by ticking.

 Can a account member be associated with more than one Plan type?

Yes, we can definitely have a member of an account dimension associated with more than one Plan type. This is again a design prerogative, there is no fixed rule. If we think that a member's presence is needed in both the Plan types, then we can assign it to both of them.

- **Aggregation Options**: We had already covered 'aggregation' in the previous section. So this can be ignored.

- **Source Plan type**: Optimization is the key and we'll understand its importance as we gain experience with Hyperion consulting. This option is strictly applicable only for an application for more than one plan type. We have learned that a member can be assigned to more than one plan type. Though, it can be associated with more than one plan type, it has to have only one source plan type. This way, we have a situation where we can have members associated with multiple plan types, but their source plan type has to be only one. This is, in a way optimized manner of having members, else there is no point in having the same member with source in all Plan types, which means, it's stored in all the data types.

- **Smart List**: Smart lists are covered in *Chapter 9, Data Forms*.

- **Data type**: The data type selection plays role in the display of the data values. Again, the selection of 'account type' does by default select the data type. Selection of account type is very important as it indirectly sets many other field properties.

  - **NonCurrency**: Displays the data values as numbers that is, numeric values only. This is the default for the account dimension member, whose account type is Saved Assumption.

  - **Currency**: Displays the value in default currency. We need to recall that there is always a default currency of a Planning application. In PandB case, it's USD. If we still don't remember, then refer back to *Chapter 4*. This is the default data type for the account types of Expense, Revenue, Asset, Liability, and Equity.

- ○ **Percentage**: This makes the data values to be displayed in percentage.
- ○ **Smart List**: Displays the values of the smart list. We are going to learn about smart lists in *Chapter 9, Data Forms*.
- ○ **Date**: This selection makes the values display as dates.
- ○ **Text**: Displays the values as text.
- ○ **Unspecified**: Displays the values as an unspecified type.

From an implementation angle, we majorly use NonCurrency and Currency. We know that for convenience sake, we designed account dimensions into three major hierarchies—balance sheet, income sheet, and statistics. All members of Balance sheet would be of assets, liabilities or equity'. Hence, the data type would be 'Currency'.

For the Income statement hierarchy, the account types of most of the members would be **Expense** and **Revenue**, again for these account type selection; the data type would be **Currency** again. An expense or a revenue is always has units of currency. that is 20,000 USD profit or 10,000 USD losses that is it's always linked with currency.

All the drivers, we have collated and made a hierarchy called **Statistics**, whose account type is 'saved assumptions', for this the data type would be **NonCurrency**. Some of the drivers might be percentages; hence the percentage data type will be used.

It's better that we look at the member properties of these three major hierarchies and check for account type, variance, time balance, and currency data type. Let us spend time till we get control over and understand them all in a comprehensive picture.

The following is a tabular form, which will recap what we have learned and also give us the information about how the account type selection by default sets the other fields.

Account Type	Variance	Time Balance	Data Type
Expense	Expense	Flow	Currency
Revenue	NonExpense	Flow	Currency
Asset	NonExpense	Balance	Currency
Liability	NonExpense	Balance	Currency
Equity	NonExpense	Balance	Currency
Saved Assumption	NonExpense	Balance	Non Currency

This is the end of the **Accounts** dimension.

Entity Dimension

We sweated out a lot for the Accounts dimension so now let us directly look at the member properties of **Entity** dimension. This should be easy, as the basics that we needed have already been covered.

We see that the Entity dimension has hierarchies related to geographical location—North America, Latin America, EMEA, and APAC and also it has functions/departments such as sales, administration, and production.

The hierarchies are again designed in a manner that the roll up happens as per the budget requirements. Again it's important to know that there is no thumb rule to know what to be included or not. It's the prerogative of the Planning application designer and the budget requirement, which determines the dimension and its hierarchies.

We design the Entity dimension in such a way that it reflects the budgeting process. We'll learn all about the Budget Review process in *Chapter 14, Budget Process Management*.

Imagine a hierarchy as country, state, and city. Now, city level budget preparation will be reviewed at state level centers and the state level budget is reviewed at country head quarters. So, we need to understand the budget preparation and its review process while designing the Entity dimension. With this understanding, we will be able to create hierarchies.

Now, let us look at the hierarchies of Entity dimension of **PandB**, as shown in the following image:

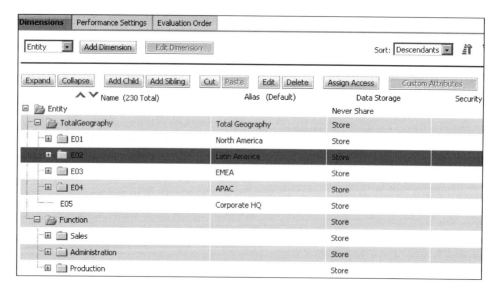

We see the main hierarchies of both geographical locations and support functions of the organization. The APAC hierarchy has Asian countries such as China, Japan, and so on, and the EMEA hierarchies includes European nations such as France, Sweden, and so on. Now pay close attention to North America and expand it to understand the hierarchy at even more granular level.

North America expands to the **USA, Canada**, and **Mexico**. We know that the USA is our favorite, so let us expand that to see East, West, North, and South, and on zooming in more, we see states such as New York.

Now, let us draw a few inferences—**USA, Canada**, and **Mexico** make up North America, and this ought to be the way for budgeting to happen, and also, budgeting is done for the east, west, north, and south centers, and at the state level as well.

We can see the part of hierarchy as shown in the following image. NY makes up for the **East Sales** and **East Sales** make up for the **USA**, which in turn, makes up for North America.

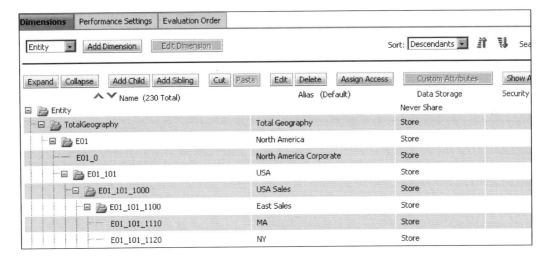

Now straightaway, let us look at the member properties of the Entity dimension member. Select member **E01** and click on **Edit** to open the member properties window.

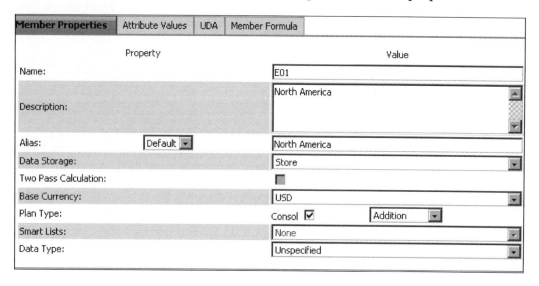

- **Name**: This is the name of the member.
- **Description**: This is a more meaningful name for the member. **North America** makes more sense than **E01**.
- **Alias**: This is another name or an alternative name.
- **Data Storage**: This is the store type. For most of the Entity members the data storage type is store type and it is set to 'never share', when it's a parent with only one child to it. We can explore other hierarchies in Entity dimension and we can see this pattern all the way through.
- **Two Pass Calculation**: We'll learn about this in *Chapter 12, Getting Started with Business Rules*.
- **Base Currency**: We'll learn more about the exchange rates and currency conversion in *Chapter 9, Data Forms*. For now, let us understand that every country has their own currency. USD is the base currency for the USA and the Pound is the base currency of the UK. Depending on the country, we set a different base currency. This is applicable only to multi-currency applications.
- **Plan Type**: We know there is only one plan in PandB, and hence, it's already ticked.
- **Aggregation**: Its addition as we see and most of them would be addition.
- **Smart Lists**: We'll learn about smart lists in *Chapter 9, Data Forms*.
- **Data Type**: We set this as **Unspecified** for Entity members.

We can see other tabs – **Attribute**, **UDA**, and **Member Formula**. Attributes are the attribute dimensions and this tab is applicable only to sparse dimensions and an entity is a sparse dimension. **UDA** is a user-defined attribute, we don't have any UDAs though and finally member formula.

This is the end of the **Entity** dimension.

Version Dimension

We have introduced this dimension already in *Chapter 3*. There are two version types, they are:

- **Standard Bottom Up**
- **Standard Target**

Refer to *Chapter 3*, *Version* section for recap of the same. Now, let us look at the version dimension of **PandB** Planning application. It has members such as working, target, variance, and so on, as shown in the following image:

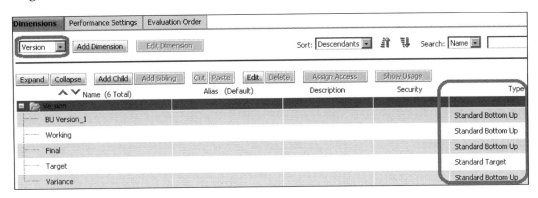

We can assume that a target version would be used to set the targets and targets are not set at base level that is at level 0. Target version enables input at all levels including the level 0 members. This is the reason why it is called Target. Its because of this property, we see **Standard Target** as the version type.

Other version members working, variance are the ones which would deal with base level members and need data entry at level 0. Bottom up version members enable input at only level 0 members. That's the reason they are called bottom up. Numbers are entered at bottom level or level 0 and then aggregated to the parent. Therefore, we see the version type as **Standard Bottom Up**.

Now, look at the member property of 'Working' member of Version DimensionVersion: It's the version member that is 'working' in the following image.

- **Type**: This is the setting that decides the type of the version. It's either **Standard Bottom Up** or **Standard Target**.

- **Enable Process Management**: We'll learn about process management later. For now, let us understand that for a version member to participate in the workflow or process management, we need to enable it .

 Version member, whose type is standard target, 'enable process management' is not an available option.

- **Data Storage**: This stores version members.

- **Aggregation**: This is set to 'ignore' for version members, as they don't make any sense in addition or subtracting or aggregating data long the version dimension Hence, it's set to 'ignore'.

Data type, alias table, description, and other fields must be boring by now, as we have understood them thoroughly by now.

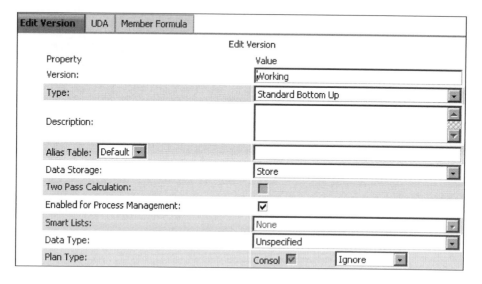

 There is no fixed number of version members we need to create, it all depends on the iterative budget process of an organization, where we are implementing Hyperion Planning. We might even make version members such as Draft1, Draft2,..., Final Draft, as per the requirements and our convenience.

Scenario Dimension

We introduced this dimension in *Chapter 3, Introduction to Hyperion Planning Dimensions*. Let us quickly recap. **Scenario** dimension members would be plan, forecast, actual, and others.

We spoke of **Entity**, **Version**, and now **Scenario**. We need to know that Entity is always associated with Scenario and Version dimension.

While we were talking of Entity dimension, we talked a little about the review process, where city budget is review at state level and then state level is reviewed by country headquarters. To generalize, entities are the ones which submit Planning data and this data is for a particular scenario and also for a particular version.

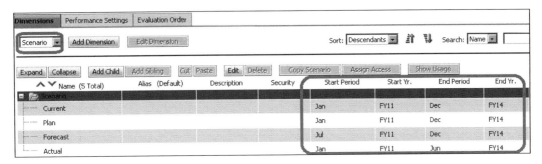

Let us elaborate, for the entity **US** in the **Current** version, the 'budget' numbers are XYZ. Or let us make other meaningful sentences, for the entity **Japan**, the **Actual** numbers for the **Final** version are LMN. Therefore, we define the intersection of Scenario, Version and Entity as a Planning unit and we'll learn about the way Planning approval and submission happens in its world in *Chapter 14, Hyperion Planning Process*.

Scenario dimension members play a major role in setting a range of years and time period ranges and this is very important. When we view a data form for a specific scenario member, then it's this settings of time period and year range, which determines where to enter data.

Let us imagine that the client requirement is to show outlook. For example Outlook3+9, it means three months of actual data and nine months of planned data. For a planner who enters data, he should be able to read the first three months of actual data and enter the plan number for the next nine months. He should not have write access to first three months and at the same time; he should be given write access to the fields from April to Dec. Then we set the range for Outlook 3+9 from April to Dec, this way, a planner can enter data only from April and not for Jan, Feb and March.

We can change the time period ranges in the later course of time also. This is important for Planning continuity. We'll understand this with an example too.

Another example would be Forecast4, it means four years of forecast. For forecasting, we always enter the future data. For Forecast4, Start year is 2010 and end year is 2013. At the beginning of the start year of 2010, forecast data is entered for 2010, 2011, 2012, and 2013. Now, after completion of 2010 , we would be changing the time range with starting year as 2011 and end year as 2014 , this way, we always give a planner the facility to enter 4 years of forecast data at any point in time.

Now, let us look at the scenario member properties. We see the scenario members as current, plan, actual, and forecast. Let us select the first member and click on **Edit** to check out its properties, as shown in the following image:

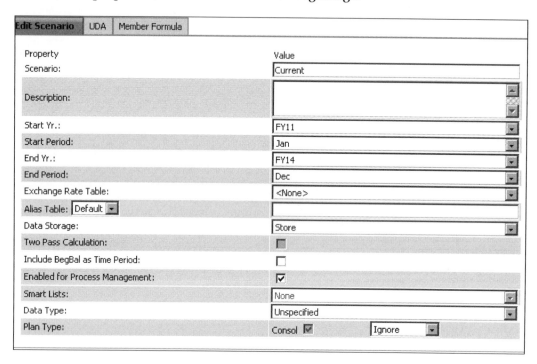

- **Scenario**: This is the name of the scenario dimension member.
- **Start Yr.**: We were trying to understand the ability of the scenario member in terms of setting the time period range. This field will have the starting year.
- **Start Period**: This field needs an input of the month, as we see in the image.
- **End Yr.**: We set the **Start Yr** and obviously we will stop it somewhere and in this field we provide the end year.

- **End Period**: We provide the ending month of a Financial Year.

  The End period is not necessarily the end month of the year. It represents the last month of the budget/plan window. For example, if the fiscal year of company ranges from Jul 2010 – Jun 2011 then:
  - Start Month: Jul
  - Start Year: 2010
  - End Month: Jun
  - End Year: 2011

- **Data Storage**: This is the store for the members of Scenario members.

- **Include BegBal as Time Period**: BegBal is a member of the Period dimension and if we want to include this in the scenario dimension, which would be useful for currency conversion, then we should tick this. We have not learned of currency conversion and exchange rate tables. Like a movie promo, let us say 'it s coming shortly'.

- **Data Type**: This is unspecified, look at the other options and you will see that scenario members need to be 'unspecified'.

- **Aggregation**: Most of the time there is no point in adding or subtracting these members of a scenario, we get absolutely nothing meaningful. What would we get by adding current and working? No, it makes no sense.

  Nevertheless, in some cases aggregation might be required. For example, a company might be applying some adjustments to the actual numbers once they are loaded into the system and they want to keep track of the original number along with the adjusted scenario. For such cases, the loaded numbers will be aggregated with adjustment entries to give adjusted actual numbers.
  - Actual ~
  - -Actual Load +
  - -Actual Adjustment +

Take a look at the member properties of other members. When we look at the member **Actual** we see a different period range that is, from Jan to June. This means that actual data from Jan to June would be editable for this scenario member.

> Plan, Actual, and Forecast are the most common Scenario members as we need a 'Plan' scenario member to enter planned or budget numbers, and the 'actual' member is need to enter acutals data, which will help in actual versus plan analysis, that is, variance analysis.

Year and period Dimension

First we shall talk about the **Year** dimension.

Year Dimension

This dimension has years and while we create a Planning application, we give information like **Total no of years** and also its Start year. The system creates **Year** dimension members accordingly. Our PandB is of a total of four years, starting from 2010 to 2013, as we see in the following image:

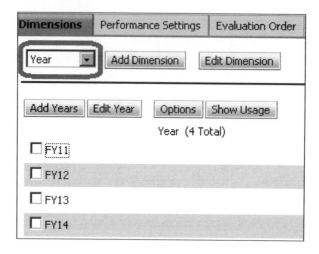

We can add more years by using **Add Years** button. The member properties of Year dimension member are quite simple. The data store is Store and Data type is Unspecified.

Period Dimension

The Period Dimension has more information to give us than the 'Year' dimension. It has summary time periods such as 'YearTotal' and Quarters and has members reflecting months too, that is, from Jan to Dec. The 'Period' dimension again is entirely created by the virtue of our selection while we create Planning application. We can refer back to *Chapter 3* to see how we had selected the correct settings to create the Period dimension.

We can see another member apart from 'YearTotal, 'Quarters' and months, it is BegBalance. This is the beginning balance, which is the amount we have it at the start of a period.

Coming to the rollup, its clear that Months are rolled up to their respective parent 'Quarters' and 'Quarters' roll up in to a 'Year' (YearTotal).

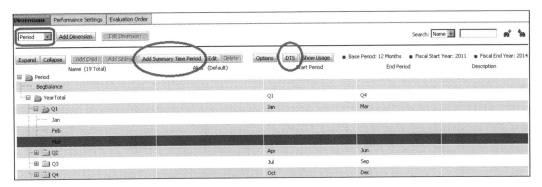

First, we'll look at the available options and then go into the member properties. There are two options – 'Add Summary Time Period' and 'DTS' as highlighted in the above image.

Add Summary Time Period

YearTotal and Quarter members are called 'Summary time period', because of the simple reason that they reflect the summarized data for the time period. Let us try to take few examples to understand more of it. **YearTotal** is the summary of all four quarters that is Q1, Q2, Q3, and Q4. Now, if our requirement needs to summarize From **Feb** to **May**, then we need to have another summary period, which should get the rolled up data of **Feb, Mar, Apr,** and **May**.

In the above case, we select **Feb** month and then select **Add summary time period**, and provide information of the new 'summary time period member name' and also provide important information of 'start Period' and 'End period', which would be 'Feb' and 'May' respectively, as per our requirement. This will cause the members to move physically from the existing hierarchy to the other to fit the new summary table.

In most implementations, we don't do this as distribution pattern is decided while we create an application and most organizations prefer regular monthly roll ups to quarters and quarters to total years.

DTS

Stands for Dynamic Time Series. Readers who are familiar with Essbase would know this concept.

This option enables dynamic calculation of period to date numbers. We use this option to show the Period-to-Date data. We need to enable DTS for members of 'Period' dimension and also need to assign generation number accordingly, which we'll see in this section

What is period to date and how is it useful for analysis?

Typically, we have months from Jan to March rolling up to Quarter 1 and the same pattern for Quarter 2, so on. If we want to know, for example, 'sales' of a 'product' from 'Jan' to 'Mar', we can look at the data of Sales against Quarter v1. But, when we need to look at the 'sales' figures from 'Jan' to 'May', as 'May' is the current month, now we have an issue. 'Jan' to 'Mar' is rolling to 'Quarter1' and 'Apr' to 'Jun' roll up to 'Quarter2'. We don't have a summary period member which summarises from 'Jan' to 'May' and we cannot create summary period member as the current month will change the moment we complete 'May' (Remember, the assumption is that the current month is 'May'). Here, In this kind of situation, dynamic time series are very handy. We use QTD in this case. We can report the data from a quarter to the current month with the help of Q-T-D.

There are several pre defined DTS, they are D-T-D (Date to date), W-T-D (Week to date), M-T-D (month to date), Y-T-D (Year to date) and finally H-T-D (History to date) likewise we have few other options too. These options are available with an assumption that Planning period dimension might have hours, days, weeks, months, Quarters and years.

How do we enable and set DTS?

Select **DTS**. It opens up a new window as shown.

Series	Enabled	Generation	Alias Table	Alias Name
Y-T-D	☐	unassigned	Default	
H-T-D	☐	unassigned	Default	
S-T-D	☐	unassigned	Default	
Q-T-D	☑	3	Default	
P-T-D	☐	unassigned	Default	
M-T-D	☐	unassigned	Default	
W-T-D	☐	unassigned	Default	
D-T-D	☐	unassigned	Default	

Now, as per our requirement, we select the series and we tick **Enabled** against the series as shown in the above image for Q-T-D.

Next is **Generation Number**. For our **Period** dimension, we have the following Generation numbers.

Generation Number	Member Names
Generation 1	Period
Generation 2	BegBalance, YearTotal
Generation 3	Q1 to Q4
Generation 4	Jan to Dec

Hence for Q-T-D, it is 3 as shown in the figure

Alias table and its name, we have been seeing it and we are happy with the default.

Save after this and refresh the database.

Now, let us look at the member properties of the 'Period' dimension.

Select the member **Feb** and click over **Edit** to get the following image:

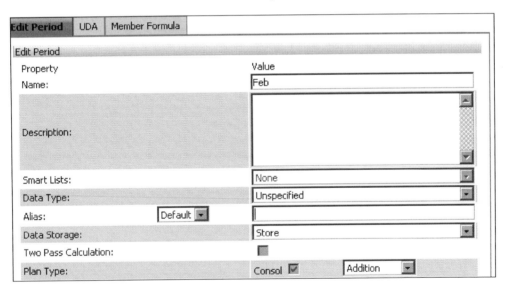

The data type is **Unspecified** and the data store is **Store**. These two are important. The consolidation operator has to be **Addition** as months have to aggregate to quarters and quarters need to roll up to 'YearTotal'. Let us move to final the dimension 'Currency'

Currency Dimension

The last dimension which we are going to talk about is the **Currency** dimension. The sample application 'PandB' has a huge list of currency dimension members within it. This is a dimension which we see only in a multi-currency Planning application.

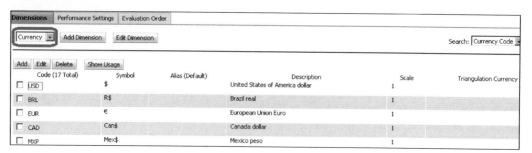

[The currency dimension members are not pre-set; we need to create these members.]

In any Planning implementation, we understand clearly about organizational structure and their currency conversion requirements. For example, if an organization which is implementing Hyperion Planning has its business run only in one country that is the US, then we don't even need to create a multi-currency Planning application in the first place. As a second example, if an organization has its business spread across three countries – the US, UK, and Australia. We understand that there would be user in the US, who would be entering data in USD, and users from UK would prefer to enter numbers in GBP while the Australian planner would budget their numbers in Australian dollars. Therefore, we shall create three members of the currency dimension as per our requirement.

Hence, the number of currency dimension members depends on the business requirement rather than any minimum count.

Let us look at the member properties of one of the **Currency** dimensioned.

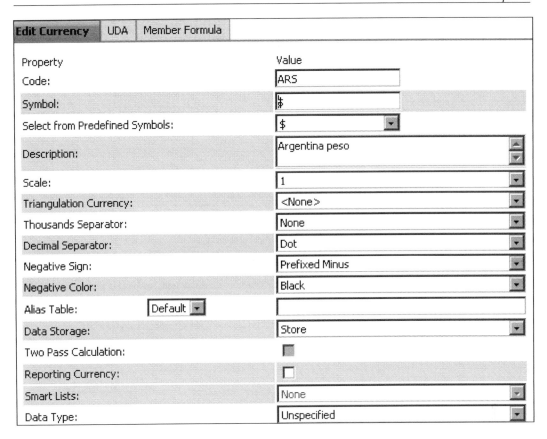

- **Code**: This is the currency name.
- **Symbol**: Planning automatically picks the appropriate symbol depending on the selection of 'Predefined symbol', which is the next field.
- **Select from Predefined Symbols**: Yes, it's understood that Planning as a system already has predefined symbols and we can pick the right ones from the list.
- **Description**: This is, as you would imagine, the description.
- **Scale**: This is for the display of the currency.
- **Triangulation Currency**: This will be explored in detail in Chapter 10, "Data forms", where will deal with exchange rates and currency conversion.
- **Thousand separators**: The separator can be comma, dot or even space, pick as per your wish.

- **Decimal Separator**: We can have comma also as a separator, but why would we want to replace a traditional dot with comma?

- **Negative signs and negative colors**: For values, when they are negative, its preferable to distinctly show this in the forms, we can color them with deadly read and also show the sign with the help of these fields.

- **Data Storage**: This specifies the store.

- **Reporting Currency**: We will cover this field in *Chapter 10, Data Forms,* when we discuss exchange rates and currency conversion.

- **Data type**: This should be set to **Unspecified**.

Performance Settings

These are the settings to improve the performance of overall Planning application. There are two sections.

The following are Essbase concepts and hence we are not going into the detail about them.

- **Dense and Sparse**: Defining a dimension as dense or sparse has a huge impact on the performance.

- **Order of dimensions**: Even the order of dimension in an outline plays an important role in an application's performance. We'll learn what is recommended and how to change the order.

Dense and Sparse

Dense dimensions are the ones which have maximum probability of occurrence in the combinations of dimensions. Generally, **Accounts** and **Period** dimensions are dense in nature. Coming to the sparse dimensions, they have lesser probability of occurrence, the examples would be **Entity** and **Custom** dimensions. The correct combination of dense and sparse dimensions would give best performance.

What performance are we talking about?

The dense – sparse combination determines the data block size and this data block can be imagined as bricks which make up the whole cube. Hyperion Planning, at its core, it's a multidimensional Essbase cube.

Therefore, every transaction, including loading, calculations and even retrieving operation would be impacted by the dense-sparse combination.

There is a whole theory behind the dense and sparse combination of a dimension and we would need to pick an Essbase book for that.

We can change density type from dense to sparse or from sparse to dense and it can be done from the tab of **Performance Settings**.

Go to **Administration | Manage | Dimensions**. Now, we see three tabs – Dimensions, Performance settings and Evaluation order. Select the middle tab that is 'Performance settings' as shown.

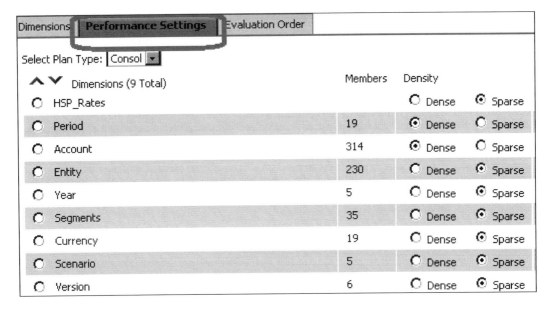

Now, Let us look at the fields in this:

- **Plan Type**: This is the plan type, as we understand that different plan types lead to separate Essbase database i.e. separate Essbase outlines. Here, in our case, we have only one plan type, the console.

- **Dimensions**: All the dimensions of 'PandB' application are displayed and there are totally 9 of them.

- **Members**: The number 19, 314, 230…etc, under 'Members' is the count of members which a dimension has. Generally, Account and Entity dimensions have more members than other dimensions.

- **Density**: Here, we can select either 'Dense' or 'Sparse' depending our understanding of dimensions.

Generally, Account, Period and HSP_Rates are always dense and the rest of dimensions are sparse in nature.

We would generally stick to 'Accounts' and 'HSP_Rates' as dense and leave other dimensions as sparse, but nevertheless, we can change dimensions from dense to sparse, or from sparse to dense, if we see performance issues.

This is not a mandatory step of implementation. By default, the system sets dimensions as **Dense** or **Sparse**. We only need to play with these if we want to improve performance.

Dimension Order

The order also impacts the performance and the recommended order would be an hourglass model. The hourglass model is the one in which the largest dense dimension is on the top and gradually moving down to smallest dense , followed by smallest sparse to largest sparse. Here, the largest dense dimension means the dense dimension which has the biggest number of members and similarly the smallest dense means the dimension which has the smallest number of members.

We can see in the above Fig 43, where up and down directions are mentioned, it's rounded. We can select a dimension and use them to move either up or down.

Evaluation Order

We have finally come to the last section of this chapter.

We have the field of 'Data type' for all the dimensions. When we create a web form and wish to view data for a combination of dimensions, then we need to tell the system which data type to use.

For example, there is an account member whose data type is percentage and an entity member **US**, whose data type is **Currency**. Now, we are looking at the form which has these two members along with other dimensions too. Now, are we not confused in understanding what data type would be reflected when we look at the data values. The order is the key here, if the **Account** dimension is above the **Entity** dimension in the evaluation order, then the **Account** dimension has precedence over the **Entity** dimension.

Another example, say we have an **Account** member set to **Percentage** as its data type and it is used in a form. To display the member using percentages, we need to place the **Account** dimension above in the data type evaluation order.

It's common when users set the data type (for example percentage) to then complain that they don't see the percentage values in the form, the simple reason is they have not set the evaluation order correctly.

How can we include the dimension in evaluation order and how do we change the order?

We were talking of second tab in the previous section of **Performance Settings** the 3rd and final tab is **Evaluation Order**.

1. Go to **Administration | Manage | Dimensions**.
2. Now, of the three tabs, select the last tab 'Evaluation Order' as shown.

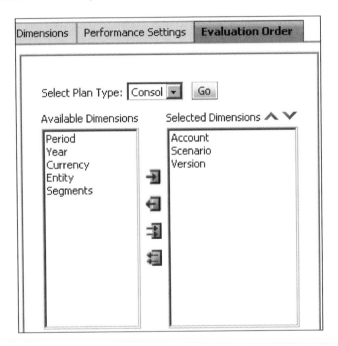

We see all arrows like helpers; we can see the **Available Dimensions**, which can be sent under **Selected Dimensions**. Selected dimensions are the ones, which are part of 'Evaluation Order'. Within the selected list of dimension of **Evaluation Order**, we can order them by using the arrows beside **Selected dimensions**, which is highlighted.

We'll again visit evaluation order, when we create data forms and witness the behaviour of data types as per the evaluation order in *Chapter 9, Data forms*.

Summary

In this chapter, we have learned the settings of all standard dimensions and also discussed in detail which settings would be appropriate to select, for a given a situation/requirement.

We understood the typical hierarchies of Accounts dimensions, for example: Balance Sheets, Income Statements, Cash Flows, and Statistics. We also understood the importance of Account Types and how they impacts the settings of Time Balance, Variance, and Data Type.

We explored each and every setting option starting from Accounts Dimension and moving on to all other standard Planning dimensions.

We spoke of Dimension settings, Performance settings and Evaluation order at the end. We used the Planning application PandB all through this chapter and gained more insight into the Planning application and its dimension settings. We should feel like designers for a while. It's been a tough water to cross so let us move ahead to next chapter where we'll learn all about metadata upload.

7
Loading Metadata

The loftier the building, the deeper must be the foundation be laid.

— *Thoman Kempis*

In Chapters 4 and 5, we learned to create Hyperion Planning application and we dived deep into the settings of Planning application and dimension properties in *Chapter 6*. The next, obvious step is to load metadata and data into the Planning application. In this chapter, we'll learn how to load metadata into a Planning application.

Before we get into the chapter, let us take a look at a possible conversation between Hyperion Planning consultant, who is already at a client's place and had started Hyperion Planning implementation.

Client: *Hi, what's the update on the project? What's happening? There has been no news from you.*

Hyperion Planning consultant: *Hi. As we had updated you, we have installed and configured Hyperion Planning along with the complementing products. As a part of the first phase of the project, that is, requirement gathering, we have started talking to the relevant departments/divisions to understand their as-is budgeting process. We have also started gathering budget templates or spreadsheets, which you guys are currently using for budgeting.*

Client: *Okay, I understand. User interviews are all about talking. Tell me what is happening with the application. I see the whole team busy with the application; what are they up to?*

Hyperion Planning consultant: *As the very first step of any Hyperion Planning implementation, we have to finalize the dimensions and members, that is dimensional structure. We need to load dimension and members on already created Hyperion Planning application, which is synonymous to metadata load. Therefore, we are at the metadata load stage.*

In this chapter, we shall cover the following topics:

- **What is metadata**: This section introduces the metadata of a Planning application.

- **Create Planning Application**: We'll create one more application for metadata load purposes. Therefore, in this section, we'll assume a client requirement and create a new Planning application accordingly.

- **Metadata load**: This section will explore the metadata load process using outline load utility.

- **Dimension load**: In this section, we'll look into each Standard Planning Dimension and load the metadata. We will start with the Account dimension.

What is metadata?

We'll first understand what metadata and data are.

Dimension names, member names and their properties all constitute metadata. Let us take an example. The value of Net sales for the Apple iPhone in January in New York is $1000. Here, Metadata elements are 'Net sales' (member of Account dimension), 'iphone' (could be the member of 'Product' dimension), 'January' (member of 'Period' dimension and 'New York' (possibly the member of 'entity' dimension).

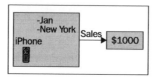

Now, what is data?

It's easy to say that it's **$1000**. It's the value, which is the data.

Now we know, when we were talking of all dimensions (standard and custom), we were talking of the metadata. Have we ever wondered why the member names of Account dimension are crazy? Consider 12345 for the Income statement in our previous sample application of PandB.

Let us explore this in more depth. From implementation angle, after we create Planning application based on the understanding of the Planning requirement of an organization, the next step is to create metadata and freeze dimension structures. While creating metadata, we typically refer to the COA (Chart of Accounts) of the organization and most of the time we get help from the finance team of client in getting the chart of accounts. We keep the same naming convention of the chart of accounts. Nevertheless, we give aliases as per our understanding. Hence, we see that crazy numbering.

PandB application has been a good friend to us so far, so let us give it a break for a while and play with a new Planning application. We'll create a new Planning application in this chapter and load its dimensions and members, along with its properties and that's what the metadata load is.

At the same time, it would make us more fluent in creating Planning applications; the more the merrier.

Create Planning Application

Before we start learning about the metadata load of a Planning application, let us create one more Planning application and use it all through this chapter. Wondering why are we doing this? The simple answer is, the sample application PandB already has its dimensions and members in it and we stand no scope to add new dimensions/ members from scratch. Hence, let us create a new application.

Before we create an application, let us assume the requirement and then we'll create a Planning application accordingly. We have two sections:

- Requirement: We'll assume the requirement of an IT company, which will act as a base for application creation in the next section

- Planning Application creation: In this section, we'll create a Planning application as per the requirements

Requirement of Planning

Imagine that we are a consulting team and we have gone to client's office to implement a Hyperion Planning and budgeting solution. The consulting team goes to see the client, after successful presales and sales meetings. Though we know that the presales team has promised magic in the form of Hyperion Planning and we know that all those promises aren't true, we are consultants in the end.

Let we have a client and we know their requirements. It's an IT company, whose business is into BPO and KPO. We can call it a lazy IT company because it makes profits because of the outsourcing business. All that company needs is intelligent tongues rather than brains.

Now, we'll start socializing with the teams and we always get one gentleman in Planning implementation, who has a universal name **SPOC (Single Point Of Contact)** from the client's side. He is our saviour for everything; he ensures that we interview the user community across the departments of the organization and also helps in understanding their budgeting. We need to agree that there was a little bit of sin committed by our sales team too.

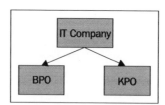

We'll understand the organization and its budgeting requirement through our interaction with all the departments/divisions, as we will always have the dimension structure and its design at the back of our mind.

We will first figure out the organization structure in terms of its spread into different geographical regions. This will help us design the dimensions of 'entity' and 'currency'. We'll also learn how their budgeting is done, some companies might be interested in budgeting at every project level, where we need to include project level information in our Planning application and accordingly need to create a dimension and its members.

This client, where we are going to implement Hyperion Planning and Budgeting, has its reach and business in countries such as US, UK, and Australia. Like any typical IT organization, even this company has support functions such as general administration, HR, and so on. It has very few loyal clients and would like to budget as per the clients. Hence, we need to include the company's client information and we can create a custom dimension for them.

They are interested in budgeting for about five years duration and are interested in looking at the monthly and quarterly levels, this information will help us in determining the Year and Period.

As budgeting is a control mechanism, their requirement is to enter a plan number, do variance analysis every quarter, and post the forecast numbers. This makes our scenario dimension members as actual, plan, and forecast. Let us keep the requirement simple and create an application.

We'll make many Planning applications of this sort throughout the later course to it understand better.

From the mentioned requirements, we'll start designing the dimensions and its members in Excel notepads. Using pen and paper is not a bad idea either. We'll make a list of dimensions and design additional custom dimensions looking at the requirements.

 Note: The design is the prerogative of the Planning designer, who goes to the client. This section gives examples of the cases and designing is purely subjective.

From the requirements, we should be able to create an application. Hopefully we have not forgotten to create an application, remember we had done it in *Chapter 5, Creating First Planning Application*. Refer back to refresh, as we are going to create another application right now; but this time, it's not going to be a sample application.

Let us go through the steps of creating a Planning application very quickly now and going forward, we are not going to repeat the instructions of application creation in the subsequent chapters.

Planning Application creation

Log in to Oracle EPM Workspace or the Planning App wizard and create a data source. We need to remember that every Planning application needs a relational data source. If it's Oracle, we need to create a new schema and if it's SQL server, we need to create a new database and also need to ensure that the database user is given the role of DBO/DBA before we can use him in the application creation process.

Now we'll see the application creation process. In the classic wizard, in the very first tab, **Select**, we give the basic information such as name of the **Data Source** (we see source name as **Out**. This is another source created; refer to *Chapter 5* to look at how to create source. It's the first thing to do before application creation commences), **Application name**, **Description**, **Shared Services Project**, **Instance** application type and **Calculation Module**.

 Application Type has always two options—**Sample** and **General**. Select **General**, as we are not creating a sample Planning application.

All these fields have been discussed at length in *Chapter 5*. Refer back if you need information about any of the fields.

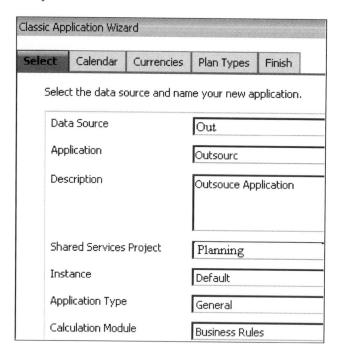

The **Application** name is **Outsourc**. If you're wondering why the 'e' is missing; it has nothing to do with numerology.

There is a limitation in naming a Planning Application; it can contain a maximum of eight letters.

Click on **Next** to go to next tab, **Calendar**. Had we selected **Application Type** as **Sample**, we would have got default selected values for all the tabs of **Calendar**, **Currencies, Plan Types**, which was the case when we first created our old friend PandB application in *Chapter 5*. It's not more of the same, we have to provide information in all the tabs, as we know the requirements this time and we have to create an application appropriately. In the **Calendar** tab, we need to provide information as shown next. If we recall the requirement of the client, they want their bidget for five years, with the five year period divided into months and quarters. We are good with the **Base Time Period** set to **12 months.** Moving towards the right-hand side, set the **Total Years** to **5**, as per the client's requirement. The **Start Year** is set to **2010** as shown in the following image.

We need to note that in real-life implementations, clients/organizations typically need to do budgeting for more than five years. Even though they might not do budgeting for all years, they want a scalable and flexible application that can adapt to their future requirements. Hence, an intelligent user will always ask for a Planning application for more years than they initially want so that the application can support his future needs. To this requirement, our smart Hyperion consultant will respond by informing the user that additional years can be added at any point in time, without requiring much technical expertise.

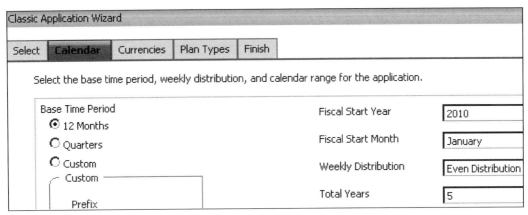

Click on **Next** to provide information about the default currency. As the client has its spread in other countries such as UK, US, and Australia. Planners from these countries would be budgeting and entering data in their local currencies. Hence, we'll create a multi currency application with the default currency of the application set to USD, as shown in the following image:

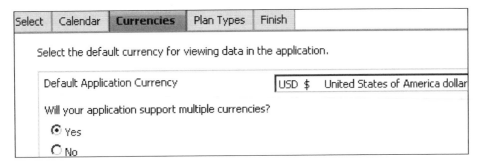

For **Plan Types**, we'll have only one plan type. Check the boxes accordingly. We need to remember that we are creating this application to demonstrate the metadata load. Hence, let us not complicate the design of Planning application. Check **Plan Type 1** and uncheck all the other plan types and don't bother to care about other modules mentioned below the standard plan types.

We usually name an appropriate Plan type something like FINPLAN, unlike Plan1 as shown in the following image:

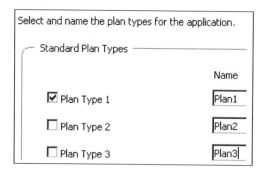

Click on **Next** to view the summary of our new Planning application Outsourc. Look at them and check whatever is needed as per our requirements and click on **Finish** to initiate application creation. It takes some time to create an application and finally it congratulates us by giving the following message:

Now, we will create a database as the next step after application creation. Log into the newly-created Outsourc application through workspace. We need to create the database for the newly-created Planning application. Go to **Administration | Application | Create Database**. In the **Create Database** page, check **Database** and click on **Create**, as shown in the following image:

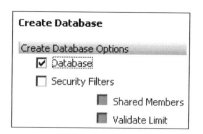

It will throw us a caution and then run some 20 steps before finally saying that creation is complete and the status is a 'Success'.

Good job; we have created one more Planning application Outsourc. Now, let us talk of the metadata load in the next section.

Metadata load

We first need to understand the utility "outline load utility" and next we need to know the 'flat file' structure, which can be fed to the utility to load metadata.

Hence, we need to understand two important things in this section, they are as follows:

- Outline load utility: This section, we'll understand about where the utility is located and its parameters
- Flat file: We'll understand the basic structure of a flat file that can be used to load metadata

We can add dimensions and their members manually, but it's not practically possible to add an individual member and set its properties. We have some hundreds of members for the 'Account' dimension and also for Entity dimension. Therefore, it's not possible to add/maintain members/hierarchies manually.

We'll use a utility named "Outline Load utility", which can be used to load metadata.

> Outline load utility is applicable only for Classic Planning applications and not applicable for Performance Management applications.
> **Data Integration Management (DIM)** and ODI adapter are also applicable to only classic Planning applications as of now.

There are many other products/tools that are capable of loading metadata. A few examples are ODI, DIM, and HAL.

HAL (Hyperion Application Link) was very popular, but it's no longer supported and not advisable for the current version of 11. Nevertheless, there are instances where HAL did work flawlessly in a few versions of 11.

> Let us not make a mistake of going with the product which Oracle Hyperion does not support. So, HAL for version 11 has to be avoided.

ODI is the new hero who is getting all the attention these days and it was some other product—which was "sunopsis" earlier—but Oracle savoured the meal and had it all and labelled it as "Oracle Data Integrator". This product is capable of loading metadata from flat files and also from the relational databases into Planning applications.

When a customer buys Oracle Hyperion Planning, ODI is bundled along with it. Hence, we can use ODI for data and metadata load. But, we need to realize that the licence will only permit us to use ODI until the time the target system is Hyperion Planning application.

But for time being, we'll use the utility which comes with the software of Planning. See, we are consultants and already thinking of saving money for the client by not investing any extra money on other products/tools. But, in real-life implementations, we typically use ODI to load metadata from source systems.

Outline load utility

We generally have few standard questions, when it comes to utilities:

- Where is the utility located?
- What is the syntax and parameters used?

Location of the utility

The outline load utility is in the following location:

`D:\Oracle\Middleware\user_projects\epmsystem1\Planning\Planning1.`

We can navigate there and check if it's present.

Syntax and parameters

The syntax and parameters are given below:

```
OutlineLoad [/S:server] /A:application /U:username [/I:inputFileName/
D[U]:loadDimensionName| [/N]    [/

C] [/F] [/K] [/X:exceptionFileName]    [L:logFileName]
```

For the list of all parameters, Refer to *Appendix B, Utilities* section, which has information about all the utilities of Planning application.

- `/S:server`: Hyperion Planning Server name. The default is localhost, so if we are running this on the same server as Hyperion Planning, there is no need to mention this parameter.

- `/U:userName`: Username, used to log into the Planning application. In our case, it would be admin.

- /I:InpuFileName: The CSV filename (flat file) and the complete path of it.

  It is important to note that we need to mention the complete path of the file containing the metadata to be loaded

- /D:loadDimensionName: It's the dimension name, whose members, including hierarchies, parent-child relationships and all relevant properties are to be loaded. In case of account dimension member metadata load, we shall select 'Account' as the loadDimensionName.

- /D[U]:To load custom dimension. It's exactly the same as /D option. The only difference is that if the dimension does not exist prior to loading, a new custom dimension will be created with the specified name.

- /N: This property checks the flat file whether it is correct to load. This property makes it to parse without actual metadata load. This property is best to include and run for the first time to check the flat file, if it's error free.

- /C: This property is used to refresh the database that is, refresh the cube. We know that after members are added, we need to refresh the database. This property will take care of it.

- /F: While refreshing database, we can even create security filters. This property does that.

- /K: This property locks the dimension to which we are adding members.

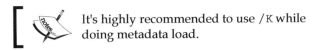

It's highly recommended to use /K while doing metadata load.

- /X:exceptionFileName: We know that while we load there would be errors and exception and to capture these exceptions we set a path and also file name with .exc file extension.

- /L:logFileName: As the name of the property suggests, this is the log file which details the status and other information of the metadata load. We provide both the path and the filename with .log as the file extension.

Flat file

Before we upload metadata, we design Planning application in terms of its dimensions. We'll decide on how many dimension our application should have and how many custom dimensions does it need. Let us get back to our outsourcing IT Company. We had understood the requirement, and now we need to have a few additional custom dimensions, which are Clients, Products, and others. As their budgeting requirements demand them, we will add them.

We need to take the utmost care when designing and deciding entity dimensions, as it's the key for process management.

We'll go step-by-step and dimension-by-dimension. First, we'll load Accounts dimension along with its members and properties and followed by other dimension such as Entity, Currency, Scenario, and so on. We all know that Accounts dimension always gets more importance and attention.

If we remember, we spent a lot of time in the previous chapter learning the settings/ fields of a account dimension member and they are many common settings/fields such as storage type, alias name, description, aggregation operator, and so on, which are common to all other dimensions. Now, we'll look at the common properties which would be applicable to all dimension members in a flat file and see if we still need any further explanation after our detailed *Chapter 6, Settings*.

The common properties that are applicable to all dimensions in a flat file are discussed next:

- **Parent**: This is the parent of the member. For example, Parent of 'Statistical Driver' is Account, while parent of the member 'Assets' is 'Balance Sheet' as per our Account dimension.

- **Alias**: This is the alias table and we have been happy with the default all through.

- **Valid for consolidation**: This is not applicable to a Hyperion Planning application.

- **Data storage**: The possible values are Store, Dynamic Calc, Dynamic Calc and Store, Shared, Never share, and Label only. Refer to *Chapter 6* for reference.

- **Two pass calculation**: If the member needs two pass calculation, we set 'true' for the member, else, it's false.

- **Description**: This is the description of the member.

- **Formula**: This is the member formula.

- **UDA**: These are User defined Attributes.

- **Smart List**: Smart lists will be discussed in more detail in the chapter titled "Data forms"

- **Data Type**: The possible data types for a member are Currency, Non_currency, Percentage, Smart List, Data, Text, and unspecified. Refer to *Chapter 6, Settings*.

- **Operation**: This property helps in updating the members, deleting the members. The possible values are Update, Delete Level 0, Delete idescendants, and Delete descendants.

- **Process Management Enabled**: We can set it to either 'True' or 'False'. Process Management will be covered in *Chapter 14, Process Management*.

- **Plan Type(Plan1, Plan2, Plan3)**: This determines which plan type the members is going to use and accordingly we provide a Boolean value (True or False) to the respective plan type

- **Aggregation**: The possible aggregation options are + addition, - subtraction, * multiplication, / division, % percentage and ~ ignore. We explored this in *Chapter 6* in detail.

But there are a few properties that are specifically meant and applicable to a few dimensions only. An example of that kind is time balance, it's applicable to only account dimension members.

Dimension load

In this section, we'll go by one by one dimension and understand the metadata load process of all dimensions. To start with, we'll pick the Accounts dimension.

Account Dimension

We had already gone through individual field/ setting of account dimension member in the previous *Chapter 6, Settings*, to name few of the fields, they are Alias, Data Storage, Data Type, and so on. Here, in this section, we are loading metadata that is, members of account dimension members through a flat file with the help of the utility. The flat file should also have the information of member properties such as Alias, Data storage, Data type, and so on. Hence, we not only load members of a dimension. But also load their properties

Before we can create a flat file, we should be able to understand parent-child relationship. As we know, everything in our hierarchies is going to be in relationships. As smart consulting team, we generally make a parent-child relationship before we create a flat file to load.

For a typical Account dimension, as we already know, it would have balance sheet, income statement and statistical drivers'. We'll leave cash flow and statistical drivers for a while for the purpose of metadata load in this chapter. We can upload the members of these accordingly, when we need to.

For the Balance sheet, we'll assume a few members such as 'fixed assets', 'goodwill', and 'investments', which are part of 'Assets'. 'Shareholders funds' and 'long term creditors' are a part of 'liabilities'.

For the Income statement, we need to finally compute the 'net income'. In the following image we can make out the hierarchical relationships and also pay attention to the 'aggregation operator'. 'Net Income' is calculated by subtraction 'income taxes' from 'Net income before taxes'. Likewise, other hierarchies are created for 'Net income from Operations', 'Gross Profit', and 'SGA'.

For metadata load demonstration purpose, let us load a few members for 'statistical drivers' hierarchy, which would be 'headcount' and 'billing rate'.

After understanding the relationships, it's easier to make a flat file. Few of the mentioned examples, 'Income statement', 'Balance sheet', and 'statistical drivers', are the immediate children of 'accounts' dimension. 'Gross profit', 'Sales', and 'COGS' are the children of 'Net Income from operations'. We'll elaborate and make a hierarchical structure as shown below.

Take some time to understand the hierarchies. Pay close attention to the aggregation operator, which is mentioned to the right-hand side of every member in the following image:

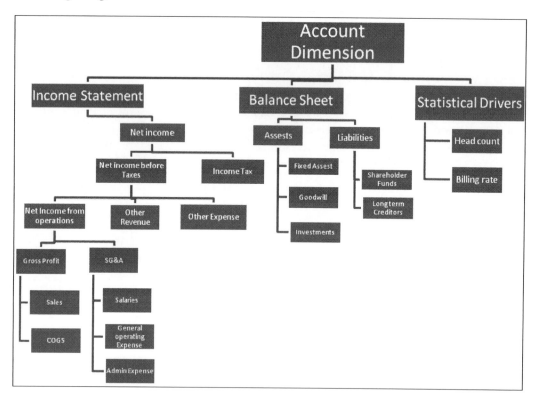

Account Dimension structure

Now, let us look at the basic structure of Accounts dimension in a flat file:

Account, Parent, Alias: Default, Alias: T1, Valid For Consolidations, Data Storage, Two Pass Calculation, Description, Formula, UDA, Smart List, Data Type, Operation, Account Type, Time Balance, Use 445, Use 544, Use 554, Skip Value, Exchange Rate Type, Variance Reporting, Source Plan Type, Plan Type (Plan1), Aggregation (Plan1), Plan Type (Plan2), Aggregation (Plan2), Plan Type (Plan3), Aggregation (Plan3), AttribDim1, AttribDim2

Look at the structure; most of them are already explained in the common properties. There are a few that are specific to account dimension, and they are Time Balance, Skip Value, Exchange Rate Type, and Variance Reporting.

Not every field is compulsory to worry about. The following table gives information about the member properties and their default values. It also provides information as to whether it's a mandatory field or not:

Property Name	Default value	Compulsory	Possible values
Account		Yes	
Parent	Dimension Root	No	
Alias	None	No	
Data Storage	Inheritance, Never Share	No	Store, Dynamic Calc, Dynamic Calc and store, Shared, Label
Two Pass calculation	Parent Inheritance	No	True, False
Description		No	
Formula		No	
UDA		No	
Smart List		No	
Data Type	Inheritance, Currency	No	Unspecified, Currency, Non-currency, Percentage, Smart List, Date, Text
Operation	Update	No	Delete level0, delete idescendants, delete descendants
Account Type	Inheritance, Revenue	No	Expense, Revenue, Asset, Liability, Equity, Saved assumption
Time Balance	Depends on the Account Type	No	Flow, First, Balance, Average
Use 445/554		No	True, False
Skip Value	Inheritance	No	Missing, None, Zeroes, Missing and zeroes
Exchange Rate Type	Inheritance, Average	No	None, Average, Ending, Historical
Variance Reporting	Inheritance, Non-expense	No	Non-expense, Expense,
Source Plan Type	The first plan Type	No	
Aggregation		No	+', '-', '*' '/', '%', '~' and Never
Attribute dimension Name		No	

Let us read the table for a while. It starts with the Account property, which is compulsory. Next is Parent, we give the parent of the account member, but in if we don't give any, by default it's understood that the account member is the child of the root dimension, that is, the Account dimension.

Alias, by default is set to 'None'. Data storage, the member, takes the data storage property of its parent, if the parent is the root, then the default data storage type is 'Never Share'. Wherever, we see 'Inheritance' for 'Default values', the understanding is that the member takes the property of the parent. We see the same for Data type, Account type, Exchange Rate Type, and Variance Reporting. All of these properties, inherit the property of the parent as their default value. We also see Currency, Revenue for Data type and Account type for their default value; these default values apply only when the members are direct children of the root dimension such as "Income statement", which is the child of Account dimension.

 Most of the property fields are not compulsory, as we see in the earlier table.

Account flat file creation

In this section, we'll fist see the flat file creation for account dimension members and then we'll run the utility to load the metadata. We will be using Microsoft Excel.

- Flat file creation
- Run the machine

Flat file creation

Now, let us attempt to create our first row in the flat file to load metadata. Let us take the member 'Income statement' as the child of Account dimension parent. Refer the hierarchal diagram for reference, while making the flat file.

We'll try to make a row and then start with other rows. First and foremost thing is to write headers in a Notepad/Excel, which ever is comfortable for us. For example, let us make a header row for 'Income statement' as shown as follows:

```
Account Parent Data Storage Description Data Type Account Type
Aggregation (Plan1)
```

There are a few important properties such as Time Balance, Skip Value, Exchange Rate Type, and Variance Reporting. These values depend on the data type selection. For example, an account member with 'expense' account type has by default Variance as 'expense', Time Balance as 'flow', Exchange Rate type as 'Average', and currency type as 'Currency'. We learned all about these settings in the previous chapter of *Settings*, under the *Accounts* section. It is recommended to refer to that once.

For our metadata load purpose, we are happy with the default Time Balance, Skip Value, Variance Reporting, and so on. Therefore, we are not including them as headers. Now, let us make a row for 'Income statement' account member.

Account	Parent	Data Storage	Description	Data Type	Account Type	Aggregation (Plan1)
Income Statement	Account	Dynamic Calc	P and L statement	Currency	Revenue	~

Spend a little time to read all these fields.

Likewise, we'll make the flat file for all the members for Account dimension. Generally, the Account dimension has many hundreds of members, we have considered only a few for tutorial purposes.

The flat file would look as shown below. We should first understand the relationships between the members and visualise the parent-child relationship. We achieved that with the help of hierarchical image. Then, we translate that into a flat file, which can serve as ammunition to load the metadata flat file though the utility.

We see in the file that **Income Statement** hierarchy related members are rounded in the bigger ellipse and **Balance Sheet** hierarchy related 'account' members in smaller ellipse. Pay attention to the Aggregation, which decides the roll up. At the bottom, we see a few **Statistical Drivers**, as shown in the following image:

Account	Parent	Data Storage	Description	Data Type	Account Type	Aggregation (Plan1)
Income Statement	Account	Dynamic Calc		Currency	Revenue	~
Net Income	Income Statement	Dynamic Calc		Currency	Revenue	+
Net Income before taxes	Net Income	Dynamic Calc		Currency	Revenue	+
Net Income from Operations	Net Income before taxes	Dynamic Calc		Currency	Revenue	+
Gross Profit	Net Income from Operations	Dynamic Calc		Currency	Revenue	+
Sales	Gross Profit	Store		Currency	Revenue	+
COGS	Gross Profit	Store		Currency	Expense	-
SG&A	Net Income from Operations	Dynamic Calc		Currency	Expense	-
Salaries	SG&A	Store		Currency	Expense	+
General Operating expenses	SG&A	Store		Currency	Expense	+
Administrative expenses	SG&A	Store		Currency	Expense	+
Other Revenue	Net Income before taxes	Store		Currency	Revenue	+
Other Expense	Net Income before taxes	Store		Currency	Expense	-
Income Tax	Net Income	Store		Currency	Expense	-
Balance sheet	Account	Dynamic Calc		Currency	Asset	~
Assets	Balance sheet	Dynamic Calc		Currency	Asset	+
Fixed assets	Assets	Store		Currency	Asset	+
Goodwill	Assets	Store		Currency	Asset	+
Investments	Assets	Store		Currency	Asset	+
Liabilities	Balance sheet	Dynamic Calc		Currency	Liabilities	-
Shareholders funds	Liabilities	Store		Currency	Liabilities	+
Long term creditors	Liabilities	Store		Currency	Liabilities	+
Statistical drivers	Account	Dynamic Calc		Non-Currency	Saved Assumption	~
Headcount	Statistical drivers	Store		Non-Currency	Saved Assumption	~
Billing Rate	Statistical drivers	Store		Non-Currency	Saved Assumption	~

Creating flat file is strictly a view through a Planning designer's eyes.

Save this file as a CSV file. Its location is `C:\Accounts.csv`. We'll be using this location address in the next section.

Run the Machine/Utility

We have flat file `Accounts.CSV` file and we know the utility to use to load metadata. In this section, we'll run the utility using the flat file to load the metadata into the account dimension.

Let us do it in steps.

1. Log in to the Outsourc Planning application and see its Account dimension. It has absolutely no members as of now.

2. We run the utility through the command prompt (Windows is the assumed operating system). Go to **Start | Run, type** cmd here to open the command prompt.

3. Now, navigate to the following location `MIDDLEWARE_HOME\user_projects\epmsystem1\Planning\Planning1`.

4. In our system, we installed Planning on E drive. So the path is

   `E:\Oracle\Middleware\user_projects\epmsystem1\Planning\Planning1`. it is shown in the following screenshot:

```
C:\WINDOWS\system32\cmd.exe

E:\>cd E:\Oracle\Middleware\user_projects\epmsystem1\Planning\planning1
E:\Oracle\Middleware\user_projects\epmsystem1\Planning\planning1>_
```

5. Run the utility using the following syntax. In the following line, we see that `Account.csv` flat file is in the `C:` drive and the `outlineLoad.log` file and `outlineLoad.exc` are also located in the very `C:` drive.

```
C:\WINDOWS\system32\cmd.exe                                          _ □ X

E:\Oracle\Middleware\user_projects\epmsystem1\Planning\planning1>OutlineLoad /A:
outsourc /U:admin  /I:c:\Account.csv /D:Account /L:c:/outlineLoad.log /X:c:/outl
ineLoad.exc_
```

6. It will ask for the password. Provide the password for the user 'admin' to log in to the Outsourc application. But when we type we don't see anything being reflected on the screen. Don't worry, that's how it is supposed to work. Provide the password and press *Enter*.

7. Go to the location of logs and check both `outlineLoad.log` and `outlinLoad.exc`. They give information of how many rows been processed and how many have been successful. The failed rows are also mentioned along with the reasons for failure in `outlineLoad.exc` file.

> Fields in flat file are case-sensitive. Even the system reads the difference between 'non currency' and 'Non-Currency' (the latter is the right one). Another example is that the header 'Aggregation(Plan1)'is different from 'Aggregation (Plan1)'. These are very trivial to our eyes, but very important to the utility. Therefore, be careful in creating flat file. Else, we'll end up looking into logs and debugging. Nevertheless, logs are pretty comprehensible and direct to debug.

8. Now, log in to the Outsourc application again and we see all the members of Account dimension as shown in the following screenshot:

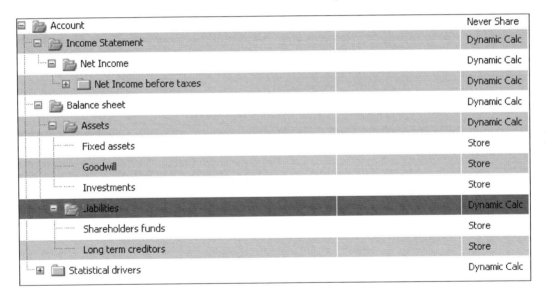

9. Now, let us move ahead with other dimensions. As always, we work enough with Account dimension. This makes working with the other dimensions a bit easier.

Currency Dimension

Currency Dimension flat file structure

This dimension is specific to multi currency applications and we see that the Outsourcing IT Company has its reach in multiple countries like US, Australia, and UK. Therefore, we had created Outsourc as a multi currency Planning application and In this section we'll load the currency members of GBP (for UK), AUD (for Australian dollar).

First, let us take a look the basic structure of the flat file needed for Currency dimension member load:

Currency, Parent, Alias: Default, Alias: T1, Data Storage, Two Pass Calculation, Description, Formula, UDA, Smart List, Data Type, Operation, Symbol, Scale, Triangulation Currency, Reporting Currency, Thousands Separator, Decimal Separator, Negative Style, Negative Color

Most of them are already explained and understood under Account dimension such as Parent, Alias, and so on. We'll pick and learn which are specific to the Currency dimension.

The following table provides the information of the property types as shown. Let us read the table and understand the properties. Its starts with 'symbol', it's required only when we want to give our own currency symbol. If we want to include GBP, we need not give a symbol; system is smart to pick the symbol by itself, unless we fancy to give our own symbol. Next is 'Scale', its possible values are from 0 to 9. Value 0 corresponds to 1, Value 1 corresponds to 10, Value 2 corresponds to 100, and so on. We'll learn about Triangulation currency and reporting currency in *Chapter 10, Data Forms*.

For 'triangulation currency', we need to give the currency symbol, as its possible value. 'Decimal separator', 'negative style', and 'negative color' are self-explanatory.

Property Name	Default value	Compulsory	Possible values
Symbol		No	
Scale	No scale	No	0 to 9.
Triangulation Currency	None	No	Currency
Reporting Currency	False	No	True, False
Thousand seperator	None	No	none, comma, dot and space
Decimal seperator	dot	No	dot and comma
Negative style	prefixed	No	prefixed, suffixed and parentheses
Negative color	black	No	black and red

Flat file and metadata load

For the Outsourc application, we'll load two currency members 'GBP' and 'AUD', as 'USD' is already added.

Why is USD member already loaded as a Currency dimension?

A Planning application has a default currency, and for the Planning application Outsourc, the default currency is 'USD'. We made this default currency selection while creating the application.

Let us take a look at the flat file for two members:

Currency	Parent	Data Storage	Description	Data Type	Triangulation Currency	Reporting Currency
GBP	Currency	Store	Great British Pound	Unspecified		True
AUD	Currency	Store	Australian Dollar	Unspecified		True

Save this as `Currency.csv`. Let us save it in `C:` drive and we'll accordingly give the syntax of the `outlineLoad` utility.

Now, run the utility using the following syntax:

Shoot the command and provide the Planning application password and press enter to start Currency dimension members upload. After successful load, log in to the Outsourc Planning application to view the newly added members. Now, let us move on to other dimensions.

Entity Dimension

As a part of understanding the organization structure, we need to understand what departments, divisions or geographical location needs to be considered for Entity dimension. Designing Planning dimensions is our responsibility as a part of implementation team; we cannot expect the clients or the user community to understand the dimensions and their usages/properties.

Generally, like Account dimension, Entity dimension also has many members. But we'll simplify for metadata load purposes by loading few members.

For the Outsorc application, we'll consider the entity dimension members as geographical location i.e. US, UK and Australia. Budgeting is done at state level and city level in US i.e. In "North Carolina" state , the city of "Charlotte" are to be included. Hence, we'll load the metadata accordingly.

Before we start the metadata load, we'll take a look at the properties and the basic structure of entity dimension in the flat file.

Entity Dimension structure

Entity, Parent, Alias: Default, Alias: T1, Valid For Consolidations,

Data Storage, Two Pass Calculation, Description, Formula, UDA, Smart

List, Data Type, Operation, Base Currency, Plan Type (Plan1),

Aggregation (Plan1), Plan Type (Plan2), Aggregation (Plan2), Plan Type

(Plan3), Aggregation (Plan3), AttribDim1, AttribDim2

There is only Base Currency, which looks like a new entrant. Otherwise, all the other properties are already discussed. Every entity member has a Base Currency. As a part of budgeting, planner/users from different countries participate. Now, every country has its currency and we need to understand that American planners will enter information in their base currency i.e USD, while an English planner will enter the budgeting figures in their own base currency of GBP.

Let us quickly make a flat file, shown as follows:

Entity	Parent	Data Storage	Description	Data Type	Base Currency	Aggregation (Plan1)
UK	Entity	Store		Unspecified	GBP	+
US	Entity	Store		Unspecified	USD	+
North Caroline	US	Store		Unspecified	USD	+
Charlotte	North Caroline	Store		Unspecified	USD	+
Australia	Entity	Store		Unspecified	AUD	+

Save the file as Entity.csv to the C: drive so that we can use the address of the flat file to load metadata using the outline load utility.

By now, we should be pretty comfortable with the outline load utility command prompt line. For the last time, let us take a look at it for entity dimension:

This will successfully load entity dimension members.

Scenario and Version Dimension

Scenario Dimension

From the requirements of Outsourc Planning application, we have seen that we need 3 Scenario members that is, Actual, Plan, and Forecast. We'll create an Actual scenario members so that actuals can be loaded into first Quarter of FY10 that is, 2010. Coming to the 'Plan' scenario member, we'll wish planner to enter only 2010 years plan number from Jan to Dec. Finally, let us provide Forecast numbers for all five years. Therefore, the planner should be able to enter forecast values from 2010 to 2014 and for all months. We'll try to create members accordingly. Before we start loading the metadata, let us take a look at the basics structure of Scenario dimension.

Scenario basic structure

Scenario, Parent, Alias: Default, Alias: T1, Valid For Consolidations, Data Storage, Two Pass Calculation, Description, Formula, UDA, Smart List, Data Type, Operation, Start Year, Start Period, End Year, End Period, Exchange Table, Include BegBal, Process Management Enabled, Aggregation (Plan1), Aggregation (Plan2), Aggregation (Plan3)

We need to recall *Chapter 6*, where we learned all these individual settings of Scenario member. The following table gives information of additional properties that are specific to the Scenario dimension. It gives details of the property name, default values and possible values.

Property Name	Default value	Compulsory	Possible values
Start Year	First Year of the application	No	
Start Period	First Period of the application	No	
End Year	Last Year od the application	No	
End Period	Last Period of the application	No	
Exchange Table	None	No	Exchange rate table name
Include BegBal	False	No	True, False
Process Management Enabled	False	No	True, False

Now, create a flat file for the Scenario dimension members. We create three members and we know that actuals have be loaded only from January to March of 2010 , while plan numbers can be entered for the entire year of 2010 from January to December. Forecasting can be done for all years from 2010 to 2014 for all the months. Spend some time observing the same in the following table:

Scenario	Parent	Data Storage	Description	Data Type	Start Year	Start Period	End Year	End Period	Include BegBal	Process Management Enabled	Aggregation (Plan1)
Actuals	Scenario	Store	Actual Data	Unspecified	FY10	Jan	FY10	Mar	True	True	~
Plan	Scenario	Store	Planned Numbers	Unspecified	FY10	Jan	FY10	Dec	True	True	~
Forecast	Scenario	Store	Forecas Values	Unspecified	FY10	Jan	FY14	Dec	True	True	~

Now, the next step is to shoot the utility to load these members. The command line would be as shown next:

```
C:\WINDOWS\system32\cmd.exe

E:\Oracle\Middleware\user_projects\epmsystem1\Planning\planning1>OutlineLoad /A:
outsourc /U:admin /I:c:\Scenario.csv /D:Scenario /L:c:/outlineLoad.log /X:c:/out
lineLoad.exc_
```

After this, log in to the Planning application and check if the new Scenario members are created. If it fails, we know which logs to look into. Next, we'll look into the Version dimension.

Version Dimension

In any organization's budgeting, the client starts with strategic Planning at a very high level and then moves to operational Planning at granular level. We have already learned that there are two kinds of Version dimension members. They are bottom up and target. We'll also create two version dimension members Draft1 and Draft2 with bottom up and target as the types respectively.

Version basic structure

Version, Parent, Alias: Default, Alias: T1, Data Storage, Two Pass Calculation, Description, Formula, UDA, Smart List, Data Type, Operation, Version Type, Process Management Enabled, Aggregation (Plan1), Aggregation (Plan2), Aggregation (Plan3)

Not many new properties or surprises here. We will list the properties that are specific to Version dimension only.

Property Name	Default value	Compulsory	Possible values
Version Type	Bottom Up	No	Bottom Up, Target
Process Management Enabled	False	No	True, False

Let us create a flat file to load the members of Version dimension. We'll create two members for now, Draft1 and Draft2. It should be pretty easy to do. As Draft2 is of Target version type, we cannot enable process management.

Version	Parent	Data Storage	Description	Data Type	Version Type	Process Management Enabled	Aggregation (Plan1)
draft1	Version	Store		Unspecified	Bottom Up	True	~
draft2	Version	Store		Unspecified	Target	False	~

Save the file as `Version.csv` on the C: drive and run the utility as shown in the following screenshot:

```
E:\Oracle\Middleware\user_projects\epmsystem1\Planning\planning1>OutlineLoad /A:
outsourc /U:admin /I:c:\Version.csv /D:Version /L:c:/outlineLoad.log /X:c:/outli
neLoad.exc
```

If we weren't lazy and did not do anything wrong, the members will load successfully.

Let's take a recap. We have loaded members for the Account, Entity, Currency, Scenario, and Version dimensions.

As per the requirement of Outsourc, it needs two custom dimensions—Clients and Projects. We'll create one custom dimension of Clients along with its members in the next section.

Custom Dimension

We'll create custom dimension Clients. The IT company has a few loyal clients and would like to include these clients as a part of their budgeting process. Let us assume the clients are called Client1, Client2 and Client3. Let us first see the basic structure of a custom dimension:

User Defined Dimension Name, Parent, Alias: Default, Alias: T1, Valid For Consolidations, Data Storage, Two Pass Calculation, Description, Formula, UDA, Smart List, Data Type, Operation, Aggregation (Plan1), Aggregation (Plan2), Aggregation (Plan3)

The first property 'User defined dimension name', we'll set it to Clients and proceed with other properties, which should look familiar by now at least.

We'll make a sample `Custom.csv` file as shown next. There is no dimension called 'Client' so far, but after running the load utility, it creates both the dimension and its members.

Client	Parent	Data Storage	Description	Data Type
Client1	Client	Store	Client1	Unspecified
Client2	Client	Store	Client2	Unspecified

Now, we run the utility using the following syntax. There is a slight difference when you create a custom dimension Client and load its members. We have circled it in the following screenshot:

```
E:\Oracle\Middleware\user_projects\epmsystem1\Planning\planning1>OutlineLoad /A:
outsourc /U:admin /I:c:\Custom.csv /DU:Client /L:c:/outlineLoad.log /X:c:/outlin
eLoad.exc_
```

This should successfully load the custom dimension and its members.

Before we summarize, let us log into Oursourc Planning application and see all the dimensions. Now, before we end the chapter, take a final look at all the flat files that were helpful in building metatdata—`Accounts.CSV`, `Entity.CSV`, and so on—and at the Dimensions and its hierarchies in our Planning Application of Outsourc as well.

Summary

In this chapter, we discussed metadata load and how can it be done from implantation perspective. We learned about the utility "outline load utility", which is capable of loading metadata. We even discussed other options for loading metadata. We learned how to design hierarchical structures before we can create flat files to load metadata.

We saw the metadata load of all Planning standard and custom dimensions. We created an application Outsourc and used it to load the metadata.

In the next chapter, we'll learn about data load in Planning application.

8

Mastering Data Forms

Every farewell combines loss and new freedom.

— Mason Cooley

This quotation is not always true, as we are moving a little far from Excel spreadsheets with the new freedom to work on Web-based Data Forms, we are not at a complete loss as Planners can still work on Smart View.

Please join us in welcoming Data forms and bid good bye to Excel sheets for now. For Excel loyalists, who are the majority in reality, Hyperion offers Hyperion Smart View, which can be called an extended Planning add-in to Excel.

Let us read a possible conversation between a novice Planning developer and an experienced Planning project manager.

Planning developer: *Sir, now that we have collated all the Budget Templates (Excel sheets) from the client and created a Planning Application along with Metadata, what is the next step?*

Project manager: *We have to create Data Forms. It's a pretty easy task to develop.*

Planning developer: *Yes, I have read about Data Forms. It looks very easy; all I need to do is select the page, row, column and POV. Is that correct?*

Project manager: *Yes, it is easy in terms of development. But, remember it is very important to create Data Forms keeping the end user i.e. Planner in mind. As we understand that it is not technically challenging job to create Data Forms. But, it is very important to create a Data Form which makes sense for a Planner from his Budgeting Perspective. You need to translate the Business Requirement of Budgeting Data entry into creation of Data Forms. It can be rather challenging.*

Yes, in this chapter we are going to talk all good about Data forms. Once upon a time, Financial Planners used to work only on Excel-based Planning templates for their budgeting, and of course we all know how difficult it is to maintain the consistency of the data stored by these excel templates and aggregation of the data received from various budget sources, considering that movement of Excel templates between multiple users/departments during the budgeting flow.

We, the Hyperion consultants, have already created the skeleton by the name of Hyperion Planning. We created this skeleton in the previous chapters (*Chapter 4* and *Chapter 5*), where we created Planning application and later we learned about the metadata load process, in *Chapter 7*. Now, we need to select the skin and present it in the form of data forms for the end users to access.

We'll cover the following in this chapter:

- **The importance of data forms**: We'll start this chapter by talking about data forms and how good they are over Excel sheets and also how useful these data forms are in the budgeting process.
- **Data forms**:
    - ° **Basic structure**: We'll start by understanding the basic structure of a data form before we create one.
    - ° **Data form properties**: In this section, we'll understand the properties/settings and options of a Data Form.
    - ° **Data form creation**: After understanding the theory, we'll create the forms and have some fun.

Importance of Data Forms

Data forms are spreadsheet-like grids but the major difference is that they are a Web-based grid and these data forms are connected to an Essbase Database at backend, which act as a central repository of all budget/actual/forecast related data. While the user/planner interacts with the data forms the data is fetched/saved back to the Essbase database. While in the case of spreadsheets, all data resides inside the spreadsheet itself and it makes it increasingly difficult to maintain the correctness of the data, considering the data resides in distributed manner in many spreadsheets. This is the key difference which eliminates all sorts of data consistency and aggregation issues with spreadsheets.

Now, let us get into the shoes of the implementing team. When we visit a client to implement Hyperion Planning, they first present us with a lot of budget templates, which are mostly in Excel format.

These Planning templates are the Excel sheets which the clients must have been using to suit and cater to their budgeting needs. We are going to refer these templates and make data forms in real implementations.

 The data forms are used by planners to enter data and update data, and also by big bosses to analyze data.

How do planners access the forms over the web when they are spread over different countries?

Data forms can be accessed over the web by using the browser. They can also be accessed by using the Hyperion Smart View client for Microsoft Excel.

What we, as an implementing team do is make the Workspace URL available on the Internet (we know that one can access Hyperion Planning through the workspace). This way, Planners from different locations can log in to this Planning application and access their relevant data forms and provide their planned numbers.

When planners submit their numbers, the data is saved in an Essbase cube, which is a centralized data repository for our Hyperion Planning application. It sounds so simple; it's like a simple website on the Internet and planners can access anywhere in the world with only one basic requirement—Internet connectivity.

Now, imagine budgeting in Excel—the data is not saved in any repository; it's everywhere and anywhere, and lying around in every single Excel sheet. It's manually driven and a very tedious activity. Imagine how much of a pain it would be to make the right Excel sheet made available to some one in the other country.

After realising the importance of data forms, we'll straight take a look at few data forms which are already available in the sample Planning application 'PandB'. We'll put our old friend **PandB** Planning application back to work.

It's common to ask a candidate in an interview about the differences between Excel-based budgeting and Hyperion Planning. We should know the answer to that question now.

 For users who are still comfortable with Excel sheets, Planning is closely integrated with Microsoft office and planner can be used with Excel using Smart View.

Data Forms

- The basic structure of a data form: In this section, we'll see how the data form looks. We'll cover the basic elements of a data form before we start creating one.

- Data form properties: In this section, we'll take a look at all the properties and options of a data form.

- Data form creation: In this section, we'll create both simple and composite data forms.

Basic structure

Let us start by understanding the basics:

- Data form and folders: We will see how folders are used in organizing/ categorizing data forms

- Data form structure: We'll view the typical data form structure

- Data form and folders.

We know that we have not created any data forms yet, but the PandB application is a sample application with a few data forms already available. Let us make use of it.

Log in to PandB Planning application. Go to **Administration | Manage | Data forms and Ad hoc Grids**.

In the following screenshot, we see the folder structure of data forms. There are a few data forms that are collated in relevant folders.

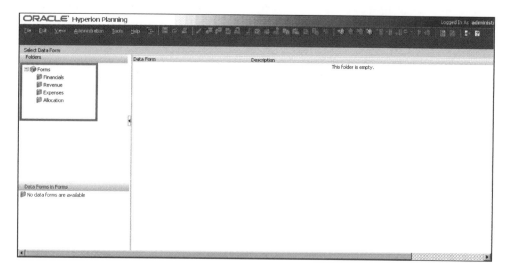

We can have the relevant forms in appropriate folders, as shown in the next screenshot. As we see in the following screenshot, we can have all revenue-related forms in `Revenue` folder. Therefore, when we create forms, it's a good idea to create folders also to save forms within them.

It makes a lot of sense, if we think from an implementation angle and user access perspective, to have a folder structure such as **Financials**, **Revenue**, **Expenses**, and **Allocation**. The **Financials** folder will have financial data forms such as income statement, balance sheet, and cash flow. While the folders **Revenue** and **Expenses** will have all revenue-related forms and expense-related forms respectively. The following screenshot shows that we have three data forms related to revenue, and hence they are grouped in **Revenue** data form folder.

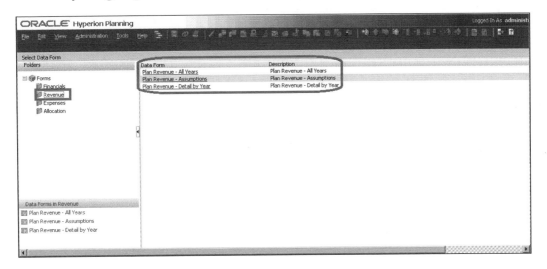

As we can see, balance sheet, cash flow, and income statement are the data forms in the `Financials` folder. We can also see a description and instruction for every form. We'll find out how get the instruction and description later in this chapter.

 It is recommended to use folders for organizing forms based on their relevancy. This organization of data form folders enhances application usability.

Data form structure

Let's open the data form from the **Revenue** folder, whose name is **Plan Revenue –
All Years**, which we can see in previous screenshot.

As we can see, there are pages, rows, columns, and POV (Point of View). This is
all we have in a data form. They sound very basic, but we'll spend some time in
understanding more, which will be useful in the next topic, which is data form creation.

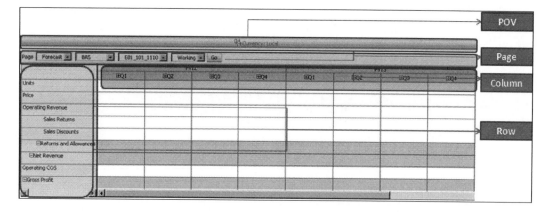

- **Page**: This consists of drop-down lists. Each drop down contains a list
  of selected members from a particular dimension. For example, the drop
  down in the Plan Revenue data form contains Version, Scenario, Entity,
  and Segment dimension members as page dimension and contains a list of
  members of these dimensions. The benefit is that **Page** enables users to select
  relevant members from each of the drop downs and then click on the **Go**
  button to modify/view data for that particular combination of members.

- This usually has member combinations. In the image above, the page
  selection has members of **Scenario** (Forecast is a member of the Scenario
  dimension), **Segment** (BAS is member of the Segment dimension), Entity
  (E01_101_1110 is member of Entity dimension) and **Version** (working is a
  version dimension members) dimensions from left to right.

- **Rows** and **Columns**: Rows include **Account** dimension, whereas
  columns include Year and Period dimension members, as shown in
  the previous screenshot.

It's recommended to create data form with **Account** dimension
members as rows and Year, period dimension members as rows and
the left out dimension members to be a part of POV.

- **POV** (Point of View): Point of view has the static member selection of dimension members. If we are still confused between Page and **POV**. Let us elaborate, **POV** is always static in nature and pages are always dynamic. Dynamic implies that they are drop-down lists and we can dynamically select/change the member selection. Whereas, **POV** members are static and fixed in nature. In the previous image, **POV** has only the currency dimension and its selected member is Local.

- Now, we can change the Scenario dimension from Forecast to Plan, it's dynamic; but we cannot change the member selection of POV.

> If we did this carefully, we ensured that all the dimensions have participated in the data form. This is mandatory. We have freedom to select dimension members as **Page**, **Rows**, **Column**, or **POV**, but we cannot leave any dimension without participation. It's against the very basic definition of Essbase multidimensionality.
>
> In a data form, it is important to note that each dimension can appear only in one of the sections of page, column, row, or POV.

Now, in next section, we'll look into the properties of a data form.

Data form properties

We'll first understand all of the properties and available options in a data form. We can make use of the PandB sample application for this purpose.

The data form has the following sections:

- **Properties**. The basic details such as **Name**, **Description**, and **Instructions** are provided in this section.

- **Layout**: **Point of View**, **Page**, **Row**, and **Column** are selected in this section. We'll explore these in more detail in this section.

- **Other Options**: In other options, we learn about other settings; including **Precision**, Display properties, printing Options... etc.

- **Business Rules**: The last section talks how we assign a business rule to a data form and what options are available in a data form for business rule execution.

Go to **Administration | Manage | Data forms and Ad Hoc Grids**. We select **Revenue** data form folder and can see its related data forms in the next screenshot:

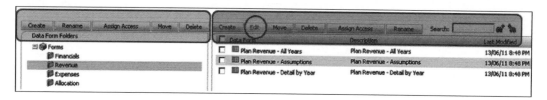

Pay close attention to the top of both the data form folders and data forms; we have the options **Create, Rename, Assign Access, Move,** and **Delete**. There is additional **Edit** option on the top of data forms, as its applicable only to data forms. The options for data form folders and the options of data forms are rounded (highlighted) in the previous screenshot.

Now, select/tick a data form and select **Edit**, which is an option available on the top of the data forms to understand the properties of a data form. It leads to a new window.

Properties

In the first tab of **Properties**, we see the following information:

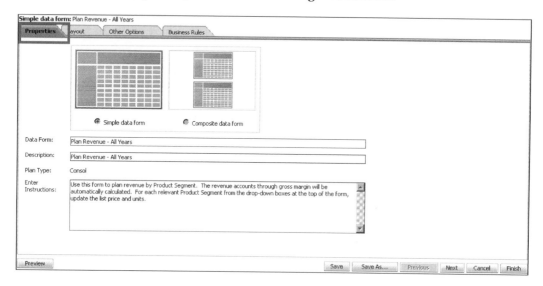

Simple data form and **Composite data form**: There are two types of data forms that can be possibly created—**simple** and **composite**. Here, we see that **Simple** has been enabled, suggesting that, this form is of simple data form case.

Now, what is a composite data form?

A data form is a display of simple single grid structure. But, when user requirement becomes greedy, they wanted to see multiple data form in a single display, that is, several data forms display simultaneously. This can be achieved using a composite data form. We'll create and learn more of it in the next section *Data form creation*.

- **Data Form**: This is the name of the data form.
- **Description**: This is the description of the data form.
- **Plan Type**: We know that a Planning application can have multiple plan types and a data form is always associated with a plan type.

 Different Plan Types would have different dimension structure, hence a data form needs to be associated with a plan type before we can complete its creation.

- **Enter Instructions**: Here, we provide instruction to the Planner, this gives them information of what the data form is meant for, which would help a Planner understand that they need to enter the data into it.

Remember, we have seen View instruction and description when we first saw the list of data forms in the *Data form and folder structure of basic structure* section.

Layout

In **Layout** tab, we see POV, page, column, and row. Towards the right-hand side, we see a few properties for rows and columns.

 The new and very useful feature of the **Layout** tab is **Validation Rules**. This new feature is available in Hyperion Planning 11.1.2.

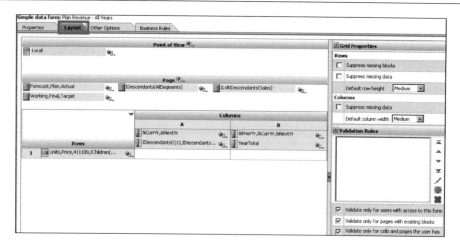

There is member selector icon, which will help in selecting members. It is located to the right-hand side of every dimension. It looks like the following: .

If we pay attention, we have **Validation Rules**, we'll learn more about these in the next chapter, *Data Entry*. This is very interesting and pretty useful concept.

Other options

Within **Other Options**, there are many options; we'll cover section by section, starting with Precision.

Precision Options: This property decides the number of decimals. We need to recall that we have set the data type to **Currency**, **Non-currency**, and **Percentage** for many dimension members.

As we can see, we need to set **Minimum** precision and **Maximum** precision.

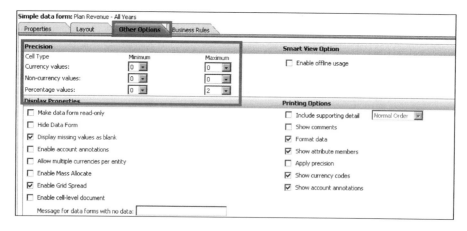

How does min and max precision work?

Let's consider an example; to explain, if 50 is the data value and it's of currency type. If we had set **Minimum** as **0** and **Maximum** as **1**, then the value displayed is 50.0. But at the same time, it allows users to enter a value with a max of 1 decimal, that is 50.1.

Now, if **Minimum** is **2** and **Maximum** is **4**, then the entered 50 will be displayed as 50.00 as **Minimum** is 2. In this case, it lets a user enter a value with maximum of four decimals that is, even if a planner enters 50.12345, it will be displayed as 50.1234 as the **Maximum** is 4.

These options become handy when the values have decimals, for example, 100.1234 is the value and we set its min precision as 0 and **Maximum** as **3** , then the displayed value is 100.123 and for the same value , if the **Minimum** precision is **6**, then the displayed value would be 100.123000.

Smart View Options

Enable **Offline Usage**: This option will enable offline usage.

> **What is offline usage?**
> Hyperion Planning gives us a facility to user for the work on data forms even when they are not connected to the Planning server. This is termed as **offline usage**.

Display Properties

The following are the display properties for data forms. Before, we start with these properties; let us make it clear that most of the properties will be discussed along with examples, in the next chapter, *Data Entry*.

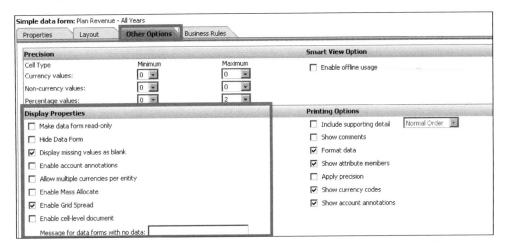

- **Make Data form read-only**: If we enable this option, the whole data form becomes read only with gray color cells and would not permit us to enter data or edit data.

 The **Make Data Form read-only** property is not applicable to composite data forms.

- **Hide Data Form**: This property hides the data form as the name suggests and this is applicable only in the case of composite data forms. An example could be hiding single forms that have been used for creating a composite form and the user does not require access to the single forms separately.

- **Display missing values as blank**: If we observe, though the data forms do not have any data, they don't show us #missing in their cells; rather, they all show us nothing. They are blank. This is because of this property. It's a pretty useful property; imagine how ugly a data form would look with #missing on every entry.

- **Enable account annotations**: An annotation means a piece of critical commentary or an explanatory note. We can give these comments to account members and we need to enable to annotate. We can give a text comment, URL, or a link to a document for annotation. We'll see this with an example in next chapter *Data Entry*.

- **Allow multiple currencies per entity**: Let us explain with an example. For US entity, the data needs to be entered in a data form in USD, which is its local currency. Likewise for UK, GBP is its local currency. This option enables input in multiple currencies apart from the local currency.

- **Enable Mass Allocate**: We can allocate or spread data across multiple dimensions using this feature. We'll see this property along with an example in the next chapter of *Data Entry*.

- **Enable Grid Spread**: Within a data form, we can increase/decrease the values of the current cells by a specific amount or percentage across all the dimensions using this option. We'll see more about this property along with an example in the next chapter.

- **Enable for ad-hoc**: This is an interesting and useful property. As per the requirements, we'll design and provide data forms for our planner. As we know, users can sometimes be greedy; they always want more. They would like to change the row to a column or page dimension to row/column. They may even want to keep or remove a few members. This can be achieved with the help of this property.

The best part of this property is that the user not only can make the changes in the data form right then, but also can save it with a different form name if he loves it too much. We'll see more of this in next chapter.

- **Enable Cell-level document**: We can give our user the flexibility to add or edit a document at an individual cell level. This way, users can add a document at cell level too. Don't we think it's too much to handle, we generally don't enable this property.

- **Message for Data Forms with no data**: When a form does not have valid rows, it gives us the message "**There are no valid rows of data for this Data Form.**" If we want to change the content of the message, then this property is handy.

Printing Options

The Printing Options help in deciding what properties or content should be there as a part of the print. The options are shown as follows:

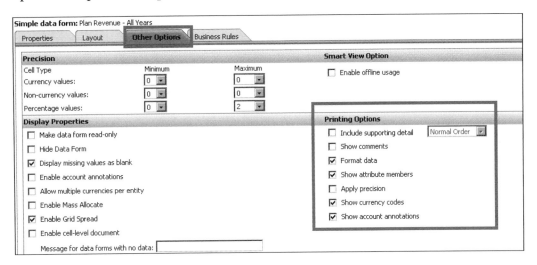

Business Rules

We'll be writing Business rules, and yes, we'll be writing many of them. We'll discover more of it in *Chapter 15, Business Rules* and *Chapter 16, Advanced Business Rules*. For now, we need to understand that we can associate or attach a business rule to a data form.

In simple way, we insert data into data form and calculation is performed on the fed data with the help of business rules. Hence, we associate business rules with the data form.

In this tab, we see the list of available business rules and the selected business rule. We'll select one business rule from **Business Rules** and 'push' it to **Selected Business Rules**. After doing this, select it and click on **Properties**, which is right below, as shown in the screenshot:

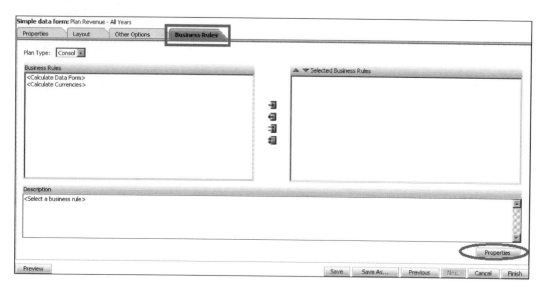

Selecting properties would open a new window and it has the following options

- **Run on Load**: When a planner opens a data form, the business rule gets executed in this kind of run. It means to run a business rule upon the loading of the data form.

- **Run on Save**: After planner enters data in a data form, he got to save data. With this **Run on Save**, the business rule gets executed when the data is saved in the data form

- The other two optional options of **Use Members on Data Form** and **Hide Prompt** are applicable to business rules, which have Runtime prompts. We'll see them in next chapter. Snub them for a while.

 Most of the time, **Run on Save** and **Run on Load** are recommended when the business rule execution does not exceed more than 30 seconds. If we realize that rule execution is taking more time, then launching it manually is recommended.

By now, we have understood almost all the properties of a data form. In the next section, we'll attempt to create data form all by ourselves.

Data Form creation

In this section, we will first understand few important considerations, which act as prerequisites and then understand the important concept of Relationship Functions. These functions will be used in the subsequent *Data form creation* section.

- Considerations
- Relationships
- Data form creation
    - ° Simple data form creation
    - ° Composite data form creation

Considerations

There are a few very important considerations. We need to understand them before we create a data form. Now, we need to use our knowledge of dimension and member properties, which we have learned in previous chapters.

Most of the data forms primarily serve the purpose of data entry.

- Version dimension: There is bottom-up and target version and we need to know that for bottom-up, the data entry is possible only for bottom level or level 0 members.

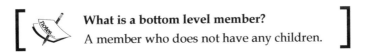

What is a bottom level member?
A member who does not have any children.

Now, there is target version, for which data entry is possible at every level—both at parent and for level 0 members.

- **Currency dimension**: We may have a single currency application or a multi currency application. In a single currency application, we don't have an issue as for different entities; we would be entering data into a single currency. We have a concern, when the application is a multi currency application, let us consider an example, imagine we have three currencies—UK pound, US dollar, and Australian dollar. Now, when we create a data form, we need to be careful as for entity US, we cannot select the currency of Australian dollar or UK pound to enter data. They would become only read-only forms that way. We can enter data values only in local currency members. It's obvious as a US planner can enter in his local currency of US and not in UK pound, but can if this planner wishes to view the data form in UK pounds currency, then he can select UK pound and then the currency conversion has to happen. We are yet to explore currency conversion; we will do more of it in next chapter anyway.

- There is a default member in the currency dimension called **Local**, which is meant to be used for inputting all numbers related to all entities and based on the base currency of the selected entity the system automatically enters the input currency in the HSP_InputCurrency member and value is saved in the HSP_InputValue member.

- **Scenario dimension**: We were talking of members such as plan, actual, and forecast for scenario dimension. It's more of the dimension design consideration rather than data form design consideration. If actuals have to be entered only for the very first quarter, we create actual member with the time period spanning from January to March. This way, when a planner selects 'actuals' in the data form, he can enter data only from January to March and the cells of other months would be read-only.

- The design considerations are:
  - Always keep dense dimensions in rows and columns (which means **Account** and **Period**) and sparse dimension in Page or POV
  - It is recommended that you keep scenario, version and Year dimension in page
  - When we create a composite data form, it's better not to include more than two simple data forms in one composite data form

- There are few other design considerations which we'll learn about in the next chapter.

Relationships

We'll understand the relationships available before we start with the data form creation.

What is the purpose of these Relationship Functions?

While we create a data form, we need to select Dimension members and there may be many members to be selected. We can select members of a dimension one by one, or with the help of Relationship functions, we can select a members and select an appropriate Relationship function to select other members as well.

We can see a table that provides information about all the available relationships.

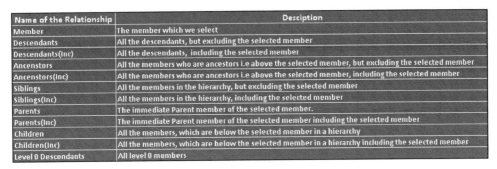

Name of the Relationship	Desciption
Member	The member which we select
Descendants	All the descendants, but excluding the selected member
Descendants(Inc)	All the descendants, including the selected member
Ancenstors	All the members who are ancestors i.e above the selected member, but excluding the selected member
Ancenstors(Inc)	All the members who are ancestors i.e above the selected member, including the selected member
Siblings	All the members in the hierarchy, but excluding the selected member
Siblings(Inc)	All the members in the hierarchy, including the selected member
Parents	The immediate Parent member of the selected member.
Parents(Inc)	The immediate Parent member of the selected member including the selected member
Children	All the members, which are below the selected member in a hierarchy
Children(Inc)	All the members, which are below the selected member in a hierarchy including the selected member
Level 0 Descendants	All level 0 members

Let us understand these relationships with a simple example of typical hierarchy of **Income Statement**, whose parent-child relationship is shown in the following screenshot:

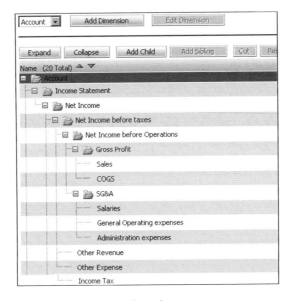

Now, let us go through the relationships one-by-one, with the help of an example. Before that, spend considerable amount of time at the table given earlier.

To start with, we'll take the following:

- **Member**: If we select a member Sales and select the relationship **Member**, only 'sales' member is selected in the data form.

- **Descendants**: If the selected member is **Net Income**, and the relationship is 'Descendants', the included members in form are all the members right from Net Income before taxes to Income Tax, right from top to down. But, the member 'Net Income' wont be part of included members of Data Form.

- **Descendants (Inc)**: The only difference between Descendants and Descendants (Inc) is that the latter includes the selected member. If we consider the same example of **Net Income**, then along with **Net Income** member, Net Income before taxes to Income Tax are included in. We need to note that **Inc** stands for 'include'.

- **Ancestors**: If the selected member is 'Sales' with this relationship, the included members are **Gross Profit**, **Net Income** from **Operations**, Net Income before taxes, Net Income and Income statement.

- **Ancestors (Inc)**: Again, the difference is inclusion of the selected member that is if 'Sales' is selected member, the included members in the data form are Gross Profit, Net Income from Operations, Net Income before taxes, Net Income and Income statement along with 'Sales.

- **Siblings**: Siblings are brother and sisters. If selected member is 'Salaries', then the included members in form are 'General Operating expenses' and Administrative expenses'. The main requirement is that their immediate parent is the same which will make their generation the same but their level might still be different.

  For example one of the siblings might have children but the other might not so this will result in a different level number for each of the siblings.

- **Siblings (Inc)**: Yes, we have understood this by now, with the selected member of **Salaries**, the included members would be Salaries, **General Operating expenses** and **Administrative expenses**.

- **Parents**: If the selected member is **Sales**, the included member in the form is **Gross Profit**. Now, we all should take a look at the difference between **Ancestors** and **Parents**.

- Parents (Inc): With selected member as **Sales**, the included members would be 'sales' along with **Gross Profit**.

- **Children**: If the selected member is **Gross Income from Operations**, the included members are **Gross Profit, SG&A, Other Revenue** and **Other Expense**. It includes only its immediate children. Now, we should have understood the difference between children and descendants.

- **Children (Inc)**: We should know what this is by now.

- **Level 0 Descendants**: This would select all level 0 members.

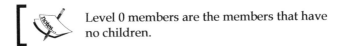
Level 0 members are the members that have no children.

If the selected member is **Net Income**, the included members in the form are **Sales, COGS, Salaries, General Operating expenses, Administrative expenses, Other Revenue, Other Expense** and **Income tax**. Notice that none of these members have any further children.

Let us get started with data form creation and understand the missed concepts, if any.

Sample data form creation

Let us do the Simple data form creation in steps

1. Log in to the Outsourc Planning Application. Go to **Administration | Manage | Data forms and Ad hoc Grids**. For the application Outsourc, we see no folders and no data forms as of now.

    First, we'll create a folder. There is an option to create data form folders as shown in the following image:

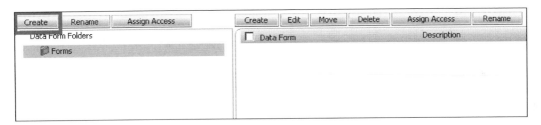

Select **Create**, which will lead to a pop up, where we need to provide name of the folder. For tutorial purposes, let us give the name of the folder as **Test Folder** as shown below.

It'll create a folder. Next, select the newly created folder, that is **Test Folder**, and then click on **Create** data form, as shown in the following image:

2. Now, we are getting into the core steps of data form creation. After we clicked on **Create**, it opens a new window, where we are supposed to provide information about the data form.

We have an option to **Assign access**, this is used for user provision. Not all forms can be made visible to every planner or user. For example, critical revenue data forms should not be made available to a HR planner and there are a few data forms that are strictly meant for CFO, which should not be made accessible by other users. We'll learn about security in *Chapter 9, User Provisioning and Access Rights*

In the first look, its surprises us, as we don't see all the tabs of the data form (as in case of **Layout, Other Options, Business Rule**, and others), which we had seen while understanding data form properties. As we move ahead by providing information, the other tabs would unwind.

We'll provide the very basic information such as the name, description, and instruction, as shown in the following image:

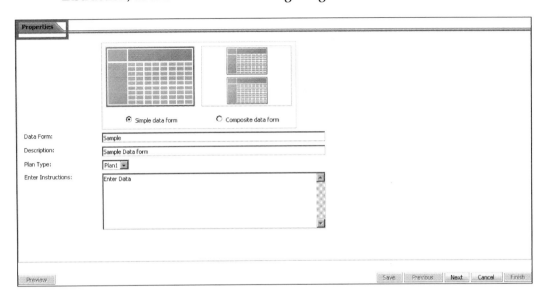

> It is important to note that we selected **Plan Type** as **Plan1** in the image above. Now, we need to understand that in case of a Planning application with multiple plan types, we create data forms with reference to different plan types.

3. Now, click on **Next** to move ahead to the next tab of **Layout** in the data form creation. By default, all the dimensions are under "Point of view". We have to move them as per our design requirement. As we had learned before that Accounts dimension members are recommended to be in rows and Period, Year dimension members be in columns and rest of the dimensions be in page or POV. We will stick to this recommendation.

How can we add Account dimension to the Row section?

Oh, it's very simple; use drag and drop to make life easier. This is an enhancement in 11.1.2 version again.

The earlier versions of Hyperion Planning used to have different layout, where we need to select dimension from drop down, but in this version, it is a simple drag and drop. Select ▓, drag and drop it either in page, row or column. ▓ is used for dimension selection. Drag and drop for all the dimension as shown in the following image. We had not selected any dimension for **POV**, **Scenario**, **Entity**, **Currency** and **Version** dimensions are dragged to Page and it's displayed as a drop down list.

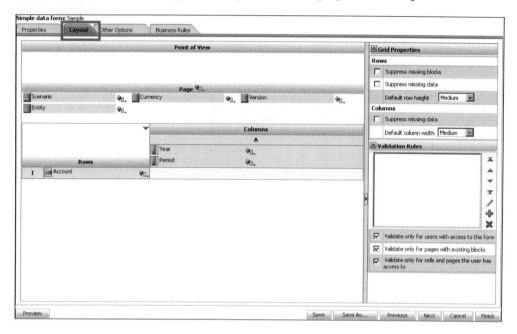

For columns, we can move dimensions up and down, try that out by right-clicking on a dimension, we can see the options for moving them down and moving them up.

Now, after selecting the dimension in terms of design, we need to select members within a dimension.

In real implementations, our dimension structure would be more elaborate with hundreds of account and entity dimension members. We would have different department, division and geographies and we would definitely not want all of the planners/users to view data or forms in entirety. Hence, we would create forms addressing the specific needs of a unit. For example, we would create few set of data forms for HR department, which would members of Account dimension, which would be of HR departments' interest and their relevance. Therefore, member selection of a data form is done keeping in mind the form and the specific users/planners that are going to view/enter data.

How do I select members within a dimension?

You should be able to see the member selector icon ✱▣, to the right-hand side of every dimension in Page, Rows, Column, and POV. If we take the cursor above, it would give us a message to select members. Select member selector icon ✱▣, to pick the member of a dimension.

We'll start with **Account** dimension member selection. Click on the 'member selector icon', which is to the right-hand side of the Account dimension and we see a new window opening. We intend to select all the members of our Account dimension. Hence, right-click on **Account** as shown in the next image, which will give the options of relationships as shown:

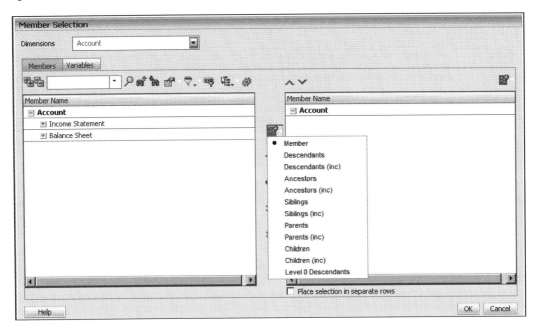

Now, we want to select all the members of **Account** dimension. Therefore, select 'Account' and choose the relationship as **Descendants**. Remember, we read about these these relationships before in the *Data form creation* section.

Now, it should look as shown next:

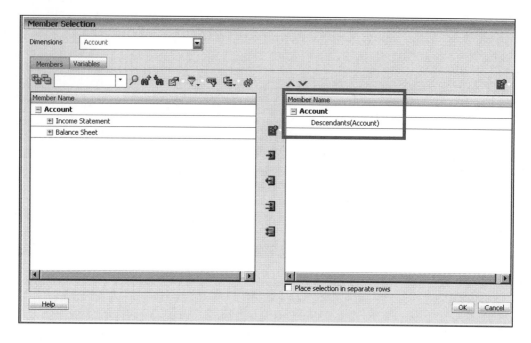

1. Before we move ahead with other dimensions, we should notice a few important options in the Member Selection window.

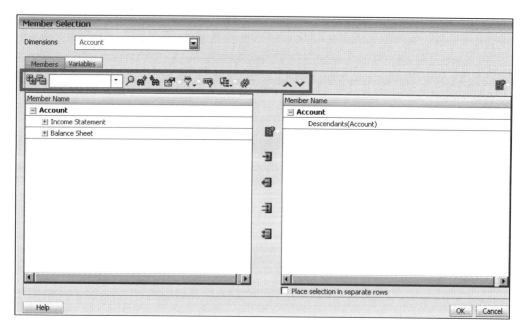

Let us start from the left-hand side and work our way to the right-hand side.

- ○ : This is to expand or collapse the members in a dimension.

- ○ This is to search a member in a dimension. We type the member and search either up or down in a dimension. We can search by name, alias, UDA and description. We can also use wildcards for searching.

> The **Search** option is very handy when we have hundreds of members in a dimension. We cannot practically expand the whole outline to select a few members.

- ○ : This is a display property. We have few possible display options. They are **Member Name**, **Alias**, **Member Name: Alias**, **Alias: Member Name**.

- ○ : This is one of the new features and it is a very good feature. It's the **Keep only by levels or generations** option. Sometimes, we need to select all level 1 members in a data form. Now, imagine the pain it takes to select all level 1 members without this option. We need to go to every individual hierarchy and select level 1.

> **Keep only by levels or generation** is a new option in 11.1.2 and it's very helpful.

- ○ : The last option is a **Refresh** option, as we can make out from its face.

2. Let us move ahead with member selection of other dimensions:

   - ○ For the **Period** dimension, we select all the descendants of 'Year Total' member.

   - ○ For the **Year** dimension, select **Siblings (Inc)** of **FY10**.

   - ○ For the **Scenario** dimension, select all the descendants, that is, the descendants of **Scenario** dimension.

   - ○ For the **Entity** dimension also, select all the descendants of Entity Dimension.

   - ○ For the **Version** dimension, select **draft1** and **draft2** members individually.

   - ○ Finally, for the **Currency** dimension, select all the descendants of the dimension.

In the end, it would look like the following image.

 The selection of members of a dimension depends entirely on the requirement of the data form. Here, the budget templates which the client provides are very handy, as they give us most of the information about what members need to be included in a data form.

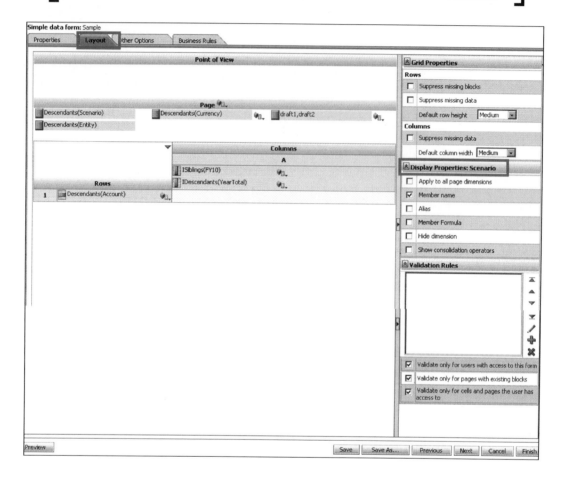

As we select dimension, we see the grid properties changing and we can set as per our requirement. If we remember, the member names of Account dimension are numbers and their aliases are more meaningful. Likewise for every dimension, we can choose whether to display member name or alias name in the data form.

Generally, for the **Account** Dimension, we would prefer to have aliases in the data form rather than names of the members. In the image above, for the Scenario dimension we have selected 'Member name'.

3. For all the dimensions, we can set Grid properties, Display properties. For that, select the dimension first and set the properties accordingly as we can see in Fig 22. We'll learn about validation rules in the next chapter **Data Entry**.

4. Click on **Next** to move to the next tab of **Other Options**. Enable/check the options as shown in the following image. The options of **Enable Account Annotations**, **Mass Allocate**, and **Grid Spread** will be covered next.

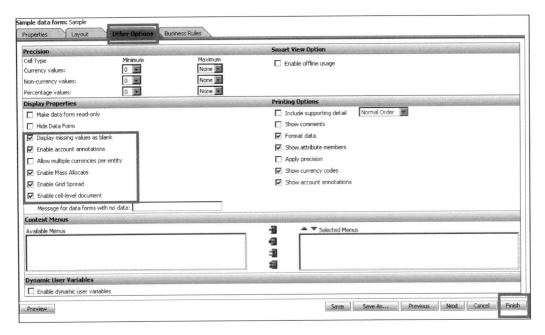

Move ahead by clicking next and finish. We'll learn about Business Rules later in the *Chapter 15, Business Rules* and *Chapter 16, Advanced Business Rules*.

5. After we finish, we get a success message as shown next:

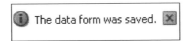

6. Now, let us straight away open the 'Sample' data form. On left hand side of the page, we see the Data form Management folder. **Expand Forms | Test Folder**. Now, select **Test Folder** to see the form in the *Data Forms in Test Folder* section, as shown next:

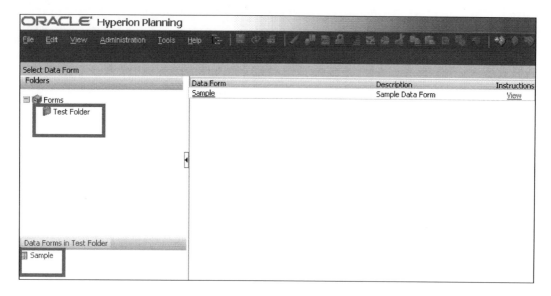

7. Now, select the **Sample** data form to open it. It gives you the following message:

This is a message that we get when we select many members in our data form. As we have created our sample data form with all the possible members, our form is huge with many members. But in real implementations, we would have specific set of members to be selected.

Select **Yes** to continue.

Sometimes, when you open the form, it throws an error "The data form is invalid". Most of the time, this happens when the Meta data has not been updated. For example if we have added a few members in the dimensions of a Planning application and created data forms, but we have forgotten to refresh the database.

Sometimes, when the data form is very large, we need to increase the JVM maximum size to improve performance.

How do we increase the JVM?

Go to the registry entry of `HKEY_LOCAL_MACHINE\SOFTWARE\`
`Wow6432Node\Hyperion Solutions\HyperionPlanning\`
`HyS9Planning`. Increase `-Xmx`. By default, it will be `-Xmx512m` Try
increasing to `-Xmx1024m`.

Do ensure that you restart the Planning web app service (Hyperion
Planning – web Application) after the changes.

7. We'll finally see our data form that we created, shown as follows:

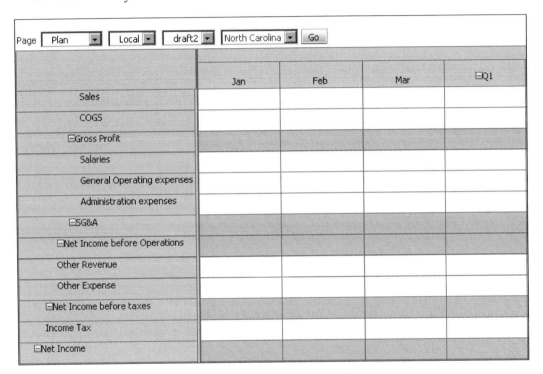

We have now successfully created our first simple data form. In the next section,
we'll learn how to create a composite data form.

Composite data form

In this section, we'll create our first composite data form. As composite form is a combination of data forms. It is required to create when we need to provide a data form to the end user, which is combination of multiple forms. It should be pretty easy to combine the already-created data forms.

We'll make use of out **PandB** application for this. The reason being, we have many forms already available in **PandB** application.

Let us do it in steps again:

1. Log in to **PandB** Planning application and go to **Administration | Manage | Data Forms**.

2. From the data form creation page, select **Create** to get the following image. We need to select the **Composite Data** form and provide the basic information as shown in the following image:

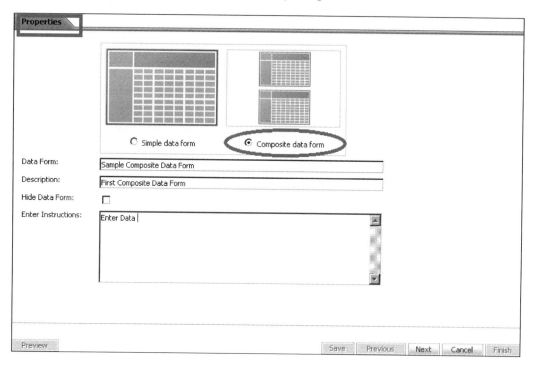

What is **Hide Data Form**?

Hide Data Form would hide this data form. If we recall, after we created the Simple data form, we selected the folder and saw the data form. But, when we hide it, it's not visible. We need to note that by hiding the form, we hide it from the users in the main interface, it still remains visible in the administer form interface for an administrator to manage.

3. Click on **Next** to go to the **Layout** tab.

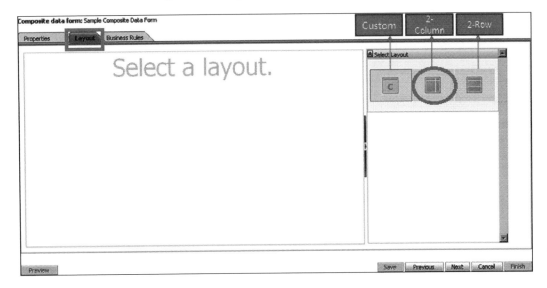

In **Layout** tab, we select the layout and the available layout options are as follows:

  ○ **Custom**: In this layout, we can split horizontally and vertically into different sections as per our own wish.

  ○ **2-Cloumn Layout**: This layout selection creates two sections with division in between i.e. in 2 columns.

  ○ **2-Row Layout**: In this layout, it splits horizontally and creates two sections, one over the other.

We'll make a simple composite form which has three data form and the lay out would be two-columned lay out. Hence, select the 2 - column lay out by clicking on it as shown in the.

After going to the **Layout** selection, it would look like the following screenshot. We need to focus on **Section Properties**, which is right below the layout selection.

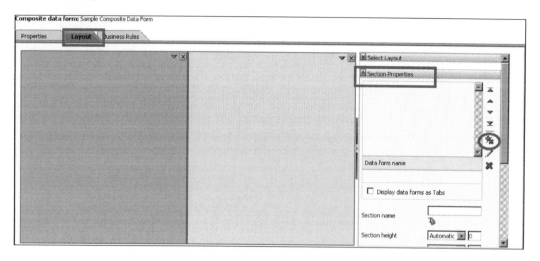

This is the place where we select the data forms with the help of 🧩.

Select 🧩 and it will lead to a 'data form selection' window, where we need to pick forms. We have selected all three 'Revenue' data forms. We need to remember that there are three data forms in the Revenue data form folder already. After the selection of the data forms, the **Layout** tab would appear as shown in the following screenshot:

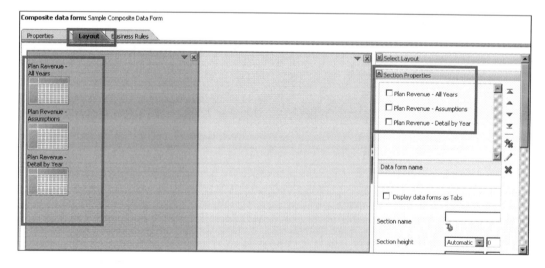

4. Now, we see all the 3 data forms are in the first section. We'll drag and drop the third data form, that is, **Plan Revenue- Detail by Year** to the right most section. Also, as we see **Section Properties**, we can name sections. We have two sections and which are split vertically, we name the sections **Section A** and **Section B**.

5. After dragging and dropping the form to Section B (assuming that the right-most section is named Section B), it would look like the following screenshot:

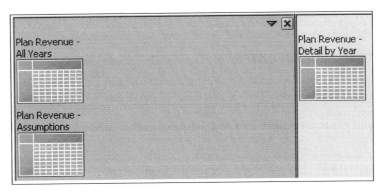

6. Leave the rest of the properties and click on **Next** and **Finish**.

7. We get a message that the data form is saved and if we open it to view, it should look like the following screenshot:

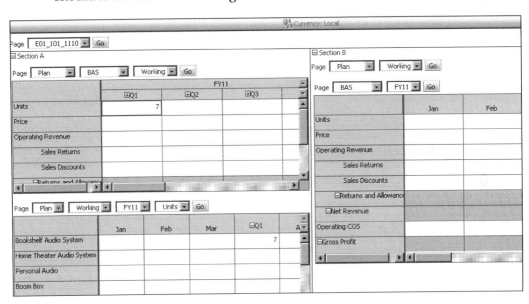

This is a composite form, where we have three simple data forms in it. Finally, we have created our first composite form.

Create more composite data forms with different layouts and explore other properties to become more fluent.

> From a real implementation's perspective, it is better to avoid Composite data forms. The reason being, as it is combination of multiple data forms, it generally takes more time as data has to be retrieved for all combinations of all data forms of a Composite data form. Hence, there might be performance issues and the planner/users may not be pleased with them. Hence, Simple Data forms are preferred over Composite Data forms.

Summary

In this chapter, we started with the basic differences between data forms and Excel-based budgeting templates and realized the benefits of data forms not only in terms of easy user access but also other aspects of maintenance and data integrity.

We moved next to the basic layout of a typical data form and explored all the properties and available options available within a data form. We also learned about design considerations and recommendations before we started creating a simple data form. We successfully created our first data form and we also learned all about composite data form.

In next chapter, we'll take a step ahead by understanding how to enter data into the data forms. It will be an interesting chapter, where we will learn how planners use the system from a data entry perspective.

9
Data Entry

Appearances are not held to be a clue to the truth. But we seem to have no other.

— *Ivy Compton-Burnett*

In the previous chapter, we learned how to create data forms, we'll continue our journey with data forms, but this time we'll learn about data entry in the data forms. You must be wondering that data entry should be as simple as typing numbers in the available cells in a data form. Yes it is true, but there are few other important concepts such as Data Spread, Supporting details, and Time balance-related data entry, which we would learn in this chapter.

Let us take a look a possible conversation between a Hyperion consultant and their client.

> **Client**: *I know you guys are working very hard on the implementation. But, I am afraid to say that our users are comfortable with the existing spreadsheets for budgeting. I am not sure how they are going to adapt to this new tool.*

> **Hyperion consultant**: *We understand that this is a difficult area and that is the reason we have our Planning application well equipped with multitude of options which will help a Planner/user enter data easily.*

> **Client**: *But there seem to be so many options such as Grid Spread, Mass Allocate, and what not. How can we ensure that all of these technical things are comfortable for the end user?*

> **Hyperion consultant**: *Yes, it is one of the main concerns and we do cover all of these topics as a part of End User Training. We need to note that end user training sessions are part of any typical implementations.*

As the proverb says 'Appearances are not held to be the clue to the truth'. Yes, we admit it but to the end user, the appearance of the Data Form is their only clue for going ahead.

We will cover the following in this chapter:

- Data entry: We'll start with the basic data entry into Data forms and understand how Planning dimensions would impact the data entry.
    - Scenario: We'll see how scenario dimension would impact Data entry behaviour
    - Version: We'll see how Version dimension members can impact data entry in this section
    - Entity and currency: We'll see how the dimensions Entity and Currency dimension influence data cells for data entry operation
- Data spread: There are many data spread options in Hyperion Planning. We'll explore them in this section.
    - Time Balance.
    - Miscellaneous options.
- Grid Spread.
- Annotations and Cell level documents.
- Supporting details.

Data entry

We'll start the chapter with data entry operation. We, as a consulting team implementing Hyperion Planning, create forms so that planners/users can enter data, for example to provide their budget numbers. These data forms are prepared based on the budget templates of an organization. We will see how the same data entry behaves with her friendly Planning Standard dimensions in subsequent sections.

Dimensions and data entry

We'll see how the data cell nature changes with different dimension member selection. The dimensions that would make an impact are as follows:

- Scenario
- Version
- Entity and Currency

Scenario Dimension

Open the 'sample' data form of the 'Outsourc' Planning application, which we created in the previous chapter. Before we study the nature of data form with respect to Scenario dimension, we need to recall that we created three members (Current, Actual, and Plan) to the Scenario dimension. It's better to quickly go to dimension properties and check them.

How do we look at the member properties of the Scenario dimension?

We actually mastered this and have seen these properties many times in earlier chapters. Go to **Administration | Manage | Dimensions** and then check the members of Scenario dimension.

Now, we observe that every member of Scenario dimension has **Start Yr.**, **End Yr.**, **Start Period**, and **End Period**, as shown in the following image:

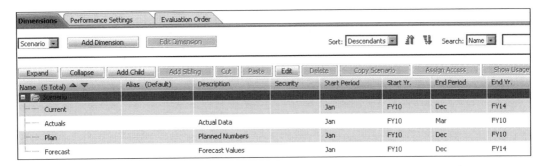

The **Start Period**, **Start Yr.**, **End Period**, and **End Yr.**, which are the properties of each and every Scenario dimension member determines the data entry in a data form.

From the previous image, we can see the **Start Period**, **Start Yr.**, **End Period**, and **End Yr.** properties and we can conclude the following

- For the Scenario dimension member Current, the data in the data form can be entered from the years FY10 to FY14 and for all the months, that is from January to December.

- For the Scenario dimension member Actual, the data in the data form can be entered only for FY10 and for the months between January and February.

- For the Scenario dimension member Plan, the data in the data form can be entered only for FY10 and for all the months; that is from from January to December.

- For the Scenario dimension member 'Forecast', the data in the data form can be entered from the years FY10 to FY14 and for all the months, that is from January to December.

The year and Period range of Scenario dimension also determines, whether or not the cell is enabled for data entry or ready-only.

There are few colors in a data form—yellow, grey, dark yellow.

What are these changing colors from light yellow, gray?

Data forms are like chameleons; they have different colors and these colors have different meanings too. Their characteristics are highlighted with the help of colors. To start with, here are a few colors:

- Light yellow: The cells with the color can be entered with data.

- Grey: These cells are read-only and not meant for data entry.

- Dark yellow: After we enter data values, the cell changes its color from light yellow to darker yellow. This is to tell us that the data has been entered but not yet saved. Saving data in a form means storing data into Essbase cube.

- Blue: The cells with blue are for supporting details, which we will see in the later part of the chapter.

- We'll now see the same in the data form, Sample of Outsourc Planning application which demonstrates similar behavior. Open the data form Sample data form and from the drop down of Scenario Dimension Page, first select Plan and observe the data form as shown in the following image:

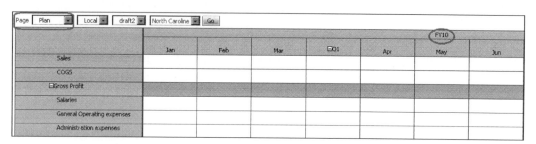

We observe that for FY10, the cells are in yellow color, signifying that the data can be entered from January to December. Now we can relate the same thing to the properties of Scenario dimension member.

Now, select **Actuals** from the drop-down menu of Scenario dimension. We know that for the **Actuals** member, the start year and end year is **FY10**, and the Start and End Periods are January and March.

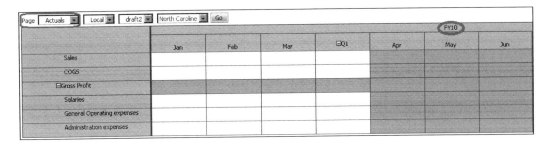

We see that for FY10, the data can be entered only from January to March and the rest of the periods are grayed, that is read-only.

To validate our understanding even more, we can see the data form for other years—FY11, FY12, and FY14. Move towards the right-hand side of the form, to see the periods of FY11 and other years such as FY12, FY13, and FY14. The cells of other periods/years should reconfirm our understanding of the Scenario dimension member's impact on the data cells.

The data form with Plan as the Scenario member for years FY11 and other years would look like the following image:

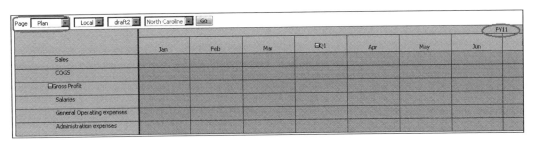

We know the reason, to repeat, FY11 year is not in the range defined in the member 'Plan' of 'Scenario dimension.

Therefore, the Scenario member property of Year and period range does impact the data entry area.

If we are told of a requirement like a planner should be allowed to enter for a limited period only and the rest should be read only. Then we know the requirement in terms of what should be the time period, which planners/users should be allowed to enter data. Based on this, we design the dimensions and data forms.

Typically, a planner would need to refer to the previous year's actual data to plan the current year budget. Let us elaborate. Let us image a firm, which had incurred general administration expenses of 1000 USD last year, FY10, which is actual. Now, when a planner is planning FY11, he keeps the actual of FY10 — 1000USD as a reference and might plan to spend 900 USD. Here, in this simple case, we should create a data form and se the properties of Scenario members (Actuals and Plan) in a manner that the planner has read-only of FY10- Actuals but should be able to enter data for FY11- Plan.

Now, we must feel like we have mastered the 'Scenario' dimension in terms of designing, given any requirement. It's a good feeling, let move ahead to other dimensions.

Version Dimension

There are two members that we had created for the Version dimension in *Chapter 7, Loading Metadata*. They are as follows:

- Draft 1 (whose type is Standard bottom up)
- Draft 2 (whose type is standard target)

Recall that with the standard target version dimension member, planners can enter data into both bottom level and parent members, whereas the standard bottom up member selection would allow data entry for only bottom level members i.e. level 0 members.

Now we'll try to validate our understanding first by selecting a parent member of a dimension in the data form.

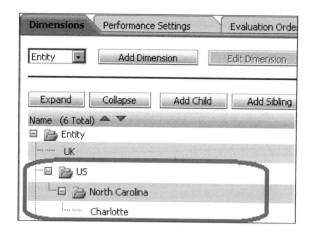

We see three cases in this section:

- Case 1: Standard Bottom up in combination with a Parent member of the Entity dimension
- Case 2: Standard Bottom up in combination with a Level 0 member of the Entity dimension
- Case 2: Standard Target in combination with a Parent member of the Entity dimension

Case 1

We have seen that **Charlotte** is a Level 0—bottom level—and North Carolina and US are Parent level members. Hence, when we select Draft 1 with the combination of North Carolina, then we should not see any data cells in the data form in yellow (to enter data).

Let us look at the form sample with draft1 with parent level member North Carolina as a combination. We will see that all the cells are read-only.

As draft1 is of standard bottom up, for which one can enter data only at the base member level (Level 0 members) and North Carolina is not a level 0 in our case. Hence, we cannot enter any data in the cells.

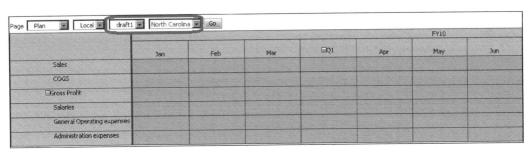

Case 2

Next, we will select the same draft1 with a bottom level member of Entity dimension **Charlotte**, as shown following image:

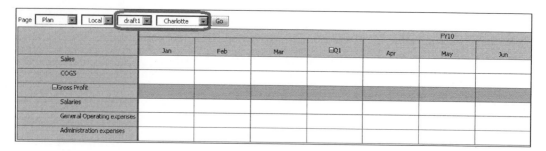

Yes, this time a planner can enter data into the cells. Draft, which is of bottom up in combination with **Charlotte** (it is a level 0 member of Entity dimension) lets users enter data.

Case 3

Now, we shall see the last case of draft2, which is of standard target. The Version dimension members in combination with both level 0 and parent members should let a user/planner enter data. Let us see with an example using the same sample data form.

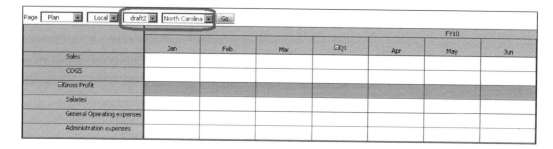

We see that all the cells are open for data entry. We also need to note that even when we select Draft 2 in combination with Charlotte, the data cells behaviour in terms of data entry remains the same.

Now, we have understood very clearly how to design Version dimension members during an implementation, knowing its impact in terms of Data entry in a data form

Entity and Currency Dimension

In all our previous chapters, we have been postponing Exchange rates and Currency Conversion topics so far. In this section, we'll learn both of the most awaited concepts.

In the process, we'll cover the following topics:

- Triangulation
- Exchange Rate table
- Currency conversion calculation
- Data entry

We understand the that budgeting of an organization which is spread across multiple nations demands users to do their budgets in different currencies, and we can easily create a multi currency Planning application for these kinds of client requirements.

For example, the base currency of Australia is the 'Australian Dollar' and the base currency for the US is the USD (US dollar), when Australian users do their budgeting, they would definitely prefer to enter the data forms in their local currency. But if we want to view the same data entered by Australian planners in USD, then there is a need for currency conversion and we will need to know the exchange rate between the USD and the Australian dollar.

Another case woudl be if, there were a US company and it has company branches in the UK, Japan, and India. In this case, budgeting data is entered by planners in UK Pounds, Japanese Yen and Indian Rupees. With the help of currency conversion, the management which is headquartered in USA would prefer to see the entire budgeting information of all countries: the UK, India and Japan in the currency of the USA.

The currency in which planners would be entering is always their Local Currency. The currency in which one would prefer to view the data in forms or reports is called the Display Currency. The display currency is also termed as the Reporting Currency.

Remember that every Planning application has a default currency, and the application which we created has its default currency set to USD. This is set when we create the Planning application.

 Data values are never entered in the Reporting Currency, they are always entered in 'Local Currency' and then with the help of exchange rates, currency conversion happens.

In the previous example of US Company, the default currency of the Planning application would be USD; Reporting currencies can be any currency in which we would prefer to view data in a form or report, which can be in INR, UK Pounds, Japanese Yen, or some other currency. We need to note that Hyperion supports all major currencies.

Triangulation

Triangulation is the concept that helps us convert one currency to the other. We set the triangulation currency and then we enter the exchange rates to convert from the local currency to triangulation currency.

For example, we have three currencies: the UK Pound, US Dollar, and INR. We set and define one of the currencies as the 'Triangulation currency' and set exchange values from every currency to the triangulation currency.

For example, if the USD is the triangulation currency, then we set exchange rates from INR to USD, and also from UK Pounds to USD. Now the conversion from INR to UK pound (or GBP) happens automatically because of the triangulation currency of USD.

Now let's do some math to demonstrate the triangulation method.

We know that:

> 1 INR = 0.0215 USD
>
> 1 GBP = 1.5476 USD

Now, we don't need to know the conversion from INR to GBP. With the help of the triangulation currency, to convert from INR to GBP, it would be 0.0215/1.5476.

> 1 INR = 0.0215 / 1.5476 GBP
>
> 1 INR = 0.01389 GBP

Now getting back to the Planning application, by default in exchange rate table, the triangulation currency is assumed as the Planning applications default currency (which is USD in our application). Else, we can set a currency as the 'Triangulation Currency' and we can set the exchange rates accordingly.

 We need to note that Planning application's default currency is the default triangulation currency and we cannot select a default currency as triangulation currency deliberately.

If you're wondering how the exchange rate table looks, we have waited long enough; let us find out in the next section.

Exchange Rate Table

We'll make use of our dear application Outsourc, it's a multi currency application and we have 3 currency dimension members USD, GBP and AUD which are for United States dollar, Great British pound, and Australian dollar. We have created all of these currency dimension members as 'Reporting Currency' in *Chapter 7, Loading Metadata*, which means that we can view data forms in all of these reporting currencies.

Now go to Account dimension and look at the properties of member Sales. Every Account dimension member property has the field **Exchange Rate Type**, as shown in the following image:

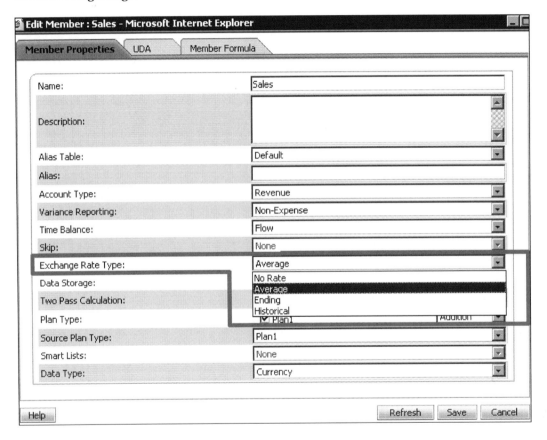

 The selection of Exchange Rate type depends on the Account type.

Here is the list that gives you information about the account type and its default exchange rate type.

Account Type	Default Exchange Rate Type
Expense	Average
Revenue	Average
Asset	Ending
Liability	Ending
Equity	Ending
Saved Assumption	No Rate

 Exchange rate types are not applicable to the account dimension members if the Planning application is a single currency application. I hope we remember this.

It's important to know these details before we start creating our first exchange rate table.

Creation of Exchange Rate table

Now let us create our first Exchange rate table. We need to know that every exchange rate table has to be associated with a Scenario Dimension member. We'll do that after we create an exchange rate table.

 Every exchange rate table ought to be associated with members of a Scenario dimension.

Go to **Administration | Manage | Exchange Rates**. As we have not created any tables so far, we see empty list as shown in the following image:

We can see the options of **Create, Edit**, and **Delete**.

Click on **Create**, which leads to a new pop-up window. Give a name and description, as shown below. Click on **Save**.

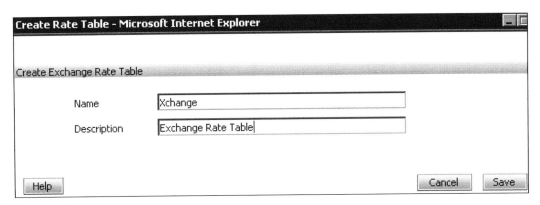

After saving, the new table gets created, as shown in the next figure, but we have not given the exchange rate information yet.

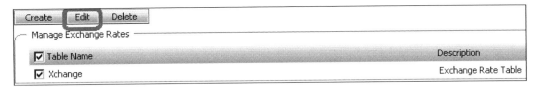

Select the **Xchange** table by checking it, and then select **Edit**. This leads to a new window as shown in the following image. It has two tabs—**Rate Table** and **Exchange Rate**.

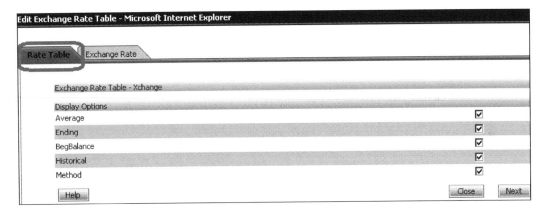

Now, if it's a feeling of déjà vu, it's good, thanks to our memory. It is because, these are the options namely, Average, Ending, and Historical, which we had seen for the 'Exchange Rate Type' for an Account dimension member. Now, we know that there are many members of Account dimension and with the different account types; we have different exchange rate types of Average, Ending, and Historical. Therefore, let all of them be checked, including Method and BegBalance and click on **Next** to go to the next tab, Exchange Rate, as shown in the following image.

It is blank as of now and we need to fill in the details:

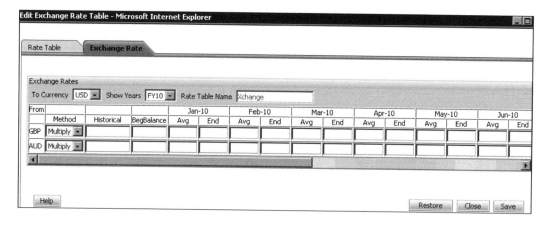

Now let us spend some time on the following image below. We need to recall that none of the Currency dimension members have been selected or nominated as 'Triangulation currency'. But, we know that by default the default currency of a Planning application is the triangulation that is USD in our case.

Hence, we see that we need to provide exchange rate values from GBP to USD and AUD to USD.

Next, we have Year selection. We selected FY10 in our case. For the method, we have two options — multiplication or division.

Now it's turn to fill exchange rate values. We know that 1 GBP = 1.64270 USD and 1 AUD = 1.07200 USD, hence we fill this information accordingly. Remember the triangulation rule and that's why there is no necessity to give any exchange rate between GBP and AUD, not that we have any option to do so.

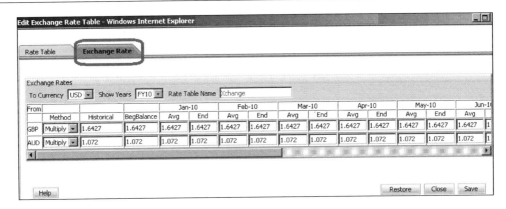

Save it after providing the information as shown and close it.

This is the end of exchange rate table creation.

Association of Scenario dimension member

In this last step, we associate the newly-created Xchange exchange rate table to Scenario dimension member of Plan. For that, go to the member properties of Plan member of Scenario dimension and select the newly created table, as shown in the next screenshot. Select **Xchange**, as shown:

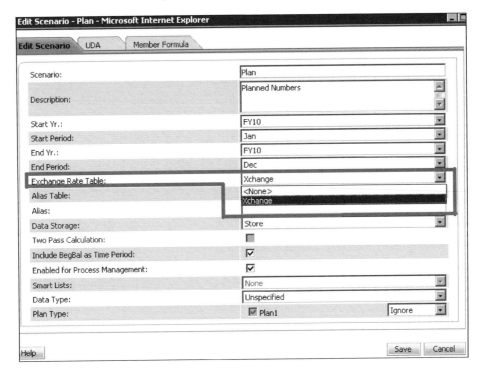

After creation of the exchange rate table or editing of the same, the database needs to be refreshed. Go to **Administration | Database**, check all of them, and refresh the database without fail.

Currency conversion calculation

We have done good job so far by providing exchange rates and creating the exchange rate table. The next task is to create calculation scripts or business rules which are responsible for exact currency conversion.

The best part is that the Planning application creates these rules by itself. Thank god!

Now got to **Administration | Manage | Currency Conversions** and provide a name and description as shown in the following screenshot:

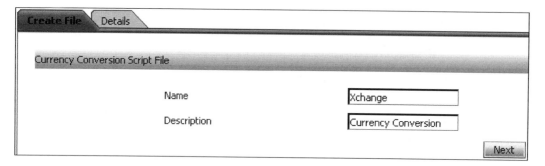

Move ahead by clicking on **Next** and select **Currency**, **Version**, and **Scenario**, members shown in the next screenshot. The currency conversion would be applicable only to these combinations. Hence, we need to be careful in this selection. This selection will create business rules which will convert the currencies.

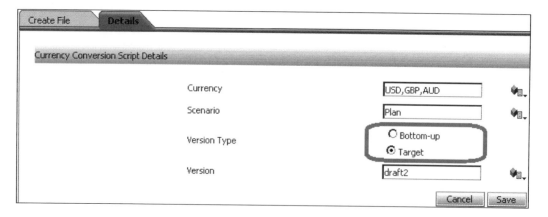

We select all three currency members (USD, GBP, and AUD). and Plan for Scenario dimension. We need to recall that the created Exchange rate table has been associated to Plan scenario member. Refer to Association of Scenario Dimension Member for the same.

We can see in the previous screenshot that we have two options of Version types and we also need to remember that Draft1 is of bottom-up type, while Draft2 member is of the Target type. Therefore, possible options of a Version dimension member would depend on the selection of version type. In our case, we will select Target type as shown in the previous screenshot. Hence, we can only select Draft2.

Upon saving it, it will show a quick message indicating that the conversion script has been created successfully.

This step successfully creates two calculation scripts or business rules by names HspCRtT and Xchange.

Why two rules? What are they supposed to do?

The first rule HspCRtT is responsible for copying the exchange rate values from table to Account dimension member, that's the reason we define every account member with exchange rate type. The next rule is the core rule, "Xchange", responsible for the actual currency conversion.

We know that business rules are not yet explored. We will do that in Chapters 15 and 16.

As we selected Version type as Target, the rule created was HspCRtT, if the version type is bottom up version, then the rule would be HspCRtB.

Business rules association with data form

We already learned that business rules are associated with data forms, but have not explored rules in much depth. Before we enter data into data forms; we will associate the newly created business rules in the above section to convert currencies.

For this, go to **Manage | Data form and Ad Hoc Grids** and edit the Sample data form. Go to the last tab of **Business Rules**, which would look like the following image:

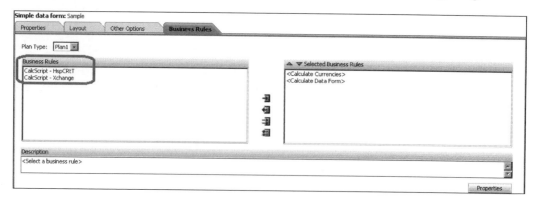

We see the newly created business rules rounded in the previous screenshot. Now, push the two scripts HspCRtT and Xchange to the right-hand side to make it as selected business rules as shown in the previous screenshot.

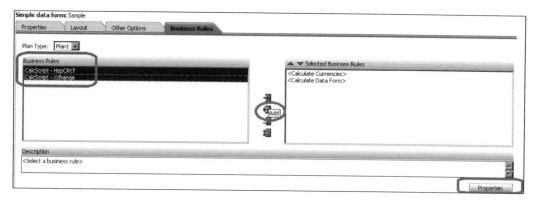

Post addition of the Business Rules, click on **Properties**, which will open a new window. Select **Run on save** as the option for the business rule execution, as shown in the next screenshot.

What does **Run on save** mean?

When data is entered into a data form, the data is not only saved but all the four business rules will be executed at the point of saving the entered data. This way, a user/planner need not explicitly run a rule, rather the Business Rules are run upon saving. Hence, it is 'Run on save'.

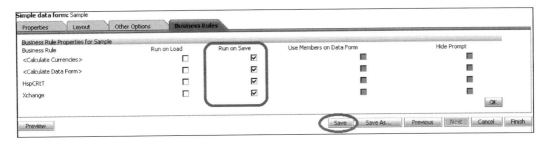

Click on **Save** and open the data form Sample.

Data entry

Currency conversion calculation was done for all currency members, 'Draft 2' member of Version which is a 'standard target' type, Scenario member of 'Plan'. This information is useful in selecting the combination of Pages in the data form as rounded in the below image. If we select any other POV or combination, of course the currency conversion would not work.

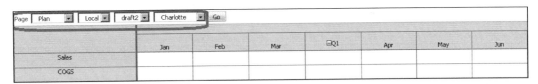

As we learned, we always enter data in local currency and the form is reflecting 'charlotte' of US entity with Scenario member Plan and draft 2 for Version dimension. We need to be careful in selecting the combination of dimensions, which needs to be the same with regard to the currency conversion scripts, which we created earlier.

Now, let us enter a value of 10 for Sales in FY10 for January month and hit *Enter* to view the cell turning darker yellow. This is to mean to us that data has been entered but not yet submitted/saved, as shown in the following image:

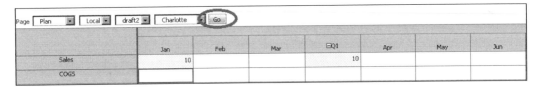

Now, we click on **Go**, or use **Save** button shown in the next screenshot to save and run the business rules, which were associated with the form Sample. Remember that Business Rules were set to run on save. It would take few moments and return with the following message.

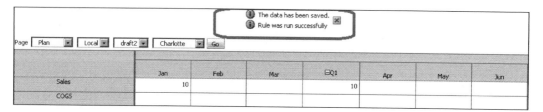

Now, let us view the form with different currencies. Our requirement is to view the same 'Charlotte' data which was entered in USD (which is it local currency) in GBP.

Hence, change the Currency member selection from 'Local' to 'GBP'; we know it's a simple drop-down. As shown in the following image, we could see the sales of January in GBP as 6.44 .Here, we'll validate the value as per our exchange rates.

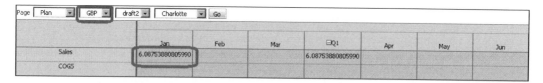

Recall the exchange rate table and the exchange rate between USD and GBP, it was to convert from GBP to USD, the value needs to be multiplied by 1.552. Quickly look at the exchange rate table to confirm the same point. Now, with that logic (mentioned in the following diagram):

We need to compute, how many GBP for 10 USD, which is 10 USD * 1 GBP / 1.64270 USD = 6.0875 GBP.

1 GBP = 1.64270 USD
(1 GBP * 10 USD)/1.64270 USD = 10 USD

1 GBP = 1.64270 USD
6.0875 GBP = 10 USD

Now, we'll check the 'charlotte' values in 'AUD'. Remember that we set to convert from AUD to USD; the value needs to be multiplied by 1.07200

Hence, 1 AUD = 10.8929 USD

Then, How many AUD's = 10 USD, Therefore the value is 10 USD * 1 AUD / 0.8929 USD = 11.1994 AUD, as shown in the following image.

Let us put it all in steps:

We see the same in the data form in the following image:

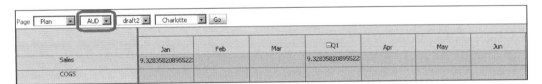

- Therefore, we are able to enter the budget numbers in local currency i.e. USD for the entity 'Charlotte' and view the same data of USD in GBP and also in AUD. Now, we can rightly say GBP and AUD are Reporting currencies, as one can view in these currencies.

- The same can be replicated with other cases, where we can try entering data for UK in local currency and then view the same data of UK in USD and AUD. It's better to practice before we move ahead with other sections.

- This is the end of most awaited section about currency conversion. Now, we should be confident to tell our clients that if their requirement involves different currencies, we have got our solution ready.

So far, we have learned about the basics of entering data into a data form and also seen the currency conversion and now we'll move ahead to the Data spread.

Data spread

In this section, we'll learn how the data within a data form spreads across different periods or entities. These options are handy to the end user/planner in terms of filling in data forms.

 Typically, we have User Training as a part of Hyperion Planning implementation to train users how to use these options.

The following concepts will be explored as a part of data spread:

- Time balance: In this section, we will explore all the option of Time Balance, which will impact the way the parent values are reflected. We'll see how data is spread depending upon the time balance property.

- Miscellaneous options: There are some important options in the Hyperion Planning application, which we'll explore in this section:
  - Grid spread
  - Annotation and Cell Level docs
  - Supporting details

Time balance

If we had observed more closely, when we entered data for Jan in a data form, automatically the value was reflected for Quarter 1. It is because, January, February, and March should sum up to Quarter 1; that's how we had designed the Period dimension with the help of the Aggregation option.

Now, let us think the other way, we should be able to enter data at levels of Quarters and Years and data should spread into the levels of months and quarters. We have not seen a setting for data spread so far, but yes, we can achieve this and we'll learn how to do that in this section.

The data spread can be categorized into two cases

- Case 1: Data form in which there is no data and needs to be entered for the first time.

- Case 2: Data form in which there is already data and we are going to re enter on the top of the existing values in a form.

In case 1, where we are entering data for the first time i.e. cells are blank, then the deciding factor is the 'Account type' of the member.

The 'time Balance' property of the Account dimension member depends on the Account type, here is the table which provides the information of Account type and its default Time balance property.

Account Type	Time Balance Property
Revenue	Flow
Expense	Flow
Asset	Balance
Liabilities	Balance
Equity	Balance
Saved Assumption	Balance

In case 2, where there is already data in the cells of data form , then the deciding factor for data spread is Time Balance. We covered this back in *Chapter 6, Settings*. If you have forgotten any of the details, it would be wise to refer back to that chapter before proceeding.

Case 1

Now, let us take a look at the data form and we'll enter data at higher period levels such as Quarters and Year total and then observe how the data values are spread.

 We need to note that typically planners/users enter planned numbers or budget figures with reference to the previous years' actual data. Hence, we usually create data forms with Actuals of Previous year and Plan of Current year.

For demonstration purposes, let us consider Sales and COGS members, which are of Revenue and Expense account type respectively and the flow is its Time balance property.

Next, we'll take 'Fixed Assets', which is an account member of 'Asset' account type and its time balance property is 'Balance'. We can take a look at these member properties to re-clarify the same.

Go to the member properties of the following dimension members.

- Sales
- COGS
- Fixed assets

For sales, the member properties are shown as shown in the following image. We see both the **Account Type** and its **Time Balance** property:

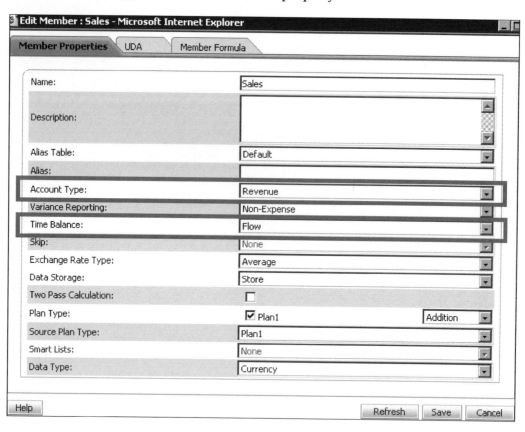

On similar grounds ,check for COGS Account dimension member, whose **Account Type** will be **Expense** and its **Time Balance** property is **Flow** again.

Now, let us finally check the **Account Type** and **Time Balance** property of **Fixed Asset** member. We can see its **Account Type** is **Asset** and **Time Balance** property is **Balance**. If its Time balance property is anything else, change it to **Balance** and refresh the database.

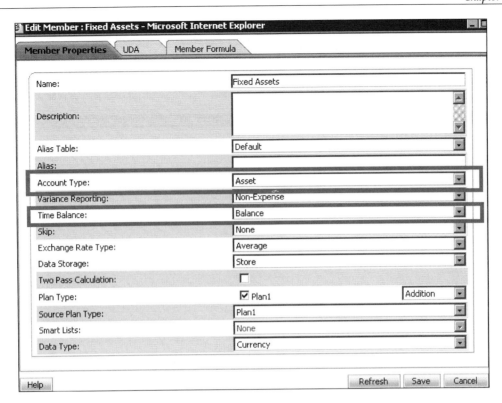

Now, we'll start filling in the cell values as shown in the following image, starting with **Sales, COGS,** and finally **Fixed Assets**. This way, we can witness the **Time Balance** property of both **Flow** (for **Sales** and **COGS**) and **Balance** (for **Fixed Assets**).

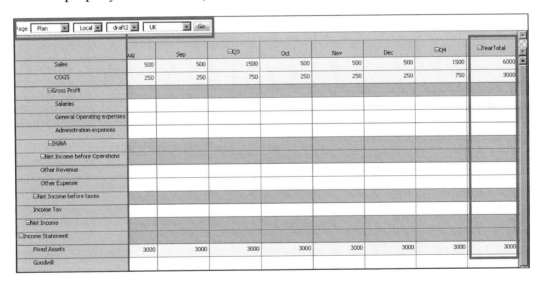

Enter data for **Year Total** as **6000** and **3000** for **Sales** and **COGS** respectively. Also enter **Fixed Assets** of **3000** again at **Year Total** as shown in the previous figure.

As we enter this data, we can see the data being spread across the quarters and months.

Now, the observation is that Account types of **Revenue** and **Expense** would distribute values proportionally.

6000 is divided into four quarters and quarter value is 6000/4 = 1500 and 1500 is again proportionally distributed to three months of a quarter i.e. 1500/3 = 500, which we see in the previous image.

Now, when it comes to the account members whose Account type is Assets, Liability, and equity, they are distributed with the same number. This is in case of fixed assets.

For fixed assets, when we enter **3000** for **Year Total**, the same values is distributed all across the quarters and periods.

Therefore, the important conclusion is Account members whose 'time balance' property is Flow and Account type is **Revenue** and **Expense**, the values are distributed proportionally, whereas members which time balance property as 'Balance' and account type as 'Asset', Liability, and equity, the same values are distributed all across the base level members.

Case 2

In this case, we already have data values for the cells in the data form and we are going to enter values at quarter or Year total level over the existing values and observe how the value would be distributed. In the previous case, it was lesser complex, as they were not any values already in the form.

Let us straight away understand the time balance properties with examples. We introduced and learned of different kinds of Time balance properties in *Chapter 6, Settings*, in this section, we'll demonstrate with a few examples.

We know that sales is an Accounts member with time balance property as Flow and Fixed assets is another member with time balance property as Balance.

We'll enter data values into cells as shown in the following image, be careful with the combination before we enter.

For sales, first enter values for months January, February, and March and as we enter 10, 15, and 20 respectively the Quarter 1 values is added to 45, as shown.

For Fixed Assets, enter the same values for January to March, but we observe that the Quarter 1 value is not the summation but the last months value, that is March value as shown, because Fixed assets is of Balance.

> Time Balance property of Balance is synonymous to Time Balance last.

After entering these values, don't forget to click on **Go** to save. Now, we have a data form where values already exist and now, we'll play around by entering data at the Quarter level and seeing how the monthly values change.

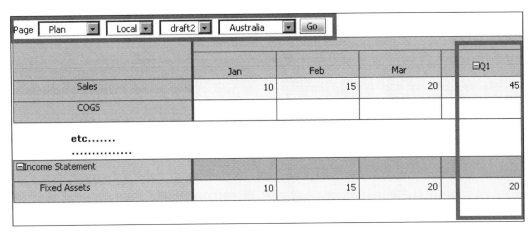

Now, after saving the form, we'll enter values at Q1 over the existing value. This time, we will enter 90 for Sales and also for Fixed assets. We can see how the data is distributed for Sales and Fixed assets as shown in the following images:

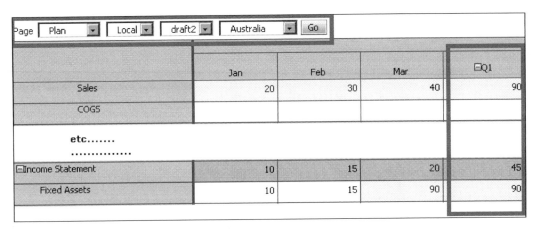

This is how the data is spread depending on the time balance property. Now, let us make a table that explains all the Time Balance properties.

Time Balance Property	Jan	Feb	March	Quarter 1
First	20	30	40	20
Balance	20	30	40	40
Flow	20	30	40	90
Average	20	30	40	30
Weighted Average_Average	20	30	40	30
Weighted Average_Actual_Actual	20	30	40	30

Now, we'll write an expression for these Time Balance properties:

- First: It's for the first month, January, hence 20

- Balance: It's also called time balance last, i.e. the last month. Hence, 40 , which is the value of March

- Flow: $20 + 30 + 40 = 90$.

- Average : $20 + 30 + 40 / 3 = 30$

- Weighted Average_Average : $(20 * 31) + (30 * 28) + (40 * 31) / 31 + 28 + 31 = 30$

- Weighted Average _Actual_Actual: $(20 * 31) + (30 * 29) + (40 * 31) / 31 + 29 + 31 = 30$

If you are still not clear on these properties, I would strictly recommend that you refer to *Chapter 6* first and read about the time balance properties and then come here to look at the examples.

Miscellaneous options

There are a few more spread options and other options in Hyperion Planning and we'll talk about them in this section.

We need to recall from the previous chapter of data forms when we were looking at the properties of a data form, we defined mass allocate, grid spread, ad-hoc analysis, account annotation, and cell level doc, but we did not spend enough time to understand. We'll explore these in this section.

Though, we have not explored but we ensured that we ticked or enabled all of these options for our sample form. We'll use the Sample form of Outsource for demonstration of these options.

Before that we will go to the properties of Sample data form to confirm if the data form has been enabled with Grid Spread, Account annotation, Mass Allocate and Cell Level Document.

Go to **Administration | Manage | Data Forms and Ad hoc Grids**.

Select Sample data form and click on **Edit** to view its properties.

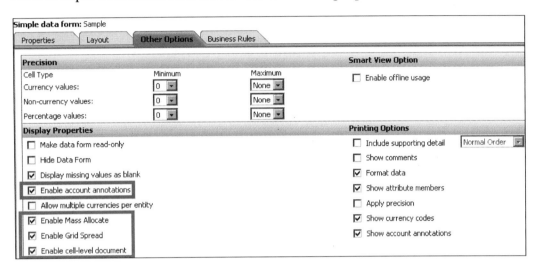

In case if any of the rounded options are not checked we need to check then and save before we jump to next section. We'll take them one by one. The first one is Grid spread.

Grid spread

When a user working on a data form wants to change the data value by increasing/decreasing by a percentage or wants to change it by an amount, then this option is handy.

 The prerequisite for Grid spread is to enable this option, when we created the data form.

We enabled this option in *Chapter 8*, when we created the Sample data form.

Now, open the data form Sample and select Sales values for Q1 (90) as shown in the following screenshot, right-click and navigate to **Adjust | Grid Spread**. We will also see mass allocate. We will explore this option in next section.

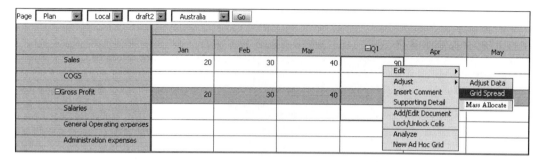

It pops up a new window of 'Grid Spread'. The cell value is 90 and we'll do two things now, we'll first adjust the value and then we'll spread the adjusted value.

1. We'll adjust the value by increasing the cell value by **45** as shown and click on **Adjust**. After clicking on **Adjust**, we can see the adjusted value of **135**.

2. We'll use **135** as the new value to be spread to the target cells of January, February, and March. There are three spread options. With the existing values of Jan = 20, Feb =30 and March = 40 in the form we'll see how the spread options would change.

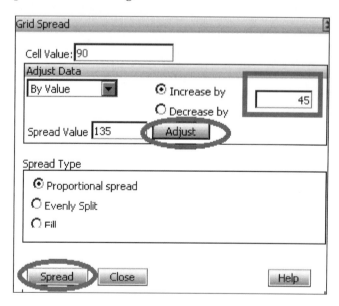

Now here is the table that shows the nature of spread type and how the values would vary with the options.

Spread Type	Description	Example
Proportional Spread	Spread proportionally as per the existing target values	Jan=20*135/90 = 30 Feb=30*135/90=45 March=40*135/90=60
Evenly Split	Spreads the values equally to the target cells	Jan=45 Feb=45 March=45
Fill	Replaces the spread values in all the target cells	Jan=135 Feb=135 March=135

We selected **Proportional Spread** as the spread type and click on **Spread**. The following image gives the new values. The new values are as per our understanding of the previous image.

Page	Plan	Local	draft2	Australia	Go
		Jan	Feb	Mar	⊟Q1
Sales		30	45	60	135
COGS					

We should explore and test all other spread types in Grid Spread before we proceed to the next section.

Mass allocate

There is another spread option that is called **Mass Allocate.** It also has the same story; this is one of the options that needs to be enabled when we create a data form. If you need a quick refresher course, take a look at the image in the *Miscellaneous options* section.

We can see this **Mass Allocate** option, as shown in the following image, when we right-click a cell in the Sample data form.

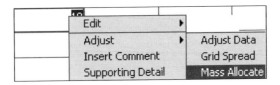

The options are similar to what we have seen in **Grid Spread**, we are not getting into details of it, it will turn into a help book rather a implementation book.

There are few differences between **Grid Spread** and **Mass Allocate**. We'll see this straightaway on the data form. Imagine a form, whose period member selection is Q1, January and February (March is not selected in the form). First, we'll use **Grid Spread** as an option and would spread value of **30** with the help of the option **Evenly Split**. We'll enter data at Q1 and spread it to January and February, as shown in the following image:

⊟Q1	Jan	Feb
30	15	15

Remember, the cells are still in dark yellow, telling us that it is not yet saved and we need to save the form to store these values.

Now let us look at the same example but with **Mass Allocate** with same **Evenly Split** option.

⊟Q1	Jan	Feb
30	10	10

We can see that it's in lighter yellow. It means that it's already saved in the form and the values are stored in Essbase. We also observe that January and February has been spread with 10 and not 15. Here is the explanation: With **Mass Allocate**, its spreads to the descendants, even though they are not a part of the data form. In our case, March is not a part of data form, but it's a descendant of Q1.

One more difference is, after we mass allocate, the data is immediately saved without giving the user a chance to look at the values in cells and saving it later.

These are the major differences between **Grid Spread** and **Mass Allocate**.

As consultants, it's easy for us to work on these options of **Grid Spread, Mass Allocate,** and others, but we should be prepared to spend hours together to explain these simple concepts to the users. Users are so much in love with Microsoft Excel that it takes time and pains to make them forget about their beloved darling Excel.

As values are saved after spread in case of **Mass Allocate**, there is no looking back or undo. Therefore, use **Mass Allocation** with caution.

Mass Allocate is very handy when we spread the data across the dimension. In typical implementations for top-down budgeting, data spread across the Entity dimension is very handy.

Finally, before we go to next section, we need to note that we can find the options **Grid Spread**, **Adjust**, and **Mass Allocate** if we go to **Edit**, as shown in the following image:

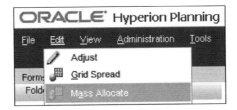

Annotations and cell level documents

In this section, we will see more options that will help an end user to enter the data into the data form.

Account annotation

As defined earlier that annotation is additional explanation or critical commentary. We can provide the same for account and we do it with the help of account annotation. This is very handy to a planner, as he gets additional information of how to enter and what to enter in the data form.

To write an annotation, open the data form and go to **View | Edit Account Annotations**, as shown in the next figure:

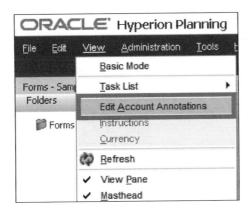

As we select, we can see that a new column emerges, right to the account members for us to type in our comments, or provide a URL to navigate. This new column, which is marked, gets created and the reader might need to scroll down to spot this new column.

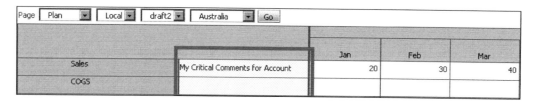

Next time, when a user/planner opens the same data form, he can view the account annotations given by previous user.

 For Account annotation, we need to design a form in which Account dimension members are always in rows.

Cell level documents

If we had enabled the option for cell level documents, we can add document at cell level. But, these documents need to be stored in the workspace and we need to give the URL of the document.

What URL can we provide to attach a file?

The files are uploaded first to the workspace and then we can pull the URL from the workspace and attach it here in a cell level document.

This might seem a little confusing, so let's work through it in steps.

1. Log in to the Workspace and go to **Navigate | Explore**, as shown in the following image:

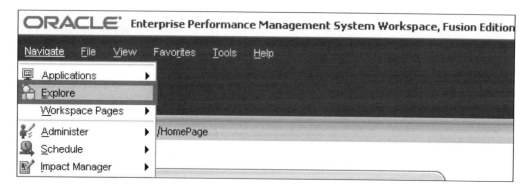

2. After we select 'explore' we see a list of files and reports. Now, we are going to import an Excel sheet from the local system in to workspace. Right-click on it to bring up the option menu. Right-click only after we select **Explore**.

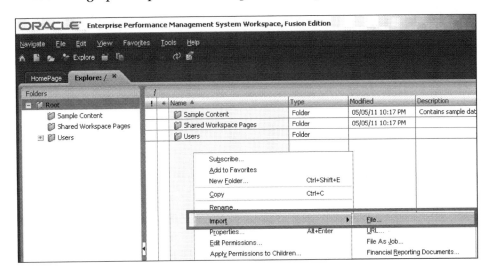

3. We'll import a file by browsing and picking the test file, called `Test.xls`. It is assumed that we had already created a file called `Text.xls`.

4. Now, right-click on the imported file `Test.xls` to get URL by selecting **E-Mail Link**. We get the URL here. Copy the URL as we are going to use it in the Planning web form.

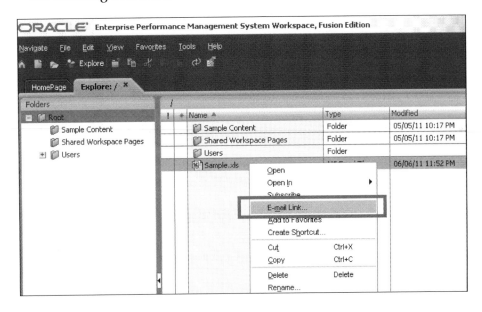

5. Now, go to the data form 'sample', where we want to add cell-level document (the document here is Test.xls, which we had already imported into workspace and have saved the URL).

6. Right-click on a cell in the data form. You will see the option to add/edit document as shown:

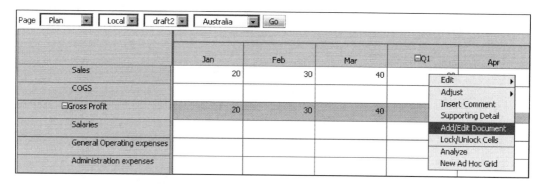

7. It pops a new windows and we need to paste the URL, which we had copied from the workspace in the space bordered and click on **Submit**.

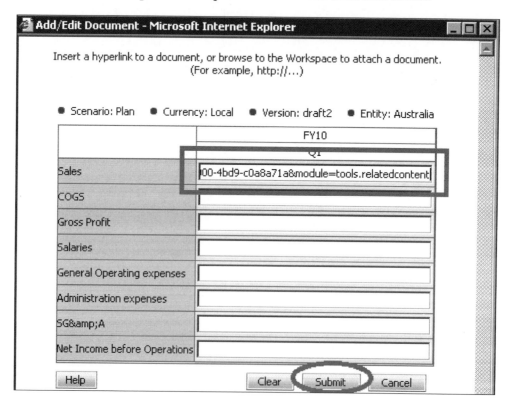

8. Now, we see that the cell (that is Sales in Q1) has a small green hat in the sample data form, this is to signify that it had cell level document. We can scroll our mouse on the cell to see the message that cell document has been attached, as shown in the following image:

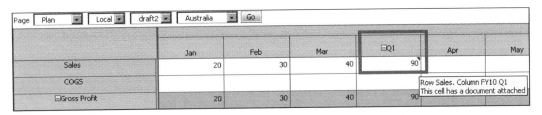

9. Any planner/user can now access the data form and open the document by right-clicking on the cell top bring up the **Open Document** option.

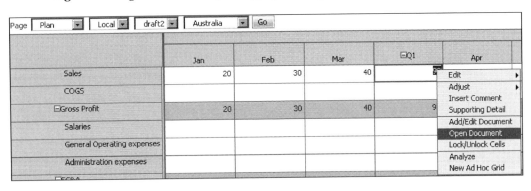

This will open the `Test.xls` document.

Supporting details

In the process of giving additional details to the users/planners, we had discussed about annotation and cell level documents. Now, as we give more and more options to the users, they will demand even more, that's how it is in reality.

But there are few features, which are truly needed to the decision makers and managers to understand numbers and make reports more transparent. Supporting details is one feature, which is aimed at that factor.

Imagine a data form in which we have provided information on the travel expenses of a team which had gone on a project to US. When the manager looks at the travel expense figure, he might get surprised with the number and would definitely like to know the break up and also more details about it. 'Supporting details' does exactly this. It is capable of breaking the expense into various sections and explain at a granular level charges such as air fare, hotel fees, transport charges, and so on.

The support detail option provides information with the items/members, which are not a part of our Planning outline. This way, supporting detail information does not disturb the metadata or outline of Planning, as they are no way related.

Now, we'll see in our Planning data form, how to create supporting details and also see its secret built-in calculator, which is the important feature of supporting details.

In our Sample data form, let us image that **Salaries** in the month of **Jan** is **100**, as shown in the following image. We need to enter the value of **100**.

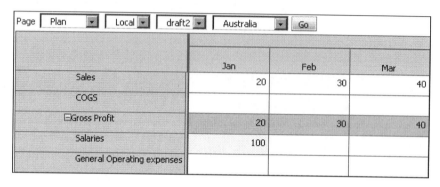

Now we know we are going to provide supporting details of this 100 for Salaries. Hence we need to create supporting details for this cell value.

As usual, all the options are available when we right-click. Hence, right-click in the cell to get the supporting details option, as shown in the following image.

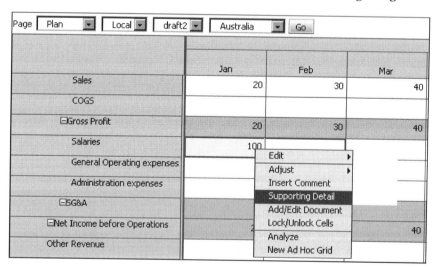

Now, we'll create supporting details for **100**, supporting with more information as to how we arrived at this figure of **100**.

There are 10 resources and the salary per resource is 10. Therefore, 10*10 =100. This simple logic is put in supporting details. Let us read from top to down.

The first line of Resources is just a label and then we have the number of resources, where we need to enter **10**. Next, one more label **Salary** and it has a child **resource** called **salary.** Finally, we need to multiply these two elements and this is done at parent levels, that is, resources * salary. Therefore, we see multiplication as the sign against salary.

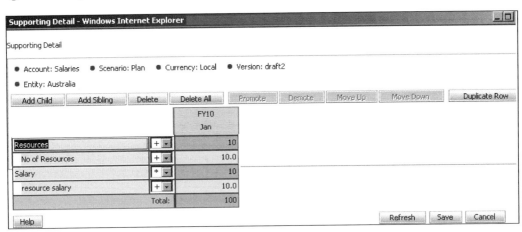

As we save this, we can see the cell color turning into blue.

Page Plan ▼ Local ▼ draft2 ▼ Australia ▼ Go	Jan	Feb	Mar
Sales	20	30	40
COGS			
⊟Gross Profit	20	30	40
Salaries	100		
General Operating expenses			

Now, we know, when the cell is of this color, users should be informed that it has supporting details to look into.

Another example of supporting details

We'll understand more of supporting details with the same old example of expense. Let us be clear of the situation. Say, there is a team of five developers from the US, who went out station for a project for 10 days. We have a data form that gives the travel expense amount of 10100 USD. The manager already might have frowned after looking at this number. Now, we'll make him comfortable, if not happy, by providing supporting details.

As shown in the following image, it starts with air fares, as there are five resources and their ticket count including return tickets would be 10. We provide rate per ticket as well.

Next is the hotel stay. Five people will need five rooms. The best part is that they get a corporate discount, which can make the manager happy. Hence, this discount amount needs to be subtracted and we did that. The last item is the local transport. We know that our resources are very accommodating and could manage our five resources in just three cabs, as shown in the following image.

Therefore, we were able to break the expense amount of 10100 USD.

Air Fares	+ ▾	5000
No of tickets	+ ▾	10
Rate per ticket	* ▾	500
Hotel Stay	+ ▾	5000
No of days	+ ▾	10
Daily hotel rate	* ▾	100
No of Rooms	* ▾	5
Hotel corporate discount	- ▾	500
Local Transport	+ ▾	600
No of days	+ ▾	10
Transport rate per day	* ▾	20
No of cabs taken per day	* ▾	3
	Total:	10100

It starts with **Air Fares**, whose expense is 5000 (as there are 10 tickets and rate per ticket is 500).

Next is the **Hotel Stay**, which is 5000, as the number of days the team stays is 10 and daily hotel rate is 100. And finally, the number of rooms taken are five, then 10*100*5= 5000.

The good news is that we have a corporate discount, which is 500. Hence, that's subtracted.

The last expense item is Local Transport, which includes **No of days**, **Transport rate per day**, and **No of cabs taken per day**.

Finally, the total expense is 10100 USD.

Summary

In this chapter, we have successfully understood the whole process of data entry. We started the chapter understanding the influence of the standard dimensions of Hyperion Planning application on Data entry into the Data cells of a Data form. Next, we have learned the currency conversion techniques within the Hyperion Planning application. As a part of currency conversion, we have created an exchange rate table and also had seen how the conversion rules are created and run in a data form.

We have also seen multitude data spread options and other options such as Mass Allocate, Cell Level Document, and Annotations.

Conclusively, it's important to make sure that users understand these options and also make them comfortable with using these options. That's what matters at the end.

In the next chapter, we will learn about 'Data Validation Rules'. It's a new feature of the Hyperion Planning 11.X version.

10
Data Validation Rules

Contradictions do not exist. Whenever you think you are facing a contradiction, check your premises. You will find that one of them is wrong.

— Ayn Rand

In the previous chapter, we have learned data forms creation and entering data with the help of different techniques available within Hyperion Planning application. Now, we'll come out of the small world of data forms and talk big of organizational policies and practices. Wondering, what we are talking, yes; we are going to talk of a new feature, which is in 11.1.2 of Hyperion Planning, which is 'Data Validation Rules'.

Let us take a look at the conversation between Oracle Sales guy and a prospective customer of Hyperion Planning.

Oracle Sales: *We have many features and functionality in new Hyperion Planning and Budgeting product.*

Customer: *I have heard and was part of the demo already. But we have a challenge and I would like to ask if that can be addressed with this Hyperion Planning product.*

Oracle Sales: *Please go ahead sir.*

Customer: *I want to have a functionality which can align according to my company policy. For example, we had spend 1000 USD last year in the month of Jan on General expenses on a department A, we would like to notice it in the web form if this year's expenses exceed more than last years. This way, we should be able to monitor our expenditure as well.*

Oracle Sales: *Yes, the new feature of 'Validation Rules', which is available from 11.1.2 Planning product, does exactly the same.*

We know that understanding the business requirement is more important than knowing an individual feature or option or even a new property in any tool/ product. Now, let us try to understand how important policies of a company can be incorporated in a planning application and how can we implement the same using data validation rules.

The following topics are covered in this chapter of data validation:

- **Why validation rules**: In this section, we'll introduce the concept of validation rules and we'll try to connect these rules with a typical organizations policy.

- **Validation Rule creation**: We'll understand the rule creation process in this section.

- **Condition values**: There are many conditions, which needs to be understood while we create rules and we'll explore this in this section.

- **Policies and validation rules**: Conclusively, we'll talk of how effective the validation rules were able to help organizations adhere to their policies with the help of two organization policies

Why validation rules

A policy is a course of action to determine decisions. That's the definition of a policy. Let us understand this definition with an example. An organization, that was affected by recession in the year 2009 decided not to spend too much this year. Hence, this organization decides not to budget anything which is not more than 10 % of last year's actual amount (we know the difference between actual and budget, let us take an example , we budget/plan 5000 to spend this month , but at the end of the month, we realize that actually we had spent 6000. Here, 5000 is budgeted and 6000 is actual). Here, in the given example, not to spend more than 10% of previous year's actual amount is the organization's policy, that is, if the organization had spend 100 USD then the new policy should not let to spend more than 100 + 10 = 110 USD.

 Validation rules can incorporate both policies and practices of organizations in planning system.

A 'practice' can be as simple as our next example- we need to highlight the 'travel expense' amount in red , if the amount exceeds 100 $ for any department is a practice of an organization. This way, when a planner looking at a data form ,which has department information, would see few data cells in red , whose department's travel expense has exceeded 100$.

Hence, when an organization has taken a decision to highlight the departments exceeding an amount of 100 $ for every department's travel expense, whenever this kind of exceptional spending happens, we are helping management know easily and effectively with the help of validation rules.

In any organization, there is a definite hierarchy and there is always a boss over the other. Bosses have to approve of the budgets set by their subordinates. Now, any organization decision of their policies has to be upheld very strictly by these bosses or managers and they have to disapprove of the budgets if their respective departments or division does not adhere to the guidelines or policies of the organizations.

Now, with the help of validation rules, we can even set a mechanism not to promote the budgets to the manager for their approval in case of violation. For example, we can use our validation rules not to promote a department budget to the manager in case the expense exceeds beyond 1000 USD. It's possible. Anyways, we'll learn more of the approval cycles and its process in detail in *Chapter 11* and *Chapter 12*.

In cases of violation, we, with the best of our abilities, can highlight it to the management by coloring our forms in red or by generating validation messages. We can also not allow planners from submitting their budgets if in case of any violation as we just understood. Now with this basic introduction, we'll start creating validation rules and also see how to set conditions within validation rules in next section.

Implementing validation rules

In a validation rule, we need to set few conditions and upon failing to meet these conditions, an action has to be taken. Here, action would be as simple as coloring cells in a red color or providing validation message or even not letting that department from promoting its budget to the next level.

Now, as we understand that we need to define conditions. The basic question would be:

Where do we set these conditions?

Yes, it's the very basic question and the answer is, we do create validation rules within data forms and set conditions in the 'validation rule' of data form.

Now, without talking any more let us go to data form and understand directly from the application.

Go to our old friend 'Sample' data form from the 'Outsource' Planning application. Hold on; don't open the Data form, First we shall look at the option of creating the 'validation rule'. Hence, we need to go to the properties of the data form.

How do we go to the Data Form Properties?

1. Go to **Administration | Manage | Data forms and Ad hoc grids**.

2. We see the folders and data forms, which were created before. Now select any data form, for example, **Sample** as shown in the following screenshot and select **Edit**.

3. It leads to a new window of its properties. We can see a tab **Layout**; this is where we would be dealing with **Validation Rules**, while we create validation rules, we'll embed conditions inside it. Let us now create new data form and say bye to **Sample** for now.

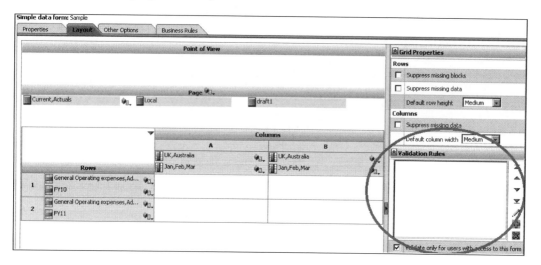

Creation of Data Form

Let us create a new data form and name is Valid.

As we see in further, we have selected all planning dimension for rows, columns and in pages. There are no dimension members left to be selected for **POV** (**Point of View**).

Now, let us start selecting the dimension members starting with "Scenario".

- For the **Scenario** dimension, select **Actuals** and **Current**
- For the **Version** dimension, we have selected **Draft1**
- For the **Currency** dimension, select **Local**

We need to be careful with rows and columns. First rows, we selected two dimensions – **Account** and **Year**. When we are selecting the **Year** dimension, we select two years: **FY10** and **FY11**, but we would prefer to have them in two rows. To achieve this in two rows, we need to tick a separator as shown in the following screenshot and highlighted in red.

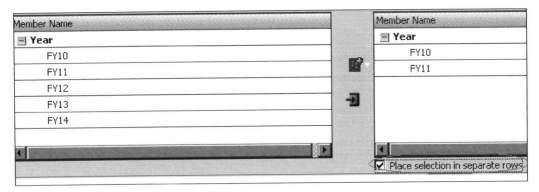

- For the **Account** dimension, select **General Operating expenses** and **Administrative expenses**.

Now, moving to our columns, we have two dimensions - **Entity** and **Period**. As we had ticked **Place selection in separate rows** for Year dimension, we would employ the same with **Entity** dimension selection. We would have **UK** and **Australia** as the selected members but this selection is in separate columns. For the **Period** dimension, we would select **Jan, Feb,** and **Mar**.

- For the **Entity** dimension, select **UK** and **Australia**.
- For the **Year** dimension, select **FY10** and **FY11**.
- For the **Period** dimension, select **Jan, Feb**, and **Mar**

At the end, if we had selected as we wanted to, our Layout should look like this with A and B as two columns and **1** and **2** as two rows.

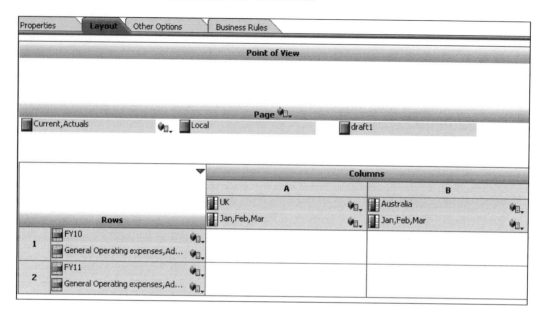

Now save the Valid Data form and open it. It should be as shown in the next screenshot. Correlate the layout and the data form shown in the next screenshot. We have A1, A2, B1, and B2. A1 is in red, A2 is in blue, B1 is in yellow and B2 is in green in the next screenshot.

A1 comprises of all combinations of data cells of **General Operating Expenses** in the Year 2010 in UK for the months of **Jan**, **Feb**, and **Mar**. It also includes **Administrative expenses** in the Year 2010 in UK for the months of **Jan**, **Feb**, and **Mar**. Likewise, we have other regions like A2, B1, and B2, which can be understood.

Therefore, we have two columns and two rows as per the layout of our form.

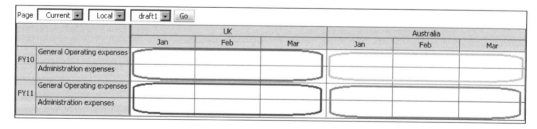

The understanding of these A1, A2, B1, and B2 is extremely important as we are going to explain validation rules with the help of these reference regions in the subsequent sections. Next, we'll create our first validation rule and learn about condition values after that.

Validation rule creation

Now, we need to juggle between opening data form and **Layout** properties of the data form. As we make changes in the **Layout** properties or **Validation Rules** of the 'Valid' data form, we save it and then view the data form to check the rule impact. Be ready for lot of clicking business.

To create a validation rule, go to the **Layout** tab of data form properties of **Valid**, as shown in the following screenshot:

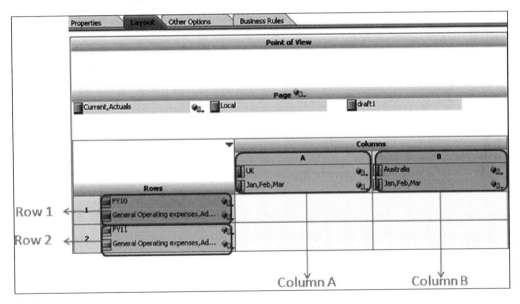

We are going to spend all our time in the **Layout** tab of data form properties to create our validation rules right-click on **Page** or **POV**. We shall get the following screenshot:

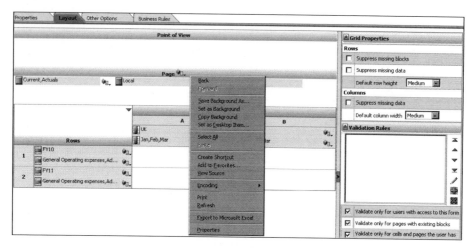

We don't see any 'validation rule' option in the preceding screenshot.

 Validation rules cannot be created for POV and Pages. They can only be created for rows or columns. They can also be created by right-clicking on the grid or on a particular cell.

Hence, when we right click on POV and Page as shown in the following screenshot, we don't get the option of **Validation rules**.

Now, right-click on Row-1 and select **Add/Edit Validation rules** as shown in the following screenshot. If we are still not very clear with Row-1, Row-2, Column A, and Column B, just go few pages back to refresh your memory.

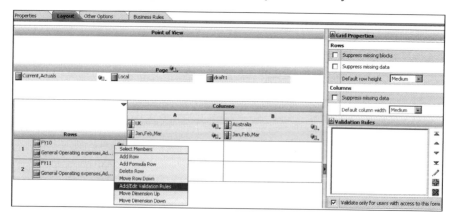

It opens a new window telling us that there are no validation rules at this level, as shown in the next screenshot. Select **Add Rule**.

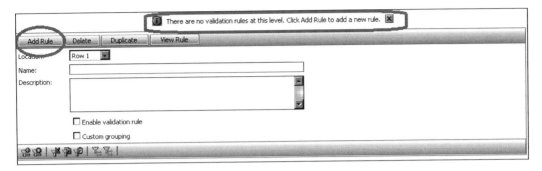

Click on **Add Rule** as the very first thing. This will lead to the following window where a default **IF** condition is present.

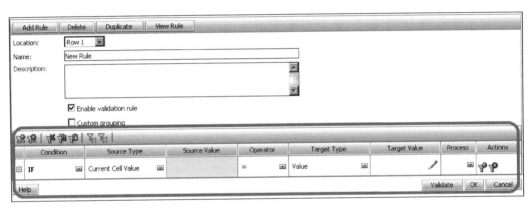

1. **Location**: This is the location in data form where we would want the validation message or data cell color to be shown as an indicative of a violation or when the set condition is met. It is **Row 1**, as we have right-clicked on **Row 1** to select **Validation Rule**. It is automatically populated based on where we right-clicked.

2. **Name** and **Description**: Give the name and description as shown in the screenshot.

3. **Enable validation rule**: If this check box is ticked, the created validation rules will be active. Generally, we create validation rules to check if the rule is a valid one and enable it only when we want it to be active. This is quite a handy option. In our case, enable it right now.

4. **Custom grouping**: This option is to group the condition which we are going to set.

Now, the below part of the validation rule is the place, where we are going to set conditions. Here, our first and simple requirement in the form of policy is to show the data cells in red when the **General Operating expense** or **Administrative expense** exceeds more than 50 for any location (for example, UK or Australia of our entity dimension) for FY10. Now, let us reframe the same requirement in an If-Then statement.

If the data cell values are more than 50, then we need to paint the cell in red. Yes, this is simple, but we need to tell Hyperion Planning the same, and it does not understand simple English in the way we do.

Let us get back to our validation rule creation.

1. **Condition**: This is what we start with. It's a drop-down list and we can see other options under condition, which are: **IF, else if, else, then, range**, and **check range**. We'll learn about the other conditions in the next section, but for now select **IF**. We always start with **IF**.

2. **Source Type**: A rule is always tested or evaluated. Hence, we select source type as the place or location in data form, where a rule needs to be evaluated. **Source Type** and **Source Value** in collaboration are used to specify the cells, columns, or rows whose values needs to be to be validated or in other words against whose values the condition needs to be evaluated. There is quite a long list of source types; we'll try to learn as much as possible without making this chapter a feel of a Help file. For now, select **Current Cell Value**,

3. **Source Value**: Based on the source type selection, we would get options for **Source Value**. If we had selected **Source Type** as **Column value** for example, we would have got source values options as **A** and **B**, as columns are divided into **A** and **B**. Hope we have not forgotten that already. We don't have to select a source value as **Source Type** selected by us was **Current Cell Value**.

4. **Operator**: This option should be self explanatory. Select **>** to see the list of all available operators as shown in the following screenshot:

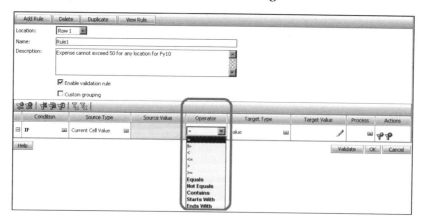

5. **Target Type**: Now, let us recall our requirement. If **General Operating expense** or **Administrative expenses** exceed **50** for **FY10**, we need to highlight the field in red. Hence, we know that if the target value is more than 50, then it's a violation. As we know that the source value should not exceed 50 it means that we have to compare the source value with an absolute value rather than with another column, row, or cell. Therefore we will select **Value** as the **Target Type**. There are other options like cell value, column value, row value, and cross-dim member. As per our requirements, if we want to set condition that it should not exceed a particular cell value or row value, and then we would have opted for other options. But, in our case, it's a known and specific 'value'.

6. **Target Value**: This depends on the selection of **Target Type**. If we had selected cell value, we would have got options of **A1**, **A2**, **B1**, and **B2**. If we had selected **Target Type** as column value, we would have got options of **A** and **B**. As we selected **Value** as the **Target Type**, we will have to provide an absolute value over here, against which the source value will be compared. In our case, the target value will be **50**.

7. **Process**: If we have more conditions to be written in our validation rule, we can add them by selecting either AND or OR under process and continue. But, in our case, we have only one simple condition. Hence, leave it with no selection as shown.

8. **Actions**: We have two options – 'add' a condition or 'delete' a condition. Let us recall our 'IF – THEN' statement. That is, if the data cell values are more than 50, then we need to paint the cell red. Of that statement, we are able to complete only first half of it. We have to complete the second half of what has to be done, when the condition of 'IF' is met. Hence, we select 'add a condition' which is 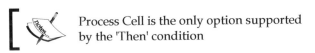. After we select it, we get a second row.

In the second row, as we see in the screenshot, we select **THEN** as the condition and as we select **THEN**, we see the **Process Cell** automatically selected. It means to say that if the condition is met then process the data cells.

> Process Cell is the only option supported by the 'Then' condition

Now, we are left with the last step of how the cell should be processed if the value of **General Operating expense** or **Administrative expense** is more than 50. For that, select 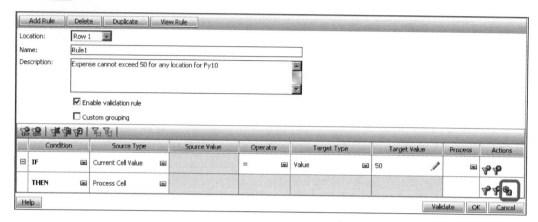 in the **Actions** column as highlighted in the screenshot

When we select the **Process cell** icon, it opens another window, where we select the background color as red and also give a validate message that says that the **General Operating expense** and **Administrative expense** should not exceed 50 for FY10. Users/Planners who view the data form will get to see the validate message when the entered value exceeds 50. This way, we can show a cell in red and also provide some information as to why it is a violation by showing a message.

There are few other options for process management, which we'll learn in *Chapter 11*. Leave it to **None** as shown in the screenshot.

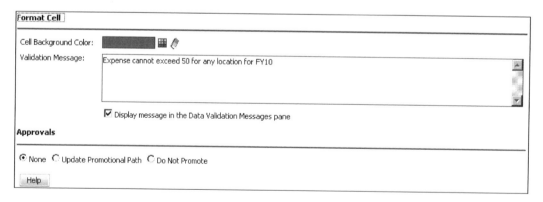

Now 'Validate' the validation rule by selecting the **Validate** option as shown in the screenshot. We should ideally get the message "**Rule has no errors**". Save the form, it's important.

Validate rule testing

Now after all the hard work of creating 'Validation rule', let us open the data form **Valid** and check if the validation rules is actually effective and working. Open and view the data form **Valid** and enter the data as shown in the screenshot:

Page Current Local draft1 Go		UK			Australia		
		Jan	Feb	Mar	Jan	Feb	Mar
FY10	General Operating expenses	70	50	100	6	80	
	Administrative expenses	45	60	40	55		
FY11	General Operating expenses	60					
	Administrative expenses						

Now, the values are not yet saved. Click on **Go** to save the entered data and we will see validation rules getting into action and highlight the data cells whose values are more than 50 as we had wanted. Now, as we pay closer attention to other data cells that is **General Operating expenses** in FY11 in Jan is 60, but it's not highlighted in red. The reason is the location, which we had selected while creating the validation rule as **Row 1** and Row 1 is highlighted in yellow in the next screenshot, it does not include FY11 at all.

> The source type is like the area which is meant for testing a condition, whereas Location is the area which is actually colored or reflected with validation messages. Source type also has an impact on the validation colors. As it can be seen in the screenshot, color is set to red only for those cells for which the condition is met rather than the entire row because the Source Type was set equal to Current Cell Value.

Page Current Local draft1 Go		UK			Australia			Data Validation Messages
		Jan	Feb	Mar	Jan	Feb	Mar	
FY10	General Operating expenses	70	50	100	6	60		Expense cannot exceed 50 for any location for FY10 [5]: 1, 2, 3, 4, 5
	Administrative expenses	45	60	40	55			
FY11	General Operating expenses	60						
	Administrative expenses							

OK, this is a good job. But we'll delete all the data cells from the data form **Valid** now, as we are going to use the same form for understanding of other concepts as well. Therefore, wipe it off clean by selecting individual data cell and keep clicking **Delete** and then finally click on **Go**.

While we were creating validation rules, we came across conditions; we are going to explore that part of validation rules in more detail in the next section.

Validation rules and conditions

Broadly, there are three different types of statements used while creating a condition. They are:

1. **If, Else, Else if**
2. **Then**
3. **Check Range** and **Range**

If, Else, Else if

All conditions must start with an IF statement and must also include the THEN statement. When we select **IF** as the condition, the immediate responsibility is to select **Source Type**. The possible values are:

1. Current Cell Value
2. Cell Value
3. Column Value
4. Row Value
5. Cross Dim Member
6. Member Name
7. Member
8. Account Type
9. Version Type
10. Variance Reporting Type
11. UDA
12. Attribute

Now, we need to understand when to use which option; whether to use 'Currency Cell Value' or 'Cell Value'. This understanding is the key for us to create any further validation rules. We'll create a validation rule with these options and quickly check in our forms, what impact those options will have. Let us start with Current Cell Value.

Current Cell Value

We created our very first 'Validation Rules' using this option of 'Current Cell Value'. We need to pay close attention to the basics when we are talking about these options. 'Location' and 'Source type'. With 'Current Cell Value', every individual cell in the scope of the selected location is checked against the condition and the color will change to red if the condition specified in the THEN condition is med, as we saw in the earlier example. We need not bother much with this, we can straight away move on to the next option, 'Cell Value'.

Cell Value

Go to the edit properties and **Lay out** tab of **Valid** data form and right-click on **Row 1** and select **Add/Edit validation rule**. We are going to edit the previously created rule, that is, **Rule 1**.

Now, we are going to talk of three different cases.

Case 1

As of now **Location** is **Row 1** and we are going to change the validation rule a little. We change **Source Type** to **Cell Value** and **Source Value** is selected as **A, 1**. The rest of the rule is the same as shown in the following screenshot:

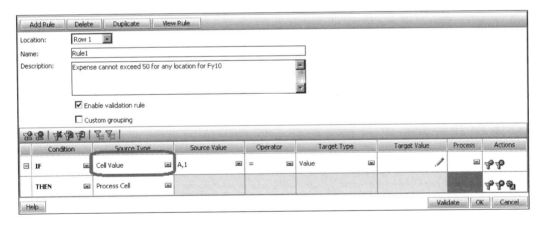

Save it and let us look at the data form.

Here, **Source Value** is **A, 1** and **Location** is **Row 1**. We enter numbers as shown. The area rounded in blue is **Source Value**, that is, **A, 1** and rounded in red is location **Row 1**.

Page	Current	Local	draft1	Go			
			UK			Australia	
		Jan	Feb	Mar	Jan	Feb	Mar
FY10	General Operating expenses	10	10	10			
	Administrative expenses	5	5	5			
FY11	General Operating expenses						
	Administrative expenses						

As we save the values, we could see that the whole Row 1 is painted in red as shown in the previous screenshot because the condition checked in **A, 1** is met.

How is the Cell value condition checked?

The cell value condition is different from 'Current Cell Value'. Here, the cell value, that is, **A, 1** is checked with its summated values; that is, the sum of values of all data cells which come in A, 1 and checked if that total value is more than 50. Hence, we see 10 + 10 + 10 + 5 + 5 + 5 = 55 and if the condition is met, we should see some red color.

Upon saving the form, we could see the complete Row 1 in red. Of course, the whole Row 1 would be in red as the condition is met and the location mentioned in the rule is 'Row 1'. Hence, the complete Row 1 is highlighted.

Page	Current	Local	draft1	Go			
			UK			Australia	
		Jan	Feb	Mar	Jan	Feb	Mar
FY10	General Operating expenses	10	10	10			
	Administrative expenses	5	5	5			
FY11	General Operating expenses						
	Administrative expenses						

Case 2

Let us spend a little more time and explore more of it. Now, delete all of the data cells in the data form 'Valid', save it, and bring back in the clean slate status. Now, we'll enter data for **Australia** entity member for the month of **Jan**, **Feb**, and **Mar** as shown in the following screenshot:

Page	Current ▼	Local ▼	draft1 ▼	Go						
			UK				Australia			
			Jan	Feb	Mar		Jan	Feb	Mar	
FY10	General Operating expenses						50	50	50	
	Administrative expenses						50	50	50	
FY11	General Operating expenses									
	Administrative expenses									

Click on **Go**. This time, we see no red colored cell. It's all because the selected **Source Value** was **A, 1** in our rule. But, we see the cell value of B, 1 as **300** (50 + 50 + 50 + 50 + 50 + 50), which is irrelevant to our rule.

Therefore, the source type and source value play an important role in what needs to be checked against the condition to display a different color in the given 'location' of the validation rule.

Case 3

In the last case for **Cell Value**, we will change validation rule a little bit as shown in the following screenshot. We'll change the **Location** this time. We'll change it from **Row 1** to **Cell B, 2** as shown in the following screenshot:

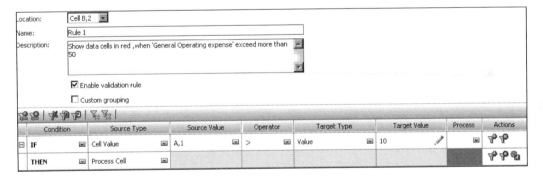

Validate it and save the data form. Now open the **Valid** data form and enter numbers for **Jan, Feb**, and **Mar** for **UK**. The cell value is 10 + 20 + 10 + 10 + 10 + 10 = 70 as shown in the next screenshot. As the location mentioned in the rule is 'B, 2', we see B, 2 getting colored in 'red'.

Page	Current ▾	Local ▾	draft1 ▾	Go				
			UK			Australia		
		Jan	Feb	Mar	Jan	Feb	Mar
FY10	General Operating expenses	10	20	10			
	Administrative expenses	10	10	10			
FY11	General Operating expenses						
	Administrative expenses						

After these three cases, we should be very clear with Source Type and Location. By now, we are clear about what changes would cause which area in the data forms to change color.

With that clear understanding, let us march on to other options.

Column value

Now, we'll again change the validation rule. But this time we would find it difficult to locate the rule to edit on the **Lay out** tab of data form properties. All through so far, the validation rule was with location 'Row 1'. Hence, when we right-click Row 1 and go to **edit validation rule**, we were able to open our validation rule. But this time as the location is 'B, 2' its hiding somewhere else.

As we see in the following screenshot, B, 2 is shaded in green, as shown in the following screenshot and we can see a message highlighting the validation presence if we hover the mouse over it. These four boxes literally mean A1, A2, B1, and B2, which are rounded in red, as shown in the next screenshot. Therefore, when we create validation rules with locations set to any of these cells, we need to go to those cell locations to edit the rules.

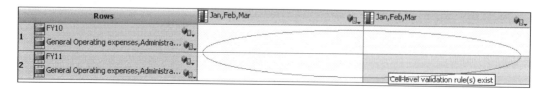

We'll start by exploring the **Column Value** starting with a few different cases.

Case 1

We'll change the validation rule and make it with **Location Row 1** and **Source Value** as **B** and **Source Type** is **Column Value** as shown in the following screenshot:

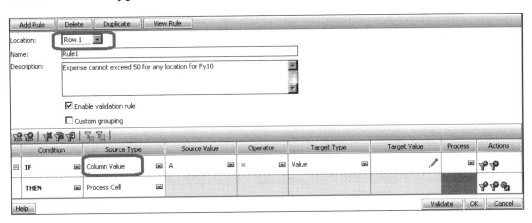

Now, look at the data form and enter the data as shown. The area rounded in red is the **Location**, that is, **Row 1**. The area rounded in blue is column A and the area rounded in pink is column B, which is colored. Now, we entered data as shown in the screenshot; **20**, **30**, and **10**.

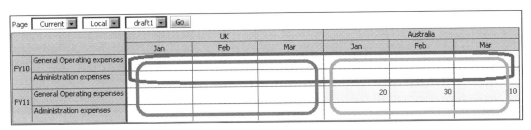

When **Column Value** is selected as the **Source Type** and **Location** is set equal to a **Row**, all the cells in the current row are being evaluated and the selected columns are added for getting to the Source Value.

As the **Location** was set equal to **Row 1** the condition will be evaluated for both the General Operating expenses and the Administrative expenses sub-rows in Row 1 and in both cases the condition will evaluate to false because there are no numbers in column B for these rows.

The Current row is actually the row of the current cell being evaluated as part of the specified Location scope.

		UK			Australia		
		Jan	Feb	Mar	Jan	Feb	Mar
FY10	General Operating expenses						
	Administrative expenses						
FY11	General Operating expenses				30	20	10
	Administrative expenses						

We see no impact of the validation rule. The reason behind this is though 30+20+10, that is, 60 is the column value but the area of interest is Row 1, which was highlighted in red earlier. As this column value is out of our area of interest or interest of validation rule, the rule has no impact.

Now, let us do a little tweaking. Enter the data for **FY10** for **Australia** for **Jan**, **Feb**, and **Mar** as **30**, **20**, and **10** respectively as shown and save it to get the below image. It's in red from UK –Jan to `Australia_Mar` as Row 1 is the set location in the validation rule.

Page	Current ▾	Local ▾	draft1 ▾	Go			
		UK			Australia		
		Jan	Feb	Mar	Jan	Feb	Mar
FY10	General Operating expenses				30	20	10
	Administrative expenses						
FY11	General Operating expenses				30	20	10
	Administrative expenses						

Now, let us extend our case 1 even further. Enter data for Administrative expense for FY10 as shown, by entering data for **FY10** for **UK** as **10, 20**, and **30**. The validation rule does not impact any value, as the data cells entered are for column A and our source value is Column B.

Page	Current ▾	Local ▾	draft1 ▾	Go			
		UK			Australia		
		Jan	Feb	Mar	Jan	Feb	Mar
FY10	General Operating expenses				30	20	10
	Administrative expenses	10	20	30			
FY11	General Operating expenses				30	20	10
	Administrative expenses						

But the very same value entered for Australia would impact the whole row as shown in the screenshot. The entered values are circled in the following screenshot. This time the validation rows show their presence because the entered values are for Column B.

Page	Current ▼	Local ▼	draft1 ▼	Go					
			UK			Australia			
		Jan	Feb	Mar	Jan	Feb	Mar		
FY10	General Operating expenses				30	20	10		
	Administrative expenses	10	20	30	10	20	30		
FY11	General Operating expenses				30	20	10		
	Administrative expenses								

Case 2

Too many cases and conditions are boring now. That's fine; we'll do little more and then be confident that we know it all. In case 2 of column values, we'll change the rule a little bit.

Now we know where to right-click to edit the validation rule. The previous rule was on the location Row 1. Hence, we right-click 'Row1' in layout properties and edit the validation rule.

We'll change the location from **Row 1** to **Column A** and the rest of the rule is the same. Before we start entering the data cell values, we'll clean the slate by deleting the cell values and save.

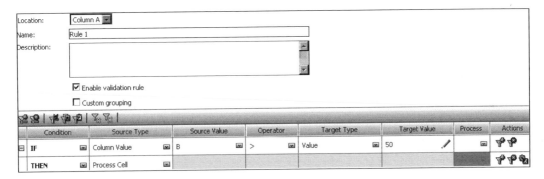

Now open the form and enter the data values for Jan, Feb, and Mar for Australia as shown in the screenshot. Now the source value is B, which is circled in blue in the next screenshot and location is **Column A**, which is rounded in yellow.

In this case, the column value is calculated for B and their values are 10 + 20 + 21 = 51, 10 + 20 + 10 = 40, 20 + 30 + 5 = 55, and finally 30 + 20 + 0 = 50. Hence, we have only two column values, that is, 51 and 55, which meet the condition of greater than 50. Therefore, we see the respective rows in 'Column A' in red as shown in the next screenshot.

In the next screenshot, we see the entered values and the highlighted red cells. The entered data is in column B and highlighted column is A, which is the location in our 'Validation rule'.

Page	Current ▾	Local ▾	draft1 ▾	Go					
			UK			Australia		
		Jan	Feb	Mar	Jan	Feb	Mar
FY10	General Operating expenses				10	20	21
	Administrative expenses				10	20	10
FY11	General Operating expenses				20	30	5
	Administrative expenses				30	20	0

On similar lines, we shall move further with our experiments to 'Row value' it's on the similar lines of 'Column value'.

Member name

If the requirement is to highlight the cell values in red, when the value is equal to the value of a particular member, for example, **Administrative expenses**, then we would create the rule as shown in the following screenshot:

Condition		Source Type		Source Value		Operator		Target Type		Target Value		Process		Actions
⊟ IF	▾	Member Name	▾	Account	▾	**Equals**	▾	Value	▾	"Administrative expenses" ✎		▾		🖉 🖉
THEN	▾	Process Cell	▾											🖉 🖉 🖉

Now, we know when we need to implement a client policy which states to highlight the Administrative expenses in the data form. Hence, we need to create a rule to highlight all the values when it's equal to any of the existing Planning dimension members, that is, in our case it is the Administrative expenses member of the Account dimension.

Member

This time, if the client decides to be even stricter and stingier, and wants to monitor their administrative expenses and wants us to highlight in red irrespective of its values being high or low. We know that **Member** is the answer for us and would create the validation rule as shown in the next screenshot in which the member **General operating expense** will be highlighted in red everywhere in a data form.

Condition		Source Type		Source Value		Operator		Target Type		Target Value		Process		Actions
⊟	IF		Member		Account		In		Value		General Operat...			🖉 🖉
	THEN		Process Cell											🖉 🖉 🖉

In the previous validation rule, every time when the account member is **General operating expense**, the cell is highlighted in red as per our condition.

Yes, we are not continuing with other options of **Source Type**, else well end up boring and make it a help guide. Let us get back and see the next condition **THEN** in our next section.

It's strongly recommended to spend substantial amount of time in terms of playing around with the difference source types and target types and understand how these changes would impact the cells in data forms.

Then

The 'Then' condition is always used to process a cell. Hence, the moment we select **THEN** as the condition, the source type is seen as **Process Cell**. We have seen this in many validation rules already.

Range and check range condition

When our requirement is to highlight when the cell value lies in between a specific range we can create a validation rule using range condition as shown in the next screenshot:

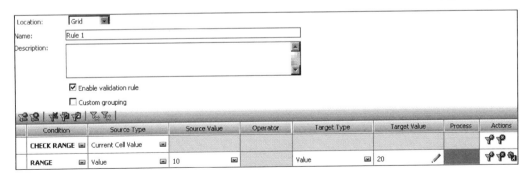

Location:	Grid
Name:	Rule 1
Description:	

☑ Enable validation rule

☐ Custom grouping

Condition		Source Type		Source Value		Operator	Target Type		Target Value		Process	Actions
CHECK RANGE		Current Cell Value										🖉 🖉
RANGE		Value		10			Value		20			🖉 🖉 🖉

Now, in the preceding rule, we have selected **Location** as **Grid** to apply to the whole data form and every data cell which falls in the range between 10 and 20 will be lighted in red. Check the same in data form.

 When Check range is evaluated, the min value is considered as >= and the second value as <, that is, greater than or equal to 10 and less than 20.

If the organization is interested in seeing the sales amount of a specific range of all the location or departments, we know what to do now.

Policies and validation rules

Organization policy needs to be understood clearly as the very first thing. Once we understand the policy, we need to create data form in a manner that we can write a validation rule to get the policy alive.

From the previous sections, we have understood how data cells of rows and columns dance to the tunes of validation rules, which is important to understand.

 We generally change the design of the data form to create a validation rule to suit to the needs of the organization policy.

Finally, we are able to see how the broad-level organization policies can also be incorporated in the granular validation rules in our Hyperion Planning application.

Therefore, common policies like flagging the cost in the data form in red when the cost increases more than the actual cost value of last year or policy like the bonus expense of a department has to be flagged in green if it falls in a specific range.

This way, we can imagine our requirements and can create validation rules to suit to the business needs.

Policy 1

This organization which we are going to talk about does not want to spend more money in the form of salaries. Though, the market is good, the organization comes up with the policy that the actual 'Salaries' expense should not exceed more than the current/planned salary expense and when its violated, they would like it to be flagged in red and monitored. No organization wants to spend more than what they planned for.

Now, we'll create data form and then create the validation rule accordingly. We'll create a simple data form firstly.

We'll give it a name, **Pol1**, and its layout is as shown in the following screenshot. We should be able to create the data form Pol1.

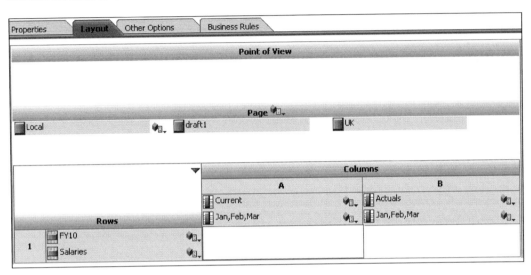

Now, we'll create the validation rule for the Policy 1 on the data form Pol1. As we see, the location is set as Cell A, 1.

The logic is, firstly we need to select member name **Salaries**, which is a member of **Account** dimension and we need to add one more condition that this member **Salaries** value, when it is greater than **Actuals** values , is shown show anger by turning red i.e. if the Actual expense is greater than the budgeted/planned expense. As we see the next rule, the same is conditioned.

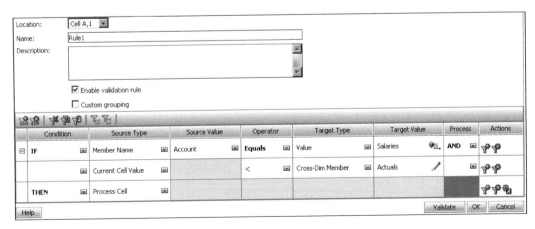

Look at the data form by entering data values into the form to feel happy that our rule is actually effective and working. We observe that Actual salary expenses in the month of **Jan** and **Mar** are more than what has been planned, that is, the current one. Hence, we see the cell being highlighted for **Jan** and **Mar** as shown in the following screenshot:

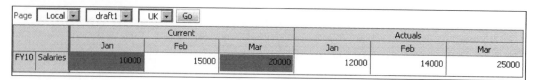

Therefore, the first policy is kicked into the system. We'll see one more policy of a greedy organization.

Policy 2

Now, let us take a more complex policy and try to create a validation rule for it. Organizations generally rely a lot on their last year's actual data. Not that they don't know of their current year, but they know what happened last year and the actuals are also available to them. That's why we always see managers looking for year-on-year reports. Performance of an organization can be gauged and said that it's growing only if they keep growing year on year. Of course, no company would target its revenue anything lesser than what was achieved last year.

Now, here is an organization and it sets a policy and wants to flag the numbers in red, when the Planned sales value of a month of a location falls by more than 5% of previous year's actuals. It's a genuine concern to any organization if their revenues drop when compared with the last year's actuals. Now, we know the requirements and are ready to act.

Let us stick to the old saying – a good start is half done. To incorporate this kind of policy, the good start would be to create a data form.

Data Form creation

It's a little complicated in this case. We have 'current' budget number and 'actual' numbers, but we need to think of how to get the value of 'decrease/increase in percentage of sales'. We know very well that we don't have any member which can give us directly the values of 'increase/decrease in sales percentage'. We need to create a 'formula column' in this case.

To do this, you will need to remember what we learned about 'formula columns' and 'formula rows' in *Chapter 8, Data Forms*.

Select rows and columns as shown and we'll create a formula column too. We have selected only Jan, Feb, and Mar and account member is Sales. Let us stick to a simpler form for now. When we actually implement, anyways, we'll end up creating complex ones.

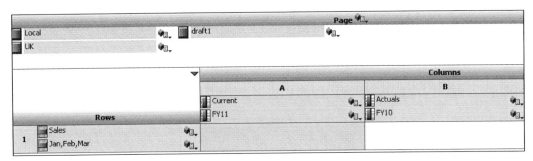

Now, right-click on a column B and select **Add Formula Column** as shown in the screenshot. The addition of the new column is for the variance analysis. Let us elaborate a little more. We have **Current** and **Actuals** as the members of Scenario dimension, which are separated into two columns, A and B. Now, let us as add one more column, C, which is custom-made and will have the label of **Variance**. This column will compute the difference between Actuals and Plan/Current.

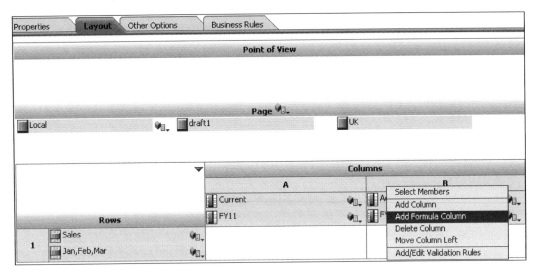

Give the names of two rows which are blank as of now, as shown in the following screenshot.

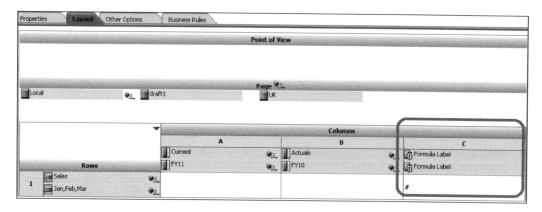

Name them **Variance** and **%Increase/Decrease of Sales**, as shown in the next screenshot. Now, we need to pay close attention. As we name the Formula label l in Column C, we need to observe the formula, which is rounded in the following screenshot:

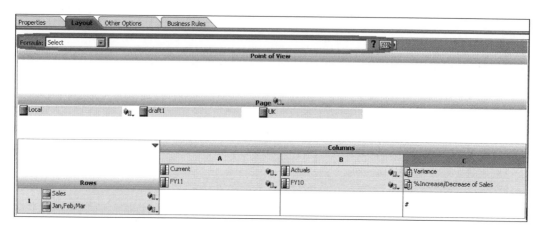

Now, we'll take a moment in understanding the formula.

The % increase/decrease of sales from previous years actual and current planned values of FY11 = (Sales of Actuals – Sales of Current / Sales of Actuals) * 100.

Actuals is Column B, **Current** is Column A. Now, we can write the formula as ([A]-[B]/[B]) * 100. Don't forget to save it. It's the most important thing.

Now, we have a new column which will give us values of percentage increase/decrease of sales. Now, it should not be difficult to write a rule.

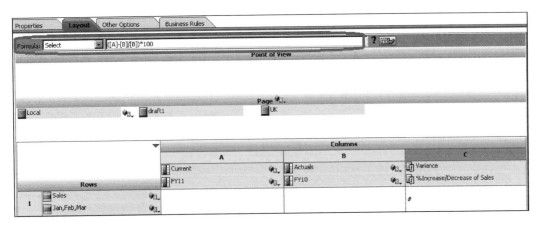

Validation rule

Right-click and write the rule as shown in the next screenshot. We first selected the account member **Sales** as shown and then added a condition in the second row that value of C column, when it is less than or equal to "-5", then flag the cell in red. The value of C column is '% Increase/decrease of Sales'.

With the given formula, we might end up getting negative numbers or positive numbers. For example, Last year's actual was 100 and FY11 current value is 80; it means to say that the sales have fallen by 20%. Now, let us use our formula, that is, (80 – 100 /100)* 100 = - 20. Hence, a negative value here means a decrease in sales percentage and the positive number would be an increase in sales percentage. Therefore, we need to flag cells in red only if they are less than or equal to -5.

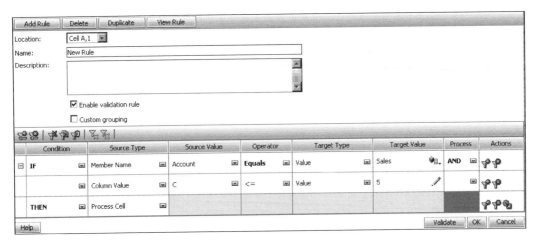

Save you changes and run the data form to see the outcome of both the newly added formula column and validation rule.

We see newly added column and also its values of 20, 10 and -10 with the entered values for Jan, Feb, and March for both **FY11** and **FY10**. Look closely, **FY11** are the current budget values and **FY10** is the previous year's actual values. We can see the **Current** values flagged in red when the **Sales** values for the **Current** year, that is, **FY11** for any month has fallen more than 5% of actuals of **FY10** as shown in the following screenshot:

Page	Local ▾		draft1 ▾	UK ▾	Go		
			Current		Actuals		Variance
			FY11		FY10		% Increase/Decrease of Sales
	Jan		120		100		20
Sales	Feb		132		120		10
	Mar		126		140		-10

We see that **Sales** in the month of March has fallen more than five percent and it is rightly flagged in red.

We'll stop here. We should now be confident in our ability to listen to any new organization policy and to incorporate into our Hyperion Planning application. It's surely going to take some time, but we will be able to do it.

Summary

In this chapter, we learned how we can incorporate organization policies into Hyperion Planning application with the aid of 'Validation Rules'.

We have created many validation rules with different requirements and understood the very important 'Conditions' in validation rule.

Finally, we have learned that when a violation happens, we have our Planning system, already made smart enough to highlight in a color or give message to the management or even stop it from getting into subsequent process of getting approvals. In the next chapter, we'll learn all about 'Security' within a Planning Application.

11
Security

Security is not something that you buy, it's something you do

— *Mark Mellis*

In the previous chapter, we learned about 'Validation rules'; we'll learn all about security in this chapter. Someone once said "the ultimate security is ones understanding of reality". Let us explore what in reality Hyperion Planning has to offer in terms of security.

We shall take a look at the conversation between two gentlemen. One is a Hyperion Consultant implementing Planning at a client office's and the other person is the client-side project owner.

Client: *I was wondering if Hyperion Planning can provide any security, as currently we have spreadsheet based budgeting and we know it is not protected.*

Hyperion Consultant: *Of course, yes, setting up security is a part of any Planning project implementation and we should do it.*

Client: *Can you tell me more about it.*

Hyperion Consultant: *Yes. We have many users and we understand the sensitivity of budget numbers as they cannot be shared and accessed by everyone in the organization. Hence, we provide access to planners/users so that they can only access what they are supposed to access, and that way the whole data integrity is upheld.*

We'll learn the following in this chapter:

- **Security**: In this section, we'll learn how different users and groups can access the Hyperion Planning application and how we can design security in general to achieve our goals.

- **Application Creation**: We'll quickly create one more Planning application and a set of users. We will then try to understand how different users with different roles can access the Planning Application.

- **User Authentication**: In this section, we'll learn of the process of user creation in Shared Services and also learn how to provision a user to a Planning Application.

- **Users and tasks**: This section explores all the available Planning roles and explains how different tasks can be performed based on the assigned roles to a user.

- **Data Security**: We'll learn about how the data at cell level is secured and we'll see different types of access and inheritance options available in this section.

- **Object Security**: In this section, we'll see how Planning objects like a data form and task list can be given access to the users. We'll also create a sample form and play around with different users.

- **Import Security**: There is a utility which is a much needed one to import security. We'll learn how to use this utility to load security in this section.

Security

Setting up security is a mandatory step in a typical Hyperion Planning implementation. While implementing, we'll get to know from the clients about the user community, and who will be accessing the application. If the client organization has offices in several different countries and the budgeting numbers are entered by users from across the globe, then it's our responsibility as consultants to set up security in such a way that all these globally spread users/planners can access the application.

As a part of budgeting, we would be looking at numbers not only at the department/ division level; it would roll up at the top organization level and it would be very obvious to state that the data of the whole organization cannot be made available to all the users/ planners. Let us elaborate a little on the same. Consider two persons, the first one is a CFO and the second one is the 'sales head' of a particular region. The CFO, being the decision maker and big man, needs to have access to the data of all countries and regions, whereas the 'sales head' should be given access only to his region/department.

In short, we cannot have an organization where 'Watchman' and 'Chairman' have the same power or privilege.

While we set up security, as a part of Planning implementation, we create users and also groups.

Why do we need user groups?

In cases where a set of people (that is users/planners) need to be given similar access rights, we can create groups and give access to this group, rather than giving each individual user access.

We'll progress to the next section, where we'll create our last Planning application. We'll look at this application closely and create users appropriately and then sort out access in the later sections.

Application creation

This section has two subsections; firstly we'll assume some requirements and then create a Planning application serving the needs of the assumed requirements:

- Requirement.
- Application Creation.

We have created two applications so far; a sample application by the name of "PandB" and another application called "Outsourc". Now, we will create one more Planning application.

As we know the procedure for creating an application, we'll spend more time on understanding the requirements rather than the steps of making the application.

To create the application, we need to assume some requirements. So, straight away let us look at the requirements.

Requirements

This time, we'll imagine a fictional consulting company whose name is 'Sargod Consulting Ltd'. This is a US-based firm which does consultancy in Oracle Hyperion products. Now, we are going to create a Planning application for this firm.

This firm is spread pretty much into every direction of the US; hence it has its offices in the eastern, western, northern, and southern regions of the country with respective states of Mascachusetts, New York, and Pennsylvania from the East, California, Colorado, and Washington from the West, Illinois and Minnesota from the North, and Florida and Texas from the south.

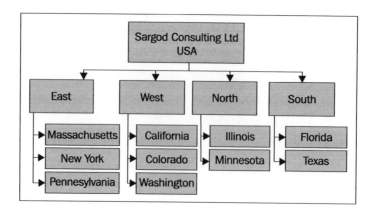

This organization will be Planning for four years, starting from Jan 2010.

This firm, "Sargod Consulting" has a small set of very loyal clients which the firm has been serving for many years. Considering this important factor, the firm would be interested in their budgets for these clients. Annually, the firm spends a lot in terms of resources, travel, and so on, on these dedicated clients and the firm would definitely be interested in knowing how much they are budgeting and how effective these clients have been in terms of filling their pockets in the form of billing to the clients.

These clients are in various industries; they are Ford in the Automotive industry, Citibank in the Financial services industry, Pfizer in the Healthcare industry, Walt Disney in the Media and Entertainment industry, British Telecom in the Telecommunication industry, and finally British Petroleum in the Oil and gas industry. We'll capture the details of these clients in a custom dimension—'Clients' in our Planning application.

Application creation

We'll create this new Planning application by name 'SRGD'. We know by now that the creation of a database for a Planning Application is the pre-requisite and we should have created a data source by name 'GD' as shown and used in the Planning application creation. We are not going to get into the step-by-step process of Planning application creation as we have done it multiple times before.

As we can see, it's a four year plan and the default currency is USD with a single plan type, Plan1, as shown in the following screenshot:

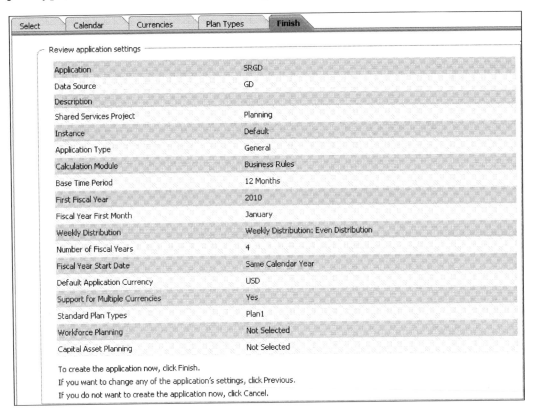

Metadata load

The next step to completing our Planning application is to load metadata. We'll quickly go through the dimensions one by one. We are not going to go in details of the process of metadata load that is the dimension build process, as we already learned how to do that in *Chapter 7, Loading Metadata*. We'll load metadata for several dimensions— the Accounts, Entity, and Custom dimension—Clients. Coming to Scenario and Version, we'll create two members each.

- **Account**: Create a flat file for the Account dimension as shown in the following screenshot and load the flat file with the content given. Refer back to the Account dimension metadata load in *Chapter 7, Loading Metadata* before you go ahead.

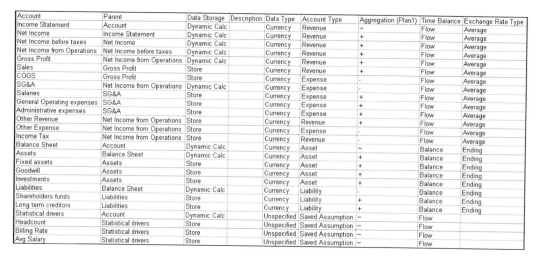

Account	Parent	Data Storage	Description	Data Type	Account Type	Aggregation (Plan1)	Time Balance	Exchange Rate Type
Income Statement	Account	Dynamic Calc		Currency	Revenue	~	Flow	Average
Net Income	Income Statement	Dynamic Calc		Currency	Revenue	+	Flow	Average
Net Income before taxes	Net Income	Dynamic Calc		Currency	Revenue	+	Flow	Average
Net Income from Operations	Net Income before taxes	Dynamic Calc		Currency	Revenue	+	Flow	Average
Gross Profit	Net Income from Operations	Dynamic Calc		Currency	Revenue	+	Flow	Average
Sales	Gross Profit	Store		Currency	Revenue	+	Flow	Average
COGS	Gross Profit	Store		Currency	Expense	-	Flow	Average
SG&A	Net Income from Operations	Dynamic Calc		Currency	Expense	-	Flow	Average
Salaries	SG&A	Store		Currency	Expense	+	Flow	Average
General Operating expenses	SG&A	Store		Currency	Expense	+	Flow	Average
Administrative expenses	SG&A	Store		Currency	Expense	+	Flow	Average
Other Revenue	Net Income from Operations	Store		Currency	Revenue	+	Flow	Average
Other Expense	Net Income from Operations	Store		Currency	Expense	-	Flow	Average
Income Tax	Net Income from Operations	Store		Currency	Revenue	-	Flow	Average
Balance Sheet	Account	Dynamic Calc		Currency	Asset	~	Balance	Ending
Assets	Balance Sheet	Dynamic Calc		Currency	Asset	+	Balance	Ending
Fixed assets	Assets	Store		Currency	Asset	+	Balance	Ending
Goodwill	Assets	Store		Currency	Asset	+	Balance	Ending
Investments	Assets	Store		Currency	Asset	+	Balance	Ending
Liabilities	Balance Sheet	Dynamic Calc		Currency	Liability	-	Balance	Ending
Shareholders funds	Liabilities	Store		Currency	Liability	+	Balance	Ending
Long term creditors	Liabilities	Store		Currency	Liability	+	Balance	Ending
Statistical drivers	Account	Dynamic Calc		Unspecified	Saved Assumption	~	Flow	
Headcount	Statistical drivers	Store		Unspecified	Saved Assumption	~	Flow	
Billing Rate	Statistical drivers	Store		Unspecified	Saved Assumption	~	Flow	
Avg Salary	Statistical drivers	Store		Unspecified	Saved Assumption	~	Flow	

- It is assumed that the reader saved the flat file by the name of `accounts_1.csv` on the `c:` drive of his machine. After creating the CSV file, we can execute the following command to load the metadata:

- **Entity**: We looked at the business of "Sargod Consulting firm"; it has offices in all the corners of US. Hence, we load the appropriate file as shown in the following screenshot:

Entity	Parent	Data Storage	Description	Data Type	Aggregation (Plan1)
USA	Entity	Dynamic Calc		Unspecified	+
Eastern Region	USA	Dynamic Calc		Unspecified	+
Massachusetts	Eastern Region	Store		Unspecified	+
New York	Eastern Region	Store		Unspecified	+
Pennsylvania	Eastern Region	Store		Unspecified	+
Western Region	USA	Dynamic Calc		Unspecified	+
California	Western Region	Store		Unspecified	+
Colorado	Western Region	Store		Unspecified	+
Washington	Western Region	Store		Unspecified	+
Northern Region	USA	Dynamic Calc		Unspecified	+
Illinois	Northern Region	Store		Unspecified	+
Minnesota	Northern Region	Store		Unspecified	+
Southern Region	USA	Dynamic Calc		Unspecified	+
Florida	Southern Region	Store		Unspecified	+
Texas	Southern Region	Store		Unspecified	+

And the command prompt code would be:

- **Scenario and Version**: We'll create just two members for Scenario dimension. If someone guessed it, they are 'actuals' and 'Plan'.

- For member 'Plan', the start year and end year is FY10 and the period range would be from Jan to Dec. The data store is 'Store'. Coming to the other member 'Actual', its start year and end year is FY10, but the period range is from Jan to March and the other properties of storage are of 'Store' type. The dimension can be viewed in the following screenshot.

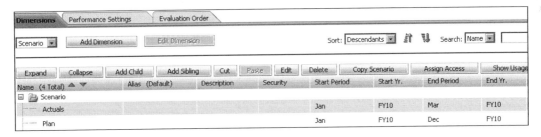

- For the Version dimension, we'll create V1 and V2. V1 is of 'Standard bottom up' with data storage as 'Store', while V2 is of 'Standard target' with same data storage property.

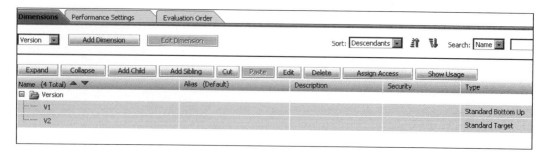

- **Custom dimension**: This would be the list of dedicated clients which the firm is interested in budgeting for annually as mentioned in the requirements.

Clients	Parent	Data Storage	Description	Data Type	Aggregation (Plan1)
Automative	Clients	Dynamic Calc		Unspecified	+
Global Motors Ltd	Automative	Store		Unspecified	+
Financial Services	Clients	Dynamic Calc		Unspecified	+
Enti Bank Ltd	Financial Services	Store		Unspecified	+
Health Care	Clients	Dynamic Calc		Unspecified	+
Global health Ltd	Health Care	Store		Unspecified	+
Media and Entertainment	Clients	Dynamic Calc		Unspecified	+
Global entertainment Ltd	Media and Entertainment	Store		Unspecified	+
Telecommunications	Clients	Dynamic Calc		Unspecified	+
Global Teleco Ltd	Telecommunications	Store		Unspecified	+
Oil and Gas	Clients	Dynamic Calc		Unspecified	+
Global Petro Ltd	Oil and Gas	Store		Unspecified	+

And the command prompt lines are as follows:

We had run the `OutlineLoad` utility to load metadata for Acconts, Entity, and Clients dimension. The other two dimensions, Scenario and Version, have been manually added.

As we added them manually, we need to refresh the database without fail before we proceed any further. This is important.

Good, we have created our last application, which is 'SRGD', and we shall take a look at the dimensions, if they look as smart as our requirement.

User authentication

What does a user need in order to access a Planning Application?

The user needs a valid username and password.

When we create a user in Shared Services, we provide his 'user ID' and 'password' information. This is stored and when the same user tries to access the Planning application, his information is authenticated before he is let inside the Planning application. Along with authentication, the system also checks whether the user is authorized to access the Planning application or not.

In most of the implementations, it's important to see external authentication. Let us elaborate. Consider a Planning application like that of 'SRGD' which is for a company called 'Sargod Consulting Ltd' that is spread across many geographic locations and needs to be accessed by many hundreds of users spread across the globe. Now, any organization of huge size would base their employee user management on technologies such as Microsoft's Active Directory.

Now, when we are implementing our application we know that it's practically impossible to create all users individually and provision them and then assign member level access manually. We generally try to connect our Shared Services to their Active directories and pull out the users from their AD's only.

 The main advantage of using users defined in Active Directory is that the users will be able to use the same credentials for logging into Planning applications that they use to log into other organization resources/applications because the password management is done using AD not Shared Services.

We create groups, and then later we assign group level access. This way, we can manage the security well.

User creation

There are members such as New York, California, Washington, Texas, Southern Region, Northern region, Western Region, and USA, as a part of the Entity dimension. Imagine that in real time, planners or users from one region should not be allowed to view budget data of other regions. For example, New York data should not be accessible to the planners who are responsible for California, Washington, and so on. But, the USA head, being the head of all the regions, should be given access to data of all states and on similar lines Western region head should have access to the data of western states like California, Colorado and Washington, but at the same time the California planner should be gives access to only his state of California but not to other states or other regions.

Now, let us refine our discussion point to the Eastern Region and its states. Let us imagine budget owners of these regions. For the US, the owner is 'US_owner'. For the Eastern Region, the budget owner is 'East_owner'. 'Mass_owner' heads Massachusetts, 'New_owner' heads New York, and 'Penn_owner' heads Pennsylvania, as shown in the following screenshot:

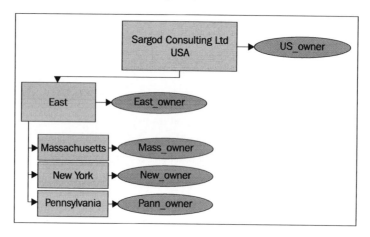

In the 'user creation' section, we'll create these users: East_owner, Mass_owner, New_owner, Penn_owner, and US_owner

With that basic understanding, we'll create a few users now and provision them to the newly-created Planning application 'SRGD'.

> We need to remember that user management is done with the help of Shared Services and we are going to create users also within Shared Services.

Let us do it in steps.

User creation

1. Log into Shared Services, whose URL is. `http://localhost:28080/` `interop/index.jsp.`

2. Using 'admin' and 'password' as credentials.

3. Expand **User Directories** | **Native Directory** | Users. Here, right-click on 'New' as shown in the following screenshot:

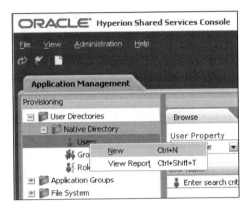

4. This will open a new window in which we'll provide information about a user. As shown, we have created a user by name 'US_owner' and the password is 'password'. Let us not waste our time in providing optional details such as the first name, last name, description, and so on. Now, click **Save**. If we are curious, we can change 'next' to discover to make our newly-created user as a part of a group. For now, we are not interested in groups or making users a part of groups. Hence, save it.

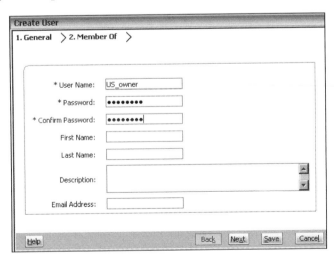

5. It will give us a message that 'US_owner' has been created. We need to create a few more users. Hence, make use of the option 'Create Another' as rounded in the following screenshot:

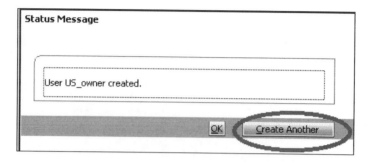

6. Likewise, create new users for East_owner, Mass_owner, New_own, and Penn_user and for simplicity's sake stick to the password of 'password' for all the users.

User provisioning

So far, we have only created users, now we are going to provision the Planning application 'SRGD' to the created users. If we try to log into the Planning application at this junction with the created users, of course the application won't let us log into it, for the obvious reason that we have not provisioned the users to any of the Planning applications. If we try to login into the Planning application 'SRGD' using the credentials of 'US_owner', we would get the following error message:

Let us see how to provision a user with the following steps:

In a typical implementation, we usually create multiple groups and do provisioning to groups and then add users to the groups. For example, we have many users/planner, who belong to the HR department and Finance department. We would encourage to create groups like HR and Fin and then provision these groups, that are HR and Fin, and then we would add the Planners/users of the HR Department to the HR group. Likewise, users of the Finance team will be added to the Fin User group.

1. Go to Shared Services, select 'users' under the Native directory, and type in the name of the user in 'user filter' as rounded as shown in the following screenshot. After you provide the name, select **Search**.

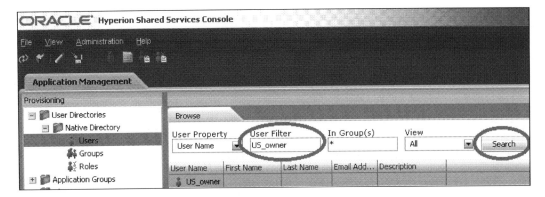

2. Now, right-click the user and select 'provision', as shown in the following screenshot:

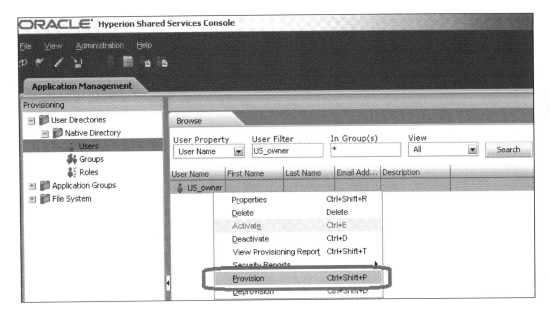

3. After selecting 'provision', a new window will open. In this window, we'll expand the folder 'Planning' to find our application 'SRGD' and expand 'SRGD' as shown to view the roles which can be provisioned. For example, Administrator, Cube creator, Planner, and so on. We'll learn all about each of these roles later, but for now select 'Planner' and push it under 'selected roles' as shown in the following screenshot:

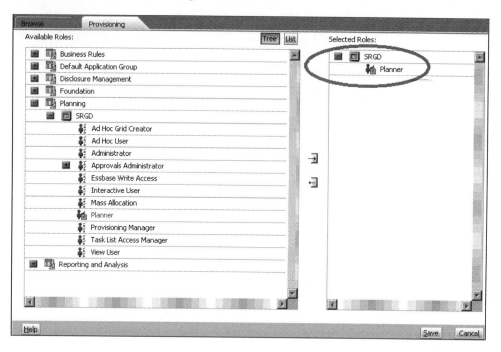

4. Repeat the steps of provisioning the 'Planner' role to other users: East_owner, Mass_owner, New_own, and Penn_user.

 We need to Refresh Security after provisioning users. Hence, we need to refresh the Security of the 'SRGD' application now.

Now, try to log into the 'SRGD' application with the user name **US_owner** and the password **password**. We might be surprised to see an error message, as shown below.

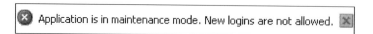

Application is in maintenance mode. New logins are not allowed.

When a baby is newly born, it's kept under medical supervision, likewise, when a new Planning application is created, planners are not allowed to access it. It's only accessible to administrators by default. Hence, we get that message of 'maintenance mode'.

Now, we'll learn how to make this Planning application accessible to users, other than administrator.

1. Log in to the SRGD application with username **admin** and password **password**.

2. After we are logged in, go to **Administration | Application | Settings**, it opens a new window in which we are going to change 'Enable use of application for', from 'administrators' to 'all users' as shown in the following screenshot:

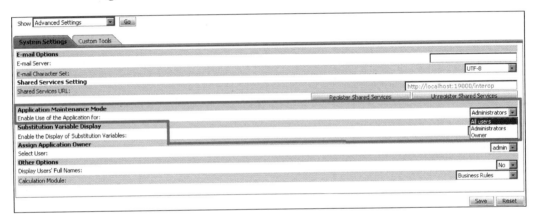

3. Select **Save**.

4. Now log out before we attempt to login as 'US_owner'.

5. Now, try to log into SRGD with the user ID **US_owner** and the password **password**. This time, it will be successful.

Users and tasks

What does a user do within a Planning application?

A user would perform tasks.

What kind of tasks does a user perform?

Yes, we'll stop answering in a primary school kid fashion. Many times, we have gone to 'Administration' and selected management of data form, dimensions, and so on. These are all tasks which one does in the Planning application like accessing and entering data into the data forms.

Not every task can be done by every user/planner. Let us explain with an example, there is a Planning administrator and there is one planner whose primary responsibility is to enter budget values into the data form which he has access to. We cannot let this planner add dimensions or members to the existing dimension structure. If every planner has access to change the dimension structure, then every user will start adding or removing members and it will no longer be a Planning application, it would soon turn into an unplanned garbage application.

Hence, we ensure that not all tasks can be performed by all users. The administrator would be creating forms and adding metadata, and so on, while a lazy planner can only access the already created forms and enter data and submit it. Here, in this simple example, we mentioned two user types: Administrator and Planner. These two are the roles. Hence the role of a user determines the tasks, which he/she can perform.

Is the US_owner user an Administrator or Planner?

We know that we have provisioned him in the 'Planner' role section. But another way to easily identity him is when we log into the Planning application of 'SRGD' using the credentials of 'US_owner'. We don't even see the option of 'administration', as 'US_owner' is a planner and he has no tasks to perform which are part of 'administration'. We can log in again to verify that, as shown in the following screenshot:

With that basic understanding let us look into all the available roles for the Planning application.

Planning roles

1. **Administrator**: He is the big boss, he can do everything. He can create and manage Planning applications; he is the one who initiates the budget process (workflow), which we will learn in chapter "".

   Now, let us hurt the ego of the 'administrator' by reminding him that he also cannot do a few things. Yes, we are talking about the 'Planning owner'. To the big boss 'administrator', there is a big daddy 'owner'.

What is the difference between administrator and owner?

The owner can delete the Planning application, while the administrator cannot. Now, we'll do one more experiment. Create another user 'Test' (with password **password**) in Shared Services and provision him the role of 'administrator' to 'SRGD' application.

How can I find out who is the owner of a Planning Application?

Good question. Log in to 'SRGD ', using the credentials of 'admin' and go to **Administration | Application | Settings**.

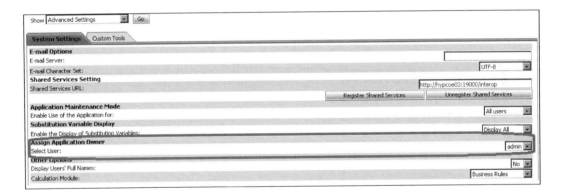

We see 'admin' as the current application owner. Hence, 'admin' is the owner and he is the only one who can change the owner from one to the other.

Now, we can log off and log in to 'SRGD' using the 'test' user (who is 'SRGD' administrator)

Go to **Administration | Application | Settings** again. Now, the 'Test' user is not an owner, he is only an administrator. Hence, he would not be able to see the details of 'Assign application owner' shown in the following screenshot:

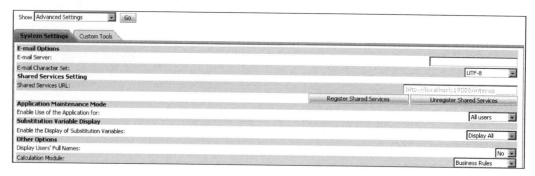

 Also, an administrator cannot do mass allocation, he needs to have the role of mass allocation to do that.

Therefore, we can laugh at the 'administrator' role and conclude that a user with an administrator role cannot assign the ownership of a Planning application from one user to another.

2. **Analytic Services Write Access**: This is applicable to the users who already have the role of 'Planner' or 'interactive user'. This role of 'analytic services write access' lets a user use third-party products to write data back into Essbase.

 A Planning Application by default doesn't let a user write data directly to Essbase using any other utility a part of Planning Data Forms. For e.g. if a planner has write access to some accounts for a particular department, he will be able to enter data for those accounts using Planning Data Forms but he will not be able to do so using Hyperion SmartView for Excel.

To enable write access to Essbase directly using any available utility such as Smart View user should be provisioned with this role.

3. **Interactive user**: This user can create/update data forms, smart view sheets, business rules, and task lists. Quite a powerful role, as the user with this role can create many important Planning objects like forms, rules, and task lists.

 This role is typically assigned to the head of departments/divisions.

4. **Manage models**: This role is dead. It's no longer a valid role, though we see it as a possible role under a Planning application. Hence, let us not bother about it.

5. **Mass allocation**: We learned about mass allocation in *Chapter 9, Data Entry*. We know that it's a little risky to give a role of mass allocation. Hence, this is a specialized role, which even needs to be assigned to an administrator to perform 'mass allocation'; he does not have this by default.

6. **Planner**: He is always in the majority. He can only enter data and submit forms, run business rules, and view and use task lists. He does not have enough power to create any of these objects though. But, in any implementation, we would find that many of the users are planners.

7. **Provision manager**: We have very comfortably logged into Shared Services and had created few users and also provisioned the 'SRGD' application to the users. We were able to do so only because the user 'admin' has already the role of 'provision manager'.

 We should log into Shared Services, search for 'admin', and right click to select 'provision'. We can see that the provisioned roles of the admin user are 'administrator', 'provision users', and 'Mass allocation'. These three roles are hence defined as power roles.

8. **View user**: These are the users who can only view the forms and data, rather than entering data.

Now, when we set up security in any implementation, we can easily make out that a lot of users would be 'Planners' and a few of them would be 'Interactive users', who head departments/divisions, who can create forms, rule, and so on. Coming to the owner, there is always one owner. Yes, we can change the ownership of an application from one to the other. But, it's only the current owner who can do that. Next comes the 'administrator', there may be more than one of these. In a typical implementation, many users can be viewers as well.

Therefore, we understood that users with appropriate roles can perform relevant tasks.

Data security

We can assign rights in Planning at the individual dimension member level. Let us manually assign access of one of the dimension members and in the process, we'll learn what we need to know.

Access rights assignment

Go to **Administration** | **Manage** | **Dimensions**, select the 'Account' dimension, and expand it as shown in the following screenshot. We can see that even at the level 0, that is 'Sales', we can assign access.

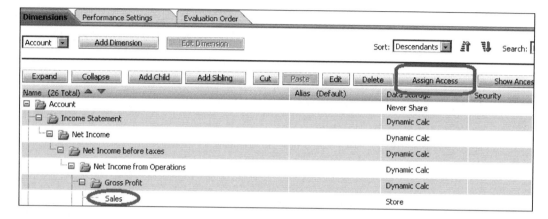

Click on **Assign Access** to open a new window.

We have not assigned any users to the member 'sales' so far. Hence, we see no users in the assigned list.

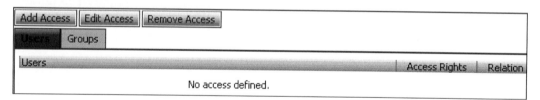

Types of access

Now, select 'Add Access'. We see the list of users as shown in the following screenshot; these are the list of users which we had created in the previous section of 'User creation' and were provisioned to this Planning application—'SRGD'.

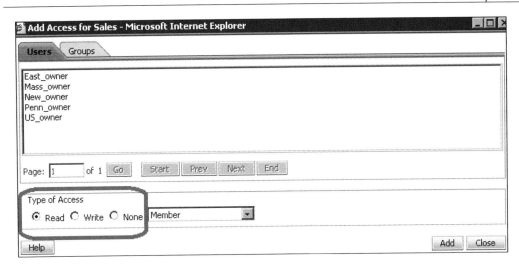

There are three types of access:

1. **Read**: A user can only view the data in a form but cannot enter or edit the cell value.

2. **Write**: A user with this access type can enter and also edit the data values.

3. **None**: Neither read nor write.

Select 'US_owner' and select 'write' for Type of access rounded in red as shown in the following screenshot. Click on **Add**. We do see a list of options ranging from 'Member' to 'Descendants (as shown in the following screenshot). These are inheritance options which will be explored in next section.

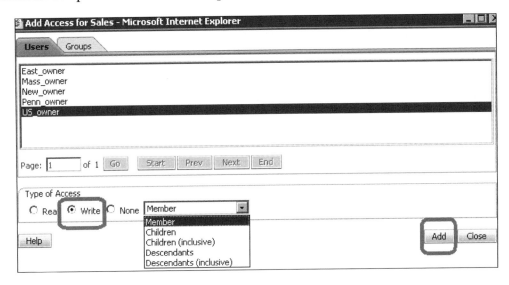

Now, select the **Add** option. It will show the message "Adding of Users/ Groups succeeded". Now, select **Close**.

Finally, after adding US_owner as the user who has write access to the Account dimension member 'sales', it would look like the following screenshot:

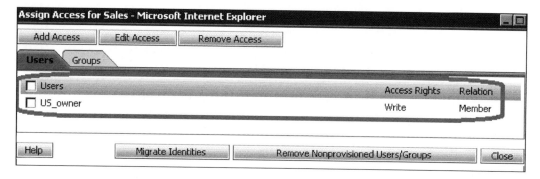

Relation / inheritance

We have one more important concept of 'Relation' or 'inheritance' options.

- **Member**: If we want to assign access only to the selected member then this option will be used. In our case we wanted to assign user 'US_owner' write access to the 'Sales' account, therefore we selected the option 'Member'.

- **Children**: If we want to give access to a user of all the children in a hierarchy. For example, if we intent to give 'write' access to both members – 'COGS' and 'Sales, we should select the member 'Gross Profit' and give write access to its children (the children of Gross Profit being COGS and Sales).

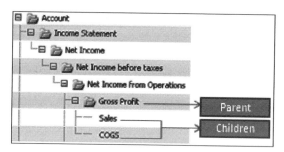

- **Children (inclusive)**: Let us consider the same example given in 'children'. If we intend to give access to children along with its parent, we should select the parent that is Gross profit in our case, and select 'Children (inclusive) as the relation, which would allow the user to access not only COGS and Sales, but also their parent 'Gross Profit'.

- **Descendants**: We know the difference between children and descendants. Children are the immediate members within the hierarchy, whereas descendants are all the members which are under a specific member. The children of 'Net Income from operations' are Gross profit, SG&A, other revenue, and other expense. Whereas the descendants of 'Net Income from Operations' would be Gross profit, Sales, COGS, SG&A, Salaries, General Operating expenses, administrative expenses, other revenue, and other expense. Now, we know the difference pretty well.

- **Descendants (inclusive)**: Inclusive includes the selected dimension member. Descendants (inclusive) is just like Descendants but it also enables access to the selected dimension member.

We can have groups and we can assign rights at group level also. But in a case when an individual, who is part of a group, has different rights on the same resources/artifacts than that of the group rights, then individual rights definitely would override group rights

Also, assume a user who is a part of group1 and group 1 has read access for a particular dimension member, and the same user is a part of group2 and group2 has been give 'None' access of the same dimension member. In this kind of situation, this user would have 'None' access. Therefore, when there is a clash between 'None' and 'read', 'None' wins. If there is a clash between 'Read and 'write', the winner is 'write'.

Object security

Here, the objects are the data form and task lists. Not every form can be made available to all the users. There are few set of data forms, which are meant for the HR team and likewise there are few other sets of data forms meant for other divisions/ departments like Finance. Hence, Users can access data forms, but only the ones they have been granted access to. In this section, we'll create one data form and try to assign the form to the users which we created.

Data Form creation

We already know how to create a data form. We'll create a form called 'test' with the layout as shown in the following screenshot:

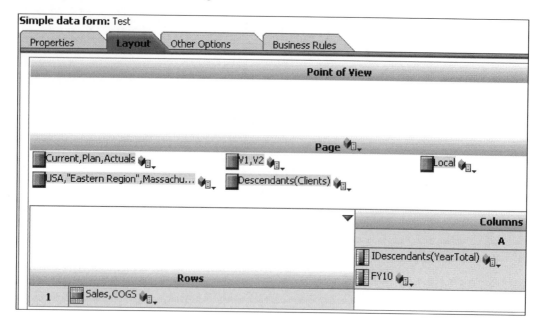

- For Account dimension, Sales, and COGS are the selected members in Rows.
- For Entity dimension, select USA, Eastern Region, Massachusetts, New York, and Pennsylvania.
- For Year select FY10 and for Period select dimension, all the descendants (inclusive) of Year total in columns
- For Scenario, select Current, Plan, and Actuals as selected members in Page.
- For Version dimension, select V1 and V2 members in Page.
- For Custom dimension 'Clients', select all descendants of 'Clients' in Page of Data form design.
- Finally for Currency dimension, select 'Local' as the member in Page.

Data Form security access

Save the form and select 'finish' at the end. Our objective is to assign data form access to a user. For that go to **Administration | Manage | Data forms and Ad hoc analysis**. Select/tick the form 'Test' and select 'Assign access', which is highlighted in the following screenshot:

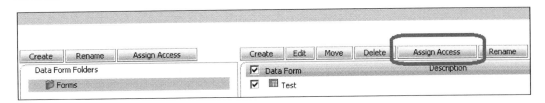

As we select **Assign Access**, we see a new window, which gives us a message 'No access defined'. It's the same window, which we had seen before while assigning user access to the 'sales' member. We should know what to do.

Select 'Add access' and select 'US_owner' and select 'write' access and add it as shown:

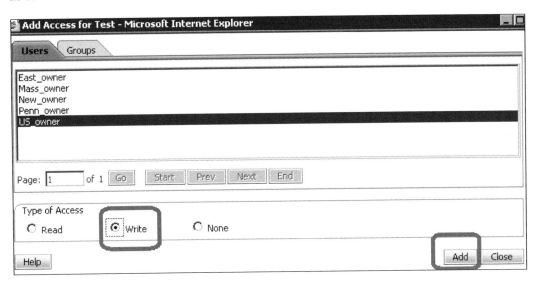

Do give the same **Write** access to other users: East_owner, Mass_owner, New_owner, and Penn_owner.

We should get the following message after data has been successfully added by the user:

Now, we can see the newly added users 'US_owner' and other list of users with 'write' access to the data form 'test':

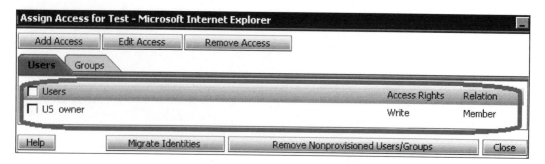

Let us do a quick recap before we move on to the next topic and get confused. First, we have given member level access of 'Sales' of Account dimension to the user 'US_owner', but we know that the only way to interact with (view/edit) data in Planning is through data forms. Hence, we created one 'test' data form and gave the same user that is 'US_owner' write access to the data form.

Data Form access

Now, log in to 'SRGD' using the credentials of US_owner (username: **US_owner**, Password: **password**) and open the data form 'test'.

To our surprise, the form slaps us with an error message:

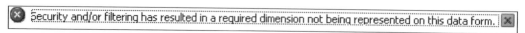

You may be wondering what could have gone wrong when we have done everything correctly, let us think again. We'll do one thing, we'll login into 'SRGD' using admin credentials and try to open the data form to test if we could open the form.

Surprisingly, the form opens flawlessly. Now, it's even more disappointing. We know the feeling when we flunk in an exam; it's a bad feeling, but if our friend passes the same exam, it's even worse. We feel the same, when the user 'admin' can open and see the darling 'Test' data form, what is wrong with the new user 'US_owner?

If we introspect, we can understand that a data form is a combination of all dimension members and every single cell value is again a combination of members, one for each of the dimensions. There is a cell which is filled with a red balloon in the previous screenshot. This cell conveys the meaning of 'Planned' 'Sales' figures of 'ford' in the month of 'Jan' in the year 'FY10' for the area 'Massachusetts' in its first version of Budget 'V1'. Here, Plan, Sales, Ford, Jan, FY10, Massachusetts, and V1 are members and the combination of all these members is what is highlighted as the red cell.

But, if we turn to flashback, we have given access to the user 'US_owner' of only the 'sales' member of Account dimension. Whereas we should give access to other members of dimensions as well to edit/to enter this particular cell in the form of a single cell value is a combination of multiple members.

Therefore, we'll assign 'write' access of Sales (of Accounts), Ford (of Clients), Massachusetts (of Entity), Plan (of Scenario), V1 (of Version) to the user 'US_owner'.

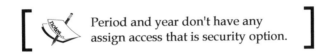

> Period and year don't have any assign access that is security option.

User access to members

Let us roll up our sleeves and start assigning access to the members of the user 'US_owner'. We had already done this for 'Sales' of Account dimension. Now, next is 'Ford' of 'clients' dimension.

Go to **Administration** | **Manage** | **Dimensions** and select 'Clients' from the drop down.

Expand the dimension to get the 'Ford' member. We could get it easily without searching much, but there is one more problem. After selecting the member 'Ford', we don't get the option of 'assign access'. Now, we are stuck big time.

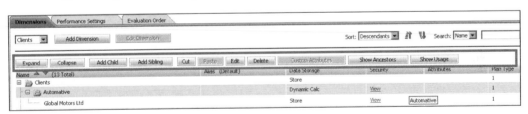

Let's check the area circled in the above picture, but there are no clues of the 'assign access' option which we could get for the 'Sales' member of Account dimension.

When we create a custom dimension that is clients in this case, we need to explicitly tell 'Hyperion Planning' that we would like to set security to the members of the dimension.

How do we set a dimension which will let us set access permission to its members?

It's not tough as it seems. We'll do that to the dimension 'clients'. Let us do it in steps:

1. Go to the Dimensions homepage and select the dimension name 'clients' and click on the 'edit' option as shown in the following screenshot:

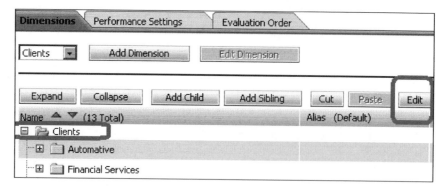

2. Now, it opens the properties window of 'Clients' dimension as shown. Enable the option of **Apply Security**, which would be unchecked. We will check it as shown in the following screenshot:

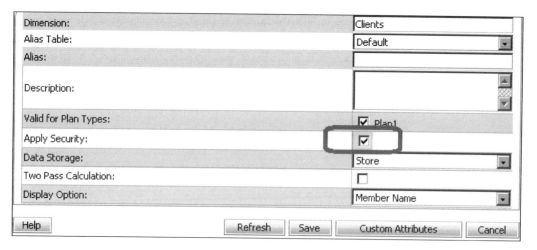

3. Select **Save** to close the window. Now, as we made changes to the properties of the dimension, which deals with security, we need to refresh the database and security.

4. Go to **Administration | Application | Refresh** application by selecting the **Database** and **Security Filters** as shown in the following screenshot:

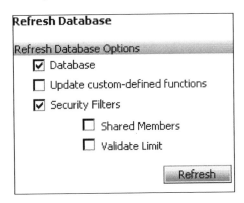

5. Now, get back to the dimension 'Clients' and the member 'Ford' to assign access to the 'US_owner' as shown in the following screenshot. We could see the option of **Assign Access** now.

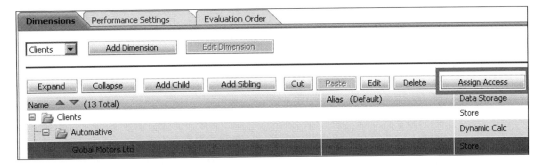

6. Thank god, we see **Assign Access** for the member 'ford' of dimension 'clients'.

7. Assign write access of member 'Ford' to the user 'US_owner'.

8. Likewise, on similar lines we'll assign member access of Massachusetts' (Entity), Plan (Scenario), and V1 (Version) to the user 'US_owner'.

9. After all of the above mentioned members are assigned successfully, log off from the Planning application 'SRGD' and now log into 'SRGD using 'US_ owner' as user and password as password and open the form 'Test'. Now, there is no error and we can see the data form.

10. There is a difference between the form we see when we log in using the credentials of 'admin' and the one we saw when we used the credentials of 'US_owner'. Before, we were able to select Versions, Entity, and Scenario from the 'Page' drop down, where as now, we don't have access to other members. Hence, we cannot select or view the other members of the dimensions of the data form.

11. Now we know that if we need to get to see the other members, which are a part of the data form, we need to provide access of these members to the user.

12. Now, for other members and other users, we need to assign access, as we had done so far for a single user.

Are we sure; if this is the only dumb way of assigning access? Of course not, we can use a utility to do that and we'll see how we can use that to provide access to other users and give access to many members of dimensions in the next section.

Import security

We have so far assigned few member level access to only one user that is US_owner. Now, we can realize that manually assigning hundreds of members of dimensions to many users is practically not possible. Also, it would be cumbersome to manually select a user and select a member and provide the access rights. Hence, we unanimously voted to use a utility, which can help us.

Do we have a utility to access member to users?

Yes, we do and the utility name is 'ImportSecurity' utility. He is our hero for now.

Where does this hero or utility reside?

He has a comfortable flat and its address is `D:\Oracle\Middleware\user_projects\epmsystem1\Planning\Planning1`.

This is with an assumption the reader has installed in D drive.

Here we can see the utility by name `ImportSecurity.cmd`.

`ImportSecurity.cmd` looks for a `SecFile.txt` to provide access of dimension members to users. We'll soon learn about `SecFile.txt`.

[This utility is also used for assigning access to data forms and task lists. Access can be granted to users as well as groups.]

SecFile

All the access rights information like:

- Which user
- To which member of dimension
- What kind of access

Has to be provided in a text file and this text file is named as `SecFile.txt`.

Why do we need to save it as SecFile.txt, why not our favorite actress' name?

We have got a reason to do that. When we run `ImportSecurity.cmd`, it looks for user access information in `SecFile.txt` and also it looks for this text file only in the particular location of `D:\Oracle\Middleware\user_projects\epmsystem1\Planning\Planning1`.

Therefore, we have two conditions:

1. We have to save the text file with the name `SecFile.txt`.
2. We got to save the `SecFile.txt` in `D:\Oracle\Middleware\user_projects\epmsystem1\Planning\Planning1`.

SecFile.txt creation

We have learned the importance of SecFile and we'll learn to create the file in this section. We need to quickly recall that we have created users East_owner, Mass_owner, Massachusetts, New_owner, and Penn_owner along with 'US_owner' and also provisioned the application 'SRGD' to these users with the role of 'planner'. We need to remember that we gave 'write' access to all the users of the data form 'test'.

Hence, we can log into the 'SRGD' application using the credentials of Mass_owner (username: **Mass_owner**, password: **password**). The system does let us login, but we wont be able to open the data form, as we have not given the dimension member level access to 'Mass_owner'.

We'll use the utility for the user 'Mass_owner' and check that actually works.

Before we start creating the SecFile, we'll understand the basic structure of the file.

SecFile Structure

The basic structure of SecFile is: `<User or Group Name>`, `<Artifact Name >`, `<Access Right>`, `<Inheritance Option>`, `<artifact type>`.

- `User or Group Name`: Provide a user or a group name to whom the access needs to be granted. User or group should already be defined in Shared Services and provisioned to access the application.

- `Artifact Name`: Provide the name of the artifact whose access needs to be granted to the user or group. The artifact can be a member from any of the dimensions, data form, data forms folders, task lists, and so on. In our case, we will be giving the member name of a dimension; we need to give the same name as it has in the Planning application.

- `Access Right`: The possible options, as we already know, the access rights are read, write, and none.

- `Inheritance Option`: Yes, we have learned of it just a little bit. The possible options would be MEMBER, @CHILDREN, @ICHILDREN, @DESCENDANTS, and @ IDESCENDANTS.

- `Artifact Type`: We understand that SecFile is used not only for member level access but also to access other artifacts like Data forms, Data form folders, and task lists.
    - For Data forms, the syntax is SL_FORM
    - For Task lists, it is SL_TASKLIST
    - For Data form folders, it is SL_FORMFOLDER

Before we start writing the content of 'SecFile', we need to make up a decision of what members are to be accessed by the user 'Mass_owner'.

We need to recall again that 'Mass_owner' is the user responsible for the 'Massachusetts' region and we'll give him access to the following members of the dimensions:

- Account: We'll give Mass_owner 'write' access to 'sales' and 'COGS'.
- Version: Both V1 and V2 'write' access.
- Entity: Give 'Massachusetts' 'write' access.
- Clients: Give 'write' access to 'Automotive' and its child 'Ford'.

Let's start with our very first line.

1. Open a text file and type the following lines: the first two lines are the Account dimension members. Next two lines are for the version dimension and its members V1 and V2. As we know 'Mass_owner' is the responsible person for 'Massachusetts', we give write access to the same. Next is the client's dimension, where we give him the access to 'Automotive' and its descendants; it has only one child that is Ford. The last line talks of the 'Scenario' dimension member, that is Plan member.

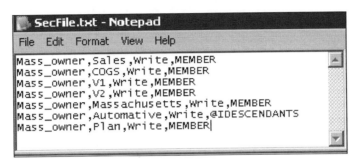

It's not difficult to make this file.

Ensure to save this file with the name SecFile.txt and save it in location D:\Oracle\Middleware\user_projects\ epmsystem1\Planning\Planning1 or <HYPERION_HOME>\ Planning\Planning1.

2. Now, go to command prompt and run the following as shown in the next screenshot. Navigate to the location D:\Oracle\Middleware\user_ projects\epmsystem1\Planning\Planning1 and execute the command by typing ImportSecurity.cmd "SRGD,admin" as shown:

3. After a few seconds, it will ask you for a password, as shown in the next screenshot. Type 'password'. We won't be able to see the letters on the screen while we type the password. But do type 'password' and press *Enter*.

```
C:\WINDOWS\system32\cmd.exe - ImportSecurity.cmd "SRGD,admin"
Microsoft Windows [Version 5.2.3790]
(C) Copyright 1985-2003 Microsoft Corp.

D:\>cd D:\oracle\Middleware\user_projects\epmsystem1\Planning\planning1

D:\oracle\Middleware\user_projects\epmsystem1\Planning\planning1>ImportSecurity.
cmd "SRGD,admin"
EPM_ORACLE_INSTANCE (D:\oracle\Middleware\user_projects\epmsystem1) is set from
JVM property[EPM_ORACLE_INSTANCE].
Th..  M.. 26 11.52:35 EDT 2011 :: The length of the string:: 1
Enter password:
```

4. It will take some time, and eventually give you a success message, as shown in the following screenshot:

```
Loaded Version of Essbase RTC: 0xb1210
Thu May 26 12:39:42 EDT 2011 :: Logged in successfully
Thu May 26 12:39:42 EDT 2011 :: Setting access controls....
Thu May 26 12:39:42 EDT 2011 :: Total Rows Provided=7 Added Successfully for=7
Thu May 26 12:39:42 EDT 2011 :: Logging off from application ....
Thu May 26 12:39:43 EDT 2011 :: Logged out of the application.
Thu May 26 12:39:43 EDT 2011 :: Import security Completed successfully.
```

We want to be sure of our security import. Hence the obvious question is: Where is the log file?

The log file can be found at D:\Oracle\Middleware\user_projects\epmsystem1\ diagnostics\logs\Planning with the log file name 'ImportSecuritylog.txt'.

 Take the utmost care in creating the SecFile.txt file as it is very sensitive.

Debugging the security errors

We'll see one of the examples, where we can go wrong while making the file. We type the first line in SecFile.txt file. Look at the following screenshots and spot the differences.

```
Mass_owner,COGS,Write,MEMBER |          Mass_owner,COGS,Write,MEMBER|
```

One can say that there are no differences. However, when we load `SecFile.txt` we will fail to import security if it has the row entries as shown in the previous screenshot on the left-hand side, marked in red.

The error message that we would get in 'ImportSecuritylog.txt' is:

```
The following access not imported:-Mass_owner,COGS,Write,MEMBER  due toInvalid Access flag found in the file
```

This is because there is a space after the first line. Take a look at the next screenshot:

```
Mass_owner,COGS,Write,MEMBER |        Mass_owner,COGS,Write,MEMBER|
```

Hence, we should avoid these errors. The right line is the one which has no spaces after the last word and cursor.

The moral of this story is to be cautious when creating `SecFile.txt`.

Now, log in to 'SRGD' using the credentials of 'Mass_owner' (username: **Mass_owner**, password: **password**) and we can open the data form and also see that the cells are in 'yellow' color conveying the message that we can write into these cells, which is what we had set for its security.

Therefore, we were able to successfully use the utility to load security of a few members for this user — 'Mass_owner'. In next section, with confidence, we'll load security for many members of dimensions for all the remaining users.

Import access rights

Finally, we have to load `SecFile.txt` for all the members of dimensions to all the users. We'll consider only a few users for now. They are East_owner, Mass_owner, New_owner, Penn_owner, and US_owner

Now, for simplicity's sake, we'll give access to all members of Account, Version, Scenario, and clients. But, we'll restrict the 'Entity' dimension.

ImportSecurity syntax

We had run the Import Security command before, but let us master it now. Its syntax is: `ImportSecurity.cmd "appname, username, password [delimiter], [SL_CLEARALL]"`.

Now, let us explore the anatomy:

- `Appname`: Hyperion Planning Application name for whom the security needs to be imported.

- `Username`: Username having rights to import security. In our case it will be 'admin'.

- `Delimiter`: So far, we have seen a simple text file where the members are comma delimited. We know that Excel is the one of the best loved products when it comes to making files like SecFile. However, it has to be `SecFile.txt` that is a text file. We can create the file in Excel and copy into the text file. This way, we will have a `SecFile.txt`, which is a text file with tab delimiters rather than comma delimiters. Now, it as CSV and rename the file to `SecFile.txt`.

  Therefore, this utility is smart and gives us few options for delimiters. They are tab, comma, space, colon and semi-colon. They are represented as `'SL_TAB, SL_COMMA, SL_PIPE, SL_SPACE, SL_COLON, SL_SEMI-COLON'` respectively within the syntax of Import security.

- `Sl_CLEARALL`: This option clears the existing access permissions before it starts importing.

User import access

Now, let us resume our activity of making the SecFile for all the users and all the dimension members. Thought we will be making only one `SecFile.txt`, we will see in this section the rows/contents in `SecFile.txt` per user.

We need to note that it's going to be one long `SecFile.txt` at the end, which will be used to run the utility.

US_owner

This user should be able to access all the members of Entity dimension, as he heads USA. Hence, it includes all the states including eastern, western, southern, and northern regions.

Now, we'll look at the file.

The first three lines rounded in red are for 'Account' dimension members. We have given 'write' access to all the members of this dimension and inheritance is all the descendants including the member that is `@IDESCENDANTS`.

Next are the rows in green, which are all the members of 'Clients' dimension; again they have the same powerful 'write' access.

Next is your Entity dimension; as its 'US_owner' the big boss of USA, we give him write access to all the descendants of USA, which is rounded in blue.

Next in yellow are the member of Scenario dimension, and lastly we have given access to the 'Version' dimension also.

Remember, this is only for one user, 'US_owner'.

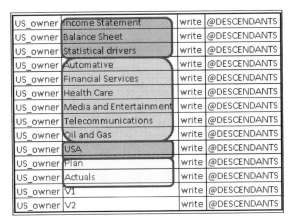

US_owner	Income Statement	write	@DESCENDANTS
US_owner	Balance Sheet	write	@DESCENDANTS
US_owner	Statistical drivers	write	@DESCENDANTS
US_owner	Automative	write	@DESCENDANTS
US_owner	Financial Services	write	@DESCENDANTS
US_owner	Health Care	write	@DESCENDANTS
US_owner	Media and Entertainment	write	@DESCENDANTS
US_owner	Telecommunications	write	@DESCENDANTS
US_owner	Oil and Gas	write	@DESCENDANTS
US_owner	USA	write	@DESCENDANTS
US_owner	Plan	write	@DESCENDANTS
US_owner	Actuals	write	@DESCENDANTS
US_owner	V1	write	@DESCENDANTS
US_owner	V2	write	@DESCENDANTS

We'll see the file for the next user, 'East_owner'.

East_owner

This owner heads the 'eastern region'; hence we see only one difference while we make a file for this user. It would look like the following screenshot; pay close attention to the marked column:

East_owner	Income Statement	write	@DESCENDANTS
East_owner	Balance Sheet	write	@DESCENDANTS
East_owner	Statistical drivers	write	@DESCENDANTS
East_owner	Automative	write	@DESCENDANTS
East_owner	Financial Services	write	@DESCENDANTS
East_owner	Health Care	write	@DESCENDANTS
East_owner	Media and Entertainment	write	@DESCENDANTS
East_owner	Telecommunications	write	@DESCENDANTS
East_owner	Oil and Gas	write	@DESCENDANTS
East_owner	Eastern Region	write	@DESCENDANTS
East_owner	Plan	write	@DESCENDANTS
East_owner	Actuals	write	@DESCENDANTS
East_owner	V1	write	@DESCENDANTS
East_owner	V2	write	@DESCENDANTS

We observe the difference. It was USA for 'US_owner', but user 'East_user' heads only the eastern region. Hence, we give 'write' access to all descendants (inclusive) of 'Eastern Region' to user 'East_user' in row 10 of the previous screenshot. Else, all other rows with an exception of the first column are the same.

Now, we are left with three more users—Mass_owner, New_owner, and Penn_owner. They are respectively responsible planners for Massachusetts, New York, and Pennsylvania. Hence, we need to assign only one member of Entity dimension differently, which is of 'Entity' Dimension. That is, we will Assign write access to Penn_user of Pennsylvania and write access to New_user of New York member of Entity Dimension.

Again, apart from Entity Dimension member access, the other rows would be the same.

Now, we are going to make one single huge file with all the security details of US_owner, East_owner, Mass_owner, New_owner, and Penn_owner.

As we had made it in Excel, we'll copy the entire content from the Excel sheet and paste it in a notepad. We know what notepad; we are talking of the 'SecFile.txt' notepad.

We need to remove the earlier entries of SecFile.txt and add all of these new entries and save it. The file now should have a total of 70 rows (5 users and 14 rows each). The text files would look like the following screenshot.

Don't make the mistake of saving an Excel file using 'save as' to .txt, because that won't work. Copy the contents from Excel and paste it in to SecFile.txt.

```
File  Edit  Format  View  Help
US_owner          Income Statement           write    @DESCENDANTS
US_owner          Balance Sheet     write    @DESCENDANTS
US_owner          Statistical drivers        write    @DESCENDANTS
US_owner          Automative        write    @DESCENDANTS
US_owner          Financial Services         write    @DESCENDANTS
US_owner          Health Care       write    @DESCENDANTS
US_owner          Media and Entertainment write  @DESCENDANTS
US_owner          Telecommunications         write    @DESCENDANTS
US_owner          Oil and Gas       write    @DESCENDANTS
US_owner          USA       write    @DESCENDANTS
US_owner          Plan      write    @DESCENDANTS
US_owner          Actuals write    @DESCENDANTS
US_owner          V1        write    @DESCENDANTS
US_owner          V2        write    @DESCENDANTS
East_owner        Income Statement           write    @DESCENDANTS
East_owner        Balance Sheet     write    @DESCENDANTS
East_owner        Statistical drivers        write    @DESCENDANTS
East_owner        Automative        write    @DESCENDANTS
East_owner        Financial Services         write    @DESCENDANTS
East_owner        Health Care       write    @DESCENDANTS
East_owner        Media and Entertainment write  @DESCENDANTS
East_owner        Telecommunications         write    @DESCENDANTS
East_owner        Oil and Gas       write    @DESCENDANTS
East_owner        Eastern Region    write    @DESCENDANTS
East_owner        Plan      write    @DESCENDANTS
East_owner        Actuals write    @DESCENDANTS
East_owner        V1        write    @DESCENDANTS
East_owner        V2        write    @DESCENDANTS
```

The previous screenshot shows a partial view of the SecFile.txt; it will run from US_owner to East_owner and we have rows for the three other users—Mass_owner, New_owner, and Penn_owner. It's a huge file and runs like a snake downwards.

 We could have created a group and assigned all users to a group and made a small SecFile.txt. Readers can try out that option.

We need to be very careful in making this file, else we'll spend an eternity checking the log and examining the file, if the security import fails.

After saving SecFile.txt, let us shoot our command as shown in the following screenshot:

```
C:\WINDOWS\system32\cmd.exe - ImportSecurity.cmd "SRGD,admin"
Microsoft Windows [Version 5.2.3790]
(C) Copyright 1985-2003 Microsoft Corp.

D:\>cd D:\oracle\Middleware\user_projects\epmsystem1\Planning\planning1

D:\oracle\Middleware\user_projects\epmsystem1\Planning\planning1>ImportSecurity.
cmd "SRGD,admin,SL_TAB"
```

Even though we give the password, the utility is dumb and it asks us to enter the password and we shall oblige and press 'enter'. It takes a few seconds, and we should be tolerant enough as there are around 70 rows. It gives the following message:

```
Wed Sep 08 17:12:02 IST 2010 :: Logged in successfully
Wed Sep 08 17:12:03 IST 2010 :: Setting  Access controls....
Wed Sep 08 17:12:04 IST 2010 :: Total Rows Provided=70 Added Successfully for=70

Wed Sep 08 17:12:04 IST 2010 :: Logging off from application ....
Wed Sep 08 17:12:04 IST 2010 :: Logged out of the application.
Wed Sep 08 17:12:04 IST 2010 :: Import security Completed successfully.
```

Wow, it did it for all 70 rows. Not bad, we did a clean job thanks to the utility. Imagine if we had to do the same for 70 rows manually. It is expected from the reader to test each of the users to whom we have assigned access, before moving forward to the next chapter.

Summary

We started the chapter understanding the importance of Security in a Budgeting Application like Hyperion Planning. We assumed a requirement of a fictional company called Sargod Consulting Ltd and created another Planning Application named 'SRGD'.

We even considered a few owners of different geographic locations, where 'Sargod Consulting Ltd' operates and identified users. These users were created in Shared Services.

We then moved on to provision the users to the Planning Application 'SRGD' and also learned about different roles in the Hyperion Planning application, which can be provisioned to a user. We have also understood the process of assigning Dimension members within the Hyperion Planning application. Conclusively, we have also learned an alternate way of using the 'ImportSecurity' utility to assign security access to users. To demonstrate the same, we have assigned security for five users at once using `SecFile.txt`.

In next chapter, we'll start looking at the management process or the workflow process.

12

Budget Process Management

A red rose is not selfish because it wants to be a red rose. It would be horribly selfish
if it wanted all the other flowers in the garden to be both red and roses.

— *Oscar Wilde*

Yes, on similar lines, not every employee in an organization can be a red rose. They
have limited knowledge and limited responsibilities. Hence, to align their budget
entries to organizational goals, managers and people with more responsibility need
to review the budget several times before finally approving it.

In the last chapter, we learned all about security in a Hyperion Planning application.
We'll learn about one of the most important topics in a Budgeting process, which is a
'Workflow process' in this chapter. We'll first understand a typical Workflow process
of an organization and then we'll bring our hero—Hyperion planning—to the front
to learn how much a Planning application can improve the Workflow process of an
organization.

The following is an example of a conversation between a client and Planning consultant.

> **Client**: *We need to bring one problem area to your notice.*

> **Planning Consultant**: *What is it?*

Client: *With our existing Excel spreadsheet budgeting. We find it extremely difficult to track the status of budgets for our departments. The person who enters budget mails to next level manager for his review takes his own sweet time before he promotes to the boss, who can approve. When we are talking of many geographies and different departments and with different people involved, we find it extremely difficult to track the status. We will never know with any certainty who is causing the delays or not doing their job correctly. Moreover, having several different spreadsheets and different versions of status reports floating around in emails is not helping our organization.*

Planning Consultant: *Don't worry. This is very common and it's not an exceptional problem only to your organization. We will be implementing the feature called 'Workflow Process', which addressed this issue. Post deployment, your management will be able to track all the department of all geographies in this Planning application right on your browser.*

The chapter is divided into the following sections:

- **Budget Workflow Process**: We'll first understand the basic Budget Workflow process of an organization.

- **Planning Unit Hierarchy**: We'll define and introduce the concept of the Planning Unit Hierarchy and understand the very basics of 'Process Management Template'.

- **Workflow Process**: In this section, we'll roll up our sleeves to start creating Planning Unit Hierarchy and also learn of alternate ways of creating Planning units using utility.

Budget Workflow Process

Let's start with some synonyms. Process management, Workflow process, or Approval process, they all mean the same. So, when one uses these terms, we know what they mean.

OK, now let us understand a typical budget Workflow process of an organization.

By the virtue of Organizational hierarchy, we definitely have a structure in which CFO, CEO, and COO are on the top of all and gradually the structure broadens itself into many 'Sales Head', 'Legal Head', 'Marketing head', and so on, where we have all VPs or heads and in the next level, we might have departmental or divisional heads. OK, we'll stop right here.

The point which we are trying to understand is that there is no equality in this unfair world and there are always few prerogative managers and even more prerogative senior managers in an organization. These managers draw higher salaries, not because they have huge tummies and are too old to do anything, but on a serious note, because they understand the organizational goals and strategy better. Hence, when we have a specific area head, for example the 'Northern region head' of the US, would be the one who needs to look into the budgets of the departments under northern part of his/her organization and has the responsibility of making sure that the respective departments or divisions submit their budgets, as far as his northern region is concerned.

Workflow Management includes mainly reviewing and approval of budgets of different departments within an organization. 'Review' and 'Approve' are just two options for now, but as we dig more into the chapter, we'll discover more options.

If we look back in time, the budgeting process was implemented mainly using Excel spread sheets. Let us imagine the old way of budget flow, where usage of Excel used to be a reality. Regional heads would submit to a country head, and the country head is the one who needs to review and approve of different regional head's submitted budgets.

In cases when the country head is not convinced with the Eastern area budget, he would request to adjust and re-submit again for his approval. Now, our valuable and antique Excel sheets and documents fly all over from country head to regional head and it might undergo few iterations, which is a common phenomena. There was a great deal of scope for errors, that is they are prone to errors in that process and would definitely take more time when the activity involves adjustment, re-submission and re-reviewing, and finally approval, which is all done manually.

Now, we are Hyperion consultants and can modestly inform the customer about a few good points of our product and we can definitely promise that the whole approval process or Workflow process be drastically brought down by XYZ % of time and that it will not be as prone to any errors. XYZ is left to Hyperion sales team to do their publicity.

In a typical budget Workflow, organizations have always seen difficulty in understanding the approval status of a specific region; this raises the concern and challenge of accountability and ownership. The management had difficulty in knowing the status of a budget of a specific region. Even if a specific problem crops up it's difficult to bring it to the notice of the higher management and get it resolved. Not that it's impossible, but the process is always sluggish and slow when an organization has grown to a massive size and spread across different continents and countries.

Let us imagine a US firm which has spread its operations to 20 other countries and let us pick one of the countries as 'India' and one of the cities in 'India' as 'Bangalore'. Now, for someone who is sitting at the headquarters of this firm in USA, it is extremely difficult to understand what is happening in the Bangalore region, in terms of its status—whether it's approved or not, who is accountable for this place, and who takes the ownership if things go wrong. Generally, the approval process of a location like 'Bangalore' includes many submissions/promotions to many users. For example, a planner enters the budget data of Bangalore and promotes it to the Indian head and after the Indian head reviews it, he/she has to send it to US head for his/her review and final approval. This path from the 'Bangalore' user to the final USA head is called the 'Approval promotional path'.

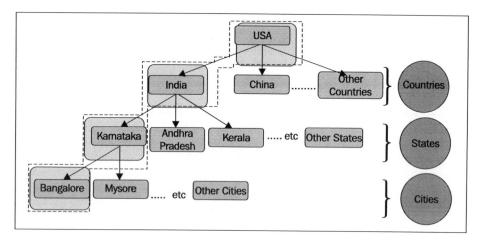

The approval promotional path is the path which gives information of all the users to whom budgets needs to be submitted/promoted in short and gives management better visibility.

It's next to impossible to get this information through e-mails or any other source and Hyperion planning. The Workflow process not only addresses all of these problem areas but also adds more features to make the whole process much simpler and more effective.

Let's make few conclusive beneficial points:

- We can easily get to know the status of every region/department/division.
- We can provide a smart visuals to provide information of the approval promotional path, even to a region of 'Bangalore' in the given example.

- Accountability and ownership is also provided, which will help the management to hold the collar of the guy, who is irresponsible and non-responsive.

We'll move ahead to the next section of understanding the 'Planning Unit' in the Hyperion Planning application.

Planning Unit hierarchy

Now, we will try to understand the concepts of a Planning application, namely, the Planning Unit, which is helpful in Workflow of Budgeting process.

- **Planning Unit**: We'll define and understand a 'Planning Unit' in a Hyperion Planning Application in this section.
- **Process Management Template**: We'll introduce three types of templates in this section and understand the basics of the same. We'll explore more of the 'Process Management template' in the following chapter.

Planning Unit

What is a 'Planning Unit'?

The definition goes as the combination of a Scenario, Version, Entity, and an optional secondary dimension. Yes, the readers must be asking themselves **"What is a secondary dimension?"**. We will come to that in a while.

This combination is the very basic unit, which plays an important role in tracing a Budget unit, that is, Planning Unit.

Let us elaborate a combination of a Scenario, Version, and Entity with the help of a simple English statement:

"First Draft" of the "New York" Budget.

Or:

"Budget" values of "New York" in our very first "Draft".

Here, in this particular statement, 'Budget' would be member of the 'Scenario' dimension, 'New York' would be of the 'Entity' dimension and finally 'Draft' would be of the 'Version' dimension as depicted in the following image:

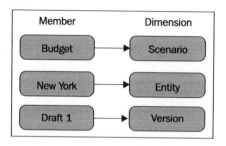

It makes sense to track this combination, to understand the status of the budget of the location of 'New York'. Hence, we always have 'Planning Unit' as the very base to submit/promote or to review/approve. We have understood a little more of a Planning Unit. But, we have not spoken anything of 'secondary dimension'.

Secondary dimensions

What is a secondary dimension and what is its relationship with a Scenario, Version, and Entity?

Here it goes: the Planning Unit was initially defined as a combination of a Scenario, Version, and Entity all through the history of Hyperion planning, but the definition has been changed and re-defined as the combination of a Scenario, Version, Entity, and secondary dimension in this new version of 11.1.2.

Now, let us get into little more details of this interesting concept of 'secondary dimension'. In real time, the Workflow process might not always stick to just the three dimensions of Scenario, Version, and Entity.

We will talk of two cases. Case 1, where there is no need for a secondary dimension and Case 2, where we would require a secondary dimension.

Case 1

Let us consider a business situation, where there is no need for the secondary dimension. There is a state **New York** of **Eastern Region**. The planner by name **NY1** takes care of entering the budget values of 'New York' and he has to promote the Planning Unit to the 'Eastern region' head, that is, **ER1** (another user). **ER1** has to review and if he is OK with the entered numbers by **NY1** of 'New York', he would approve it. In this case, we don't see the intervention of any secondary dimension as such. It is assumed that both **New York** and **Eastern Region** will be represented as members of the Entity dimension.

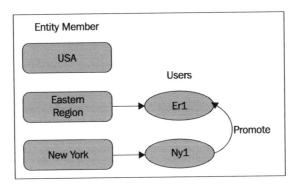

Case 2

Now, let us complicate the requirements a little more to discover the necessity of the secondary dimension in a Planning Unit. We'll consider "Sargod Consulting Ltd", where we need to budget a region of their clients and need to note that this firm is willing to have separate budget approval flows for each of its clients.

Let us elaborate, there are many resources working at the 'New York' office of 'Sargod Consulting Ltd' and they serve different clients like Global Petro Ltd, Global Teleco Ltd, and so on. Hence, the firm would be interested in planing and budgeting for how many of the 'New York' resources are going to incur how much of the expenses in the process of serving and working for the client 'Global Petro Ltd' and on the similar lines how much of 'New York' resources going to incur expense while working for another client 'Global Teleco Ltd'.

Therefore, we cannot budget just for the region 'New York'; there is a necessity to budget 'New York' along with their client 'Global Teleco Ltd' and also need to budget the same 'New York' region with another client 'Global Petro Ltd'. Now, in these kind of situation, we see the necessity for the secondary dimension 'Clients', which also needs to be promoted unlike only the 'Entity' dimension of region, as we had done previously.

Therefore, to have separate budget flows for each of the clients, we would require a secondary dimension.

Therefore, there might be two users NY1 and NY2, NY1 is responsible for 'New York' and client 'Global Teleco Ltd' and NY2 user is responsible for the same region 'New York' but different client 'Global Petro Ltd'. Both NY1 and NY2 have to effectively budget values of 'New York' but for different clients. Also, when NY1 is entering data, the system should definitely allow NY2 also to enter data. Though NY1 and NY2 are entering data for the same New York region, they are providing budget values for different clients of New York. This kind of requirement is very common and Hyperion has realized that they are already late and felt "it's better late than never" and enhanced the basic definition of a Planning Unit by adding a secondary dimension to it. If we have not understood the long paragraph theory, we'll understand when we look at the application in the subsequent sections of the chapter.

Hence, we can state the following:

"First Draft" of "New York" "Budget" for its client "Global Teleco Ltd".

Or:

"Budget" values of "New York" in our very first "Draft" for its client "Global Teleco Ltd".

And:

"First Draft" of "New York" "Budget" for its client "Global Petro Ltd".

Or:

"Budget" values of "New York" in our very first "Draft" for its client "Global Petro Ltd".

The same is depicted in the following image:

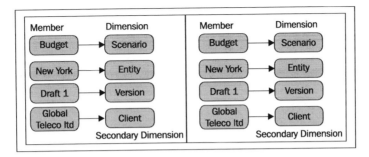

Process Management Template

The Process Management Template is the Hyperion Planning feature that enables implementation of Budget flows. They lay down the basic structure and rules based on which the budget approval process will be designed and executed.

While we create a 'Planning unit hierarchy' we need to select an important field of 'Process Management Template' and this option determines the complete Workflow. We'll see how the following three templates impact the Workflow and also understand in which cases, do we select them in *Chapter 13*. For now, we'll look at basics of the same.

Hyperion Planning provides three different types of Process Management Templates that can be used for implementing an organization budget approval flow in Hyperion Planning. This is broadly classified into three, they are:

- Bottom-up budgeting
- Distributed budgeting
- Free-form budgeting

Bottom-up budgeting

Rather than defining and then explaining with an example, let us directly understand with the help of examples. Let us consider our new Planning application 'SRGD' and its Entity dimension structure. We have always been told that the 'Entity' dimension is designed in the Planning application, keeping the budget flow of the organization in mind. Now, let us elaborate a little more on this matter.

Looking at the part of 'Entity' dimension, we see the structure is designed from Entity to USA, then from Country level USA to a regional level Eastern Region, then from regional level to state level. This is the hierarchy and it does reflect the budget flow of the firm.

In case of bottom-up budgeting, Users/Planner first enter their budgets at their respective states, namely, Massachusetts, New York, and Pennsylvania, which is the leaf level or bottom level. Then we walk upwards to the Eastern Region, whose values are rolled up or consolidated as per the organization hierarchy designed.

Coming to the approval process, as we understood in bottom-up budgeting, first the budgets at state level are submitted to the Eastern Region user (Eastern Region head) for his review and promotion. Then, after all the state-level review is over, then the USA head (who heads all the Eastern Region, Western Region, Southern Region, and Northern region) has to review and finally approve of the budgets sent by the regional heads. Now, we understood why we call it is as 'bottom-up'.

Hence, this way in bottom-up, the Planning Unit moves from a 'New York' owner to 'Eastern Region' owner and then from 'Eastern Region' owner to 'USA' owner. This movement is from person to person (from one reviewer to the other reviewer) and it's already defined in the bottom-up process management template.

> Therefore, there is an already defined promotional path from one person to the other in bottom-up process management template users have to promote the Planning Unit but the next reviewer is determined automatically based on the hierarchy.

We'll see this more clearly in an example in *Chapter 13*.

Distributed budgeting

In this budgeting, the budget values are defined at the top level first (USA level), and then it gets distributed down to the regions (Eastern, Southern, Western, and Northern). If we pick one region for example, 'Eastern Region', after 'Eastern Region', it flows further down to states of New York, Pennsylvania, and Massachusetts.

We can easily make out that this budgeting is exactly the opposite of 'bottom-up'. We 'distribute' to the next lower levels and we 'submit' to the next upper levels in 'distributed budgeting', we don't 'promote' to next upper level, as we do in 'bottom-up'.

In bottom-up budgeting, Planning Units are promoted to the next reviewer, whereas in distributed budgeting, they are distributed and submitted to the other owners or reviewers.

Submitting, distributing, promoting. It's confusing. Yes, that's true But, these concepts will be better understood when we start creating workflows, which we will do in *Chapter 13*.

For 'distributed budgeting' also, there is a definite promotional path, which decides how the Planning Unit has to be moved from one user to the next reviewer. We will see more of this in the next chapter.

 Therefore, for both 'distributed' and 'bottom-up', the promotional path is set and one need not select the next owner for the Planning Unit. It is done automatically based on the promotional path.

Free-form budgeting

As the topic heading says, it's free from. In this kind of budgeting, the planner needs to select the next reviewer unlike the 'bottom-up' and 'distributed' budgeting.

The automatic selection of the next owner is not available in this budgeting template and one has to select the next user for review explicitly. For example, in the earlier example, we saw that when the 'New York' planner after providing his budget number would promote the budget to the next user, the budget will be promoted automatically to the Eastern region head.

Whereas in the same example, in the case of free-form budgeting, the 'New York' planner has to explicitly select the next owner that is, the Eastern region head to promote the 'New York' budget for his review.

We'll see this form of budget demonstration in next chapter. Now, we have understood the basics concepts of 'Process Management Template'.

Enough of the theory, let's work on the application.

The Workflow process

To set up an Hyperion Planning Workflow process, we need to do the following:

- Create a Planning Unit hierarchy: This is the very first step in setting up a Workflow process, where we select the Entity dimension members, the secondary dimension, and other important settings.

- Assign a Scenario and Version: The Planning Unit is a combination of Scenario, Version, and Entity. In the previous section, we had saw the creation of a Planning Unit, which included only Entity dimension and Secondary dimension. In this section, we'll learn how to make a Planning Unit complete by assigning the Planning Unit Hierarchy, which was created in the previous section to Scenario and Version dimension.

- File based import/Export: In the previous section of *Creation of Planning Unit Hierarchy*, we do every selection on the planning web, which is impractical in real time. There is an alternate way of providing all the information of the Planning Unit Hierarchy and we'll learn of it in this section.

Before we start creating a Planning Unit and get into the grove of the Workflow process of Hyperion Planning application, let us first understand what exactly would be the requirement and how planning Workflow can be addressed from our Hyperion planning consulting hands.

Requirements

We are now going to talk of the requirement of the Sargod Consulting Ltd firm. We know its Entity dimension, which reflects the budget flow of the firm. Now, our requirement is to set Workflows for the Easter region, which includes Massachusetts, New York, and Pennsylvania along with its serving clients.

Sargod firm does serve its client Global Entertainment Ltd from its Massachusetts operations. Likewise, it serves its client Global Motors Ltd from its Pennsylvania office operations. Here we also need to understand that a state like Massachusetts serves its client Global Entertainment Ltd (a single state) and its resources working for one client, which is Global Entertainment Ltd. State like New York, which has many people working for the firm Sargod Consulting Ltd works for two clients— Global Petro Ltd and Global Teleco Ltd. Hence, we have Planners/Users who enter budget values of their clients (that is, the state).

Hence, we have a Planner **Walt_owner**, who is responsible for entering budget numbers of client **Global entertainment Ltd** of the Massachusetts office. Likewise, we have two planners **Petro_owner** and **Tele_owner** who are responsible for budget entry from the New York office for their clients Global Petro Ltd and Global Teleco Ltd respectively.

Once the owner of a state enters the budgets of his region, he/she needs to promote it to the regional head and then to the country head. All state budgets will be finally approved by the US head that is **US_owner**.

We know by now that the Easter region states have owners like **Mass_owner**, **New_owner**, and **Penn_owner**. We need to introduce more Planners/Users, who are functionally responsible for these geographies. These users don't enter data for their respective regions, but are responsible to the management. Hence, they review the budgets before they are promoted to the next level.

We have users like **Mass_rev**, **Penn_rev**, and **New_rev** who are responsible to review the budget numbers before it is promoted to the next level. Hence, we can call these users reviewers in our case.

Let us explore this in more detail by using the example of Massachusetts.

Global entertainment Ltd is the client of **Massachusetts**. The user **Walt_owner** is responsible for entering budget as shown in the figure and it is promoted to the user **Mass_rev** for this review. Post **Mass_rev** review, it will be promoted to **Mass_owner** and **East_owner**. Finally, it is promoted to **US_owner** for his approval. The same is depicted in the following image:

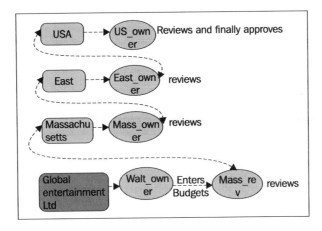

Likewise, we can also understand from the following image that two users **Petro_ owner** and **Tele_owner** would be responsible for entering budgets for their client, New York and then **New_rev** will be reviewing. Post **New_rev**, it will be promoted to **New_owner** for his/her review. After which, **East_owner** will take a look at it before **US_owner** finally approves it.

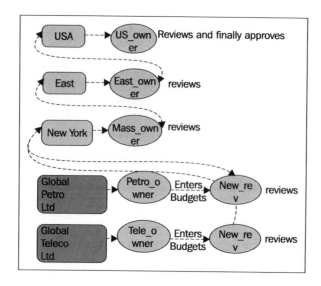

In a real life situation, the Planner who enters data is generally a small fry in the organization and the reviewer is generally his manager/boss, who reviews everything before sending the Planning Unit to next level. Again, the owner is the person who will review the numbers, even after reviewers review them, before he promotes to next level.

You may be thinking that there are too many levels of promotions and reviews. Yes, indeed it's true and it's actually necessary for large organizations.

Creation of a Planning Unit Hierarchy

Starting with the very first task of creating a Planning Unit Hierarchy in the Workflow, we need to provide information of the following tabs as shown:

- Process Management Dimension
- Primary and sub-hierarchy selection
- Assign Owners

Prerequisites

There are three sets of users:

- Owners
- Reviewers
- Users (who enter data for their respective clients)

We have already created users—US_owner, East_owner, Mass_owner, New_owner, and Penn_owner in the *Chapter 11, Security*. We also need to recall that we have provisioned these users with the 'Planner' role for the SRGD Planning application and have also assigned appropriate dimension member security access previously.

Now, we might have realized that we have to create a set of Planners/Users for 'Reviewers' and also for the users, who enter budget data for their respective clients. Hence, we will create the list of users mentioned in the following image as shown in the column **User Name**. We need to assign the role of 'Planner' to the SRGD Planning application and finally we need to assign WRITE access to the dimension member as shown in the following image:

User Type	User Name	Account	Entity	Scenario	Version	Clients
Reviewers	Penn_rev	All members	Pennsylvania	Plan	V1	Global Motors Ltd
	New_rev	All members	New York	Plan	V1	Global Petro Ltd, Global Teleco Ltd
	Mass_rev	All members	Massachusetts	Plan	V1	Global entertainment Ltd
Planners, who enter budgets.	Walt_owner	All members	Massachusetts	Plan	V1	Global entertainment Ltd
	Petro_owner	All members	New York	Plan	V1	Global Petro Ltd
	Tele_owner	All members	New York	Plan	V1	Global Teleco Ltd
	Ford_owner	All members	Pennsylvania	Plan	V1	Global Motors Ltd
	Yes_boss	All members	New York	Plan	V1	Global Teleco Ltd

We see an intruder (**Yes_boss**), he is stranger as of now, but will come handy in next chapter. As of now, create and assign him an appropriate 'Planner' role and dimension member WRITE access.

How do we provide security access?

To refresh your memory, refer to the *Import Security* section of *Chapter 11*.

It will take some time to create Users and provide appropriate security access. We need to ensure we refresh the security by going to **Administration | Application | Refresh Database** and select **Security filters**.

After completion of User security; let us start creating Planning Unit hierarchy.

Let us straight away start working on the application. Log into the Planning application 'SRGD' using the admin credentials.

Go to **Administration** | **Approvals** | **Planning Unit Hierarchy** as shown in the following image:

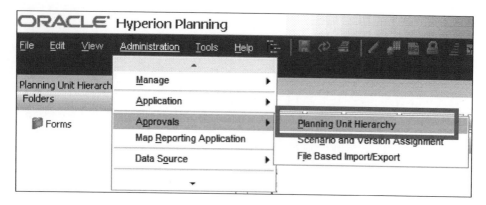

As we have not created any Planning Unit hierarchies, we will see a message that there are no Planning Unit hierarchies. Select **Create**, it shows an empty list as shown. Now select **Create** as shown in the following image:

After we select **Create**, we now see three tabs—**Process Management Dimension**, **Primary and Subhierarchy Selection**, and **Assign Owners**. Let's start with the first one.

Process Management Dimension

In the **Process Management Dimension** tab, we have to provide the following information as shown in the following image:

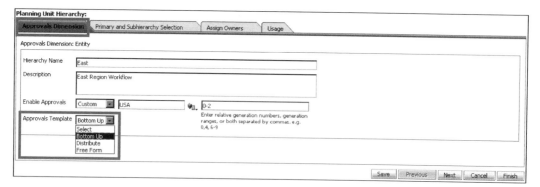

- **Hierarchy Name**: Here we give the name for the 'Planning Unit Hierarchy'. We give 'East', as we are going to create Planning Unit and set Workflow for the 'Eastern region' of the US.

- **Description**: Here we can give an appropriate description of the Planning Unit hierarchy.

- **Enable Approvals**: This is an important option, which decides which members of the 'Entity' dimension are going to be part of the Planning Unit hierarchy. The possible options are:

    ◦ **All**: When we intend to include all the members of the 'Entity' dimension, we should select 'All'.

    ◦ **None**: If we don't want any of the members of the 'Entity' dimension as a part of the process management, then 'None' is the selected option.

    ◦ **Custom**: When we intend to select few of the entity members, as we have the current requirement of only 'Eastern region' related members of Entity. Hence, select 'Custom'.

    ◦ As we selected Custom, we see the member selection space for Entity dimension, and we select USA.

- **Approvals Template**: The possible options for process management template are bottom-up, distributed, and free form. We had already introduced these. Select **Bottom Up** for now. We can change it later anyways.

Click **Next** to move to next tab of the **Primary and Subhierarchy Selection**.

Why USA?

We wanted to show the Workflow budget process for states of Massachusetts, New York, Pennsylvania to the Eastern region and from the Easter region to USA on the top. Hence, we select **USA** as the member and select relative generation number as **0-2** as shown in the image.

What is a relative generation number?

Relative generation is the condition which is evaluated over the member with an objective to select the list of members for the selection of a Planning Unit. The relative generation number is the generation number which is relative to the selected member. It determines the members which will be selected as part of the Planning Unit, starting from the selected member and up to all the members below the selected member having the provided relative generation number.

Let us explore this with the help of an example. After selecting 'Custom', we need to select a member of 'Entity' dimension. This member is called as 'Parent member'. Now, when we select 'Parent member' as USA and then set the 'relative generation number' as 0-2, the condition of 0-2 is evaluated over USA in the dimension of Entity. We can change 0-2 based on the parent member selection. It means, starting from USA as 0, select all the members within USA hierarchy whose generation numbers are 1 and 2. In our Entity dimension, with USA as selected parent member, generation 1 would be Eastern Region, Western Region, Southern Region, and Northern Region as they stand just one step below USA, and generation 2 would be children of all the respective regions.

Let us take another example, if the selected parent member is 'Eastern Region' and the relative generation number is 0-1, then the selected members for Planning Unit would be 'Eastern Region' and its immediate children of three states (as they stand only on level below and the generation number is 0-1).

Finally, if we intent to select only one specific member, we can select the member as 'Parent member' and set the relative generation number to 0.

Primary and Subhierarchy Selection

The 0-2 relative generation number of USA will result in a selection of all regions and states under USA as part of the Planning Unit hierarchy, because all the regions are at level 1 and all the states are at level 2 with USA as the selected 'Parent member'. Now, in this section, we'll de-select all other hierarchies apart from the 'Eastern Region', as we want to create a Planning Unit, which includes only Eastern region and its states.

We see many fields to be filled in this tab.

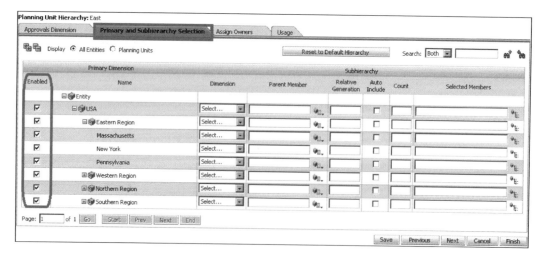

Starting with **Display** which has two radio buttons **All Entities** and **Planning Units** on the top. **All Entities** is the list of all Entity dimension members and **Planning Units** is the list of selected entity dimension members for process management.

With the relative generation number being 2 for USA, which we can see in the following image, the system picks all the Entity dimension members under and including USA. But, as per our requirements, we are interested only in the 'Eastern Region'. For that, we need to uncheck all members of Entity dimension except the Eastern Region hierarchy.

How do we uncheck them?

Right click on **Clients** and select **Exclude All Descendants** as shown in the following image:

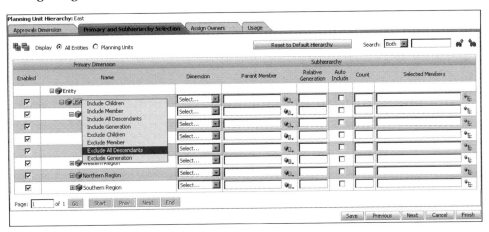

Now, select only **USA**, **Eastern Region**, **Massachusetts**, **New York**, and **Pennsylvania** as shown in the following image:

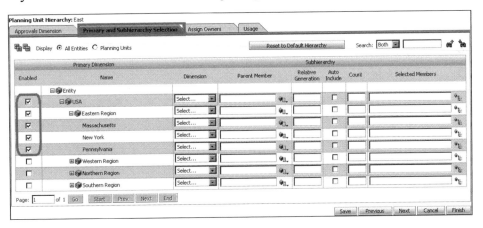

We need to recall that there are two dimensions—Primary and Secondary dimension in a Planning Unit hierarchy. Of course, the Primary dimension is the Entity dimension and we had selected the members of this entity dimension, that is, Primary dimension already, as shown in the previous figure.

Now, we need to select the members of the Secondary dimension. As per our requirement, we need to manage process which also includes Client dimension members. Therefore, Client dimension is the secondary dimension and we'll select few members of this dimension too.

We'll move from left to right in the following image:

- **Enabled**: This shows which of the Entity dimension members are selected as part of the Planning Unit Hierarchy.

- **Name**: It's nothing but the **Primary Dimension**. We know that 'Entity' is always the primary dimension and we see its members in the column under **Name**.

- **Dimension**: This is an important column. Hyperion could have labeled it as 'Secondary dimension' for better clarity. This is the secondary dimension and we need to select a dimension here before we proceed to the next column, **Parent Member**. Select the **Clients** dimension for **USA**, **Eastern Region**, **Massachusetts**, **New York**, and **Pennsylvania** in our case.

- **Parent Member**: Here, we select the parent member of the Secondary dimension. We need to make an important observation here. We cannot select more than one member under **Parent Member**.

   We have to ask to ourselves, what if we have to select two client dimension members against a same entity member such as 'New York', then how do we achieve this?

   First, let us think; if that kind of requirement is legitimate from a business point of view. Yes, the resources of the 'New York' office might be working for two different clients and it's definitely a common case. Yes, we accept the requirement and that's where 'relative generation' is helpful.

We select the 'parent member' and the 'relative generation' in a way that evaluation of the relative generation over the parent member will give the outcome, which includes our desired members for the Planning Unit. In this case, we want entity member 'New York' to have two members of Clients dimension. We would select **Clients** as the **Parent Member** as shown and set the **Relative Generation** as 2. As we set 2 over the parent member 'Clients', all the members of the dimension—'clients' fit the criteria and are selected. But, we don't want all of them; we need only two of them. There are a total of six members which comply with the condition as shown in the following screenshot. Now that we have got all of the members, we can exclude the unwanted ones in the last column, **Selected Members**. Just spare a minute, we'll get there, as we are working from left to right we cannot hop all of a sudden to the rightmost setting.

To the right of the **Parent Member**, we see the image [icon], which will help us in selecting the parent member.

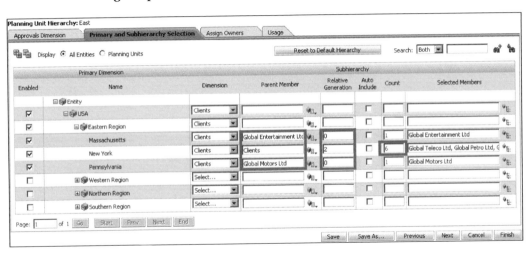

- **Relative Generation**: We learned about this a few pages ago.

- **Auto Include**: This option will help in adding the members of the dimension to be included as a part of Planning Unit Hierarchy. The inclusion is again based on the criteria set by the relative generation and the selected parent member.

- **Count**: It is the total number of selected members of the secondary dimension. In case of Pennsylvania, we have the client dimension member 'Ford' and we set the **Relative Generation** as 0, then the selected member is the single member, that is, the same parent member in this case.

- **Selected Members**: Here, it shows the list of selected members of the secondary dimension. We need to recap our requirement of selecting only two members of client dimension, namely, Global Petro Ltd and Global Teleco Ltd. We selected **Clients** as the **Parent Member** and set the **Relative Generation** as 2, which will select all members and hence we see the **Count** as 6, but we need only two. To do this kind of selection out of the total 'selected members', we have an option to limit our selection. As we see in the following screenshot:

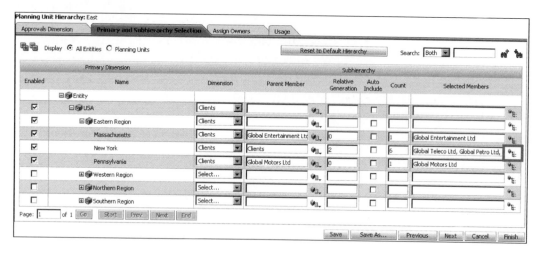

Now, it leads to a new popup, from where, we will select **Global Petro Ltd** and **Global Teleco Ltd** as shown in the following screenshot:

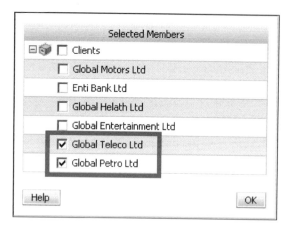

- After selecting these two clients for New York, the final screen of the **Primary and Subhierarchy Selection**' would look like the following:

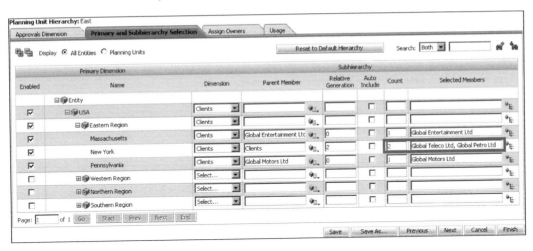

Why are we selecting 'Ford' client member for 'Pennsylvania', 'Global entertainment Ltd' for 'Massachusetts' and two other clients for 'New York'? What is its meaning from a Workflow perspective?

We are trying to demonstrate the Workflow and we have assumed the requirements of the Workflow. When we had assigned Pennsylvania to Global Motors Ltd client, the business meaning is 'Pennsylvania' office of 'Sargod Consulting Ltd' work for its client 'Global Motors Ltd' and we are going to set Workflow process for the same. The Pennsylvanian planner Penn_owner has to fill in budget details of his location serving its client Global Motors Ltd and needs to promote it to Easter Region head East_owner, which we can see in the previous screenshot.

Now, we can explain ourselves the same in case of Massachusetts and its client 'Global entertainment Ltd'. Coming to the New York location, 'Sargod Firm' has some unusual interest in Global clients of 'Global Petro Ltd' and 'Global Teleco Ltd' and we are in the process of setting the Workflow process for the same.

Here, the interesting and important observation would be that there are two planners of New York, who would be interested in budgeting for New York, Petro_owner and Tele_owner. Petro_owner responsibility is of New York and its client 'Global Petro Ltd' and Tele_owner has the responsibility of New York location of the 'Sargod Firm' as far as the client 'Global Teleco Ltd' is concerned.

We'll revisit these two owners in short while. Now, select **Next** to open the final tab, **Assign Owners**.

Assign Owners

From all the reading which we have done so far regarding the Eastern states of US, it is very clear that US_owner is the man responsible for the entire USA for 'Sargod Consulting Ltd' and then we have East_owner who heads the Eastern region of the same firm. Likewise, we have New_owner for New York, Mass_owner for Massachusetts and Penn_owner for Pennsylvania.

Before we start assigning owners—reviewers in this section—it is best to read our *Requirements* section once again.

Now, let us assign the owners of our Planning Unit hierarchy.

 It is important to note that there can only be one owner to any Planning Unit.

We will recap few important points to make assigning easier:

- We know that Penn_owner heads Pennsylvania on the whole, but within this location of Pennsylvania Ford_owner is the gentleman who has the responsibility of entering budget numbers of this location for the client 'Global Motors Ltd'. Also, it is important to note that Penn_rev is the reviewer who would review before he promotes to Penn_owner.

- Coming to 'New York', it's headed by New_owner. Petro_owner and Tele_owner are the two planners that report to him. Tele_owner is the planner responsible for the budget for New York to its client 'Global Teleco Ltd' and Petro_owner is the user who has to budget the same location (New York) but its other client 'Global Petro Ltd'. Hence, after Petro_owner and Tele_owner provide their respective budgets; they would seek the review of their boss New_rev, before it is promoted to New_owner.

- The same logic is applicable to Massachusetts, it is headed by Mass_owner and he has to review the budgets submitted by Walt_owner, who takes care of 'Global entertainment Ltd' clients to its location in Massachusetts.

Finally, we know the owner of USA is US_owner, who has the power to do the final approval of budgets of all states, where the firm 'Sargod Consulting Ltd' has its operations.

This information is enough to assign owners and reviewers:

- At the top, we see USA, the owner is USA_owner and he has the final say. He does not need a reviewer. Hence, we select **USA_owner** as the owner.

- Next is Eastern Region, its owner is East_owner, and he has to review the budgets of eastern states but has to send it to US_owner. Hence, we have selected **East_owner** as the owner for **Eastern Region**.

- For Massachusetts, the owner is Mass_owner and he will review the budgets before he sends them to East_owner for reviewing, before that Walt_owner will enter data for the Massachusetts location to its client Global Entertainment Ltd and promote it to Mass_rev. Mass_rev, as we have understood does not enter but will review before budgets are promoted to Mass_owner. Hence we see the owner as **Mass_owner** and for **Massachusetts: Global Entertainment Ltd**, the owner is **Walt_owner** and the reviewer is **Mass_rev**.

- For New York, Petro_owner and Tele_owner enter budget details of their respective responsibilities and then have to send these to New_rev, for his review before it is sent to New_owner, as he heads New York, who again has to send it to East_owner, as he heads the Easter Region. After he is done with his review, he again has to send it to US_owner and he will give final approval. This is defined as the promotion path and we can very well see this by selecting the promotion path as highlighted in the following image:

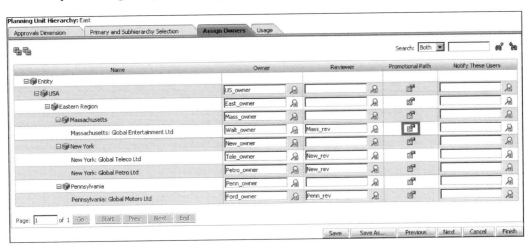

In the following image we can see the promotion path of **Massachusetts: Global Entertainment Ltd**. We can get his path by clicking on as shown in the previous image.

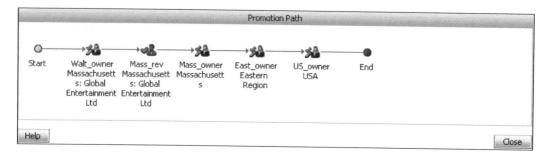

In the following image we can see the promotion paths of the New York location.

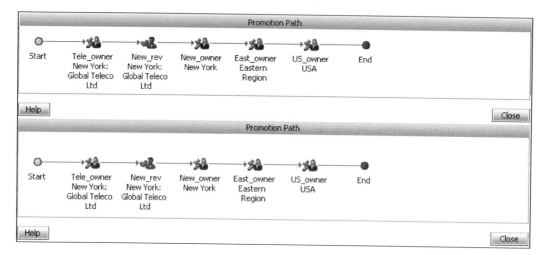

Now, try to relate the previous two images with their respective charts, which we had seen in the *Requirements* section earlier.

Now, we can read from left to right to feel comfortable that we are able to comprehend all the options. We can also see the owner as ⬚ and reviewer as ⬚ in the previous image.

> As said earlier, we can only have one owner of a Planning Unit, but we can have multiple reviewers. We can also create groups in shared services and select the group for reviewers.

The right-most column, **Notify These Users** is a very important feature of this new version of Hyperion planning. Firstly, notifications happen through e-mail. We have to configure the mail server to send e-mails to the user community.

Now, when a Planning Unit is promoted or submitted/rejected or approved, we would always see a requirement that this status has to be intimated to a specific set of people. This can be achieved with this feature of **Notify These Users**.

We can again create few groups and select the groups, which we think as per the requirements are the set of users who need to be informed all about the status and actions of a Planning Unit.

Now, let's elaborate a little on this with the help of the 'New York' location entity. We saw that there are two planners who are responsible for filling in budget details as per their client responsibilities. We can select both these users including the owner of 'New York' in **Notify These Users**. This way, when the user Petro_owner submits his budget details, the other user Tele_owner will get a e-mail saying that Petro_owner has submitted to New_rev. This is important in an organization to keep the required people informed.

When we go to a client place, they always have this requirement. Therefore, we know now that this version has something to offer to the clients. Now, we can include this point in our sales PPT presentation as well.

We have been lazy and have not created any groups. Hence, we have selected individual users for **Reviewers** and selected 'none' for **Notify These Users**.

Select **Finish**. This is the end of Planning Unit hierarchy creation.

Before we start stretching our arms and give an impression that we are tired and need coffee, we will quickly do our next section without losing any momentum.

After we select **Finish** we see the newly created Planning Unit hierarchy. We see a few other options as shown in the following image:

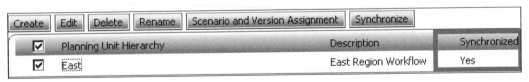

We'll discuss the **Synchronize** option and then we'll do **Scenario and Version Assignment**.

Synchronize

We define dimension members in a Planning Unit Hierarchy and it's common to expect changes in the dimensions in terms of adding and removing members, that might be with the 'Entity' dimension of geographical location or even with the custom dimension 'clients'. Let us look at this from a business point of view, 'Sargod Consulting Ltd', in the process of expanding its business might set up its offices in a new state and this new state has to be part of our Entity dimension now. Also, they might catch hold of new clients, who are impressed with Sargod Consulting firm, and then this new client also needs to be added to the dimension 'clients'. Therefore, dimension changes are expected in today's business and we cannot afford our Planning Unit hierarchies be inflexible by not updating it. In these kind of business situations, the option to **Synchronize** comes very handy.

We select member and the relative generation number for the selection of members for Planning Unit Hierarchy. If we had set a generation number from 0-4 and when a new member is added which is of generation 4, it's supposed to be included as a part of Planning Unit Hierarchy. But, it's not added automatically to the Planning Unit Hierarchy, we need to synchronize in these cases.

It's OK, but how do we get to know, if a new member is added to the dimension and it's required to be added to the Planning Unit Hierarchy?

Or:

How do we get to know, whether the planning dimension structure is in sync with the Planning Unit Hierarchy?

For the lengthy question, the answer is very simple. If we pay closer attention to the previous image, we see a column of **Synchronize** and **Yes** is marked against the Planning Unit hierarchy **East**. It conveys the message that they are in sync. If they are not, we do get to see message like **No**.

We are sometimes surprised by the application when we get a message as shown in the following image, when we try to edit or synchronize.

This happens only when someone is already working on a Planning Unit and it's being edited or synchronized. In these cases, the Planning Unit gets locked.

 Therefore, we cannot synchronize when a Planning Unit is being edited or synchronized by any other user

Scenario and Version Assignment

We have been defining the Planning Unit as the combination of Scenario, Version, Entity, and Secondary dimension. As far as Entity and Secondary dimension are concerned, we had already selected these in the previous sections while we created the Planning Unit hierarchy. Now, it's time to merge our Planning unit hierarchy (which has entity and secondary dimension information) with Scenario and Version dimension members.

For the created **East** Planning Unit hierarchy, we'll check it and select **Scenario and Version Assignment** as shown in the following image:

Selecting **Scenario and Version Assignment** will lead to the following image, where we see no **Scenario** and **Version** dimension members are selected. If we carefully keep the cursor over ![icon], we see the message as shown in the following image. Click on the message or Add button.

After clicking on **Actions**, we need to select **Scenario** dimension member first. We select **Plan** member from the list of Current, Plan, and Actuals.

Next is **Version** dimension member, select **V1**, which is a check box, tick it and select **OK**. After selecting both **Scenario** and **Version** dimension member, we can see the selections as shown in the following image

Now, there is a **Save** option, don't forget to click on that to save the assignment.

This is the end of **Scenario and Version Assignment**. To do a quick recap, we first created a Planning Unit hierarchy with the name **East** and then we assigned **Plan** and **V1** as **Scenario** and **Version** dimension members respectively.

File Based Import/Export

We have understood the importance of Workflow and even had fun creating one, but as greed is insatiable, we would be unhappy with so much clicking business in the process of creating Planning Unit hierarchy. We agree that assigning the Planning Unit Hierarchy with scenario and version dimension was easy. We just can't imagine the amount of work on Planning web if a Planning Unit Hierarchy has to be set up for the entities, which are in hundreds.

Do we have an alternative or do we need to stick to Planning Web to do, as we had done, consuming hours of time?

We are blessed. The Oracle god has showered us again with a smarter way of importing a flat file. We'll learn how to create Planning Unit Hierarchy using 'File based import' in this section.

Yes, greed is good.

File Based Import/Export

As the name suggests, we are going to import a file to load the information of Planning Unit Hierarchy. Hence, we should have a template which reflects all of the information which a Planning Unit Hierarchy would need.

Flat file creation

The flat file has the following fields and we are aware of almost all of them. We'll quickly glance through one by one. Before that it's advisable to go back and check the section *Creation of Planning Unit hierarchy*.

- **Primary Member**: Of course, we know it is Entity dimension member.

- **Primary Enabled**: Possible values are 'True' or 'False'. We would set it as 'True' for the entity dimension member, which needs to be included in the Planning Unit Hierarchy.

- **Secondary Dimension**: We have learned about this already and in our case it is 'Clients' dimension.

- **Secondary Parent**: Remember, we select the 'parent member' for clients dimension and then set the 'relative generation number', which will result in the list of selected members of secondary dimension for the Planning Unit Hierarchy. Here, we select the 'parent member'.

- **Relative Generation**: This is the numeric range and we had learned it with example in section *Creation of Planning Unit hierarchy*. We set it to 0, when we want only the selected parent member, and we set a range like 0-2 or 0-3, when we intent to select list of members which are of generation 1 or 2 or 3.

- **Auto Include**: We saw this setting and we would set it as 'True' or 'False' in the file.

- **Include**: it should be named as 'secondary enabled' on the similar lines of 'primary enabled'. This field can be set as 'True' or 'False' and this is for the secondary dimension or other way of calling it is sub hierarchy members.

- **Secondary Member**: As we mentioned before, we first select the primary members of client dimension and then set the relative generation number to get an outcome of a list of selected members of secondary dimension that is 'clients'. Here, the secondary member is the selected members of clients dimension.

- **Owner**: Here we will list appropriate owners as we can see in the following image.

- **Reviewers**: We will list the reviewers here.

- **Notifies**: These are the users, who need to be informed of the Planning Unit. We had a property of 'notify these users' while we were creating 'East' Planning unit hierarchy on planning web.

We can now create a flat file as shown with the help of the above understanding of fields. Here the requirement is to create a new Planning Unit hierarchy which includes only Massachusetts and its client Global entertainment Ltd of Eastern Region of USA, unlike all the states of Eastern region.

Primary Member	Primary Enabled	Secondary Dimension	Secondary Parent	Relative Generation	Auto Include	Secondary Member	Include	Owner	Reviewers	Notifiees
USA	true	Clients			false		true	US_owner		
Eastern Region	true	Clients			false		true	East_owner		
Massachusetts	true	Clients	Global entertainment Ltd	0	false		true	Mass_owner		
Massachusetts	true	Clients	Global entertainment Ltd	0	false	Global entertainment Ltd	true	Walt_owner	Tele_owner	

For Massachusetts, we selected 'Global entertainment Ltd' as the parent member and set the relative generation to 0 to select the same parent member. We could have achieved the same by selecting 'Media and entertainment' as the secondary parent and set the relative generation to 1.

The other fields are self explanatory.

Now, the most important point is to save this flat file as a CSV as shown in the following image. Save the Excel sheet as shown on Desktop. We can save it anywhere, there is no restriction on that front.

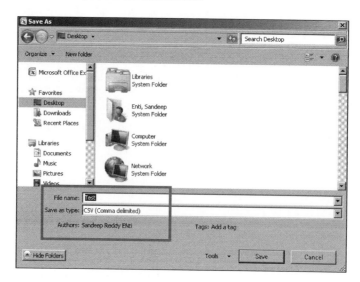

 Any flat file, which we are going to import, has to have an extension of `.exp`. Hence, after saving `Test.csv`, we will rename it to `Test.exp`.

It's extremely important to follow this.

Once, we are ready with our `Test.exp` file, we can import the flat file now. Let us do it in steps:

1. Go to **Administration | Process Management | Planning Unit Hierarchy**. Here we see already created one Planning Unit Hierarchy **East**; we are going to create one new hierarchy now. For that, select **Create** and provide the minimal information of name and description as shown in the following image.

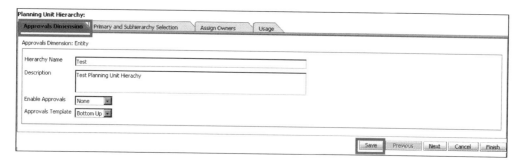

Let us not provide any more information apart from that as we are going to load Planning Unit Hierarchy information through import file option.

 File based import loads only the information of Planning Unit Hierarchy, it does not create one. Hence, before we start importing the file, we need to create a Planning Unit by providing at least the minimum information of 'name' and 'description'

2. Save the Planning Unit Hierarchy and finish. Now go to **Administration | Process Management | File Based Import/Export**. This will open a new window as shown below:

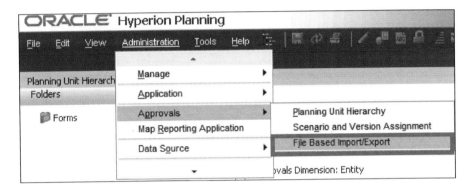

It opens a new window, where we will select the newly created Planning Unit hierarchy, namely, 'Test' and browse for the `Test.exp` file as shown in the following image:

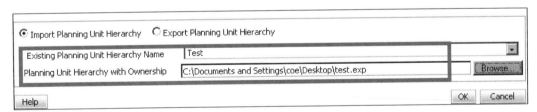

First of all, we observe that we have two options—**Import Planning Unit** and **Export Planning Unit**. Here, we are interested in importing the Planning Unit Hierarchy information. Hence select the first options.

3. The two options below are as follows:

   ○ **Existing Planning Unit Hierarchy Name**: it's a drop down list; we should see **East** and **Test** as the possible options to select. We are not interested in disturbing the 'East' Planning Unit Hierarchy. We had created a new Planning Unit Hierarchy by name 'Test'. Hence, select 'Test'. Now, we know why we created another Planning Unit Hierarchy before importing the file, as we need to select the Planning Unit Hierarchy and then import the information of the same.

   ○ **Planning Unit Hierarchy with Ownership**: Yes, we are already ready with our `Test.exp` file, which was saved to the desktop. Browse for the file and select it as shown in the previous image and select **OK** to initiate the import. If we have done things correctly, then we should get the success message as shown below:

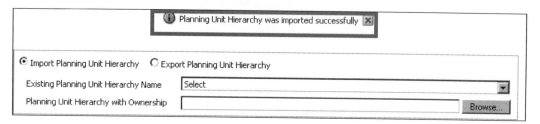

To err is human, and we might have made mistakes in making the flat file. In that case, we would get an error message.

Now, this should ring the obvious question, where do I get to see logs?

`HyS9Planning-syserr.log` is the log file name and is located at `D:\Oracle\ Middleware\user_projects\epmsystem1\diagnostics\logs\services`.

Isn't it easier than what we actually thought?

Summary

We started the chapter by learning about the importance of the Workflow process, as a part of budgeting of a firm. We defined the Planning Unit hierarchy and understood and elaborated on Primary and Secondary dimensions. We also introduced three Process Management Templates.

We assumed requirement of the firm 'Sargod Consulting Ltd'. Based on this firms Workflow requirement, we have started setting up Workflow process and had successfully created Planning Unit Hierarchy—East. Later, we assigned the Planning Unit Hierarchy to Scenario and Version dimension members as well.

Finally, after realizing that there is a smarter way of creating Workflow rather than heavy duty clicking business, we have explored an alternate approach of 'File based Import/Export' and we have created another Planning Unit Hierarchy 'Test' at the end.

The game is still on, we need to accept the fact that we have just started understanding things and in next chapter, we'll advance into process management. In this chapter, we set up process management and in next chapter, we'll learn how to use it.

13
Mastering Budget Process Management

The secret of getting ahead is getting started. The secret of getting started is breaking your complex overwhelming tasks into small manageable tasks, and then starting on the first one.

— Mark Twain

If we thought we had mastered the Workflow processes in a Hyperion Planning application, we're in for some bad news. We were only half way there when we completed *Chapter 12, Data Validation Rules*. We understood the conceptual clarity of Workflow in the Budget process and we have also created Planning units such as 'East' and 'Test' in the previous chapter. In this chapter, we'll learn more about the Process Management Templates of Planning Workflow. It's like a sequel of a successful movie. Let us make this particular sequel even more interesting and a bigger hit.

Let us take a look at a conversation between a client—explaining his/her requirements to a Hyperion Planning consultant:

> **Client:** *We have understood by now that Hyperion Planning has a feature called 'workflow', which can be used to monitor the status of Budgeting. That is very impressive! But how about different budgeting workflows?*
>
> **Hyperion Consultant:** *Can you please elaborate?*
>
> **Client:** *We have multiple budgets like Strategic planning, which we typically want from a top-down kind of flow and other budgeting models, where we would prefer from bottom-up. Can Hyperion Planning fit in these kinds of different budgeting workflow requirements?*

Hyperion Consultant: *Yes, we have different templates, that is, Bottom up, Distributed, and Free form, which will address your entire workflow requirements. Also, we can have multiple planning units, as per your requirements.*

The following are the sections we will cover in this chapter:

- **Process Management Templates**: We have already introduced three kinds of Process Management Templates and discussed them in the previous chapter. In this chapter, we'll explore each and every kind of template with a demonstration.

  - **Free form**: We'll learn about this budgeting format with the help of Planning unit states and actions along with a demonstration in our application.

  - **Bottom up**: We'll learn about bottom-up in the same fashion as free form; by understanding states and actions of a planning unit and finally seeing a demonstration.

  - **Distributed**: After free form and bottom-up, we should ideally be comfortable with this kind of budgeting. But, nevertheless, we'll understand the relevant states and actions of this budgeting and we'll also see a mini demo of the same.

Process management templates

We have understood very clearly that Planning is tracked with the help of a basic unit, that is, Planning Unit, which is a combination of Scenario, Version, Entity, and Secondary dimension. Now, this Planning Unit has to move from one owner/reviewer to the other and finally needs to get its approval. We'll learn about all the different states of a Planning Unit in its journey in a Workflow and what actions need to be performed to move from one state to another. We know the final destination, the Planning Unit needs to get 'Approved'. With that strong goal statement, let us start with Planning unit states.

Before we start, we need to recall the three process management templates:

- Free-form budgeting
- Bottom-up budgeting
- Distributed budgeting

These templates indirectly influence the states and actions of a Planning Unit. We'll start with free-form budgeting in the next section.

Free-form budgeting

To understand free-form budgeting, we need to understand its actions and states. So, let us get started.

Actions and states

In this section, we'll learn about the individual Planning Unit states and actions. They are:

- **Not Started**
- **First Pass**
- **Under Review**
- **Not Signed Off**
- **Signed Off**
- **Approved**

We will first talk of the state name and the possible actions of the state. Let us start with the first state: **Not Started**.

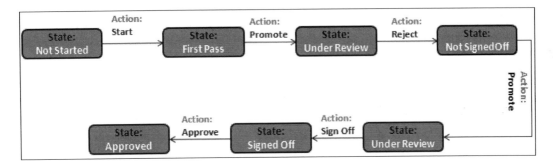

Not Started

This is the very first state of a Planning unit. This is the state which indicates that the planning unit has not turned on the engine to start. That is, the Workflow has not started. The whole review process starts from this state.

> We need to note that a Planning Unit is always started by the administrator.

Action

The only possible action which can be done is to either start or exclude. The **Start** action will initiate the Planning Unit, while the **Exclude** action will take away the Planning Unit from participating in the workflow.

The possible action in this state is:

- **Start**

First Pass

After a Planning Unit is started, it gets into the state of **First Pass**. Now, the Planning Unit is ready to be promoted to a user for its review/approval. From the workflow perspective, once a Planning Unit has started and is in the **First Pass** state, the users who have access can enter, run calculations, and promote them for review.

 In the **First Pass** state of a Planning Unit, there is no owner.

Action

When a Planning Unit is in **First Pass**, it can either be promoted or approved. The 'Promotion' action will make a user the owner of the Planning Unit so that he or she can review and edit the data, while the 'Approval' action will approve the Planning unit. In Free-form, any user can approve a planning unit after it has started. We need to recall one important point that we had learned in the previous chapter; that ownership is not automatically given to the next user in Free-form budgeting. Instead, we need to explicitly select the next owner from the list of available users, unlike how it's done in automatic fashion in Bottom-up and Distributed budgeting. We will demonstrate the same in our Planning application in a while, until then, remember the concept.

The possible actions in this state are:

- **Promote**
- **Approve**

Under Review

Once a Planning Unit is promoted or submitted to someone. Its status becomes **Under Review**. It signifies that someone is reviewing the budget data (remember, generally the data is entered during **First Pass**). Post review, it depends on the mood of the current owner of the Planning Unit, who is reviewing whether to sign off, promote to another user, or approve the budget data.

Action

When a planning unit is in the **Under review** state, the possible actions are **Promote**, **Sign Off**, **Reject**, or **Approve**. We had learned already about **Promotion** and **Approval**. The current owner can sign off a planning unit. **Sign Off** signifies that the values for the planning unit look good and it's typically signed off before the final approval.

The other action is **Reject**, if the numbers don't look too good and need some adjustment or changes, the planning unit is rejected. The planning unit is rejected to another user. That is, the ownership of the planning unit is transferred to another user so that another user can change or adjust the values and promote the planning unit again for the review process.

As we saw in the previous screenshot, the process is rejected and it leads the planning unit to the state of **Not Signed Off**.

> The **Promote** and **Reject** action will transfer the ownership from a user to the other, while the **Approve** action will transfer ownership from the current owner to the administrator, as there is nothing to be done after doing the final approval. Coming to the **Sign Off** action, the ownership stays with the current owner.
>
> Once a planning unit is promoted to the next user, the data for the planning unit can only be entered/changed by the next user. The current user, who had promoted, cannot enter or edit the data in the form anymore. For example, if user A promotes to B, the user can only edit the data of the planning unit in **Free Form** budgeting. We'll see how the data edit property varies in other templates.

The following actions are discussed:

- **Promote**
- **Sign Off**
- **Reject**
- **Approve**

Not Signed Off

It's the state of a planning unit when it is rejected, as we saw in the previous figure.

Action

A Rejected planning unit again has the same action options of **Promote, Sign Off, Reject**, or **Approve**. As we saw in the previous figure, the rejected planning unit is re-entered with the new set of values and again promoted to the next user. This time, we'll bring some smiles to the planning unit by signing it off.

The possible actions in this state are:

- **Promote**
- **Sign Off**
- **Reject**
- **Approve**

Signed Off

A planning unit, when it is signed off, is in the state of 'signed off'. There is nothing more to say about it but we can conclude by saying that 'sign off' pretty much means a happy ending.

Action

A planning unit which is in the **Signed Off** state, can possibly be promoted, rejected, or approved. We saw in the previous image that the signed-off planning unit is finally approved.

The possible actions in this state are:

- **Promote**
- **Reject**
- **Approve**

Approved

This is the pinnacle; this is where we want all the Planning units to reach. It's the final destination and once a Planning unit is 'approved', the ownership changes from the current owner to 'administrator'. Remember, that 'administrator' is the one who kick-starts it when it finally comes to him. It reminds us that admin throws the Planning unit like a boomerang, which finally returns to him.

Action

It's all over, it's finally approved and we don't want any more actions over an approved Planning unit.

 An administrator can edit data at any state and at any point of time; the state of the Planning unit does not matter.

So, we have learned about **Not Started, First Pass, Under Review, Not Signed Off, Signed Off,** and **Approved** with the knowledge of actions on planning units like **Start, Promote, Reject, Sign Off,** and **Approve.**

In the next section, we'll try to demonstrate the Free Form budgeting with the help of our Planning application **SRGD (Splicing Related Gene Database)**. Remember, we have already created a planning unit with the name **East**. We'll make use of it.

Free-form Demonstration

We'll learn how to manage the Workflow process and see how the Free Form template works in this section.

Prerequisites

The first and foremost thing to check is whether the Planning unit has its property of 'Process Management template' set as 'Free form'.

Log in to the 'SRGD' Planning application using admin credentials (**Username**: **admin**, **Password**: **password**) and navigate as:

Administration | Approvals | Planning unit hierarchy

Here, we'll find the list of planning units. We have **East** and **Test**. We'll bother only with the **East** planning unit. Check the **East** planning unit and select **Edit**. Of the properties of **Hierarchy name**, namely, **description**, enable process management, and so on, we are interested in the last property, that is, 'Process Management template'. As we know, we have three options and we need to ensure that it is 'Free form'; if it is anything else, such as bottom-up or distributed, then select **Free form** and save the **Planning Unit Hierarchy**.

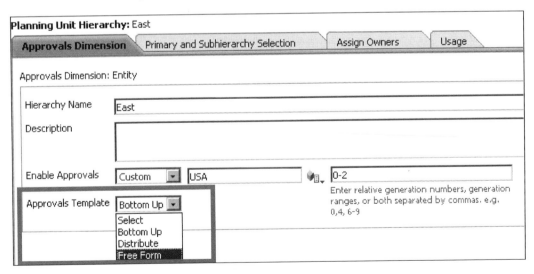

This step of selecting the right option for 'Process Management template' is important, as it impacts the whole workflow process and we are interested in demonstrating free form budgeting for now. In the later section, we'll change from free-form to bottom-up.

Starting Planning Unit

We will start the planning unit and do it in steps from now onwards.

Go to **Tools | Manage Approvals**. Selecting this would lead to a page, where we need to select 'Version' and 'Scenario' dimension members.

Here, we need to remember that after creating our first Planning unit hierarchy **East**, we had an immediate next step of assigning **Scenario** and **Version**, which we had done in the previous chapter and we had assigned Scenario dimension member 'Plan' and Version dimension member of **V1** to **East** Planning unit hierarchy. Hence, select **Plan** and **V1**, as shown in the following screenshot. Note the **Out of office Assistant** link rounded in the next screenshot.

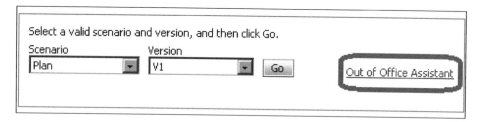

What is the out-of-office assistant?

It's common in a corporation that few of the Planners/users who are part of the Workflow process, may not be available at certain times, that is, not in the office for various reasons. From an organization's perspective, they cannot afford to wait till the Planner/user returns to their office, attending his/her personal needs. This will eventually delay the Workflow process. Therefore, in these kinds of situations, we should be able to give the responsibility to another planner who can act as an alternate reviewer so that the process does not get hampered. Using the **Out of Office Assistant** makes this possible.

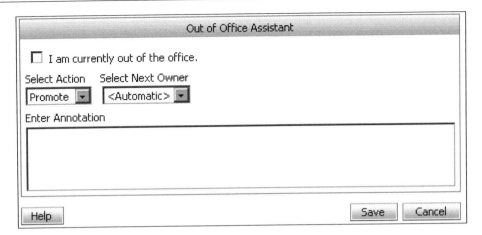

A planner/user can select **I am currently out of office** and select an alternative user to do his/her work and after this planner/user returns from the office, he/she would uncheck the option and get back into action. It's synonymous to configuring an 'Out of Office' message for our Outlook mailbox, when we are on leave or on vacation.

Now, let us not use this option as we are not leaving the book, but remember that there is an option in **Planning** which will help even when a user if out of office. Let us get back to our work now, chanting 'Show will go on'.

Post selection of **Scenario** and **Version** member, as shown in the next screenshot. select **Go**.

We start with an error already. However, 'Error messages' should not be seen as discouraging, they can be incredibly educational. We see the following message.

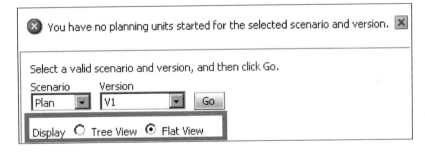

Why don't we see any planning units here?

If we understand the concepts well, we wouldn't need to ask this question. Remember, the administrator is the only one who can start a planning unit and we know that the administrator has not started any of the planning units yet.

One more question: How can an administrator start a Planning unit; he does not even get then list of planning units to start, as shown in the previous screenshot?

Here, we should pay attention to the rounded area in the previous screenshot. There are two display options:

- **Tree View**
- **Flat View**

Tree View, as the name suggests, depicts the Planning units in a tree view which shows a parent child relationship, whereas **Flat view** lists the entire element at the same level, which is flat, and one can filter the columns only in **Flat view**.

 It's only the administrator who can view both **Tree View** and **Flat View**.

Now, select **Tree View**, as **Flat View** gives no results to us.

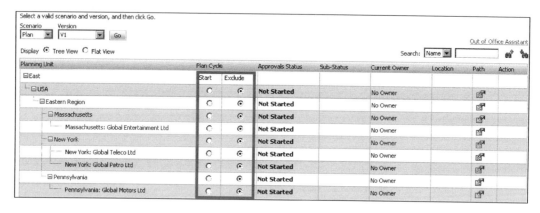

As we select **Tree View**, we see the planning unit and there are many columns, we'll go one by one from left to right.

- **Planning Unit**: It's the planning unit hierarchy, which we had created for **East**. We could also see the secondary dimension members **Global Teleco Ltd** and **Global Petro Ltd**, which are of the 'Clients' dimension, associated with the primary dimension of 'Entity', as shown in the previous screenshot.

- **Plan Cycle**: This column gives information as to whether a planning unit is excluded from the workflow and we rightly see that all of the planning units are not started and as a result are excluded. To start a planning unit, we need to select **Start** to commence the workflow process.

- **Process Status**: We have learned about the states of a planning unit; this is exactly the same. Process status reflects the planning unit state. As of now, in the previous screenshot, we see **Not Started** as the state or process status. Once it's started, it will change its status to **First Pass**.

- **Sub Status**: One can run a validation rule and decide whether to promote the planning unit or even change the promotional path. **Sub Status** gives information of the validation rule run. We see nothing at this point in time, but we will explore this in later chapters.

- **Current Owner**: It's the owner of the planning unit and as we follow the workflow, we can see different current owners. As of now, we don't see any owner, as the Planning Unit has not started.

- **Location**: This is actually the name of the Entity dimension member.

- **Path**: This is the promotional path. It's more useful in **Bottom Up** and **Distributed** budgeting as the path is already set and the ownership is transferred automatically as per the promotional path. We'll learn more about it when we explore Bottom Up budgeting in later sections.

- **Action**: Remember, we have already learned about states and actions; the latter are reflected in this column. As of now, the status is **Not Started**; the possible action is **Start** and we start it by selecting the **Start** button which is rounded in green in the previous screenshot for New York.

1. We'll start the Planning unit for **New York**. We do it by selecting **Start** against both **New York: Global Teleco Ltd** and **New York: Global Petro Ltd**.

   As we start the Planning units, we see the message "Planning unit has been started" and it's in the **1st Pass**. As we had learned that in the **1st Pass.**, there is no owner to a planning unit, hence we don't see the owner, as highlighted in the next screenshot.

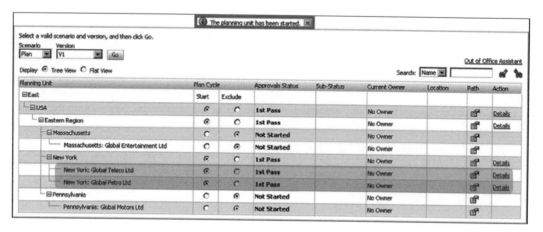

We also observe that the members like 'New York', Easter Region, and USA would also start and are in **'First Pass'**. The simple reason being 'New York' is a child of 'Eastern Region' and it's, in a way, a descendant of 'USA' too. Hence, they all get started as we see in this screenshot. All ancestors of the started Planning Units also get started.

2. During the **First Pass**, users generally enter data and promote to the next users. In 1st Pass of Free Form, we don't see any Current owner for the started Planning units in the previous image.

 First Pass is, in fact, the only state in which multiple users who have access can enter data for the same planning unit. Apart from **First Pass**, in all other states, only the current owner can enter the data and add annotations

Coming to the reviewers, they are not allowed to enter data. They can only add annotations and comments.

Requirement

We'll keep the workflow requirement simple and let us sketch the plot. The two users, **Petro_owner** and **Tele_owner**, will enter budget data of their respective planning units of **Global Petro Ltd** and **Global Teleco Ltd**, and then promote it to **New_owner**, who heads **New York** office for his review and final approval. Sounds very simple, doesn't it? Let us add more twists to our plot now; **New_owner** will get angry and reject the planning unit as he is not pleased with the budget numbers. He will send it back to the **Tele_owner** and **Petro_owner**. **New_owner** also advises them to make few specific changes. So poor hard working **Tele_owner** and **Petro_owner** will adjust the values and then promote again for **New_owner**'s review. This time, **New_owner** is happy. He signs off and finally approves it too.

This can be visualised in the following figure:

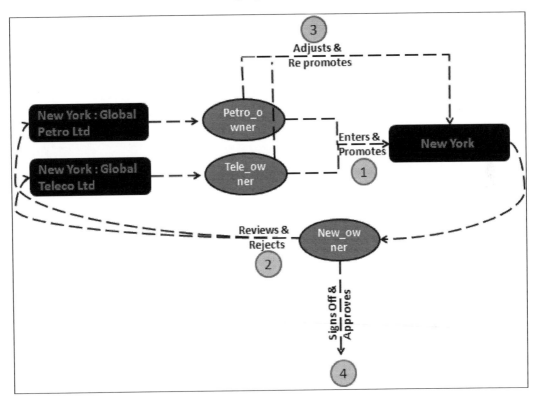

Demonstrating free-form approval template

Our two heroes, **Petro_owner** and **Tele_owner**, as per their respective responsibilities, enter data in the **Test** data form, which we had created in Chapter 11, *Security*.

Step 1

Log in to the **SRGD** Planning application as **Tele_owner** and open the data form **Test**. Select the Page dimension members, as shown in the following screenshot, such as **Plan**, **V1**, **Local**, **New York**, and **Global Teleco Ltd**. We see that the planner, **Tele_owner**, enters data into this data form for Jan, Feb, and March, as shown in the next screenshot:

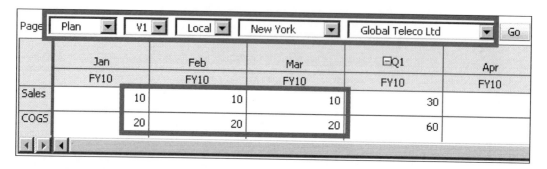

Now, log out of the SRGD Planning application, log in as **Petro_owner**, and open the **Test** data form. Do the same thing; open the data form with a different Page member selection: **Plan**, **V1**, **New York**, **Local**, and **Global Petro Ltd**. As we see in the next screenshot, **Petro_owner** will also enter data for **New York: Global Petro Ltd**.

Page	Plan	V1	Local	New York	Global Petro Ltd		Go
	Jan	Feb	Mar	⊟Q1	Apr		
	FY10	FY10	FY10	FY10	FY10		
Sales	30	30	30	90			
COGS	40	40	40	120			

Step 2

Now, we'll promote the planning units to **New_owner**, as per our requirement. Refer to the first figure under the *Requirement* section. As we have already logged in as **Petro_owner**, we will promote **New York: Global Petro Ltd** to **New_owner** first.

Go to **Tools | Manage Approvals**, select **Plan**, and **V1** as the dimension member selection of **Scenario** and **Version** respectively. Select **Go**, as shown in the next screenshot:

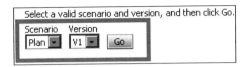

After we select **Go**, we can see the planning unit of **New York**: **Global Petro Ltd**. We know that our objective is to promote **New York**:
Global Petro Ltd to **New_owner**. Select **Details** under **Action**, as shown in the following screenshot:

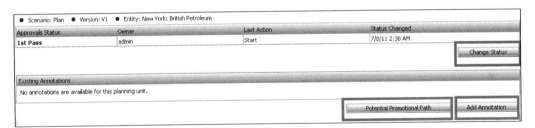

Upon clicking **Details**, we see that we have a few options. They are:

- **Change Status**
- **Potential Promotional Path**
- **Add Annotations**.

We can see this in the next screenshot:

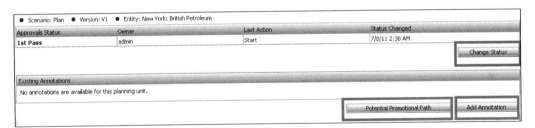

What are Annotations?

We define an annotation as additional commentary or critical information. We can add an annotation to a planning unit to help a user in determining what to do and what are the assumptions taken or anything, in short, that can act as a guideline. We'll see how these annotations come in extremely handy throughout this chapter.

We want to promote to **New_owner** and **change the status,** as is rounded in red, in the next screenshot. Select **Change status**.

It opens one more new and small window and we need to select two things—Action and Next owner. We need to select **Promote** and we rightly selected it, as shown in the next screenshot. We also have to observe that there are only two possible actions at this junction of this planning unit—it's whether to promote or approve. We'll select **Promote** and from the list of users, select **New_owner** as per our requirements. Also, we would prefer to give annotation, as shown in the following screenshot. The next owner, in this case, **New_owner**, will get an immediate e-mail notification once the change is submitted.

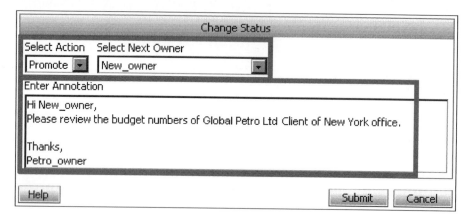

Finally, select **Submit**. After we click submit, we can see the message **Change status submitted**, as shown in the next screenshot:

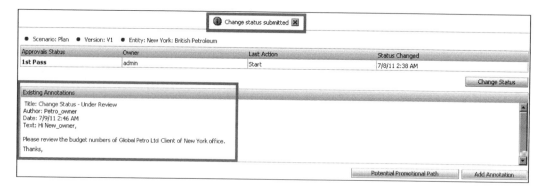

Step 3

We will do a quick recap at this point of time. Both the users, **Petro_owner** and **Tele_owner**, had entered into the **Test** data form for their respective clients, Global Petro Ltd and Global Teleco Ltd. After that, **Petro_owner** promotes the Planning unit of New York: Global Petro Ltd to **New_owner**. Now, we have to promote **New York**: **Global Teleco Ltd** to **New_owner**, as per our requirement. We need to follow similar instructions as mentioned in *Step 2* to promote the Planning unit of **New York**: **Global Teleco Ltd** to **New_owner**.

Log in to the SRGD planning application as **Tele_owner**. Go to **Tools | Manage Approvals**. Select the **Scenario** and **Version** dimension members as **Plan** and **V1** respectively, as shown in the screenshot under *Step 2*. We see the planning unit **New York: Global Teleco Ltd** in **First Pass** without any current owner. Let us promote it to **New_owner** by selecting **Details**, as highlighted in the following screenshot:

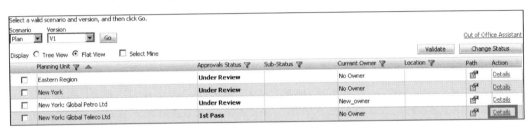

Select **Change Status**, as shown in the previous screenshot.

Now add annotations, as shown below, and promote the planning unit to **New_owner**.

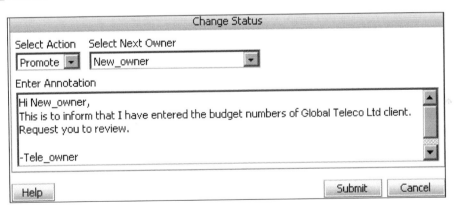

The planning unit, **New York: Global Teleco Ltd**, is now in the status of **Under Review**. To elaborate, it is under the review of **New_owner** and we can see the current owner is **New_owner**.

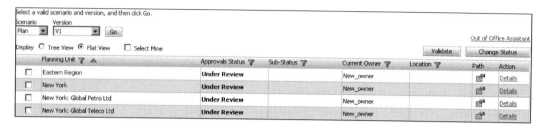

Therefore, we have successfully promoted the planning units of **New York: Global Petro Ltd** and **New York: Global Teleco Ltd** to **New_owner**. Now, we should be confident regarding how to change the status and how to promote any planning unit from a user to the next owner. After we promote, **New_owner** gets an e-mail in his/her inbox along with annotation and the planning unit information, informing him that the planning unit is under his/her review and he/she is the owner of the planning unit.

Before we go to the next step, where in we will log in as **New_owner** and review, let us log in to the SRGD application and open the **Test** data form at this junction as **Petro_owner**.

Log in as **Petro_owner** and access the form. It should appear as shown in the next image:

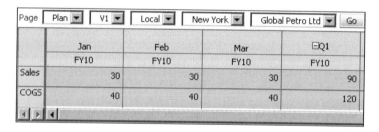

You may be wondering why is it all gray, which means that the user **Petro_owner** cannot enter or edit data in the form. This is because of planning unit promotion. Yes, indeed it is true that **Petro_owner** had the responsibility of entering budgets as far as the client **Global Petro Ltd** is concerned, but he/she has promoted it to **New_owner**. Hence, after a planner promotes, he/she will no longer have the privileges required to enter or edit data. Now, let us think about this from a budgeting angle. The **New York: Global Petro Ltd** planning unit is promoted to the **New_owner** and it is under his/her review. Hence, it's logical that no one should be able to edit while the **New_owner** is reviewing it.

On similar lines, we can try to log in as **Tele_owner** and witness the gray cells of the **Test** data form as the **New York: Global Teleco Ltd** planning unit is also under the review of the very boss of **New_owner**.

> This is extremely important that when a planning unit is currently owned by a user and he/she is reviewing it, another user should not be able to edit the data.

Step 4

Now, log off at once and log in to the SRGD application using the credentials of **New_owner**. He/she needs to know the planning units, which he/she has the responsibility to review. Go to **Tools | Manage Approvals** and select the **Scenario** and **Version** dimension members. Now, select the option of 'Select Mine', as shown in the following screenshot. This option will tick the Planning unit application to the user.

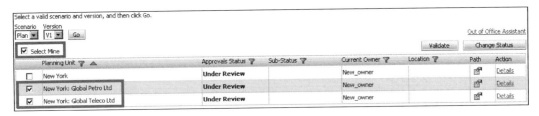

> Every time a user selects a **Manage Approval**, it's extremely important to select the option of **Select Mine** to get his/her relevant planning unit and we should stick to it all through.
>
> We don't see an option of **Select Mine** when we log in using admin credentials. The obvious reason is that the 'administrator' is the boss of all planning units at any stage, even if it's under review by an other user. In short, all planning units are his or hers.

Now, **New_owner** knows that he/she has to review for both his/her clients **Global Teleco Ltd** and **Global Petro Ltd**. In the process, he/she opens the data form **Test** to review the numbers, as shown in the next image:

Page	Plan ▼	V1 ▼	Local ▼	New York ▼	Global Petro Ltd ▼	Go

	Jan	Feb	Mar	⊟Q1	A
	FY10	FY10	FY10	FY10	FY
Sales	30	30	30	90	
COGS	40	40	40	120	

◄ ► ◄

Page	Plan ▼	V1 ▼	Local ▼	New York ▼	Global Teleco Ltd ▼	Go

	Jan	Feb	Mar	⊟Q1	A
	FY10	FY10	FY10	FY10	FY
Sales	10	10	10	30	
COGS	20	20	20	60	

◄ ► ◄

The very first observation is that **New_owner** can edit or change the numbers. The cells in the form are in a pleasant yellow than a cold gray. This reiterates the important point that the planning units are under his/her ownership, as he/she is the current owner.

New_owner is not impressed with the budget numbers, as he/she thinks that Sales should be more than COGS, else they would be making losses eventually. He/she outright rejects both the planning units. He/she wants Sales for Jan to March that need to be adjusted by increasing by 15 for all 3 months of Jan, Feb, and March send him/her back again for his/her review.

Hence, **New_owner** decides to avoid suggesting the changes.

 In real time, the reasons for rejection may be very subjective and generic, the rejected unit undergoes data adjustment and this should remind us that we had learned all about the data adjustments and changes within a data form in *Chapter 9, Data forms.*

How can New_owner reject and revert to Petro_owner and Tele_owner of their respective clients of Global Petro Ltd and Global Teleco Ltd?

Go to **Tools | Manage Approvals**.

We know that **New_owner** is not impressed with either of the planning unit numbers. He starts with **Global Teleco Ltd**. Select **Details**, as highlighted in the next image.

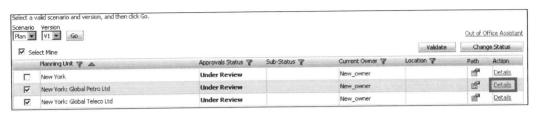

We can see the existing annotation provided by **Petro_owner**. Now, we need to select **Change Status**.

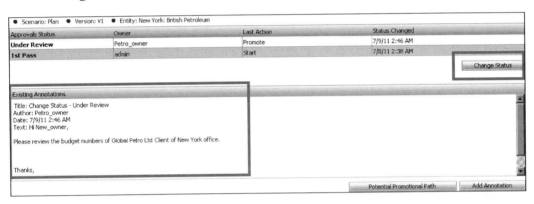

Now, click on **Change Status**. The planning unit has to be rejected and sent back to **Petro_owner**. It was very sweet on the part of the **New_owner** to add annotation regarding what is to be done to the budget values, as shown in the next screenshot:

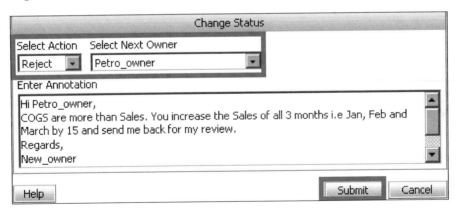

On similar lines, **New_owner** would reject the **New York: Global Teleco Ltd** planning unit to **Tele_owner**, as shown in the next screenshot:

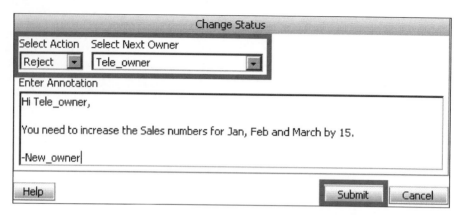

After **New_owner** submits the planning units, we can see that the planning unit status has changed in terms of ownership and also status. Status is **Not Singed Off**; this is because **New_owner** has not signed off the plan.

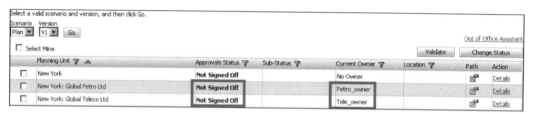

Now, we know the obvious next step, where both our heroes, **Petro_owner** and **Tele_owner**, will get busy in adjusting the numbers and promoting to **New_owner** again.

Step 5

Petro_owner and **Tele_owner**. Both of them get e-mails as **New_owner** rejects and they read the annotation and realizes that Sales cannot be less than COGS and have to change the values in the data form **Test**.

Log in to SRGD as **Petro_owner**. Open the data form **Test**. We observe that **Petro_owner** can edit the data now because he/she attained the ownership.

	Jan	Feb	Mar	⊟Q1
	FY10	FY10	FY10	FY10
Sales	30	30	30	90
COGS	40	40	40	120

We can adjust the values by right-clicking on the cell, as shown, and go to **Edit | Adjust Data**, as shown in the following screenshot:

	Jan	Feb	Mar	⊟Q1
	FY10	FY10	FY10	FY10
Sales	30	30	30	90
COGS	40	40		120

Edit ▶

Adjust ▶   Adjust Data

Insert Comment   Grid Spread

Supporting Detail   Row COGS. Column

Add/Edit Document

Lock/Unlock Cells

It opens a new window, where we will enter **15** and click on **Adjust Data**.

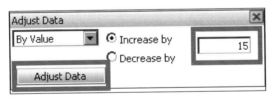

Likewise, edit all cells of **Sales** for Jan, Feb, and Mar and save the data without fail. Finally, the form should look like the next screenshot:

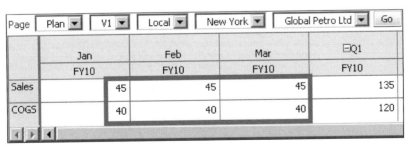

	Jan	Feb	Mar	⊟Q1
	FY10	FY10	FY10	FY10
Sales	45	45	45	135
COGS	40	40	40	120

On similar lines, log off and log in as **Tele_owner** and adjust the **Sales** numbers, as shown in the following data form:

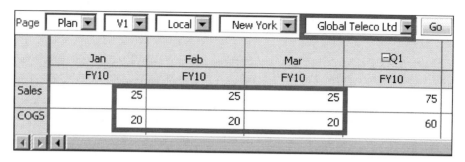

Take a look at the second screenshot, under the previous *Step 4*, to compare it with the new values. The second screenshot under the previous *Step 4* has the previous values of Global Teleco Ltd.

Now, we know that we had adjusted the numbers and the next step is to promote to **New_owner** for review and approval.

We should know by now how to promote units to different owners.

In case of the **New York: Global Petro Ltd** planning unit promotion. Log in as **Petro_owner**. Go to **Tools | Manage Approvals**. Change the status by promoting the planning unit to **New_owner** and give him/her a message, as shown in the next screenshot:

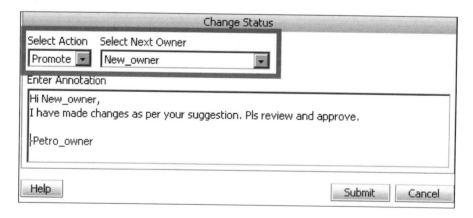

On similar lines, log in as **Tele_owner** and promote the planning unit **New York: Global Teleco Ltd** to **New_owner**.

As far as our requirement is concerned, we have completed *Step 1*, *Step 2*, and *Step 3*, which we can see are rightly ticked in green in the next diagram:

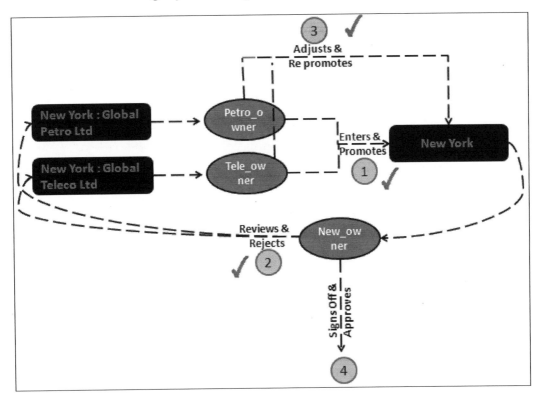

Let us recap the story. Two Planning units were initiated by **admin**, namely, **Petro_ owner** and **Tele_owner**. They entered budgets for their respective clients and were then promoted to **New_owner**.

New_owner reviewed and observed that COGS was more than Sales and rejected it, sending it back to **Tele_owner** and **Petro_owner** and instructing them to adjust it. Post adjustment, it was again promoted to **New_owner**. This is the story so far. Now, **New_owner** has to review the adjusted numbers and should ideally and happily signoff. This process was depicted in the previous figure.

Step 6

In the final step of the planning unit workflow, log in to SRGD as **New_owner**. **New_owner** looks at the budget numbers of both Planning units—**New York: Global Petro Ltd** and **New York: Global Teleco Ltd**. This time he/she is convinced and wants to approve of the planning units without hurting any more planners/ users by rejecting or promoting to other users.

We will approve the planning unit **New York: Global Petro Ltd** first. Select the appropriate planning unit, as shown in the next screenshot:

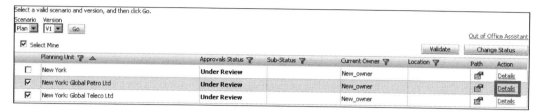

Go to **Change Status** and approve, as shown in the next screenshot. After each and every Planning unit approval, the ownership is back into the hands of **admin**. Hence, we see the user **admin**. Select **Submit** after entering annotations.

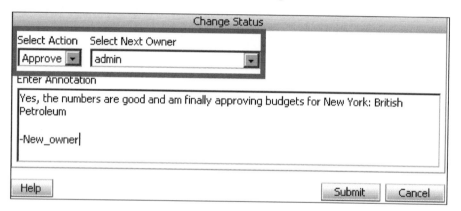

We can now see the complete history of what has happened with our planning unit, as shown in the next screenshot. It talks of **Global Petro Ltd**. This information explains the whole story in a clear manner.

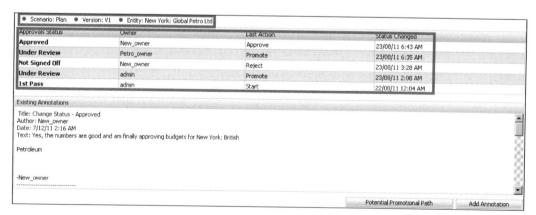

Now we see that the planning unit, **New York: Global Petro Ltd**, is approved and its current owner is **admin**.

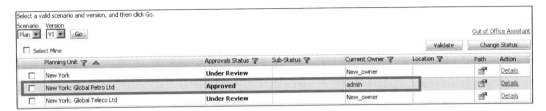

Likewise, approve **New York: Global Teleco Ltd**.

Before we end this section and head for a cup of coffee, let us quickly recap:

It starts from **Not Started** to **First Pass** when the **admin** initiates the Planning unit. **Petro_owner** then enters the budgets for his client and promotes to the **New_owner**. The **New_owner**, while reviewing rejects the budget and requests and adjustment of the numbers. **Petro_owner** adjusts the figures and promotes again to **New_owner**. Finally, **New_owner** approves, and the ownership is sent back to the administrator. This is depicted in the next figure:

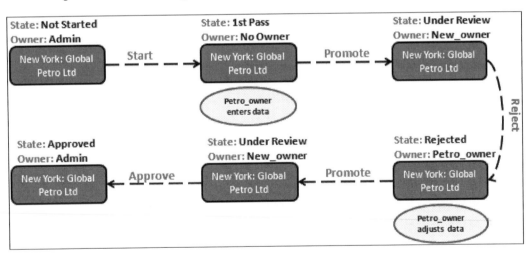

Excellent, we have done a good job so far. Let us move ahead and explore Bottom-up budgeting in the next section.

Bottom–up Budgeting

In free-form budgeting, any user who is the current owner of the planning unit can approve the planning unit. We have seen in free form that we can promote, reject or do any action and select the next owner, as per our wishes. The next owner selection is explicit and we have chosen from the drop-down list of available users. Now, we'll see how 'bottom-up' changes the way budgeting is done.

We'll start by understanding the planning states and actions, which are solely applicable in the case of bottom-up budgeting, and then hit the planning application for the demo. But this time, we'll make it quicker, as the basics of process management are already covered.

- Actions and states
- Bottom-up demonstration

Actions and states

We have already learned a few of the states and actions in the previous section of free-form budgeting. Now, we'll learn about other actions and states that are applicable to 'bottom-up'. Nevertheless, what we had learned of **Not Started**, **Under Review**, **Not Signed Off**, **Signed Off**, and **Approved** is important. We are going to learn about additional states and actions to the already-known ones. They are as follows:

- Frozen
- Take Ownership
- Originate

We will explore these options while we demonstrate them with the help of examples.

Bottom-up demonstration

In this section, we are going to see how budgeting will dance to the music of the 'bottom-up' template. For that, we have to first edit the **Process Management Template** of the planning unit **East**.

Prerequisites

We know that so far the planning unit is with the **Process Management Template** property of **Free Form**. We need to change it to **Bottom Up**. Log in as **admin** and go to **Administration | Approvals | Planning Unit Hierarchy**. Now, check the planning unit **East** and select **edit**. We see the **Approvals Template** property as **Free Form**. We'll change to **Bottom Up** and then save and finish.

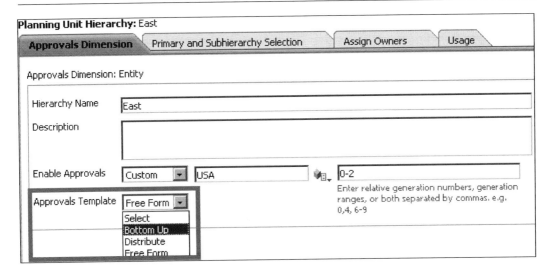

The next prerequisite is that we'll need to exclude the planning unit of **New York: Global Teleco Ltd**, as we are going to see an altogether new form of bottom-up budgeting. We have to exclude the entire planning unit, which we had started in the previous section of free-form budgeting.

Go to **Tools | Manage Approvals**.

Select the **Scenario** and **Version** dimension members and select **Plan** and **V1** as their respective members. Now, select **Tree View**. We see the planning units of New York as approved because of our previous free-form demonstration.

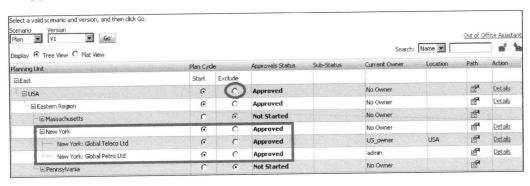

Exclude USA from the planning unit by selecting the **Exclude** option highlighted in the previous screenshot. Excluding **USA**, which is the top member of the Entity dimension hierarchy, will exclude all the members, as we see in the next screenshot. This will give us a clean slate for our bottom-up demonstration as we had dirtied it a little bit while demonstrating free-form demonstration. After exclusion, it would look like the next screenshot:

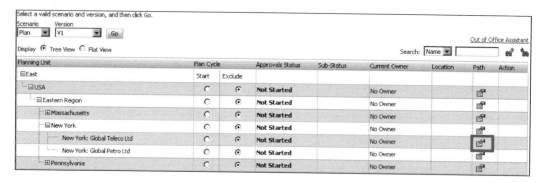

Hence, in the process of setting stage, we excluded all the planning units and also set the **Process Management Template** as **Bottom Up**.

Now, we are able to understand the requirement before starting the demonstration.

Requirement

Before the demonstration, we'll write the requirement story and the demonstration will follow the story line.

It's again the story of **New York: Global Teleco Ltd** — I guess we are already familiar with this story line. As it's a bottom-up budget, there is no freedom to promote a planning unit to any user, as we could have done in free form. In bottom up, we follow a specific path of promotion, that is, the preset promotional path. We will see the promotional path by selecting the path, as shown in the next screenshot. We'll explore the story of **New York: Global Teleco Ltd**, looking at the promotional path.

Let us remind ourselves that although we had a promotional path earlier in free form as well, we did not bother as we had all the freedom to promote to any user as we wished in free form.

Selecting the promotional path will open a colorful smart window, as shown in the next figure:

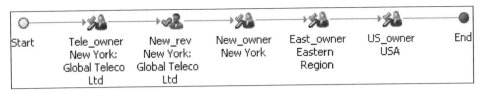

Wondering how we have got this good-looking promotional path? Let us remind ourselves that when we created the planning unit **East**, we assigned ownership and reviewers. Don't forget that we've already seen this promotional path once. If you'd like to refresh your memory, refer to *Chapter 12, Assigning Owners.*

OK, let us get back to our story. Now that we are done with the introduction, we'll get into the real plot. The **Tele_owner** is responsible for New York's location as far as his/her client **Global Teleco Ltd** is concerned. He/she has to enter data and then he/she has to promote it to **New_rev**, who will review the budgets entered by **Tele_owner**. **New_rev** will promote to **New_owner**, who happens to be the person heading all of **New York**. Hence he has to review **New York** and its client's **Global Teleco Ltd** budget data also.

New_owner, as usual, is not happy and sends back the planning unit to the inception stage, as he/she wants **Tele_owner** to re-work on this planning unit. Unfortunately, **Tele_owner** does not work on the planning unit and delays it a lot. **New_owner**, realizing the importance of time, the **New_owner** takes back the ownership of the planning unit and promotes to the next owner, **East_owner**.

East_owner delegates the planning unit to **Yes_boss** and after that he/she is promoted to **US_owner**. **US_owner** finally gives his/her approval.

The requirement plot is thick and complicated, but as we get into the demonstration, it becomes simpler.

 All through the workflow process of bottom-up, the control moves not only from one person to the other, but also from an entity member to the other or from one location to another.

In our application, we can see from the promotional path that the control gradually passes from New York to Eastern Region and from Eastern Region to USA. It's restricted and the workflow has to stick to this route only. Look at the **Entity** dimension to witness the same.

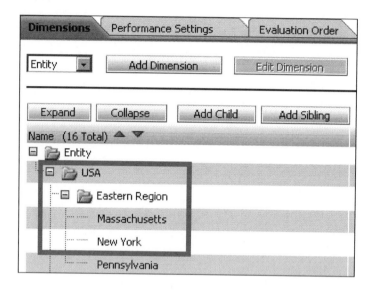

Here, we need to know that the approval of a planning unit can only be done by the last person in the promotional path, that is, **US_owner** unlike free form, where any user or current planning unit owner can approve.

In bottom-up, the planning unit has to go under the review process of all the users in the same sequential path mentioned in the promotional path, and it has to be approved by the last user only.

So the story is simple, but it has lot of reservations.

Demonstrating the bottom-up approval template

Now, let us start the demonstration of bottom-up planning, step-by-step:

Step 1

Log in to SRGD using admin credentials. We know that the admin is the person who can starts a planning unit and we will do that in the very first step. After we log in, go to **Tools Manage Approvals**. The immediate step is to select **Plan** and **V1** for **Scenario** and **Version** dimension members respectively.

It puts us into a déjà vu experience as we get the same error message, as shown in the next screenshot. It's because none of the planning units have started and we have to select **Tree view** and start the **New York: Global Teleco Ltd** planning unit. Refer to the section *Starting Planning Unit* under *Free-form Demonstration*.

Now, start the Planning unit **New York: Global Teleco Ltd**, as shown in the next screenshot:

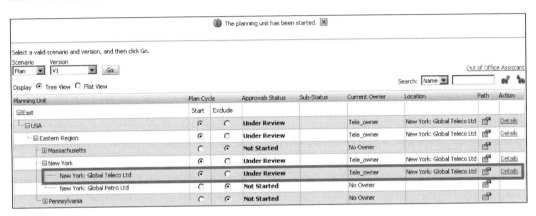

We have to make an important observation here. We see the status of the planning unit changing from **Not Started** to **Under Review** directly and the current owner is **Tele_owner** for the planning unit. We did not select the **Tele_owner** user explicitly, but we know that this information about the user is pulled from the promotional path and we give the owner and reviewer information in **Assign owner** and **review** tab of the planning unit creation , while creating the planning unit.

Hence, there is no state to **First Pass** for bottom up. As we start the planning unit, the owner is selected automatically and the state of the planning unit becomes **Under Review**.

Coming to the planning units, the parent entity member gets started when its child entity member is started.

We also see that the other planning units like New York, Eastern Region, and USA have also started, though we have started only **New York: Global Teleco Ltd**. The reason for this is that the other planning units are ancestors to the started planning unit and they would also start automatically

The last observation would be on the Location as **New York: Global Teleco Ltd**. This location is the same as we can see in the promotional path. Run to promotional path and we can see it's the very first location after **Start**. As we proceed with promotions, we would be moving from one location to another and from one owner to the other, as we can see in the promotional path very clearly.

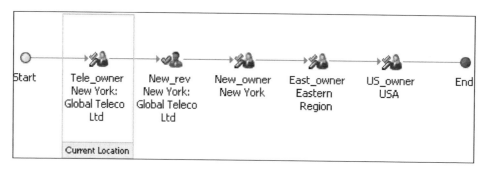

Step 2

In bottom-up budgeting, the data is usually entered only at the leaf level, that is, the data is entered only at the beginning of the workflow. Hence, **Tele_owner**, who is standing at the beginning of the workflow, has to fill in data. The other reviewers like **New_rev** can only review. They cannot edit or enter new data for the planning unit. Whereas, in free form, once a user becomes the owner of the planning unit, he/she gets the privilege to enter or edit data of the planning unit and the other users can only read the data.

Step 3

Log in to the planning application of 'SRGD' using the credentials of **Tele_owner** and open the data form with the appropriate Page member selection. We can see that the color of the data form is yellow saying that Cooke can enter data in the form. We already have numbers; we'll not waste our time and energy changing them. But, in the case of real-life implementations, **Tele_owner**, being the first owner of this bottom–up budgeting workflow, has to enter data without giving it a miss.

Page	Plan ▼	V1 ▼	Local ▼	New York ▼	Global Teleco Ltd ▼	Go

	Jan	Feb	Mar	⊟Q1	Apr
	FY10	FY10	FY10	FY10	FY10
Sales	25	25	25	75	
COGS	20	20	20	60	

Now, **Tele_owner** has to promote and he/she will do so without thinking twice about whom to promote, as in bottom-up, it will stick to an automatic promotional path. Hence, it's obvious that the next planner **New_rev** is the one that will be presented with it to review. We can take a look at the promotional path again to re-confirm the same.

After logging in to the system as **Tele_owner**, go to **Tools | Manage Approvals** with an objective to promote the planning unit to **New_rev**, as shown in the next screenshot.

Select **Select Mine** to see the appropriate planning unit of **Tele_owner** and select **Details** under the column by the name **Actions**. We know how to proceed with the status change.

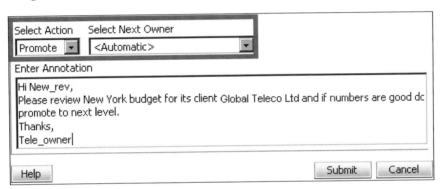

 In **Select Next Owner**, we don't see the list of users as we had seen in the case of free form. Its automatic and now we see it. We can also see the annotation in the previous screenshot. Select **Submit** and now the planning unit is promoted to **New_rev**.

Step 4

Now, log in as **New_rev** and view the budget numbers in the data form, which is read only as if **New_rev** is just a reviewer.

| Page | Plan ▼ | V1 ▼ | Local ▼ | New York ▼ | Global Teleco Ltd ▼ | Go |

	Jan	Feb	Mar	⊟Q1
	FY10	FY10	FY10	FY10
Sales	25	25	25	75
COGS	20	20	20	60

If he/she feels good about the numbers, he/she decides to promote it to the next level. Again, he/she has to go to **Tools | Manage Approvals** and select **Select Mine** and change the status, as shown in the next screenshot by promoting it automatically to the next owner and select **Submit** followed by **Done**.

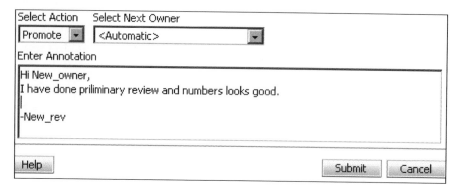

It's a simple promotion to the next level. Now, management is willing to know the exact status of the planning unit of **New York: Global Teleco Ltd**. The simple way to find out is by looking at its promotional path.

See the promotional path, as shown in the next screenshot. We can see that it is in the middle of its workflow journey.

We could see that the workflow is at the stage where **New_rev** has been promoted to the next level to **New_owner**. We can also see that the current stage is clearly explained with the 'current location' squaring the owner and location, as shown in the next screenshot:

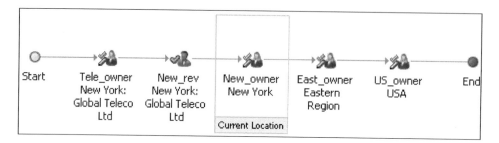

Step 5

Log in to SRGD as **New_owner** and open the **Test** data form. We see that for the combination of **V1, Plan, New York**, and **Global Teleco Ltd, New_owner** we can edit the data as well. Remember that **New_rev** can not edit the data as he/she is a reviewer and not an owner.

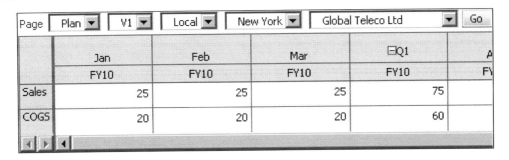

New_owner is not happy with the numbers, so he/she insists that the numbers be revisited all over again. Hence, he/she selects the action of **Originate**. **Originate** will take the status of the planning unit directly to the first owner, that is, **Tele_owner** again. He/she is being punished for his/her laziness now. Honestly, though **New_owner** can edit numbers, he/she wanted **Tele_owner** to work on it and then have it reviewed by **New_rev**. Hence he/she gives it back.

How can New_owner originate?

It's another action on a planning unit. Hence, we select **'Change Status** and select **Originate**, as shown next:

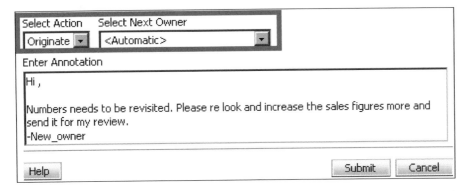

This will straightaway make **Tele_owner** the owner of the planning unit again and he/she has to take another look at the numbers and promote it all over again. After **Tele_owner** is done with his/her work, he/she cannot promote directly to **New_owner**. He/she has to stick to our conservative promotional path, where **Tele_owner** has to promote to **New_rev**, **New_rev** to **New_owner**, and so on.

We should check the promotional path and we will see that the ball came to **Tele_owner's** court again via the 'Originate' action, as shown in the following figure:

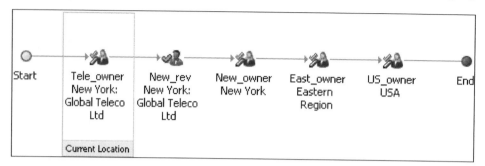

We can hate **New_owner** for his action of selecting **Originate** as that nullifies all our efforts so far. But the power is with boss, in the end.

> Therefore, **Originate** action will lead the planning unit to the inception stage where it goes to the first owner.

Now, let us see how **Tele_owner** will react to this action of **New_owner** in next step.

Step 6

Ideally, **Tele_owner** should re look in to the numbers and promote to next level. But, we can safely guess that he felt bad and we know that there are many employees in a firm, who are old and who have been with the firm for more than 10 years and they don't want to do as per any ones timelines, it becomes an ego issue. Hence, **Tele_owner** is buying time and showing off that he is an important person. Now, after waiting for few days **New_owner** decides to take ownership. We know that the current owner is **Tele_owner** but we have an option of 'take ownership' which **New_owner** can employ.

Log in as **New_owner** and select **Change Status**. As the current owner at this point of time is **Tele_owner**, we see only one possible action for **New_owner**, that is, **Take ownership** as shown in the next screenshot.

Select **Submit** followed by **Done**.

Step 7

Now, this brings us to an important question: who is qualified to take ownership? If every user could take ownership of a planning unit, the workflow would become a mess for sure. Let us answer this in a clear manner. **Take Ownership** as an action can be used only by a user who is firstly a part of the promotional path and secondly he/she is ahead in the path, as per the hierarchy. Let us elaborate with our current example, we were at **Tele_owner New York**: **Global Teleco Ltd** in the screenshot. In the promotional path, we can clearly see that **New_owner**, **East_owner**, and **US_owner** are the ones involved in the promotional path and all of these users are ahead of **Tele_owner** in the promotional path. Hence any of these users can **Take Ownership**.

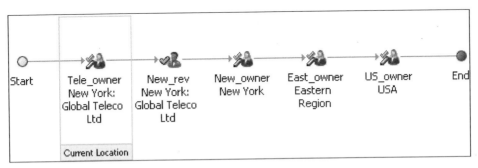

Now, let us consider a second case. Let's say the workflow is at the state of **New_owner New York**, as shown in the following image. It's only **East_owner** and **US_owner**, who can 'take ownership'. The simple reason is that both **East_owner** and **US_owner** are the only two users who are ahead of **New_owner** in the promotional path.

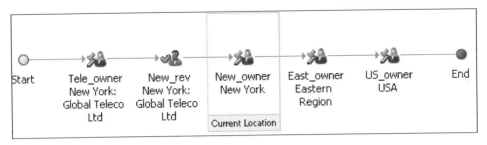

If we look from an organizational structure perspective, it makes a lot of sense also. **US_owner**, being the head of US, should have more control and should have enough power to take ownership from **New_owner**, **East_owner** and **Tele_owner**, whereas **New_owner** should not have the power to take ownership from **East_owner** or **US_owner**.

Now, let us get back to our drama, where **New_owner** is not happy with **Tele_owner**.

Step 8

After taking ownership, **New_owner** is kind of lost and does not know what to do, so he/she decides to seek the help of his/her boss and promote to the next level, that is, **East_owner**, who knows whom to delegate to.

So, **New_owner** promotes to next level, as shown in the following screenshot:

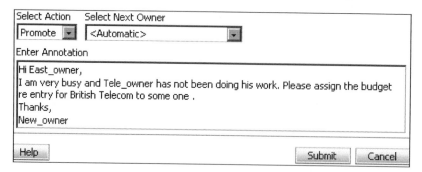

Now, **East_owner** thinks of a resource, who is always a 'yes man' and he immediately thinks of an employee by the name of **yes_boss**, who will do the work for him. **yes_boss** is young and is in the initial years of his career and it's pardonable to show a little bit of sycophancy for him. Even better, **yes_boss** is relatively free and has bandwidth to work with.

East_owner delegates the planning unit to **yes_boss**. Login to SRGD as **East_owner** and change the status, as shown in the following screenshot:

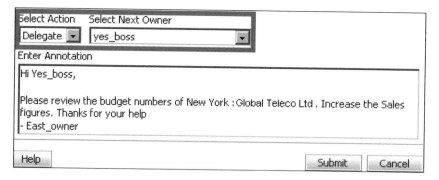

Once this has been done, **yes_boss** gets an e-mail informing him that he is the new owner of the budget. Now, it should be very interesting to see how the workflow moves from here.

Step 9

Log in as **yes_boss** and first open the data form 'test'. We see that **Yes_boss** can actually edit or enter data of the planning unit. Oh yes, we can edit and save the values in the form for the POV of **Plan, V1, New York,** and **Global Teleco Ltd**, as shown in the following screenshot:

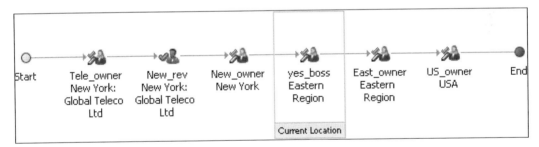

Job done by **yes_boss!**

Now, we have a question, **yes_boss** was never a part of our initial plan and was not part of promotional path. Now, where does **yes_boss** fit in the promotional path? Yes, **yes_boss** was never a part of the promotional path. But, when a users delegates the planning unit, the delegate takes the position before the user, who delegated it. In our case, **East_owner** has delegated the planning unit to **yes_boss**. Hence, **yes_boss**, being the delegatee, takes on place before **East_owner**. This way, when the delegatee is done with his job, he can promote the planning unit and the ownership back to the user who had initially delegated it to him. This is demonstrated in the below figure:

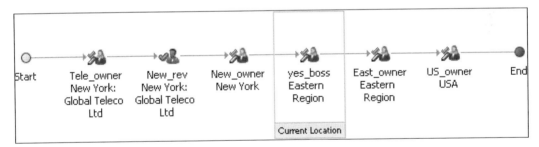

Now, **yes_**boss promotes and the ownership moves automatically to **East_owner**. We know that we have an option of 'Notify users' under the tab of 'Assign Owners', while we had created the planning unit called'East'.

yes_boss now will promote the planning unit to **East_owner**, as shown in the following screenshot:

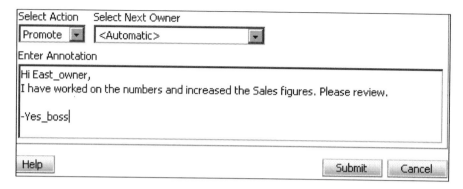

Step 10

Now, log in to SRGD as **East_owner**. We know that we are not very far from the final approval, unless **US_owner** pulls a nasty trick.

There is one more option which an owner can use, which is 'Freeze'. Freeze locks all the descending planning units of the planning unit. Let us understand this with an example. New York is a planning unit in our hierarchy; **New York: Global Petro Ltd** and **New York: Global Teleco Ltd** are the planning units under it. If we freeze the planning unit of New York, its descending planning units gets locked. Likewise, if the USA planning unit is frozen in our case, then all the planning units are locked and values cannot be edited as USA is the planning unit at the top-most level.

>
> When a planning unit is frozen by the user for a reason, then the same user can unfreeze it before he/she decides to promote it to the next level or take any other action on the planning unit. Hence the freeze action is always followed by the unfreeze action.

Then what's the point in freezing something if has to be unfrozen? Sometimes, an organization decides to stop budgeting for some reason for a while. This might be because of some serious doubts about a company's existence or some other reason. Then, in such situations, the company might freeze the budgeting process for the time being, and then it is unfrozen to proceed in future, when they have visibility of projects/production or pipeline.

Step 11

East_owner promotes to **US_owner** and finally **US_owner** signs off and later approves the planning unit of **New York: Global Teleco Ltd**. This is the happy ending of the planning unit, and finally the owner becomes the **Admin**, after final approval.

Hence, we can now understand the way bottom-up budgeting behaves with the help of the following screenshot:

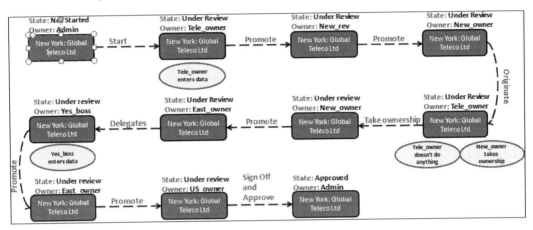

Distributed budgeting

This is the last budgeting format of the workflow in planning. This time, we won't be as elaborate as we were for both free-form and bottom-up.

Distributed budgeting is somewhat different to bottom up. In bottom up, we initiate the workflow from the lowest planning unit and gradually it gets promoted to the next level, and finally, the top level of the organization approves the budget. Now, coming to Distributed budgeting, it's the other way round. The budgeting starts at the top level of an organization and gradually moves down to the lower levels, and after reaching the lower level it takes a U turn. After budget data is captured at the lower levels, the owners submit it to the next level up in the hierarchy, and this gradually reaches the top level of an organization.

We'll see any planning unit's states and actions, which are only applicable and related to distributed budgeting. Yes, there are, which are only applicable to distributed budgeting and the explanation of those is given in the following section.

States and actions

Distributed

We have learned that in distributed budgeting, it starts at the top level of the organization, and as we proceed with the budgeting, it has to move further down to the next level of the organizational hierarchy. The movement of budgeting from the top level to the next subsequent lower level can be understood as **Distributed** and a planning unit is in the state of **Distributed** only when a user distributes it further down to the lower levels of the organizational hierarchy.

With this understanding, we can conclude that the leaf-level planning unit owners cannot distribute any further as they themselves are at the bottom level of the hierarchy. Now, we will see what kind of actions transform a planning unit into the **Distributed** status.

Action

There are five actions that we are going to talk about in this *Actions* section. They are:

- **Distribute**: The basic action is **Distribute**, which will move the planning unit ownership to the next planner, who is in the immediate next level in the hierarchy of an organization.

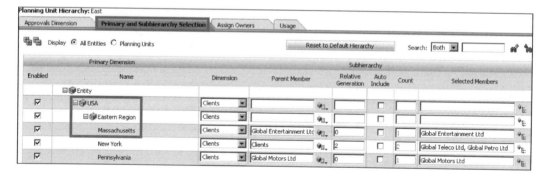

Now, go to the promotional path of **Massachusetts: Global entertainment Ltd**. To do this, go to the tab of **Assign Owners** and select the path as shown below:

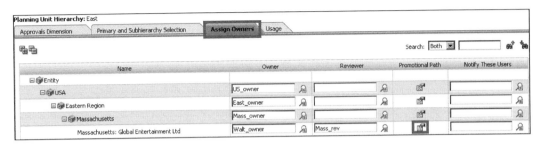

As we see the promotional path, here, we know that the leaf planning unit **Massachusetts: Global entertainment Ltd** is owned by **Walt_owner**, but when we start the planning unit, the very first owner will be **US_owner** and he/she automatically becomes the owner.

Why US owner? Good question, for that, take a look at the promotional path of **Massachusetts: Global entertainment Ltd**, as shown in the next image:

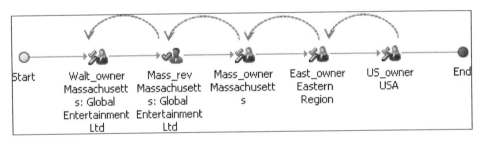

The last person in the last promotional path is **US_owner**, that is, he/she is the one who is at the top level in the organization hierarchy. In distribution, we know that it starts from the top level and hence **US_owner** would be the very first owner of the planning unit of **Massachusetts: Global entertainment Ltd** when it starts.

Now, getting back to distributed definition. **Distribute** transfers the ownership from one location to the other. For example, look at the promotional path in the previous figure. Let us assume that the planning unit of **Massachusetts: Global entertainment Ltd** has started, **US_owner** is the first owner, as we see in the figure Now, the **Distribute** action will transfer the ownership to **East_owner** of **Eastern Region**. Now, if **East_owner** of **Eastern Region** location distributes, it moves another step left - towards **Mass_owner** of Massachusetts

Therefore, the **Distribute** action moves only one step left in a promotional path.

- **Distribute Children**: This action will move towards the children of the planning unit. If the current location of the planning unit is **US_owner** and if we **Distribute children**, the control transfers to **East_owner: Eastern region** because **Eastern region** is the child of **USA**. Likewise, when the current location is **East_owner: Eastern Region** and the action performed is **Distribute children**, then the control goes to **Mass_owner: Massachusetts**. When the current location is **Mass_owner: Massachusetts**, we cannot distribute children as there are no children to **Massachusetts**. **Massachusetts** is the last child.

We can easily make out a difference between **Distribute** and **Distributed children**. The former moves to the next level and the latter logically jumps to the next child of its current location.

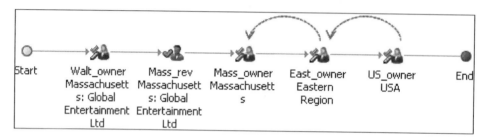

- **Distribute owner**: We know that when we had assigned the owner and reviewer, the assigned owner of the **Massachusetts: Global entertainment Ltd** planning unit is **Walt_owner** (refer to the third screenshot under the *Starting Planning Unit* section) . Now, when we start this planning unit, we learned that the owner becomes **US_owner** to start with. Now, if the action of **Distribute owner** is performed, the planning unit control comes into the hands of its owner, the real owner, or **Walt_owner**. We can see the leap in the next diagram:

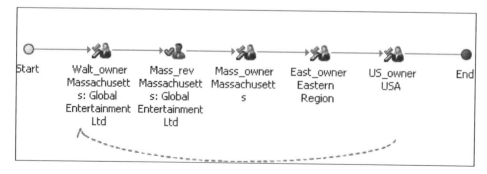

- **Submit**: We don't promote in 'distributed budgeting'; we submit. We'll understand more about why we submit in 'distributed budgeting' in the demonstration section. As we had learned that gradually the ownership moves from right to left in the promotional path and moving one step gradually as we distribute the planning unit. After it reaches the leaf level, that is, **Walt_owner: Massachusetts: Global entertainment Ltd**, it takes a U turn and then the action of **Submit** starts. **Walt_owner** will then submit and **Mass_rev** becomes the owner. It moves gradually from Massachusetts to the eastern region, from eastern region to USA, and finally reaches **US_owner**.

This is demonstrated in the following image:

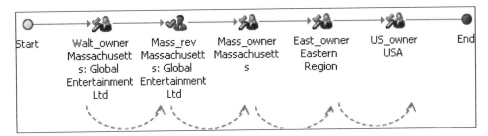

 Therefore, every **Submit** action will move one step towards the right in the promotional path.

- **Submit to Top**: When the current location of the planning unit is at **Walt_owner Massachusetts: Global entertainment Ltd**, **Walt_owner** can submit the planning unit and the control goes to next location, that is, **Mass_rev Massachusetts: Global entertainment Ltd**. However, another action, that is, **Submit to top** will submit the planning unit directly to **US_owner | USA**, who is at the top level of the organizational hierarchy.

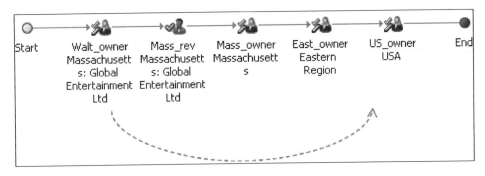

This is a smart action as it saves a lot of time of the workflow and organizations would benefit a lot too. In the end, time is money!

Distributed budgeting demonstration

We will start with understanding a few very basic English words. They are **Submit** and **Promote**.

Why do we 'submit' in 'distributed' and why do we 'promote' in 'bottom-up'?

Meaning will not only help our English, but these two words will help us in understanding these budgeting fashions.

We'll start with 'submit'. The meaning of this verb says, 'to accept or yield to a superior force, to the authority, or will of another person'. Now, let us relate it to *distributed* budgeting. In this form of budgeting, the flow starts from the top level, that is, **US_owner: USA** and it goes to the leaf level, for example, **Walt_owner Massachusetts: Global entertainment Ltd**. Now, **Walt_owner** has to submit the budgets to the next level, that is, to **Mass_rev**, or **Walt_owner** can directly submit to **US_owner** with the help of **Submit to top**. The submission of **Walt_owner** means that **Walt_owner** is accepting as per the higher authority and then seeks for final approval from the top-level management. OK, now it's clear. Let us understand the meaning of 'promote'; it says 'support a cause or further the progress of or to raise it to the next level'. In the case of *bottom-up* here, the workflow starts from the level, that is, at the **'Walt_owner Massachusetts: Global entertainment Ltd** level and it is gradually promoted to the next level so that the subsequent location owners review it and promote the planning unit in the process of raising it to next level and finally to **US_owner** for his/her approval.

The major difference, as we understand it, is in distributed budgeting, the budget values are determined by the top-level management and as the workflow progresses, the leaf level submits to the top level , that is, eventually agrees to the top-level budgets for their respective location of unit. Whereas, in bottom-up, it starts from leaf level and further goes to the top level, and as a promotion takes place, the workflow is contributed by others' reviews.

Now, we'll learn more about distributed budgeting with the help of the next image:

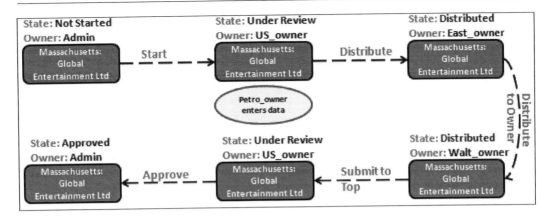

Let us follow this again in steps, but this time in the minimum number of steps:

1. The first thing we need to do is to exclude all the planning units which we had started in the previous section of 'bottom-up' so that we'll again start our work on 'distributed', like it's a clean state. We know how to do it, else run back to the early part of the 'bottom-up' section.

2. Secondly, the planning unit **East** is currently with the process management template of 'bottom-up'. Remember, we changed it to bottom-up in the previous section. We shall make use of the same planning unit **East**. Therefore, change the setting of **Process Management template** to **Distribute**. Now, we are ready.

3. Log in to the SRGD application using admin credentials and start the planning unit of **Massachusetts: Global entertainment Ltd**, which is rounded in the next image. As we start this planning unit, the whole hierarchy would look like the hierarchy shown in the following screenshot:

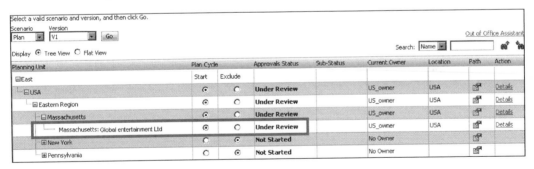

We should be paying attention to the **Current Owner** and **Location** as we progress with the workflow. The very first owner is **US_owner** and the state is **Under Review**.

Are you wondering how US_owner is the very first owner of this planning unit?

1. We need to now look at this planning unit's promotional path and we can clearly see that the top-level person in this promotional path is **US_owner**, as shown in the next screenshot:

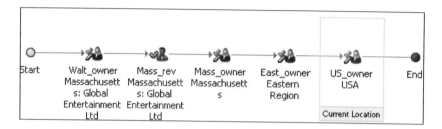

And we can also see that the very beginning is at **US_owner: USA**. This is what is shown in the first screenshot under the *Distributed budgeting demonstration* section.

2. Now, **US_owner** can distribute to the next level of **East_owner**, which is rounded in the previous promotional path image. Hence, log in as **US_owner** and distribute the planning unit to the next lower level. This is exactly shown in the first screenshot under the *Distributed budgeting demonstration* section., where after distribution of the **US_owner**, the owner becomes **East_owner** and the location is 'Eastern region'.

3. **East_owner** can again distribute to the next lower level, as per the organization hierarchy, but to save time, he distributes to **Walt_owner** and **East_owner** would be able to accomplish with the help of the action 'distribute to owner'. We can see this action in the first screenshot under the *Distributed budgeting demonstration* section and after this action, it's at the leaf level.

4. Now, **Walt_owner** cannot distribute any further as he is at the bottom-most level and he can only submit (now, we know what exactly submit means). **Walt_owner** would edit the budget values and then would submit it directly to the top level management, that is, **US_owner**. In real life situations, these short cuts are rarely present. A user would submit to the next level and the next level would again submit to his next higher level. But, for demonstration purposes that too after ourselves getting tired after looking at both free form and 'bottom-up' we can innovate short cuts like this. We can see the action of 'submit to top' in the first screenshot under *Distributed budgeting demonstration* section.

5. It's again in the hands of **US_owner** and let us consider it a happy ending by **US_owner** signing off and later approving rather than rejecting or freezing.

   Now, let us take a look at the first screenshot under the *Distributed budgeting demonstration* section, and if we are clear with this, then we'll play more on this budgeting format by spending more time and handling more options.

6. Good job! We have learned all three budgeting formats and we, as Hyperion planning consultants, can inform clients in generic fashion that for strategic planning or budgeting, they can make use of *distributed* and for operational Planning , they can can make use of *bottom-up*. There is also *free-form*, which gives full freedom to the planner.

Summary

In this chapter, we learned a lot about workflows. We started with *free form*, where we first understood basic Planning unit states and actions. Next, we assumed the requirement of free-form workflow and have seen the demonstration with the help of SRGD Planning application and Test data form.

After this, we started our work on *bottom-up* and studied more states and actions of a Planning unit. Along with the demonstration, we have also witnessed interesting business situations and how actions like *delegate* and *take ownership* can come very handy. Finally, we quickly did 'distributed' workflow demonstration, which was not difficult after having worked on two workflows already.

It has been a long chapter so we will follow up with a relatively simpler chapter, *Task Lists*, next. We surely do deserve more than coffee now.

14
Task Lists

The only reason for time is so that everything doesn't happen at once

— Albert Einstein

Yes, Einstein was right. There is a reason for sequence of tasks to happen. Everything cannot happen at once and this holds true for Budgeting processes and for Hyperion Planning applications as well.

Check out the following conversation between a Hyperion Planning consultant and a Client who is trying to explain his requirements:

Client: As we are moving from Excel spreadsheets to a web based Planning tool, I have one more requirement.

Planning Consultant: Yes, please go ahead.

Client: Our organization users are very rigid. They are not very good with new products or new interfaces. We have had some bad experiences with upgrades. We replaced a system XYZ with ABC, the solution was very good but users did not find it user friendly and eventually, we had to scrap the system. I don't want that situation to repeat itself.

Planning Consultant: We will take the utmost care in terms of making a planner or user comfortable with our Planning solution.

Client: I understand, but I want them to be provided with a lot of instructions and also a lot of navigational support within the application. Is that possible?

Planning Consultant: Of course it's possible. We have a feature called the 'Task list'. With the help of this, we will provide your users with navigational help. We will provide them with information on how to proceed and what to do so that they does not feel lost in between.

Client: Thank you.

Have you ever wondered how we actually navigate any website on the Internet (www) with ease and without any prior information about the website?

You may have to book a movie ticket, log in to your mail box, or log into a new social network website such as Google Plus for the first time. The answer is *it's not that difficult*, there is usually enough information on the web page itself, informing us what to do and how to go about it. Websites tend to be easy to navigate. They give us clear instructions of where to provide a user name or where to click or select.

We now need to assume that the end users need to be pampered, and we need to set up a Planning system that can be used with ease. It does not matter how technically sound our design for the Planning application was, with complex dimensionality structures and all our brains invested to create very appropriate Data Forms, and so on. In the end, when an end user logs in, he needs to know which form he has to open and what data has to be entered, and he should get enough instructions to do so.

We will do all that we can for the user and his ease of navigation in the name of 'Task List'. We'll learn all about Task Lists in this chapter, which is divided in to the following sections:

1. **Modes**: In a Planning application, there are 2 modes — Advanced Mode and Basic Mode. We'll learn about these modes and learn how Task Lists are related to this.

2. **Task List**:

    ○   Introduction: We'll introduce Task List and understand the very basic objective of Task Lists in this section.

    ○   Requirement: We'll assume a business requirement before we proceed with Task List creation. We'll look into the requirements in this section.

    ○   Task List creation: We'll learn through a step-by-step process of task list creation in this section and we'll make use of the SRGD Planning application.

    ○   Task List access: We'll see how a planner/user would access Task Lists in this section.

Modes

There are two modes in a Planning application, as said earlier, they are:

1. Basic Mode
2. Advanced Mode

Basic Mode

In a Planning application, as a part of Planning, Budgeting and Forecasting exercise, we want most of the planners or users to perform fewer basic tasks such as entering data into a data entry form, or promoting a Planning unit to the next level for approval rather than creating new Forms, Planning units, or making dimensional structure changes. Creation and design of the Planning objects such as Data forms, Task Lists, or Planning units is a job for consultants like us or for Planning developers. End users need not do that.

When users need to primarily work on "task lists", the Basic Mode is preferred. In this mode, a user has a set of tasks that have to be performed. Later in this chapter, we'll learn what kind of tasks a user can perform within Task Lists.

For now, login into the 'PandB' Planning application using the credentials for "admin" and go to **Basic Mode**.

How do we know which mode we are currently in, and how do we switch from one mode to another?

After logging into the 'PandB' application, go to the **View** menu as shown in the following screenshot:

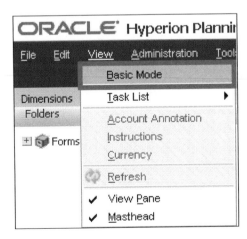

We see **Basic Mode** as the option in the previous screenshot, this answers the first part of the question: the current mode is Advanced Mode, we can switch to Basic Mode by selecting the option and we have simultaneously and smartly answered the second part of the question as well.

After selecting 'Basic Mode' we don't see the 'Administration' option active or enabled anymore, which was the key to most of the activities in terms of creating or editing dimensions, creating or editing planning units, creating or editing data forms, and so on. However, we see a task list that we have never seen so far, as in the next screenshot.

Apart from the 'Administration' option, the other main difference is that the Form or Folders display no longer appears in the left panel. We see **Task List** in place of Forms or Folders, as we can see the next screenshot.

 Creation of Data Forms, Dimensions, and members, Task Lists, Planning units or any Planning application objects can only be done in Advanced Mode, not in Basic Mode.

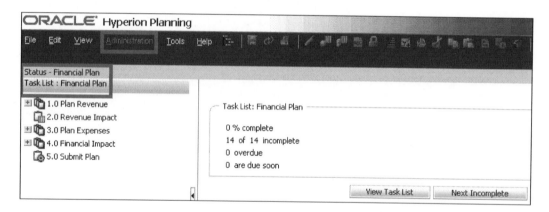

As we can see on the top panel in the screenshot, the name of the **Task List** is **Financial Plan** and many incomprehensible terms on the right-hand side. Not to worry, we will be discussing these in later sections of the chapter. We also see in the previous screenshot that the **Administration** option is disabled.

Advanced Mode

It's interesting to know that whatever we have been working with so far, that is from the first chapter up till this point, has been in 'Advanced Mode'. In Advanced Mode, we create or edit every object of a Planning application such as Data Forms, Task Lists, Planning units, and so on. Coming to Task Lists, yes, we do create Task Lists in Advanced Mode but prefer to access it in Basic Mode. Nevertheless, we can access Task Lists in Advanced Mode as well.

Now let us switch from Basic Mode to Advanced Mode and make few observations. Log in to the same application 'PandB' and switch the mode from Basic Mode to Advanced Mode. It's very simple, go to **View | Advance mode**.

Advanced Mode makes Task Lists disappear and brings back a Data Forms list, as shown in the following screenshot:

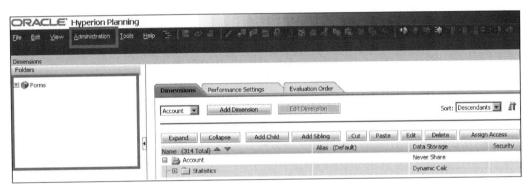

It also brings back our secret weapon, the **Administration** option, as highlighted in the previous screenshot:

 [Now, we can conclude that Task List view is in Basic Mode and the Data Forms view in 'Advanced Mode'.]

We are still trying hard to understand what Task List would comprise of. We'll learn that in the next section.

Task Lists

We began this chapter by talking about a website and how easily a user can navigate it. Task Lists also help a user by specifically listing the activities or tasks in an order meant for a user. Before we take a look at Task Lists, let us learn some more theory.

A planner needs some guidance or instructions before he enters the budget values and he also needs to perform tasks in a specific order. Here, the simple example of the order would be **'to enter budget values and promote the Planning unit to other user for review'**. Now, this simple activity can be broken down into two tasks; that is firstly entering budget values in a Data Form and secondly, promoting the Planning Unit. This sequence is shown in the following diagram:

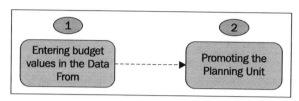

We should not promote a Planning Unit before entering budget values. Hence, the specific order of data entry in a Data Form followed by Planning Unit promotion is the right way. We achieve ordering of tasks with the help of Task Lists again. We provide users guidance before they start entering budget values in a form, and finally we can tell them to promote, and we do all of this with the aid of Task Lists.

 Hence, it's a guide to the end user in budgeting by directing the users to perform appropriate task in a prioritized order.

1. **Introduction**: In this section, we'll learn what information a task list would provide to a user.

2. **Requirement**: We'll assume some requirements before we start our Task List creation activity.

3. **Task List creation**: In this section, we'll learn the process of Task List creation.

4. **Task List access (Basic and Advanced Mode)**: In this section, we'll access the created task list both in basic and advanced mode.

5. **Task List Reports**: In this section, we'll explore an option of creating Excel and PDF reports of task lists.

Introduction to Task Lists

In this section, we'll see what a typical Task List would provide a planner. Log in to 'PandB' application ad 'admin', switch to 'Basic Mode'. We see the list of tasks on the left-hand side in the next screenshot and we can also observe that the tasks are numbered (from **1** to **5**). As we select the task, the task opens in the central workplace. A task can be Data Form entry, opening an internal website, or promoting a Planning Unit.

Let us think about this a little more. If we open a task of Data Form entry, the attached Data Form opens for the planner. Likewise, when the task is 'promotion a Planning Unit', the Approval Page opens for the planner.

We can see in the next screenshot that **Financial Plan**, highlighted in the image, is the name of the **Task List** and there are five tasks from **1.0** to **5.0**, from **Plan Revenue** to **Submit Plan** on the left-hand side of the screenshot:

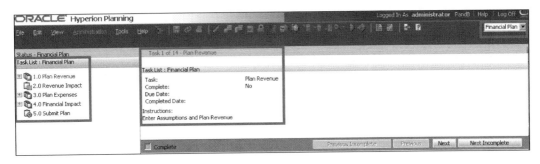

1. **Task List**: This is the name of the Task List. In our case, it is 'Financial Plan'. By now, we should know that Task List is the one which comprises of multiple tasks. In our case, Task List 'Financial Plan' has tasks such as Plan Revenue, Revenue Impact, and so on.

2. **Task**: This is the name of a task, in this case Plan Revenue, which is the very first task of the Task List 'Financial Plan'.

3. **Complete**: This gives us information about whether the task has been completed. In our case, the task has not been completed. Hence, it displays 'No'.

4. **Due Date**: For the task **1.0 Plan Revenue**, we don't see any due date. The simple reason being that this task has not been created with any due date. Typically, we set a date when a task should get over. In a typical budgeting exercise, there are multiple tasks and we do set different due dates for individual tasks. If there is a task list with two tasks:

   ° Enter budget values in Data Form

   ° Promote the planning unit

   In this simple case, we will set the due date of task 1 before task 2 as it makes sense to promote the planning unit only after budget values are entered.

5. **Completed Date**: This parameter gives information of task completion. It might happen that we had set a due date for a task, but unforeseen circumstances (read lazy planners) may cause delays which mean that the task is completed much later than the set date. Hence, we need to know the completed date, which is the actual completion of a task.

6. **Instructions**: This is a piece of information that will be useful to the user. It's a kind of guideline for a user before he starts filling in data forms. A task can also be a workflow task, report, or a business rule.

7. **Alerts**: Hyperion may have thought that words are boring and preferred colors for once. The alerts are shown in colors, and here's what each of them means:

   ° Green: The task is on schedule and the due date is not approaching immediately

   ° Yellow: Look alive, the Due Date is approaching

   ° Red: The Due Date has passed and the task has not been completed. You are late… you are late…

We know that we don't see all of these in the previous screenshot. When we create Task Lists however, we shall see all of them.

Every task that we see on the left-hand side of the previous screenshot is a link. When we say 'a link', it might be a task that is linked to a Data Form or a task, which is a link to a Planning unit promotion. The best part of a task list is that we can make different task lists to cater to different audience or set of users. For example, when a Sales planner logs into the system, he'll see the tasks that are applicable to him, while a manufacturing planner gets a task list specific to him.

There may be cases in which different kinds of budgets are done in an organization such as the annual budget, rolling forecast, and long term budget. We can create three different task lists for different sets of users based on their responsibilities - for example whether they are supposed to create an annual budget, rolling forecast, or a long term budget.

Conclusively, a task list gives an instruction to a user guiding him as to what needs to be done, and it also requests a user to specify by when a task should be done, and finally task list does alerts a user with its colorful wings. Here the wings are of red, green, or yellow. This is the manner in which task list helps a user in basic mode.

Requirement for Task Lists

Let us make our requirement very simple. The user Ford_owner is responsible for the Pennsylvania location of its client *Global Motors Ltd* that is 'Pennsylvania: Global Motors Ltd'. This gentleman, when he logs in to the Planning application, should get instructions saying that he has to enter the revenue details of Pennsylvania for its client Global Motors Ltd for the first three months of 2010 and also expense of the same.

Next, Ford_owner should able to take a look at Gross Profit and 'Net Income from operation' and he should finally be able to promote to the next user that is Penn_rev, for his review. All of this should happen in the sequence in which we had narrated the requirement.

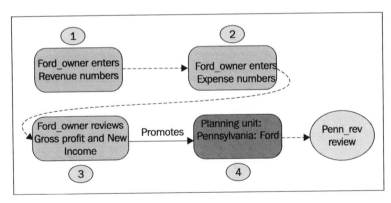

In a Budgeting exercise, time is the most important factor. Management of any firm cannot wait indefinitely for the planner to finish their tasks. Budgeting is always time-bound and it is supposed to be. Hence, we will set the time line also as a part of our requirement.

The timelines are set as per our requirements and are depicted in the following table:

Ford_owner to enter Revenue numbers into Revenue Data form by 25th July
Ford_owner to enter Expence numbers into Expense Data form by 28th July
Ford_owner to review Gross Profit and Net Income by 30th July
Ford_owner to promote the Planning unit Pennsylvania: Ford by 2nd Aug

This is the end of our requirements.

Now, we have to realize that for application 'SRGD', we have not created Data Forms where a user can enter revenue details and expense details. We'll quickly do that before we start task list creation.

Prerequisites

Creating PF_Revenue Data Form—Log in to the 'SRGD' application using the admin credentials and create the following Data forms. The first form with name PF_Revenue and the second form is PF_Expense.

For PF_Revenue, select **Sales** and **Other Revenue** for **Rows** as they are the revenue components for our application and select **Pennsylvania** and its client **Global Motors Ltd** as per our requirement. Select other dimension members, as shown in the following screenshot:

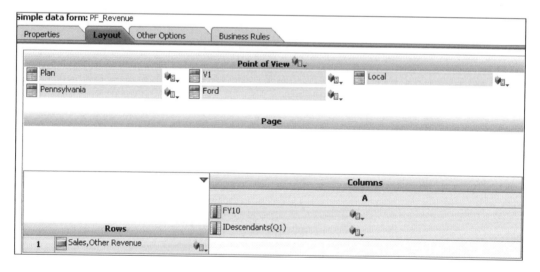

Creating PF_Expense Data Form—For `PF_Expense`, select **COGS** and **Other Expense** for Rows and other dimension members as shown in the next screenshot. Okay, these two forms will be entered first and then as per our requirements there should be one review form which shows the gross profit and net income.

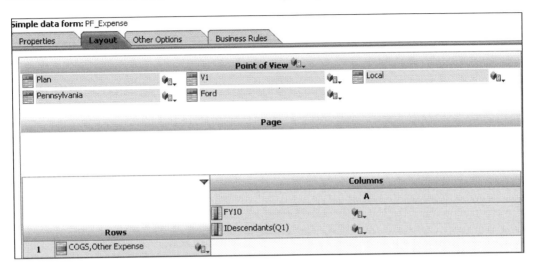

Creating Review Data Form—Now, we know we need to create one last data form, which would act as a review data form for `Ford_owner`. This is shown clearly in the next screenshot in which we select **Gross Profit** and **Net Income from operations** The name of the data form is `Review`.

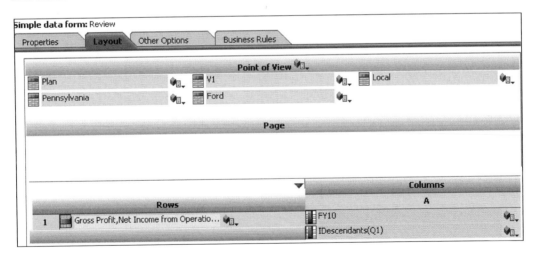

This concludes the creation of the three Data Forms.

This is all we need before we start creating our first Task List. Let us do a quick recap. We have assumed a set of requirements and created few forms, which will give life to our assumed requirement.

Security Prerequisite

Write access to the Data Forms—Are we sure that we need not do anything more before we move to the next section? Yes, we did miss something. We have created Data Forms with an objective that Ford_owner will be using them in the Task List, but we did not assign Ford_owner the write access to these three Data Forms. We'll quickly assign 'write' access of all newly created three forms to Ford_owner.

As we missed this very important point, so lets take some time to consider if we still need to do anything more as per our requirements. We said in our requirements that after entering the revenue and expense values, Ford_owner will review another data form (that is the Review Data form) and finally promoted to Penn_rev. Penn_rev will also review the numbers in the Review Data Form. Hence, we should grant 'write' access to Penn_rev of the Review Data form.

Start Planning unit Pennsylvania: Global Motors Ltd—We now need to start this Planning unit of Pennsylvania: Global Motors Ltd. We had learned already that unless an administrator starts the planning unit, it would be in a 'Not started' state, and none of the users such as Ford_owner will be able to promote to the next level.

Go to **Tools | Manage Approvals**; select **Plan** and **V1** as **Scenario** and **Version** dimension member selection excludes any Planning units started. This is an important step to exclude any Planning units that have started. We are doing this so that we can make use of the already created Planning unit—East, with an objective to change the Approval template to Bottom up.

Now, we will go to the Planning unit East and change its Approvals template from **Distributed** to **Bottom up** and save it. If we have not excluded the Planning units, the system does not let us change the approvals. It is very important to exclude the Planning units before we change the Approvals template.

Now again, we shall go to **Tools | Manage Approvals**. Select of **Plan** and **V1** as **Scenario** and **Version** dimension member and start the Planning unit of Pennsylvania: Global Motors Ltd. Log in as admin. It's assigned automatically to Ford_owner as we see in the next screenshot. It's assigned to Ford_owner because the process management template is bottom-up.

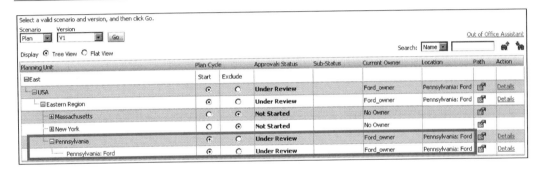

Okay, now we are good to go to the next section of Task List creation.

Creating a Task List

Let us straight away start creating our first Task List. This Task List is for the user `Ford_owner`, but in real time implementations, we would create Task Lists keeping a group of planners in perspective. For example, we would create a Task List by name HR Task List that would comprise of tasks (that is Data Forms, Planning unit promotions, and so on) related only to the HR planners or users.

We should do it in steps, Let's start:

1. After logging into the Planning application of SRGD as an admin, go to **Administration | Manage | Task Lists**, as shown in the following screenshot:

This should be similar to Data Form creation. When we first created our Data Forms, we had seen a similar screen.

We'll start with folder creation and then proceed with Task List creation. Select **Create** as highlighted in the previous screenshot, it leads to a prompt to provide the name of the task list folder. We'll give the name as `Pennsylvania`.

2. Now, we should see the newly created folder as shown in the next screenshot. Select the folder **Pennsylvania**. The selection of the folder **Pennsylvania** is important. Else, the created Task List will not be a part of the newly created Task List folder — `Pennsylvania`.

Select **Create**, as highlighted in the following screenshot:

This again leads to a prompt and we'll give the name of the task as PF. This will create a Task List by name PF. Now, check this newly created Task List **PF** and select the **Edit** option as shown in the following screenshot:

3. **Task Types and Properties**—Upon selection of **Edit**, a new window opens up and we see that the **Task List** is empty; it does not contain any tasks, as shown in the following screenshot:

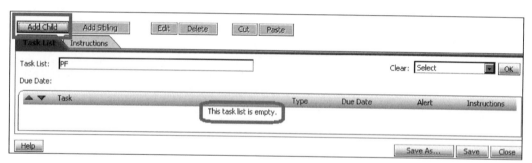

Select **Add Child** as highlighted in the previous screenshot. Now, let us get into a mode where we need to think of the user Ford_owner. We should think of making Ford_owner comfortable with the planning system and its navigation by ordering the tasks accordingly. We know that he has to fill in few Data Forms first. Hence, the very first task should give him some guidelines or some basic information for him to proceed to next task. Therefore, we shall create our first task which is informative to the user. It generally provides an overview of the Task List.

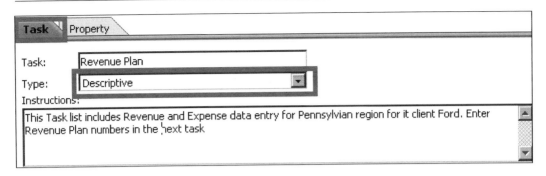

Here, let us spend some time in understanding the properties of this window in the previous screenshot:

- **Task**: This is the name of the task. In our case, we set it as **Revenue Plan** to make it relevant to the next task of entering revenue values in a form.

- **Type**: This is a drop-down menu. We can see the following options:

  - **Descriptive**: A task is descriptive when it has to provide information or guidelines to a user or planner. In our case, we want to give some guidelines to the user Ford_owner. Hence, we started with the first task of type **Descriptive** as we can see in the previous screenshot.

From an implementation perspective, it's always good to give the first task as Descriptive; it's a kind of guideline on how to proceed further with other tasks.

  - **URL**: The task is of type URL when we want the planner to visit a website. An example of this would be organizations that may have all the information and guideline documents on their internal site, and the organization's requirement is to provide the guidelines to the planning user. We can do it by providing the URL of the relevant document or website and a planner. When he starts his work in a planning application, he can go to the website with the help of this task.

In the previous screenshot, we can see two tabs—**Task** and **Property**. When we select the task type **Descriptive**, we see **Property** getting grayed out and not available. However, when we select **URL**, **Data Form** or **Manage Process**, we need to go to **Property** and need to make the appropriate selection.

The appropriate selection in the **Property** tab would depend on the task type.

To elaborate, if the Task is a URL then obviously the **Property** tab needs to have an option to provide the URL. Likewise, if the task type is Data Form, then the **Property** tab should give us the list of data forms to select.

- ○ **Data Form**: Most of the times, we want a planner or user to enter data in a relevant form. It would be very confusing for a planner to get to the right data form in Advanced Mode. In a real life implementation we would create hundreds of Data Forms and for a planner or end user; and we cannot expect him to know the names of the Data Forms. Task Lists make his life easier. We create a task and associate it with the relevant Data Form, and when a user selects the task list, he knows that the tasks are linked to the relevant forms and he can easily enter values. It's a kind of spoon-feeding which some users need. We'll see how to associate a Data Form with a task in the later part of the section.

- ○ **Manage Process**: As we said earlier, a task is a logical nexus which is just a link to either simple description, URL, Data Form or a Planning unit to manage processes.

We have just created our first task which is of the 'descriptive type' which helps as an instruction or guideline to our hero Ford_owner. We will now create one more task of the Data Form type and link it to the data form of PF_Revenue, as shown below:

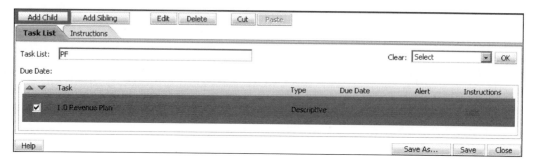

Now check the first task, that is **Revenue Plan** and select **Add sibling** as highlighted in the previous screenshot. It leads to a new window in which we give the task type as **Data Form** and provide **Instructions**, as shown in the following screenshot:

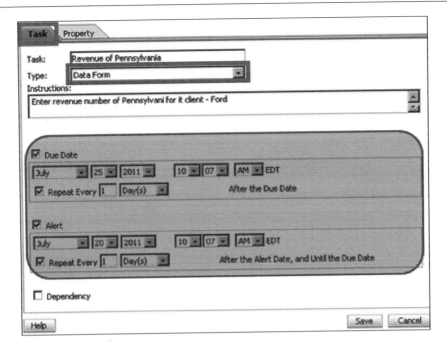

We have learned that for task of the 'data form' type, we need to select the data form to associate it with the task. Hence, post selections of **Task Type** go to the **Property** tab as highlighted in the previous screenshot, and we select the data form PF_ Revenue as shown in the following screenshot:

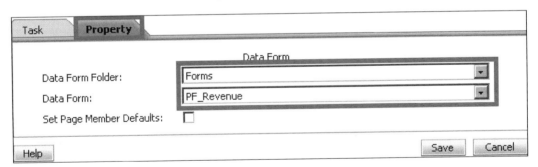

Before we save those changes, we have some work to do on this task. Select the **Task** tab.

Due Dates and Alerts

We have been snubbing a few important properties so far when we created our tasks. Check the newly created task **Revenue of Pennsylvania** and select **Edit**. We are now concerned about the lower portion of the window which has information about the **Due Date**, **Alert**, and **Dependency**.

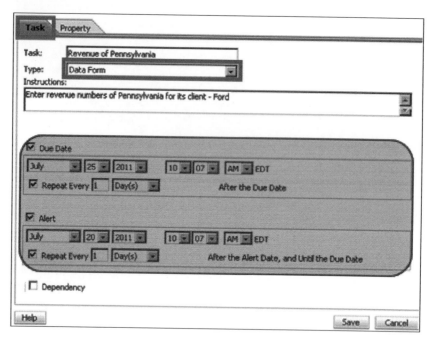

We must understand that users may be lazy and we, as consultants, need to ensure that the planning system is user-friendly in terms of navigation, and it's also equally important to get the work done in time by planners. We also know that an alarm must be set for the user community to wake them up and perform tasks. We do the same in this step. We inform the user with the help of alerts in the form of an e-mail.

 An administrator has to set up e-mail alerts and users can receive e-mail reminders about tasks when they are approaching or have passed their due date.

We alert the planner from the time of alert date and we keep alerting him till the due date is reached. After the due date has lapsed, we inform him that the task has already turned red and he needs to perform tasks quicker.

Hence, we have two dates — Alert Date and Due Date.

Due Date

We always have timelines to finish a task and we set the same for a user. We need to send e-mail reminders to users if they miss their due date, and we do that in this section. We see the due date information highlighted in the previous screenshot.

We can be very aggressive in terms of reminders; reminders can be sent every hour. In our case, the frequency is set for both Alert and Due Date. Hence, a user starts getting e-mail alerts from July 20, 10:07 AM onwards, every day, informing him that the task is approaching. If a user does not finish the task by July 25, 10:07 AM, then he'll start getting e-mails saying he has already passed the due date and again with the frequency of one day.

Alert Date

This is a date set to alert users after the alert date is over. We also set the frequency with which the alert should be sent to the user that is for every one day in our case. We have other frequency options such as hour, day, week, month, and year, that is if we intend to send an e-mail alert for every month to a user to remind him we would select the option of 'month'. The other options of day, week, and year are self explanatory.

> The Alert Date is specified in related to the Due Date. It is usually a week or two before the Due Date.

Dependency

When we mark a task as dependent, it means to say that this task is dependent on the primary task. Let us try to understand with an example: there are two tasks in our Task List and we set the second task as 'dependent'. Now, when a planner or user is accessing the second task, he will not be able to mark the task as 'complete' unless and until he has completed the primary task (which is the first task in our example). Hence, task 2 is dependent on task 1.

In our case, we have two tasks:

- 1.0 Revenue Plan
- 1.1 Revenue of Pennsylvania

We know that the task 1.0 is an instruction and if of descriptive type and will give guidance to perform task 1.1. Hence we can make 1.1 dependent on 1.0 and it makes sense.

We do this by checking the option as shown in the following screenshot:

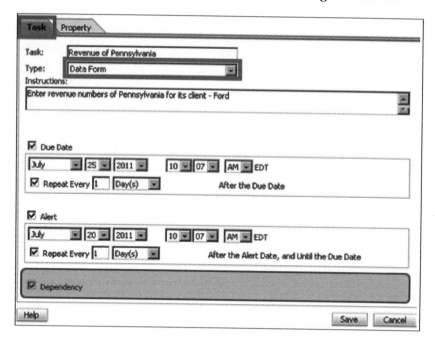

Now, let us think of an example that has three tasks—Task 1, Task 2, and Task 3. If we mark Task 2 and Task 3 as dependent then a user won't be able to mark Task 2 as complete until he has finished Task 1. Similarly, a user cannot mark Task 3 as complete until he completes Task 2. This should clearly explain the concept of dependency.

Save our changes, and we should finally see the child task as shown in the following screenshot:

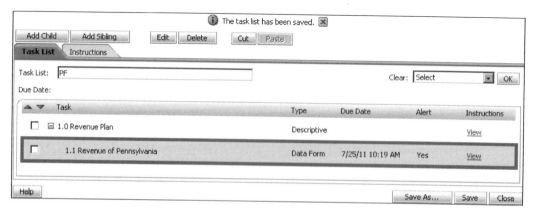

Why do we see the dates in EDT such as 10:07 EDT in Due dates and alerts?

That's an interesting question. Times are marked in EDT because the Planning application is installed on a server, whose time zone is set to EDT.

Where do we see this time zone?

Let's assume the Operating System is Windows, and when we double click on the clock it opens a pop-up that shows the time zone as follows:

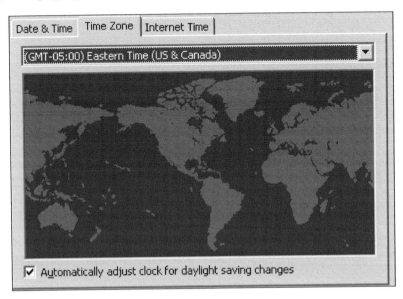

Now let's resume by checking **1.0 Revenue Plan** and select **Add Sibling** as shown in the next screenshot to create a descriptive task by name 'Expense Plan' and its instruction is relevant as shown in the following screenshot:

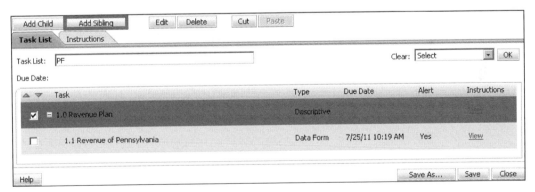

Again it's descriptive. Hence there is no need to set anything in the **Property** tab and also no need to alert a user of this task. We'll set alerts to the user for the next task which is a sub task to this task; that is, a child of this task.

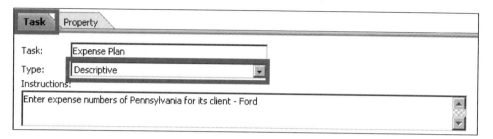

As we did for Revenue tasks, we have created a descriptive revenue task followed by a Data Form type task. We need to remember that the second task is dependent on the primary one. In this step for expense tasks, we'll create a sub task to 2.0 Expense plan that is a child task. Hence, check the task **2.0 Expense** plan, select **child**, and provide the information as shown in the following screenshot:

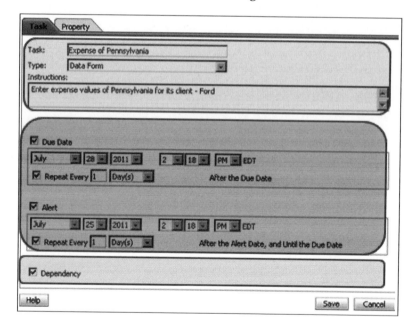

For the Due Date and Alert Date, we have taken precautions that Expense plan is done after Revenue plan; hence the dates are July 25 and 28. We need to recall that Revenue expense was supposed to be completed by July 25.

We also need to select the Data Form of PF_Expense accordingly in the **Property** tab. We should already know how to do that.

Our Task List should look like the following screenshot:

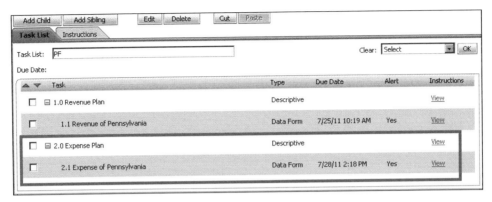

We can see the Due Date and alerts for the two tasks—**1.1** and **2.1**.

We'll now create a task that is a sibling to **2.0 Expense Plan** and will be associated with the Data Form `Review`. Now we know why the order is important to the end users. We have provided `Ford_owner` starting with instructions to fill revenue then followed by expenses and a then look at the values of 'Gross profit' or 'Net income' in Review Data form. His objective is to look at the `Review` Data Form to see whether the entered revenue and expense values have produced the gross profit and income, which is good enough to promote to next level.

Hence, we'll create a task as shown in the next screenshot. Again, we need to link it to the data form 'Review'.

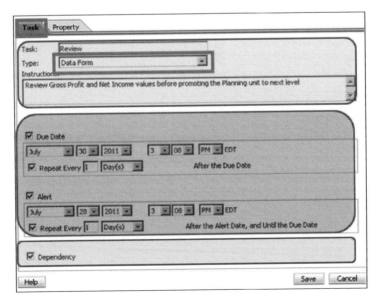

Here, we had set the alerts and due dates as July 28 and 30 respectively. Save it and remember that we need to associate the `Review` Data Form as shown in the next screenshot before we save and close this task:

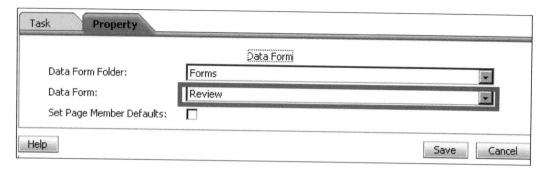

So far, we have created expense tasks, revenue tasks and review task. Now, as per our requirements for the Task List, `Ford_owner` should promote to `Penn_rev` post his review task. We can refer to the requirements section for the same.

Hence, we will create a task as shown which is of Type 'Manage' process as shown in the next screenshot, and we will set its due date as Aug 2. It implies that `Ford_owner` has to do all tasks in the `PF` task list and promote it on or before Aug 2.

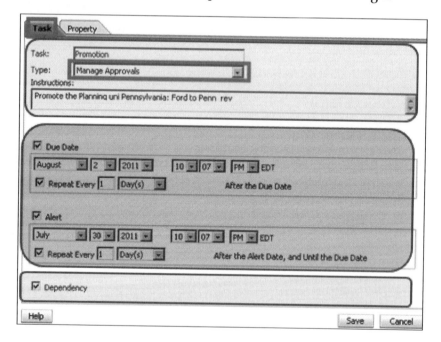

Now, we'll see the **Property** tab as we are dealing with task type of 'Manage' process for the first time.

Go to the **Property** tab and select **Plan** and **V1** because we had created a Planning unit—East earlier for these members of **Scenario** and **Version** dimensions, and we need to ensure that the Planning unit is started before we do this step. We had already started the planning unit earlier as a part of the pre-requisites.

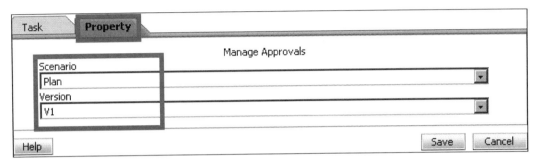

Save our changes.

The final screen of our tasks in the task list PF is as shown here. Save and close it.

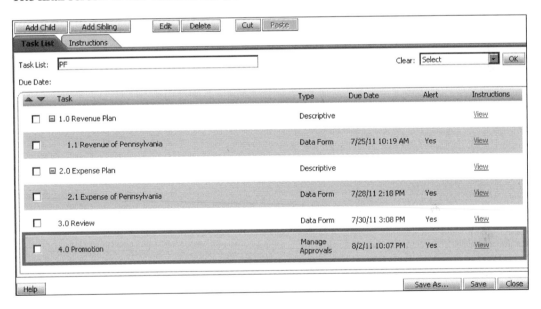

Security access for Task Lists

The administrator now needs to provide access for the PF task list to the user Ford_ owner. For that check the task list **PF** and select **Assign Access** as shown in the following screenshot:

On the security front, we had provisioned the required Data Forms (that is PF_ Expense, PF_revenue, and Review) to the user Ford_owner already. It is also necessary to provision the Task List— PF to Ford_owner for him to access. At the end, Task List is a dubious font face, but the back end reality is the Data Forms, Planning unit, and so on.

As we select **Assign Access**, a new widow will open as shown in the next screenshot. The following screenshot clearly states that it's only the 'admin' who has access rights at this point of time.

Now, select **Add Access** with the intent to provide Ford_owner access rights. Select **Ford_owner** from the list shown in the **Users** tab and select the **Add** button as shown in the following screenshot:

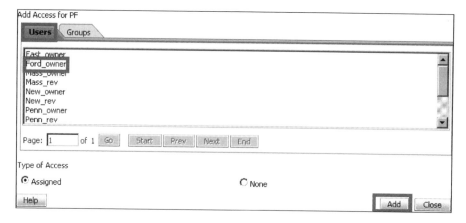

We should be presented with a success note as follows:

Close it, and now log into Planning application again as `Ford_owner` and see whether our hard work thus far is actually worth it.

> Not every planning user can create task lists. This just can't be the case. Hence, they are created only by those users who have the role of administrator or 'Interactive User'.

Accessing Task Lists in Basic Mode

In this section, we'll see exactly how a planner would experience the Tasks Lists for a Planning application in Basic Mode, and we need to recollect our litany that basic mode is for majority planners.

Now let us get the look, feel, and experience of our end user or Planner who accesses the Task Lists. We'll log into SRGD application on behalf of `Ford_owner` using his credentials (user name: `Ford_owner`, password: `password`) and embody ourselves as planner `Ford_owner`. We'll do it using the following steps:

1. First login into as `Ford_owner` and straight away put on the lenses of Basic Mode by navigating **View | Basic Mode**, and you will see the task list **PF** as seen in the next screenshot. This confirms that the security access rights for the PF Task List have been successfully given to `Ford_owner`.

   As `Ford_owner` has been granted access to only one Task List that is PF, we can see it selected by default in the next screenshot. Else, the list is always a drop-down listing the Task Lists and you have to select one.

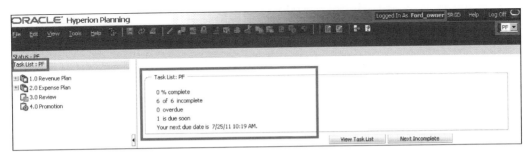

Let us pay attention to the right-hand side Task List pane which is highlighted. It firstly says that only 0% is complete and we are very well aware that we have not finished any tasks so far. Next, it mentions that there are a total of six tasks and all six are incomplete. The next line talks of Overdue, that is the tasks that are not completed on time and Planner or end user had already passed the set due date. We see **0** overdue that is none of the tasks have missed the set dates so far.

The next line tells us that there is one task which is due soon and concludes by saying that the due date was July 25, 2011. We need to assume that we stand on July 21, 2011 at this junction of time.

2. Now, go to **View | Task Lists | Task Lists** and here we can see the status in colors. Refer to the section *Introduction to Task Lists* earlier in this chapter, where we have learned that a Yellow status means that the Task is approaching (will be performed soon) and Green status indicates that it is not yet approaching and we have time for that.

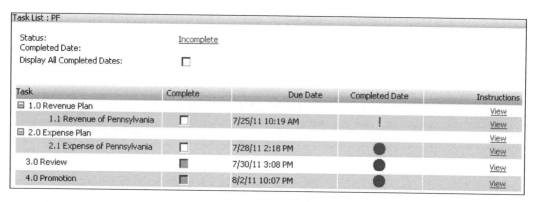

As we try to correlate, the task 1.1 Revenue of Pennsylvania which is supposed to be completed by July 25 and we are today standing on July 21. Hence, it correctly shows in Yellow whereas **2.1 Expense of Pennsylvania**, **3.0 Review**, and **4.0 Promotion** tasks still have time remaining on them.

The tasks **1.0** and **2.0** do not have any due dates as the admin has not set them, considering them to be descriptive tasks.

3. **Task 1.0 Revenue Plan**—Now let us start completing the tasks. Click on **1.0 Revenue Plan** as we can see on the left-hand side of the following screenshot:

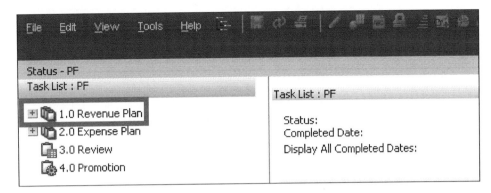

The first task, which is **1.0 Revenue Plan**, is an easy one. All the Planner Ford_owner needs to do is to read the instruction and move on to the next task. This task is a descriptive task and for this reason it has no due date. Therefore, the option of 'complete' in not available and it is grayed out as we can see in the next screenshot. Read the instructions and select **Next** as shown:

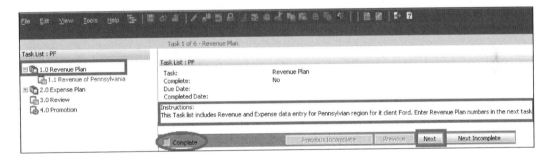

4. **Task 1.1 Revenue of Pennsylvania**—The next task is **1.1 Revenue of Pennsylvania** as shown in the next screenshot, which is associated with the Data Form—PF_Revenue and we are going to enter the values in the data form and save it. This is task 2 of 6 tasks as highlighted in the next screenshot. This task opens the Data Form—PF_Revenue and enter the values for January, February, and March of Q1 as shown in the next screenshot. We can also observe that the Entity dimension member is **Pennsylvania** and Client dimension member is **Global Motors Ltd**. This is to reconfirm that Ford_owner is entering numbers for Pennsylvania region and for its client Global Motors Ltd. After entering the numbers, we need to save without fail.

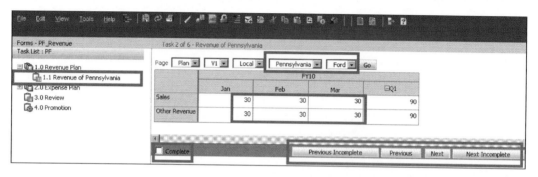

After entering the data values in the Data Form, we can go to the next task by selecting **Next**. But before that, check the **Complete** checkbox as shown in the previous screenshot and then move on by selecting **Next**.

Is checking Complete important?

Yes, it is extremely important to tick the task. Even though the task is to enter revenue values in the Data Form, the system does not have enough intelligence to understand that the planner had entered the values and a task is over. No, this is not the case; a Planner has to explicitly check the **Complete** checkbox to make the system understand the completion of a task.

One more question:

We see a few options—Previous Incomplete, Previous, Next, and Next Incomplete. What are these options?

Good observation. We will discuss them next. Most of these terms are self explanatory and we'll try to define them quickly:

- ○ **Previous Incomplete**: This option, upon selection, will take us to the task that has not been completed. Let us try to understand with our PF Task List. In our task list, we have six tasks 1.0, 1.1, 2.0, 2.1, 3.0, and 4.0. We are currency at task 1.1. Now, we know that there is only one task that is 1.0 which can be called as a previous task and we also know that there are no other tasks that precede 1.1 which are incomplete. Hence; we see the **Previous Incomplete** option grayed out.

- ○ **Previous**: This option will move control to the preceding task. Now the question would be what is the difference between **Previous Incomplete** and **Previous**? The former option will go to the previous task which is incomplete, while the latter option will go to the task that is exactly a step before or preceding the task, it does not care about the status of completion at all. Hence, 'Previous' task is an applicable option in our case at this point of time and we do see this option in the previous screenshot. We can select it and witness for ourselves how the control goes to the previous task.

- ○ **Next**: The explanation of **Previous** holds true for **Next** as well. This is the option we generally used to move on and go to the next task.

- ○ **Next Incomplete**: This is very close to **Previous Incomplete**. This option goes to the task which satisfied two conditions—tasks which are incomplete and the tasks which are after the current task in the order of a Task List.

5. **Task 2.0 Expense Plan**—After we select **Next** we will reach Task 3 of 6. Firstly, we observe that the tasks 1.0 and 1.1 are ticked in green signifying the completion of the tasks in the next screenshot. In this step, we are at task 2.0, which again is a descriptive task and it gives an instruction of what to be done in the next sub task of 2.1 as shown in the next screenshot. We also need to observe that the **Complete** checkbox is grayed and disabled, and we know the reason, it is because the task is descriptive in nature. In this task, we read the instruction and select **Next** knowing that we have to fill the expense numbers of Pennsylvania, which was clearly stated in this instruction.

Select **Next**.

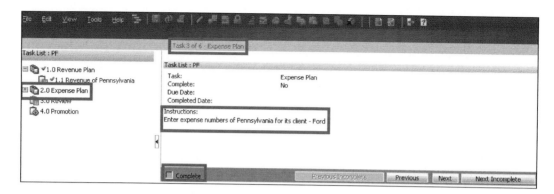

6. **Task 2.1 Expense of Pennsylvania** — In 2.1, which is task 4 of 6, we fill the expense information as shown in the next screenshot and before we go to **Next**, we need to tick the **Complete** checkbox.

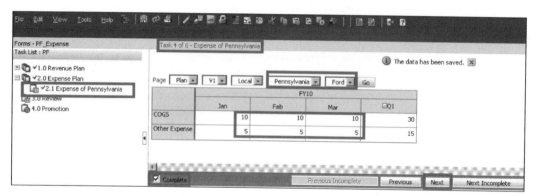

7. So far, we have completed 4 tasks out of 6, now let us see the status of the task list on the whole of PF.

How can one see the status of a Task List?

Go to **View | Task List | Status** and we can see the following status as shown in the following screenshot:

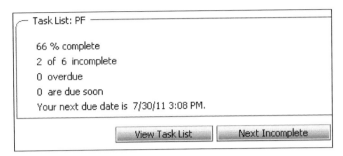

Now, we can read the status very clearly from the previous screenshot. Remember, we had looked at the status before completing any of the tasks of the Task list. Now, select **Next Incomplete**. This option should take us to the next incomplete task, which would be **3.0 Review task**.

8. **Task 3.0 Review**—The control will go to task of the Review Data Form and we need to finally look at the Net income and Gross profit. We need to realize that it's the review form and hence, it is displayed in grey.

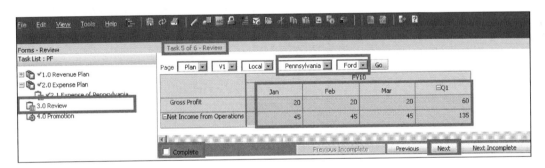

Now, we will try to understand how the numbers for Gross Profit and Net Income from Operation are calculated.

- Gross Profit = Sales -COGS

- Net Income from Operations = Total Revenue (which is Sales + other Revenue) - Total Expense (that is COGS + other expense)

We can reconfirm the same by looking at the Account dimension hierarchy as shown in the next screenshot. We have not entered values for Income Tax and SG&A in the earlier data forms, we did not consider them in the previous formulae.

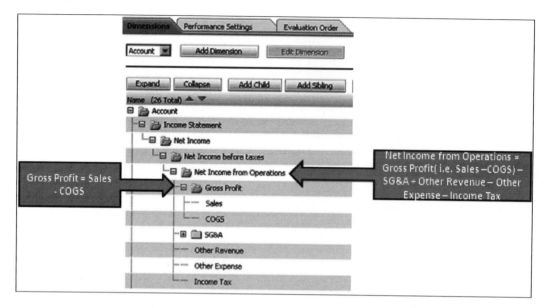

If you feel comfortable with the numbers in the Review Data Form, check the **Complete** checkbox and select **Next** to move on to the next and the final task.

9. **Task 4.0 Promotion** — In this final task of 4.0 Promotion, we get the **Process Management** screen, as we had associated the Planning unit of Pennsylvania: Global Motors Ltd to the last task. To recap the story quickly — Ford_owner first reads the instruction that Revenue numbers of client Global Motors Ltd of region 'Pennsylvania' are to be entered and in the subsequent step, he fills the Revenue Data Form and after that he reads the instruction that he has to fill the expense details of Pennsylvania, he does that in the next task by filling in the Expense Data Form. Now, after filling the two Data Forms he ought to review the Data Form — Review, which has information about Gross Profit and Net Income, and moves on with happiness to promote the Planning unit to the next level or next owner of the Planning unit that is Penn_rev. But, we need to realize that the last step of promotion is still left for us to finish.

In this last task, as we move ahead from task 3.0, we see the following task in the next screenshot. Check the **Select mine** option which will check the Planning unit Pennsylvania: Global Motors Ltd as shown:

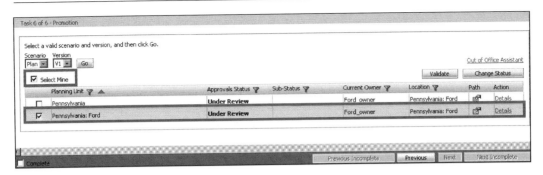

Now, go to **Details**, select **Change Status** and promote it to the next owner as shown in the following screenshot:

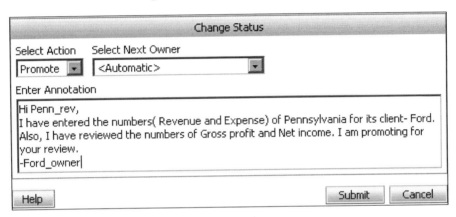

Submit it and click on **Done**. Now we can see that the Planning unit is under review and its current owner is Penn_rev, as shown in the following screenshot:

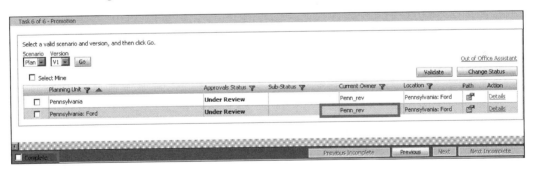

Now, check the **Complete** checkbox below to mark the end of the final task of the PF task list performed by Ford_owner.

10. Now go to **View | Task List | Task List** to see that all the tasks are completed, the task status is 'complete' and we don't see any more Red status marks against any tasks.

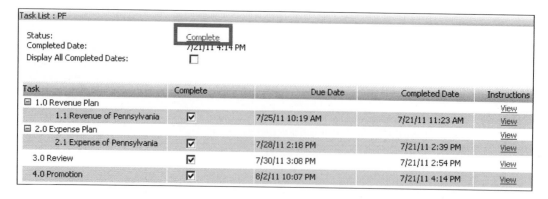

This is the end of our job on behalf of Ford_owner as far this PF task list is concerned. This what a typical planner would be doing.

Accessing Task Lists in Advanced Mode

The task list can also be accessed in advanced mode.

Log in to SRGD as admin.

So far, we have been working in Basic Mode, we will now switch over to advanced mode. Go to **View | Advanced Mode** and then go to **View | Task List |Task List**. We can see three tabs:

- **Available Task Lists**: This lists the Task Lists that are available to the user. Select the Task List folder **Pennsylvania** in which we have only one task list that is **PF**. Select **PF** and as we select it, the control goes to the **Task List** tab.

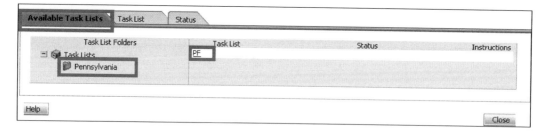

- **Task List**: This digs into more granularities by listing the tasks under the selected Task List of PF. Here, one can access the tasks on the left-hand side. A user can view Due Date, Completed Date, and also Instruction, as shown in the next screenshot. We need to know that we are on July 28, 10 AM. Hence task 1.1, which was supposed to be complete by July 25 is overdue and task 2.1, which is supposed to be completed by July 28 2:10 AM is about to approach. We can see Red and Yellow warnings for these tasks respectively.

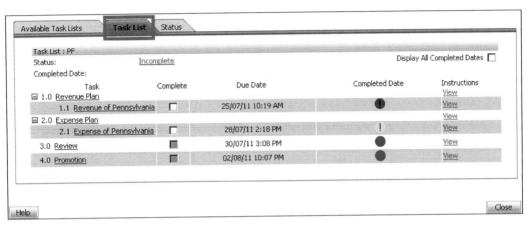

We cannot believe that none of the tasks are complete as we have completed each and every task individually. We now need to do some soul searching and figure out that we have logged in as 'admin' now but we completed all the tasks as another user — Ford_owner.

Now, we will log off and logi n SRGD as Ford_owner and go to Advanced Mode. Here we see that all the tasks are completed, as shown in the following screenshot:

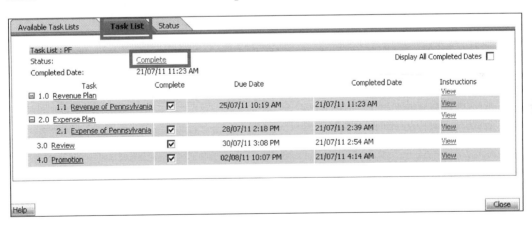

So, we can conclude that the Task List is incomplete for the 'admin' user, whereas it is complete for `Ford_owner` user.

> There are two users XYZ and ABC, both the users are assigned to a same task list. User XYZ logs in and marks a task as completed. Now, ABC logs in the application and accesses the same task list.
>
> **Here the question is – As XYZ has completed the task, would the status of task be complete or not complete for ABC?** Task List is stored at user level, which means that everybody can view their very own task list status. Hence, for ABC, the task is still not complete.
>
> Hence, this behavior of Task Lists comes in very handy when two users are responsible for performing the same set of tasks but for different entities. We can relate now as admin and `Ford_owner` are two different users with access to the same PF Task List.

- **Status**: This gives us the progress card of the tasks in the PF Task List as shown in the next screenshot. Again the status is 100% complete if we log in as `Ford_owner` and it would be 0% complete if we log in as admin.

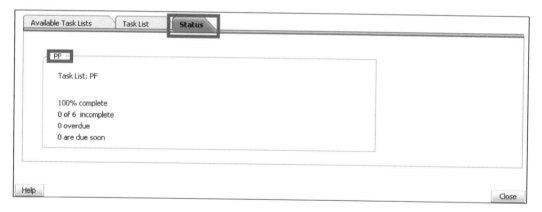

To conclude, we first select the Task List, that is PF in **Available Task Lists** tab and then we can select tasks of PF and perform based on the information of due dates and instruction in **Task List** tab. Finally, we have status tab which gives information on a task's overall progress.

Therefore, Task Lists can be accessible from Advanced Mode also.

Task List Report

There is always a requirement from management to know whether all planners have completed their tasks, and if not, which planners have not yet completed their assigned tasks To serve to these kinds of requirements, we have an option of 'Report Creation' which will provide information of planners and task list in the form of Excel report or PDF report.

Go to **View | Task List | Report** ,which will take us to the window shown in the next screenshot, select PF and move it under **Selected Task Lists** and select **Next** to proceed.

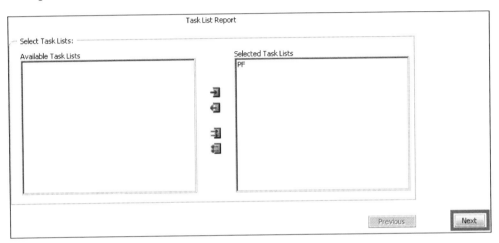

In this window, we'll see a list of users who have access to task list PF. We know that there are only two users, they are admin and Ford_owner. We'll select Ford_owner as shown in the following screenshot:

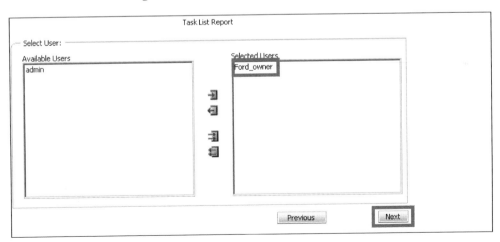

In the next step, we have a multitude of options for the report ranging from grouping results either by users or by task lists to the display options. We'll stick with the default options and select the report type as **PDF Format** as shown in the following screenshot:

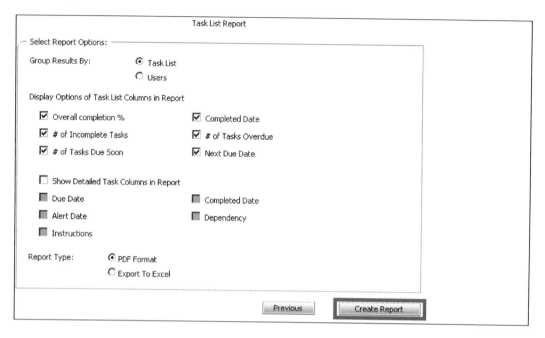

It is highly recommended that readers explore other combinations of **Select Report Options**.

Select **Create Report** to view the PDF, as you can see in the following screenshot:

ORACLE' | Hyperion'

Task List Report
Application: SRGD

Tasklist: PF
User: Ford_owner
Status: Complete
Overall Completion %: 100
0 of 6 task(s) incomplete
# of tasks overdue: 0
# of tasks due soon: 0
Next due date: 02/08/11 10:07 PM

Tasks in PF

Task	Type	Status	Additional Details	Details
Reve nue of Penns ylvan ia	Data Form	Complete	Data form name = PF_Revenue	
Expe nse of Penns ylvan ia	Data Form	Complete	Data form name = PF_Expense	
Reve nue Plan	Descriptive	Complete		
Expe nse Plan	Descriptive	Complete		
Revie w	Data Form	Complete	Data form name = Review	
Prom otion	Workflow	Complete	Scenario = Plan & Version = V1	

This is how we can create reports of task lists.

Summary

We started this chapter by exploring the two modes of Planning application—Basic and Advanced. We introduced Task Lists and also its importance to a Planner or end user. Before we jump-started the creation of our first Task List, we assumed business requirements and then created a Task List, keeping planner (Ford_owner) in mind.

Finally, we also saw how a Planner would experience task lists in a planning application by logging into SRGD application as Ford_owner in Basic Mode and Advanced Mode as well. We have also seen how to create Task List reports, which will help to trace the progress of users and also Task Lists.

In the next chapter, we'll introduce Business Rules in Planning applications. This is where we incorporate business logic into our planning application.

15
Business Rules

For the hand that rocks the cradle, is the hand that rules the world

— *William Ross Wallace*

Yes, I completely agree with William Ross Wallace on his statement, we can also say that a Business rule is like a mother and will rock the cradle of Hyperion Planning application.

This is one of the most important chapters of this book. So far, we have seen planners entering data into web data forms, but the complex activity of calculating the entered data is done with the help of Business rules. Hyperion Planning has a very powerful engine of Business rules, which are capable of handling even complex business requirements such as the allocation rules across the dimensions effectively. Hyperion Planning inherits this capability from Essbase as it is built on top of the Essbase, which, apart from storing multidimensional data, also provides a very strong calculation engine. Therefore, the analytical capability of Hyperion Planning lies in the hands of Business rules.

Let us take a look at a conversation between an Essbase developer learning Hyperion Planning and a Hyperion Planning expert:

> **Essbase developer**: *Hi, Mr. Planning expert, I have been working on Essbase for many years and I want to learn about the Planning tool.*

> **Planning expert**: *It's an ideal thing to do. I need to inform you that it is very beneficial for an Essbase guy to learn Planning.*

> **Essbase developer**: *Yes, I have heard the same. I have heard that there is this important concept of Business rules in Planning and have also heard that it's one of the important and complex topics. Is this true?*

> **Planning expert**: *Yes, I would agree that it is an important subject and I also would like to inform you that it's synonymous to your calculation scripts of Essbase. This must make you feel comfortable.*

In this chapter, we'll start our journey with the basics of Business rules and cover the advanced Business rules topics in the next chapter. We need to start the chapter with a disclaimer saying that the readers who have already worked on Essbase will find it more helpful than readers with no experience in working with the *calculation scripts* of Essbase.

Business rules are similar to calculation scripts in Essbase. We are not going to learn the basics of calculation scripts; rather, we'll stick to the Business rule angle of Hyperion Planning.

Also, Business rules can be created using the calculation manager (this is one of the modules of EPM architecture), but we are not going to talk about it, so consider it to be out of scope.

The following are the sections covered as a part of this chapter:

- **Introduction to Business rules**: We'll understand the basic needs of Business rules in this section before we dig into the details.
- **Calculation**: We'll learn the ways of achieving calculation logic in a Planning application in this section, where Business rules define one way to achieve them. The other ways are:
  - **Outline**
  - **Member formula**
  - **Business rules**
- **Business rules**: We'll learn all about Business rules in this section.
  - **Business rule roles**: First, we'll explore the roles that are applicable to the Business rules product.
  - **Business rule components**: We'll understand the basic components of a rule before we start creating our first Business rule.
  - **Business rule creation**: This section is a step-by-step process covering Business rules' creation.
  - **Business rule execution**: In this section, we'll understand how a planner would execute a Business rule.

Introduction to Business Rules

A rule, in general, is defined as a governing power or authority. It can also be defined as a method or procedure for solving a problem.

Here, we are talking about a *Business rule*. If we look at its definition, it says that Business rules are the constraints which control the behavior of the business. In our case of budgeting through Hyperion Planning applications, Business rules have more to do with business calculations.

A simple example of a calculation is to compute the travel cost by multiplying the headcount with the average travel cost per resource. This simple multiplication is also a business calculation.

Another example is of allocation of costs. In budgeting cost allocation to departments, it is important to identify the cost incurred by the individual departments. Hence, we generally write Business rules for allocation also known as allocation rules.

 Business rules were licensed separately some time back, but not anymore and that's the reason we see Business rules, when we log in to the EAS console now.

In next section, we'll explore different options of achieving calculations in a Planning application.

Calculations in a Planning Application

The calculation part of Hyperion Planning can be achieved in three ways:

- Outline or dimensional hierarchy.
- Member formula
- Business rules.

Using outline

We know that a Planning outline comprises all dimensions, members, and their respective hierarchies. Calculation is performed based on the way we design the dimensional hierarchy in a Planning outline. If we recall the two basic settings of dimension members, they are:

- Consolidation
- Storage

We learned about these two properties at length already in Chapter 6, *Settings*, under the *Basics* section. Please refer to it once before we presume our discussion.

Let us take the Account dimension of SRGD as an example and view its dimensional structure to understand this.

Log in to SRGD as an admin and take a look at the **Account** dimension hierarchy of the SRGD Planning application, as shown in the next screenshot:

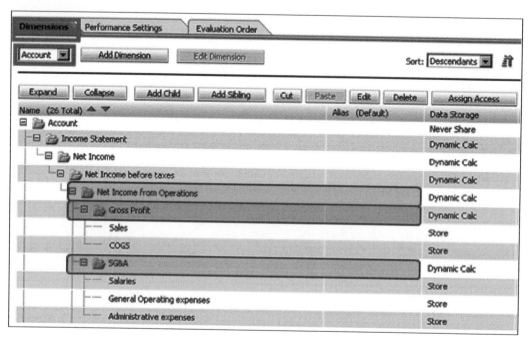

We clearly observe that the parent members in the hierarchies have the storage property of **Dynamic Calc** and the level 0, that is, leaf members have the storage property of **Store**. The reason behind this is planners usually enter data at leaf level and when a member is of the **Store** type, it has the ability to store the entered data value. In the case of members with the **Dynamic Calc** property, a planner is not allowed to enter a value; they are computed or calculated members. **Dynamic Calc** calculates at runtime every time a user accesses it and it's not stored.

We can also observe that the parent members **SG&A**, **Gross Profit**, **Net Income from Operation**, and so on, which are all parent members, are all assigned **Dynamic Calc** access in the previous screenshot.

In the designed **Account** hierarchy, most of the members have the aggregation property, either as 'addition' or 'subtraction'. If we take a look at **Gross Profit** in the previous screenshot, it has two children: **Sales** and **COGS**. We know that **Gross Profit** is calculated by subtracting **COGS** from **Sales**. Hence we would set the consolidation operator of **Sales** and **COGS,** as addition and subtraction respectively.

Now, to calculate **Gross Profit**, we need not write any formula, that is, **Sales – (minus) COGS**. We set the **Gross Profit** as **Dynamic Calc**, and in this way, it dynamically calculates its value by subtracting **COGS** from **Sales**.

In the next screenshot, we can see the **Member Properties** of **Sales** and **COGS**, and we can see their consolidation operators being **Addition** and **Subtraction** respectively.

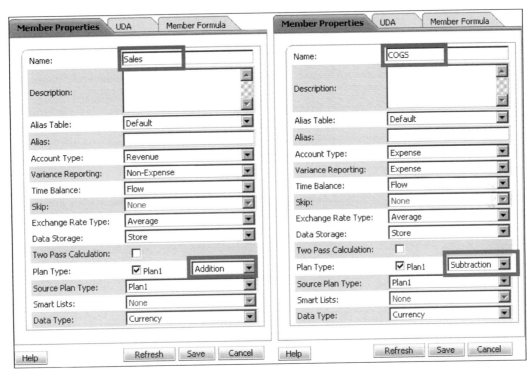

From a design perspective, it's preferred to set the parent members as **Dynamic Calc**. It is also important to note that this is applicable if the dimension is dense in nature. It is not a recommended point for sparse dimensions.

This is how we design the Planning outlines, in a manner that does calculation with the help of **Consolidation** and **Storage** properties, without using any member formulas or even Business rules for that matter.

Wherever possible, it's better to use the appropriate consolidation operator in the Planning outline. Therefore, we can achieve calculation with the help of the outline design. In the next section, we'll explore the option of member formulas.

Using member formulas

There are predefined sets of functions and operators that can be used to build member formulas. If we have a member, **Travel Expense** in our Planning application and we have two other members such as **Average travel expense per resource** and **head count**, then it's understood that the possible formula for **Travel expense** would be simple multiplication of **Average travel expense** with **Head count**. We will not create a member formula now; we will first take a look at one formula and then will try to implement the same.

We have a member by the name **Operating Revenue** in the PandB Planning application, which has a member formula. Log in to the 'PandB' Planning application as **Admin**.

Go to **Administration | Manage | Dimensions**.

Select the **Accounts** dimension. Expand the members of the dimension, as shown in the next image. Our area of interest is three members, which are highlighted in the next image:

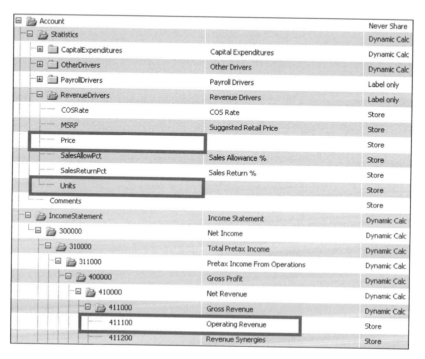

If we are in the business of selling books, then the revenue calculation would be 'number of units of books sold' multiplied by the 'price of the book'. Likewise, the 'Operating Revenue' is equal to **Units** multiplied by **Price**.

From a designing perspective, we keep the statistical drivers under one hierarchy. Hence, we see 'Price' and 'Units' as a part of **Statistics** while **Operating Revenue** ought to be a part of any **Income statement report**. Hence, we see **Operating revenue** as a part of the **Income statement** hierarchy.

Select the member **411100** and click on **edit** to view its properties. We see three tabs and the top right-hand side tab, as shown in the following screenshot, is of **Member Formula**.

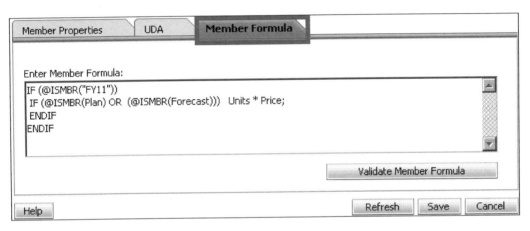

We see the member formula written for the member **411100**, as shown in the previous screenshot. We are not going to understand every line of the given syntax but if we have to put it in simple English, then the member formula means, "If the year is FY10 and if the scenario dimension member is **Plan** or **Forecast**, then the value of **411100** is computed by multiplying **Units** with **Price**".

After writing the member formula, we can validate and then save it.

This is another way of achieving calculation in the Hyperion Planning application. Now, we'll move on to the next section of Business rules.

Using Business Rules

In budgeting, the business logic requirement is not easy to achieve through the Planning outline design. We employ Business rules to implement complicated calculations.

We are not going to code in any complicated programming language for a Business rule; rather, it will be all graphical in nature. Graphical interfaces ease Business rule creation, even for users with a business (non-technical) background.

Nevertheless, Business rules can also be created by coding in all the calculations. In fact, the graphical interface also generates code behind the scenes and the user developing a rule using the graphical interface can switch to the source section for viewing the generated code. We shall see this in the subsequent sections.

Business rules make use of the predefined functions and formulas of Essbase and it's strictly recommended that you learn the calculation process of an Essbase cube. Hence, Essbase knowledge was already stated as the prerequisite for Planning.

Business rules are not created within the Planning web, unlike the outline structure or member formulas. We create Business rules through the EAS console. Nevertheless, one can create rules using the Calculation manager (which is a part of EPM architecture), but it is out of the scope of this book.

Business Rules

We introduced Business rules in the previous section, and in this section, we'll learn all about Business rules.

- Business rule roles
- Business rule components
- Business rule creation
- Business rule execution

Business Rule roles

As a movie quote goes, "With great power comes great responsibility", the Business rules are very powerful and determine the way the budgeting calculations for the organizations are performed. Hence, the rules have specific roles, and not all planners can use them. In short, it means it's not just meant for any Tom, Dick, and Harry.

We have already learned about the Planning roles of *Administrator*, *Interactive user*, and *Basic user*. Now, we are going to see Business rule roles with the same role names.

Don't confuse Planning roles with Business rule roles. We need to understand this; the Business rules and the Hyperion Planning are technically two different products of Hyperion. Hence, different products will have different roles.

Before the confusion builds any further, let us log in to Hyperion Shared Services using the **admin** credentials:

1. Expand **User Directories** to **Native Directory** and then select **Users,** as shown in the next screenshot:

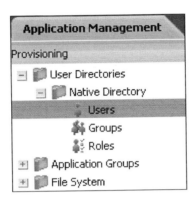

2. Now we will search for the user **admin** by typing it in the **User Filter** field and select the **Search** option. This will result in giving the following search result, as shown in the next screenshot. Now, right-click on the user **admin** and select the **Provision** option.

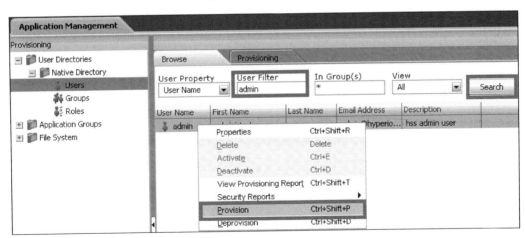

3. As we select **Provision**, it opens a new window where we can see the list of roles and their respective products. We have already learned by now that Business rules and Hyperion Planning are two separate products, and hence will have a different set of roles as well.

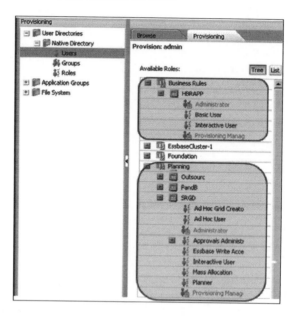

We see on the top that a Business rule is one of the products and the available roles are as seen in the previous screenshot; similarly, we can see a list of roles for a **Planning** product too, with their respective roles.

Now, let us learn about Business rules roles:

- *Administrator*: A user with the *Administrator* role can create, edit, delete, validate, and launch a Business Rule. This user can also provide *access privileges* like validating, launching, and creating to other users as well.

- *Interactive User*: A user with the *Interactive User* role is also a powerful person and is allowed to create, edit, validate, and launch a Business rule.

 An Interactive user can also provide *access privilege* to other users but cannot provide *launch* privilege; it's restricted and it can be done only by the administrator.

- *Basic User*: He/she is the user to whom the administrator gives privileges to launch or has been given the privilege to view or edit.

> We need not provision users for the Business rule roles in Shared Services in order to use Business rules with Planning. The roles are used for provisioning users to use Business rules exclusively with Essbase, not Planning. If we provision a Planning user as a *Planner* and they are given the appropriate *access privilege* to launch a Business rule, they will be able to execute Business rules. The conclusion is that for a user, who wants to access Business rules in the EAS console and wants to work like a developer, he/she would need to be given, explicitly, roles of Business rules in Shared services. Else, for a typical planner, it is not required at all.

To demonstrate the same, log in to the EAS console using **admin** credentials and right-click on **Rules**. We can see that we can select a new rule and create a rule. Log in to the EAS console using the credentials of any other users. We can use **Walt_ owner** or any other user, and we will realize the fact that this user is not permitted to create a new rule.

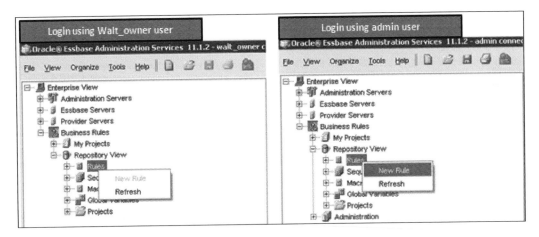

Now, the next step is to log in to the shared services and look at the roles provisioned to both **admin** and **Walt_owner**. We can see that a role of 'administrator' of HBRAPP is provisioned to the **admin** user, while none of the roles of HBRAPP are assigned to **Walt_owner**.

Business Rules components

Let us continue with the basics of Business rules in this section too.

Now, straightaway log in to the EAS console using the **admin** credentials. For that, navigate to:

Programs | Oracle EPM System | Essbase | Essbase Administration Services | Start Administration Services Console.

Now, log in to the EAS console by providing **admin** credentials.

We observe three important tabs in the next screenshot. As we expand Business rules, we see **Rules**, as highlighted in the next screenshot:

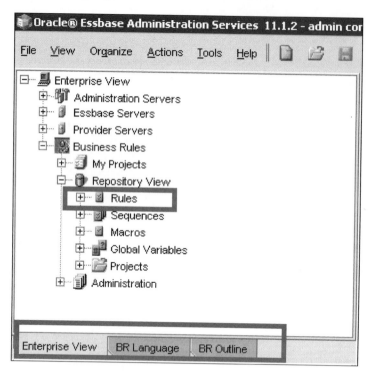

And we see the highlighted area of tabs: **Enterprise View**, **BR Language**, and **BR Outline**, as shown in the previous screenshot.

Enterprise View

The **Enterprise View** tab has whole lot of objects, starting from Essbase server, Essbase applications/databases, to Business rules objects. We create a new Business Rule from the **Enterprise View** tab and one can arrange the rules under the **Projects** folder for easier administration and maintenance. We can see the same in the next screenshot.

BR Language

As we had learned already that a Business Rule needs to include predefined functions and commands, the selection of the same can be done from the **BR Language** tab. In this section, we'll learn about the following:

- Actions
- Formulas

Select the second tab of **BR Language** and we can view the options of **Actions** and **Formulas** in the following screenshot:

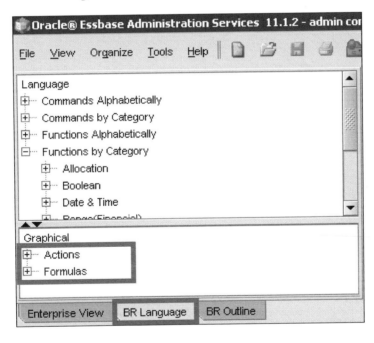

We see the commands list on the top under **Language**. There is a huge list of commands under **Allocation, Boolean**, and so on. As we move down, we can see the list of actions and formulas under the *Graphical* section.

Now, understanding functions and commands are out of the scope of this book and is practically impossible to discuss all of them, but coming to *actions* and *formula*, we can talk about them.

Actions

Expand actions and we can see the following options, as shown in the next screenshot:

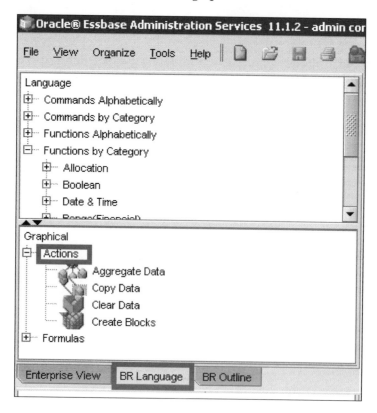

We see that Actions has four options; they are:

- **Aggregate Data**
- **Copy Data**
- **Clear Data**
- **Create Blocks**

Aggregate Data

Generally, data is entered at level 0 or at leaf level of the Planning outline. We achieve this with the help of data entry in Data forms. This data entry, in a way, is 'data loading' into the Planning application. Though data is entered at leaf levels, we would definitely be interested to view the information at higher levels. For example, a planner enters data for Jan, Feb, and March months and now, we are interested to view the information at quarter level and year level. To achieve this roll up, we need to perform aggregation.

The possible options from the action **Aggregate Data** are as shown in the next screenshot.

Dimension	Value type		Selected Values
	Not specified		

Options shown in screenshot:
- ○ Calculate entire database
- ○ Calculate entire database with two pass calculation
- ◉ Calculate portion of database specified below
- ☐ Aggregate missing values in the database
- ☐ Aggregate data up to local currency
- ☐ Optimize the calculation of formulas on sparse dimensions
- ☐ Use calculator cache High

- **Calculate entire database**: We see options starting with **Calculate entire database**. This option of the action will calculate and aggregate all the dimensions of the Planning application outline. In short, CALC ALL.

- **Calculate entire database with two pass calculation**: This option does the same as **Calculate entire database**, but it does it with two-pass calculation. Readers must be familiar with two-pass calculation, as it's one of the most important concepts of Essbase. This option will calculate all the members that are tagged as two-pass calculation in the Planning outline.

- **Calculate portion of database specified below**: We have a list of dimensions of the Planning outline and we need to specify a subset of the Planning database, that is, a few of the dimensions that we would want to include as a part of aggregation. Hence, it calculates only the subset of the database, rather than the entirety. As of now, we have not selected any dimensions or its values. Hence, we see an empty list in the previous screenshot.

 Calculate portion of database specified below is the default selection.

We see more options on the right-hand side in the previous screenshot. These are again Essbase concepts:

- **Aggregate missing values in the database**: It is SET AGGMISSG; this setting determines whether missing values are to be aggregated. Readers should be aware of this, as it is an Essbase concept.

- **Optimize the calculation of formulas on sparse dimension**: Optimize the calculation is SET FRMBOTTOMUP. This setting is generally used in very large database outlines with the intent to optimize the calculation of formulas on sparse dimensions.

- The last option, that is, **Use calculator cache** is to specify the calculator cache. The more the better. It is a SET CACHE setting.

In the above options, we have seen options determining the settings; more information of the settings can be found in the Essbase technical reference, whose URL is: `http://download.oracle.com/docs/cd/E17236_01/epm.1112/esb_tech_ref/frameset.htm?launch.html`

We know that in the sequence of events, at first, Planners or end users enter data in to the web forms. We also know that there can be a number of member formulas or Business rules created to do computation. So, when data is entered, based on the member formula or Business rules, it gets computed. For post computation, we would like aggregation to happen. Let us understand the same with an example. There is a country, which has three states. Let us name them using the following nomenclature: C1 will be country and S1, S2, and S3 will be the states, and the hierarchy will be such that S1, S2, and S3 will be children to C1. Also, note that all C1, S1, S2, and S3 are of the 'store' storage type. C1, though in this case, is parent, but whose storage property is not **Dynamic Calc**.

Now, Planners enter data for S1, S2, and S3 and if then followed by Business rule exaction. Now, to view data at C1 level, the data at S1 to S3 needs to aggregate. Hence aggregation is recommended at the end.

Therefore, when we create Business rules, aggregating data is generally the last step to impact the calculations performed over the data.

Copy Data

The **Copy Data** action copies the data from one subset of the database to the other. If we look from a budgeting perspective, actual numbers for the current years' actual months are copied to the budget or forecast scenario so that the forecast for the remaining months of the year or the budget of the next year can be created based on the actual data, and the year-to-date value can be calculated based on the actual data for the actual months as well as the forecast data for the forthcoming months.

So, in a nutshell, the copy would be from the same months/year to the same months/year, but the scenario would be changing:

- Actual to Forecast
- Actual to Budget

If we need to copy one month of data to the other, it copies between one subset and the other. Hence, we can make use of **Copy Data**.

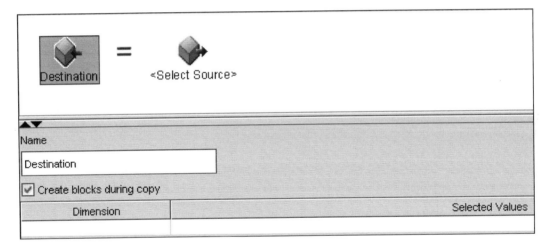

The copy data action looks like the previous screenshot. It's simpler to understand, we have a source and destination, and we know that we need to select the appropriate dimension member for source and destination to move data from one side to the other.

In these kinds of scenarios, copy data is very handy in planning Business rules.

Clear Data

As the title suggests, this action is helpful when we want to clear data from the Planning database.

It is also important for us to note that when a subset of database needs to be cleared from the Planning application, we can do so by selecting the appropriate dimensions and members for clearing. In real life, imagine that the planners have entered data for the month of August, the data representing the planned numbers. Now, management decides to go with a different perspective and decides to redo the exercise of Planning the month of August. In these kinds of situations, we can definitely delete the subset of the database, that is, only the August month Planned data with the help of **Clear Data** option.

There are two possible options, as we see in the next screenshot. **Clear cells only** is the CLEARDATA command and **Clear entire block** is the CLEARBLOCK command. These are Essbase commands and for the readers who are not familiar with them, go to the URL of Essbase for technical support.

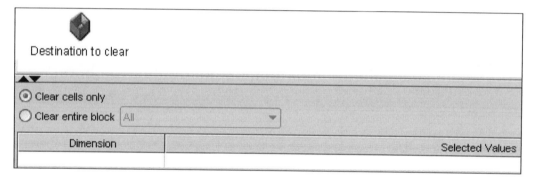

Create Blocks

Data blocks are created for the combination of sparse dimensions. We use the **Create Blocks** action to ensure that all the blocks are created from the sparse dimension combinations.

 Create Blocks actions are not applicable to the members with the property of **Dynamic calc** or **Label only** and the reason being that the block is not created as these members are not stored in the database physically, and also provide a reference to the chapter/ section where we have discussed storage types.

Formula

The following is the list of formulas that we can see in the **BR Language** tab, as shown in the next screenshot.

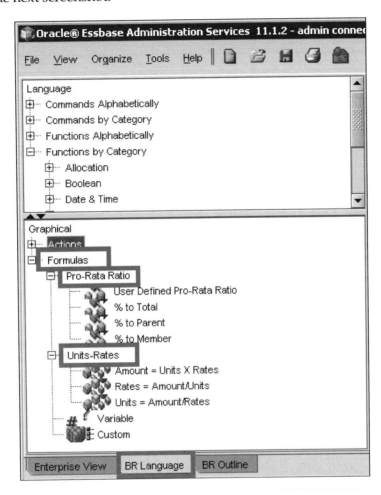

From the previous screenshot, we can see that there are two important options:

- **Pro-Rata Ratio**
- **Units-Rates**

We will explore these two options now.

Pro-Rata

Pro-Rata means 'in proportion to' or proportional ratio. It is taken as in proportion to some other member/factor. In general, **Pro-Rata** can be used in many forms and in many contexts too.

An example would be – an employee of SRGD firm is entitled to take 20 leaves a year and a gentleman joins the firm on the 5th March. Then we can calculate the leaves available to this employee, proportional to the number of days left for him in the year, that is, 20/365 * 302= 16.5.

Another example would be an even simpler one. If the interest rate is 12 percent per annum, then we can say on a **Pro-Rata** basis, it is 1 percent a month, that is, 12%/12.

Unit Rate

Firstly, rate is the ratio to compare and unit rate means how many units of a type corresponds to the other type

If the Internet cost is 100$ for 10 resources, then the rate is 100$ for 10 resources and the unit of rate would be 100$/10 resources, that is:

Units = 100$ amount / number of resources, that is, 10

Likewise, if we want to compute 'Amount', then we multiply units with the number of resources.

In **Unit-Rates**, we see three formulas as shown:

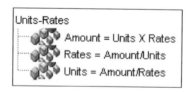

While we create a rule using any of these formulas, we select members for amount, unit, and rates, and perform computation. For example, if we want to calculate the amount of money spent on travel, that is, travel expense amount, we would multiply it as:

Average travel expense per person * number of people

Which means:

Travel expense amount = Average travel expense per person * number of people (or headcount)

Hence, we need to select the members travel expense amount, average travel expense per person, and number of people for amount, units, and rates respectively.

 When we are creating a Business rule, all we need to do is drag the appropriate command, action, or formula into the Business rule creation area. This is the ease with which a rule can be created by a user.

BR outline

The very first thing which we do while we create a Business rule is to select an outline. This outline might be of Essbase or Planning. In our case, we are interested in the Planning outline.

As we select a Planning outline, for example, SRGD – the outline of the same is reflected in 'BR outline'. Hence, BR outline gives us information of the outline for which the Business rule is being created on, and it is also helpful in looking at the outline contents, which would be very handy while we create a Business rule.

When we create our first Business Rule, we'll revisit the same tabs so that we can learn by example.

Creating a Business Rule

In this section, we'll learn how to create a Business rule in a step-by-step fashion. Before we start creating our first Business rule, we shall assume requirements and address the same by creating a Business rule.

 Business rules can be accessed not only through the EAS console, but through the Web using the URL:

`http://hostname:10080/hbrlauncher/`

The first and foremost thing before we start creating a Business rule is to get familiarized with the Planning outline. We need to be very in terms of aggregation and storage of the dimension member instances, as they would impact the calculation.

Requirement

As usual, we need to have a requirement and we shall assume the simple requirement first.

We have a planner by the name **Walt_owner**, who has responsibility of entering data for the **Massachusetts** location for its client **Global Entertainment Ltd**. This planner will enter data for the members **Avg Salary** and **Headcount** of the hierarchy **Statistical Drivers** of the **Accounts** dimension and the **Salaries** expense member of the **SG&A** hierarchy for the months of January, February, and March of 2010 should be calculated based on the values entered of **Avg Salary** and **Headcount**.

The version is **V1** and the scenario is **Plan**.

Prerequisites

Now, let us quickly create a data form as per the requirement. Log in to SRGD as 'admin' and create a data form by the name of 'Rule form', as shown in the next image:

Save the form and we also need to assign 'write' access to the data form for the user **Walt_owner**.

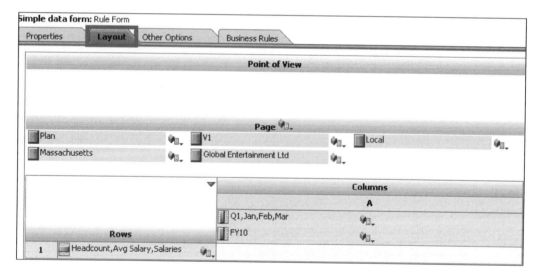

The Business Rule should not only take care of the calculating 'salary' expense, but also aggregate the value of *salary* to its parent SG&A and thereby rolling the values to PandL. It should also aggregate the values entered in January, February, and March to Quarters and Years.

Steps to create Business Rule

We'll divide the process of Business rules creation in multiple subsections as follows:

- Graphical/Source tab
- Doc
- Properties
- Locations
- Access Privileges
- Save
- Validate
- Launch

Graphical/Source

1. After we log in to the EAS console using the credentials of 'admin', expand Business rules and right-click on **Rules** to select **New rule**, as shown in the next screenshot:

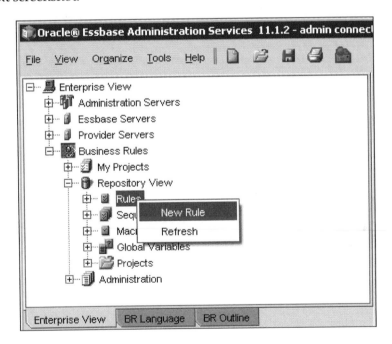

This will open the rule editor, where we observe the initial two tabs of **Graphical** and **Source**. A Business rule can made either in the **Graphical** or **Source** tab.

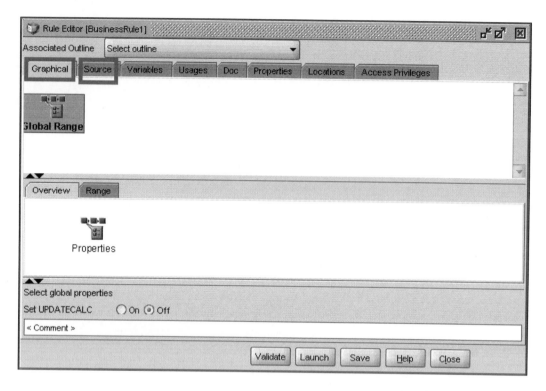

In the **Graphical** tab, we need to drag-and-drop the action, formula, or command, whereas in 'source' tab, we need to write scripts, that is, calculation scripts, which readers might have seen in Essbase. We'll stick to the **Graphical** tab for now to make the life of the rule creator easier and we will look at the **Source** tab later in the chapter.

We see the global property rounded in the above image. SET UPDATECALC is the setting to either enable or disable intelligent calculation. We are not getting into the basics or any more details of 'intelligent concept' of Essbase. As a recommendation, most of the times we can abstain from using this option for application development.

2. As said earlier, we can use the 'Source' tab to create Business rules as well. Go to the 'Source' tab and try to type some text as if we are creating a script. As we start typing, it throws an error message as shown in the following screenshot:

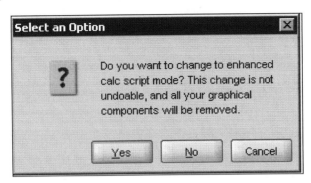

It clearly says that if we choose the **Source** tab, then the **Graphical** tab will not be available and this change cannot be undone. We'll select 'No' and get back to **Graphical** tab.

 In a real life scenario, most of the developers prefer and also use the **Source** tab to create Business rules, as they have already worked on calculation scripts in Essbase

3. In the process of creating a Business rule, the first and the foremost step is to select the outline. We can either select Essbase or the Planning outline. In our case, we have to select the Planning outline of the 'SRGD' Planning application.

Expand the drop-down of **Associated Outline** and select 'select outline', as shown in the next screenshot:

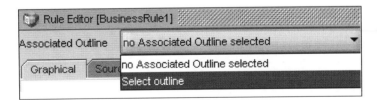

Selecting outline will lead to a new window, as shown in the next screenshot, where we can see both Planning and Essbase under **Available Servers**. Select the **Plan1** outline of the **SRGD** Planning application shown and select **OK**.

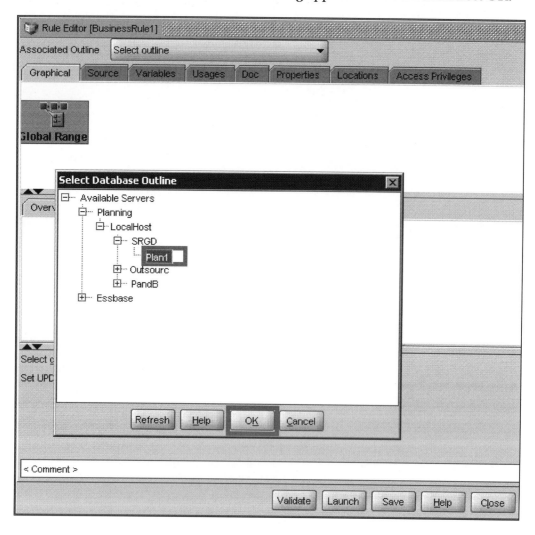

4. Now, select the **BR Language** tab to select the members and formulas by dragging-and-dropping into the rule editor.

   Drag-and-drop **Amount = Units X Rates** in the rule editor, which is under the **Units-Rates** formula, as shown in the next screenshot:

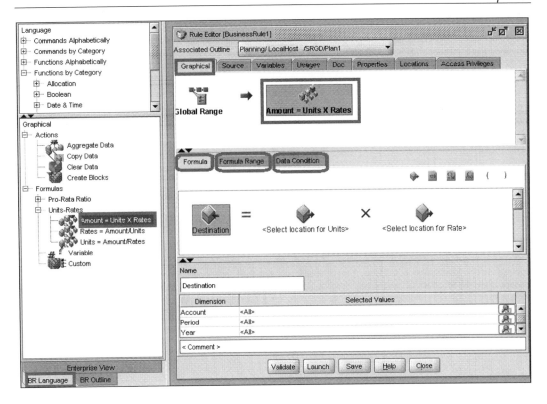

5. We see that there are three tabs in the previous image:

- ○ Formula
- ○ Formula Range
- ○ Data condition

Formula

In this tab, we need to select the members for Amount, Units, and Rates. We need to recall that the calculation that we want to achieve, as per our requirement, is:

Salary = Headcount * Avg Salary.

Now, we can relate the same with the formula. Select **Salary** account member for **Destination**, Headcount for **Select Location** for **Units**, and **Avg Salary** member for **Select Location for rates** option.

We select members as follows:

- **Salaries** of **Account** dimension for **Destination**
- **Avg Salary** of **Account** dimension for **select location for units**
- **Headcount** of **Account** dimension for **Select location for rate**

The same is shown in the next screenshot. First, we need to select **Destination** and then select the **Selected Values** of **Salaries** of **Account** dimension. Next, select **Select location for units** and then again browse for **Avg Salary** and select it. Finally, select **Select location for rate** and again browse to select **Headcount** of the **Account** dimension.

In the following image, we can only see the selection of **Destination** and its selected Account member of **Salaries**.

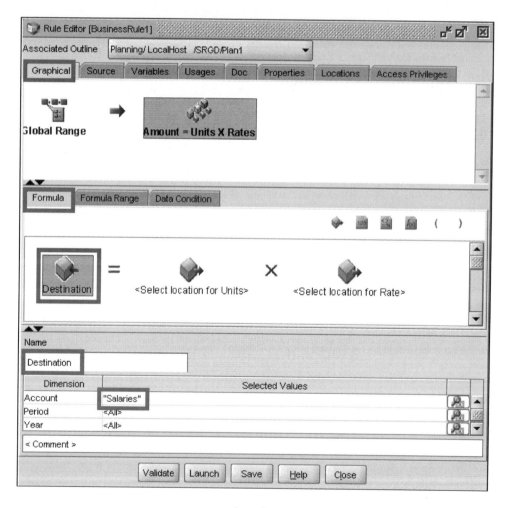

Formula Range

As per our requirement, the calculation is restricted to the **Plan** scenario, **V1** version, January to March period, **FY10 Year**, and also the client of **Global Entertainment Ltd** for the location of **Massachusetts**.

Now, in the **Formula Range**, we are going to select the members of other dimension to restrict and also make the Business rule relevant to the requirement, as shown in the following screenshot:

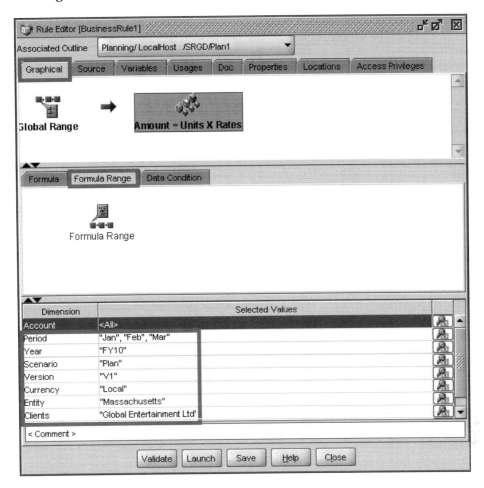

We need not select members for Account dimension as we have already selected them in the previous tab of **Formula**.

> While we create a rule, we can see the co-relation between the dimension member selection of the Data form, Rule form, and the selected values of the formula range.

Therefore, we use the formula range to restrict the computation of the Business Rule to a portion of the database, rather than the complete database.

Data condition

We can create customized formulas using this tab. The options available in this tab are:

- : This is for source. We can drag and select the members of the dimensions.

- : This drag-and-drop option will help in giving a number or a variable in our customized formula

- : This is for operators, that is, +, -, *, or /.

- : This is the selection of functions and finally we see options of parenthesis.

Hence, with the help of the options of 'Data condition', we can create our customized formulas. We'll not create any customized formulas as per our requirement of 'salary' computation.

So far, we are able to successfully embed the computation logic of salary. Now, we need to remember that **Salaries** is a child of **S&A** hierarchy and SG&A is a child of the **Accounts** dimension. We would want the value of *salaries* to be rolled up to the top-most 'account' level. Also, we would want the values for Jan, Feb and March to roll up to Quarters, that is, Quarter 1. Hence, we add the **Aggregate Data** action to the existing Business rule.

To do this, drag-and-drop the action of **Aggregate Data** from 'Actions' of the **BR Language** tab to the right-hand side, as shown in the next screenshot:

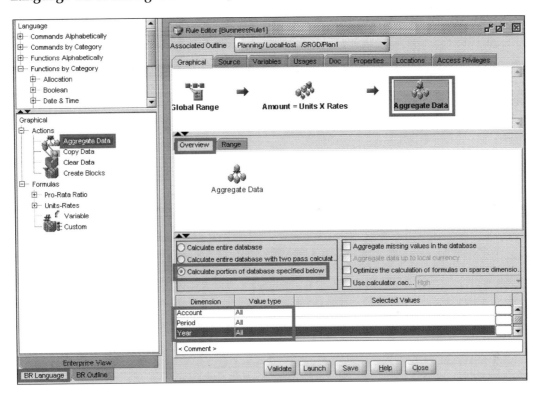

We won't aggregate the entire database; instead, we'll use a portion of the database with three dimensions, that is, **Account**, **Period**, and **Year**.

Now, before we move to the other tabs, select the **Source** tab to view the script, which got created as per our selection of formulas and members by the system.

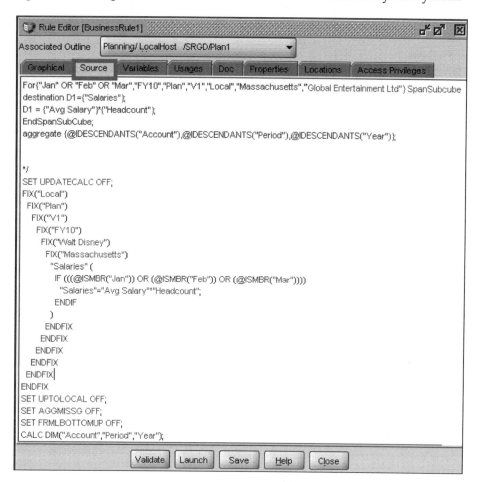

```
For{"Jan" OR "Feb" OR "Mar","FY10","Plan","V1","Local","Massachusetts","Global Entertainment Ltd"} SpanSubcube
destination D1={"Salaries"};
D1 = {"Avg Salary"}*{"Headcount"};
EndSpanSubCube;
aggregate {@IDESCENDANTS("Account"),@IDESCENDANTS("Period"),@IDESCENDANTS("Year")};




*/
SET UPDATECALC OFF;
FIX("Local")
 FIX("Plan")
  FIX("V1")
   FIX("FY10")
    FIX("Walt Disney")
     FIX("Massachusetts")
       "Salaries" (
        IF ((((@ISMBR("Jan")) OR (@ISMBR("Feb")) OR (@ISMBR("Mar"))))
         "Salaries"="Avg Salary"*"Headcount";
        ENDIF
       )
      ENDFIX
     ENDFIX
    ENDFIX
   ENDFIX
  ENDFIX
ENDFIX
SET UPTOLOCAL OFF;
SET AGGMISSG OFF;
SET FRMLBOTTOMUP OFF;
CALC DIM("Account","Period","Year");
```

Usages

There are sequences, which are a set of Business rules grouped together in an order to execute in a predefined sequence. In this tab of **Usages**, we can see which sequence the Business rule is a part of.

Yes, we have skipped the **Variables** tab, because we will learn about them in the next chapter. Till then, let us not bother ourselves with that.

 For a newly created rule, this tab will be always be empty.

Doc

We can summarize Business rule in this tab. This will help planners know about the Business rule in a simple manner without getting into the complex details of the **Source** tab or the **Graphical** tab.

We'll summarize our Business rule by typing, as highlighted in the next screenshot. Also, it is interesting to read all the information about the rule in the lower part of the screenshot.

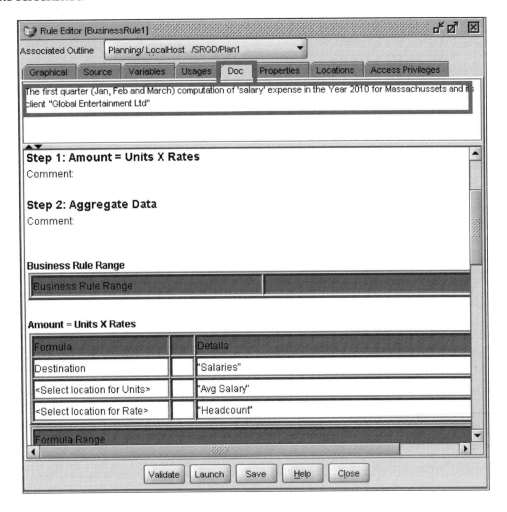

Properties

In this tab, we provide the basic information, such as the name of the rule, description, and owner of the Business rule.

There is an important option of **Locked**. This will prevent users other than **admin** from editing and viewing the Business rule, as shown in the next screenshot:

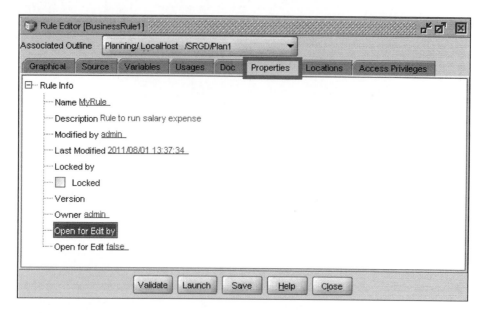

Go to the next tab, **Location**.

Location

Planners validate and execute a Business rule against a database, that is, a database location. In our case, it is the SRGD database location against which a rule is validated and even executed.

We don't see any location as of now. Select 'add', as shown in the following image, to add a location to our Business rule.

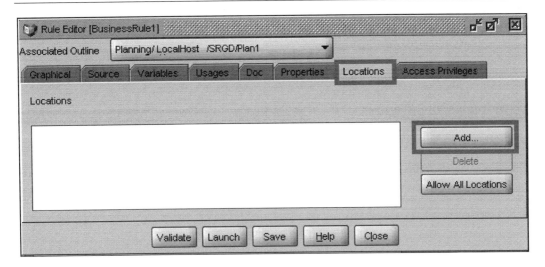

As we select 'add', it pop up a new window, and we'll select **Plan1** of the **SRGD** planning outline, as shown in the next screenshot:

Now, we'll move to the last tab of **Privilege** to assign access to the appropriate users.

Access Privileges

We grant users or groups the access privileges to Business rules in this tab. In this tab, we select the user and his/her role location (which we created in the previous step). Go to the tab and select **Add**, as shown in the next screenshot:

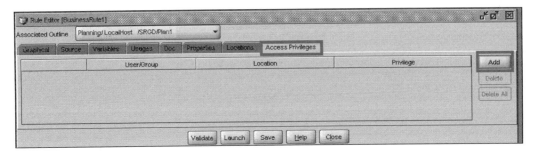

It opens a new window of **Add Privilege,** as shown in the next screenshot. Here, we have a list of all users and we know that **Walt_owner** will be the user who will execute this Business rule after entering planned numbers for **Global Entertainment Ltd client** for the **Massachusetts** regions. So select **Walt_owner**, as shown in the following screenshot:

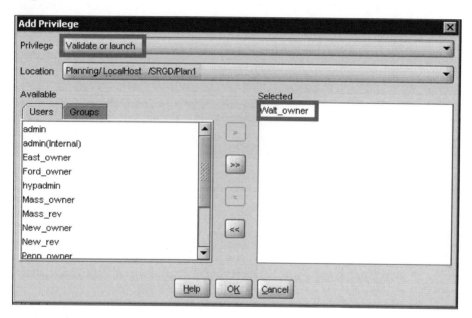

Select the location and the user **Walt_owner**, as shown, and then click on **OK**.

On similar lines, give privileges of both **Validate or launch** and **Modify rule repository objects** to the user **admin**. We are giving extra powers to the user **admin** as he/she can modify the rules in future. At the same time, we don't want a normal planner/user like **Walt_owner** to modify the rules. Hence, we have only given the **Validate** or **launch** options to him/her.

Post selection of appropriate privileges and locations for both **admin** and **Walt_ owner**, we should get the final image, as shown in the next screenshot:

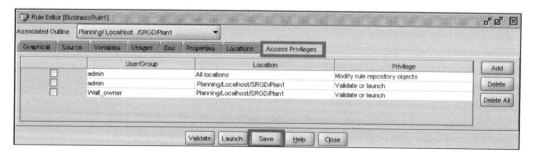

This provision of access privileges is responsible for a user (that is, **Walt_owner**) or even **admin** to execute a Business rule. It reconfirms that point that we need not assign a role of Business rule product to the planner (that is, **Walt_owner**) to execute a rule. Provision of the planner's role of the Planning product is good enough.

Save

Let us save the rule and select **Save** as we can see in the previous screenshot and it will lead to a pop-up window, which confirms the name of the rule and its description, which we had provided in the **Properties** tab.

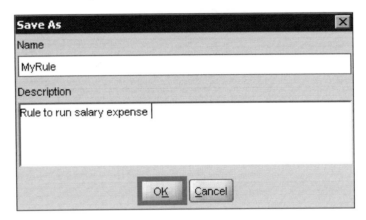

Select **OK** to complete saving our first Business rule, **MyRule**. Yes, we have created our first rule, but we would like to be sure if it is a flawless rule. To check if it is, we shall validate it, as shown in the next section

Validate

In this step, we validate the rule against the database location to see if there are any unwelcome errors. Validate will check if the members used in the rule exist in the database and also checks the syntax and returns error messages to debug.

After saving the rule, select the **Validate** button and it will rightly ask for the database location.

 A rule cannot be validated unless it is saved. Hence, we need to ensure that a Business rule is always saved before it is validated.

The next screenshot shows how a **validate** screen will look like.

Now, we need to remember that admin is the user with which we logged into the EAS console and we had already given the privilege of **Validate or launch** to the user admin already.

Select **Validate**, and if there are no errors, we will get the following message:

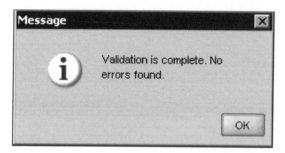

No errors found! Good, we wanted just that result. Now close the rule editor. This concludes the process of Business Rule creation, and in the next section, we will wear the mask of **Walt_owner**, enter data in the Data form, and execute the newly-created Business Rule, that is, **MyRule**.

Executing a Business Rule

In this section, we'll see how a user/planner would experience the execution of a Business Rule. In our case, the planner is **Walt_owner**.

- Data form and Business rules
- Business rule execution

Data Form and Business Rule

A planner **Walt_owner** will enter data values for **Avg Salary** and **Headcount** into the data form **Rule Form** and wishes to execute the Business rule, **MyRule**.

We had already learned in *Chapter 9*, *Data forms*, how to select a Business rule for a data form and execute the rule upon saving the data form.

Log in to **SRGD** as **admin** and go to:

Administration | Manage | Data forms and Adhoc grids.

Select **Rule form**, click on **Edit**, and go the last tab of Business rules. Here, select the rule **MyRule**, as shown in the next screenshot:

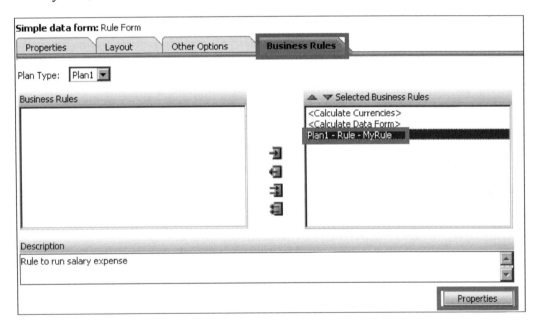

Select the rule, click on **Properties**, and tick the option of **Run on Save**.

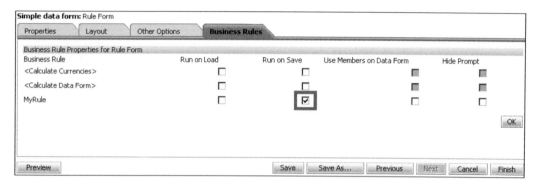

Now, we have a data form and the rule attached to it. We are good to go with the data entry and rule execution in the next section.

Business Rule execution

Now, log in to the Planning application of **SRGD** as a planner **Walt_owner** (username as **Walt_owner** and password as **password**) and straightaway open the data form **Rule Form**. The empty form looks like the next screenshot.

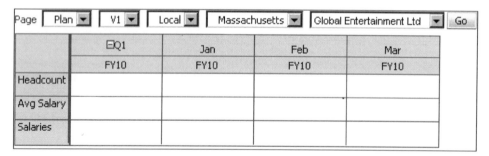

Fill in data for **Headcount** and **Avg Salary**, as shown in the next screenshot for the months of Jan, Feb, and March. Dark yellow reflects the unsaved data in the form.

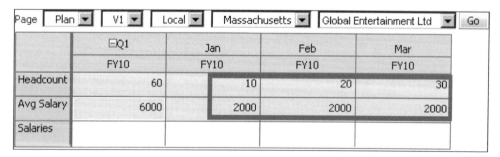

Click on the **Save** option or **Go** and we get the message, as shown in the next image. The message says that the data has been saved along with the successful run of the rule. We also see that with the help of Business rule execution the values of *salaries* has been computed.

	□Q1	Jan	Feb	Mar
	FY10	FY10	FY10	FY10
Headcount	60	10	20	30
Avg Salary	6000	2000	2000	2000
Salaries	120000	20000	40000	60000

The data has been saved. Rule was run successfully

Page: Plan | V1 | Local | Massachusetts | Global Entertainment Ltd | Go

The numbers of Salaries for the month of Jan, Feb, and March are calculated because of our **Amount = Units * Rates formula**. Whereas the number which we see in green in the previous screenshot is the result of the Aggregate Data method. Therefore, both the formula and method have come into action as far as the **MyRule** Business rule is concerned.

This is how the Business rule plays the most important role modestly in the background.

Summary

In this chapter about *Business Rules*, we started by learning the ways of achieving calculations in the Planning application with the help of Outline design, member formulas, and Business rules.

In the process of learning Business rules, we explored the Business rule roles that will take care of the security aspect of it. Later, we studied the basic components of a Business rule. After assuming a simple requirement of calculating **Salary** expense, we successfully created our first Business rule, and finally we learned the ways of executing or launching a Business rule.

In the next chapter, we'll continue our Business rules journey by working on some of the more advanced topics of these rules.

16
Advanced Business Rules

If you want a happy ending, that depends, of course, on where you stop your story.

— Orson Welles

As the proverb states, making a happy ending is in our hands, and we will stop our story right here in this chapter.

In this second chapter about business rules, we'll continue our journey and learn about the following topics:

- **Variables**: We'll learn about the different kinds of variables and also learn about using them in business rules

- **Run-time Prompts**: In this section, we'll explore the option to provide run time prompts to planners in order to allow them to select a variable for the execution of the business rule

Before we jump into the chapter, let us take a look at a conversation between a Hyperion Planning trainer and a trainee:

Trainee: *Sir, I have learned all about dimensions, metadata, and its loading, data forms, task lists, and also learned a lot about security as well.*

Trainer: *How about Business Rules?*

Trainee: *Yes sir, I have learned about Business Rules as well. However, I'm not quite confident about Business Rules.*

Trainer: *I completely understand. It's no surprise; most beginners feel the same way. Over time, with some experience, you will feel comfortable and confident with Business Rules. Don't worry, keep writing rules and you will be fine in a few months.*

Variables

In the previous chapter, we selected the appropriate dimension members and fixed them in Formula Range as per our requirement for calculating and selecting the data form `Rule Form`.

Let us take a look at this in more detail by opening the rule **MyRule**; we see that the rule has been confined to the dimension members highlighted in the following screenshot:

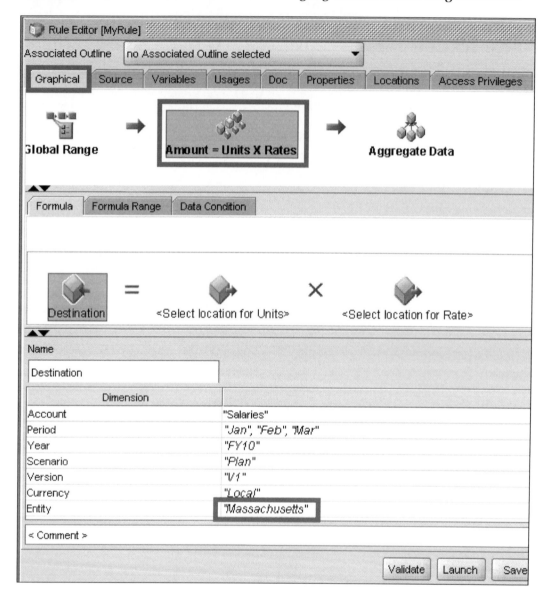

Imagine a requirement where the planner wants to select the Entity dimension member for the business rule on run-time basis dynamically, rather than fixing within the rule in Formula Range.

We see in the previous screenshot that **Massachusetts** has been selected and we know that the rule will run for this Entity dimension member only. In real time however, providing an option to a planner to select the Entity dimension member on run-time will be very handy. A planner can select Massachusetts or New York likewise.

In short, we are talking of his selection that is not fixed, but rather changeable or varying. Hence, we introduce the idea of variables in Business Rules, which will add functionality that allows planners to select a value for the variable as per their needs or requirements.

In the context of run-time prompts of Business Rules, there are two types of variables.

- Global variables
- Local variables

Global variables are applicable to all business rules, whereas local variables are applicable only to a single business rule. Global variables are available to be used for all business rules, whereas local variables are available only for those business rules in which they have been created.

We'll demonstrate both the variables in the subsequent sections.

Run time prompts

In this section, we will first assume the requirement for run time prompts and then understand in detail how Hyperion Planning application's Variables and Prompts work. We'll discuss:

- Requirements for run time prompts
- Global variables and run time prompts
- Business rules and local variables
- Business rules and data forms

Traditionally, we assume a requirement first to understand the concepts better. Let's start with the *Requirements* section.

Requirements

Planners enter the data into a data form and then save the form. The business rule, which is attached to the form, gets executed. This is the usual story that we have witnessed.

In the previous chapter, for data form `Rule Form`, the planner `Walt_owner` entered data for `Avg salary` and `headcount` for the months of Jan and Feb, and for the location **Massachusetts**, and saved the form to execute the rule. The rule runs and provides the calculated result of salary expense. This had already been demonstrated so far in the previous chapter. Now, let's complicate the requirement.

Our requirement is — we want a planner to select the location, client, and period at run time. Hence, the objective is to set system in a manner that the end user or planner gets a prompt at run-time and is requested to select which month, location, and which client wants the rule to be executed.

Prerequisites

To demonstrate run time prompts, create one more data form with the name `Rule form 2`. Select the layout and dimension members as shown in the next screenshot.

We need to pay attention in terms of selecting Client dimension members as **Global Entertainment Ltd**, **Global Teleco Ltd**, and **Global Motors Ltd**.

Also, we need to ensure that we select **Massachusetts**, **Pennsylvania**, and **New York** for Entity dimensions, as shown in the following screenshot:

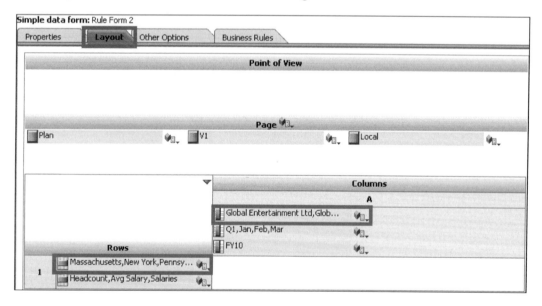

We need to ensure that the users `Walt_owner`, `Ford_owner`, and `Tele_owner` are all given write access to this new data form—`MyRule2`.

Run time prompts can be achieved with the help of both variables—Global and Local. We can create all global variables or local variables, but to explore both the variables we'll create one global variable for month, which is `Period`, and the other two variables for `Entity` and `client` as local variables.

Let us start with the global variable in the next section.

Creating global variables

There are many tabs that we'll visit during the course of our global variable's creation. They are:

- Variable
- Usages
- Properties
- Access Privileges

The Variable tab

1. First log in to the EAS console as an admin and expand the **Business Rules** as shown in the next screenshot. To create a new variable, right-click and select **New Variable**.

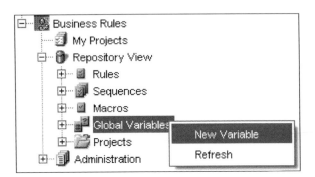

2. Clicking this opens a new window where we are going to fill in information of our first global variable.

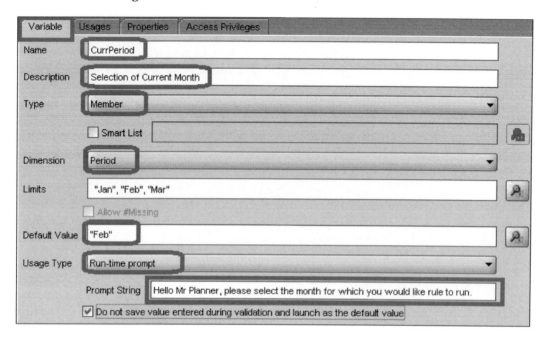

- ○ **Associated Outline**: We first need to select the outline on the top. Select **Select Outline** and do select the planning outline of SRGD.
- ○ **Name** and **Description**: Provide appropriate name and description for the global variable. We shall name it as CurrPeriod and description as Selection of Current Month.
- ○ **Type**: Next, we see a drop-down for **Type**. This is the type of global variable that we are going to create.

There are many options available here. We know that as per our requirement we need variables which would assume the values of period dimension members. Hence, we select member as the type, which means that the global variable type is a member of the selected dimension, which would be **Period** in this case.

What's the difference between the `Member` **and** `Members` **type?**

When we create a variable with type **Member**, we know that we want to prompt a planner with the member of a dimension. This member can be selected from all the available members of the dimension, whereas, **Members** is the variable type that will set the range of members of the dimension. In short, a variable with type **Member** allows only a single member from the allowed member list to be selected as its value, whereas one with type **Members** allow selection of multiple members.

In short, if the variable type is:

- ○ **Member**—only one member can be selected as variable value.

- ○ **Members**—multiple members can be selected as variable value. Which means that the rule will run for all the selected members

- ○ **Lists**—the list of members from which the member or members can be selected is determined based on the **Limits** option. The **Limits** option can be used in combination with both the **Member** and **Members** variable type, a planner can select any member of the dimension upon prompt. If the variable type is 'members', then a planner is restricted to select a member for a limited range of members of the dimension.

- **Dimension**: Select the dimension **Periods** from the drop-down. If we had not selected the outline of the SRGD planning application, we would not have got the drop-down of the planning dimensions.

- **Default Value**: We are creating a variable with the intent to provide run time prompts to the planner so as to select the desired period member from the available period members on the fly. This default value will now be the default selection of the period member of the whole list of available lists. As highlighted in the next screenshot, we need to select the default member. Click on the button and select **Feb** as the default period dimension member.

- **Usage Type**: There are three types of variables. The first two types can be called as non-run time prompt types, which are—**Use by value** and **Saved selection**. We are interested in the last option, which is **Run-time Prompt**.

- **Run-time prompt**: When a business rule is launched, that is, at run-time, the planner is prompted to provide values for the variables. This is exactly what our requirement is, and we would select this type for our first global variable.

- **Prompt String**: This is the prompt that a planner would receive at run time. Hence, we'll provide a relevant prompt string so that the planner is instructed of the period member selection, as shown in the previous screenshot.

- **Limits**: The purpose of the **Limits** option is just to specify the range of members from which the planner can select a desired member or members for rule execution. In our case, we will select **Jan, Feb**, and **Mar**.

> The **Limits** option has nothing to do with the type being selected; **Member** or **Members**. It works for both. The option is enabled or disabled is based on the **Usage Type**.
>
> It is extremely important to note that we cannot select members for **Limits** until and unless the **Usage Type** is selected as **Run-time prompt**. Therefore, first we have to select the **Usage Type** and then select the members for **Limits**, that is, the sequence is **Usage Type** selection followed by Limits member selection.

As we see in the previous screenshot, the option of **Do not save value entered during validation and launch as default value** is checked. We have already set the default value for the variable as **Feb**. Hence, when we try to launch the rule, it will prompt the planner, and the planner would see the default **Feb** member as the selected member for the variable. This option will be used to prevent the default value from being overwritten by the value selected by user during validation or launch.

We'll revisit this concept when we launch our business rule.

Usages

In the **Usages** tab, we can see which business rules are currently using the variables. Because we created a new variable `CurrPeriod` and did not include this variable in any business rule so far, we see an empty list in this tab as seen in the following screenshot:

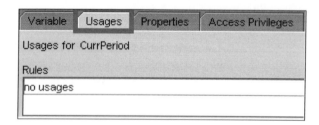

After we create a business rule and add this global variable to it, we would be able to see the rule name in the **Usages** tab. Take a look at this tab and then move on to the **Properties** tab. We will revisit this section in a little while.

Properties

The **Properties** tab looks familiar to us because we had used it while creating our first business rule. It answers a few important questions such as:

- Who is the user?
- Who last modified the rule?
- When did he modify it?
- Is the variable locked or not?

We can also see the owner information. It's editable and can be used to change the owner from admin to the other user.

Access privileges

An administrator has the provision to grant privileges that allow other users to modify the variable. He also has equal power to remove privileges already granted to any users. As we logged in to the EAS console using admin credentials, we can perform any of these mentioned actions.

We are not interested in providing any user with the privilege to modify this variable. Hence, leave this tab without any changes.

Save and close the window. As we try to save our changes, it will pop up the following window:

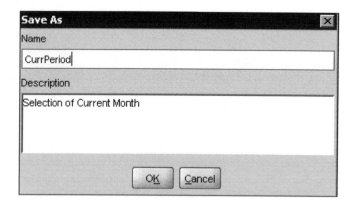

Select **OK** and save it.

We have now successfully created our first global variable. In the next section, we'll create two local variables as we create a business rule simultaneously.

Business Rules and local variables

In this section, we'll create two local variables. Local variables are applicable to and can only impact a business rule as they are created within a business rule. Hence, we'll create a new rule along with two local variables.

> There is no difference between a local and global variable in terms of functionality. The only difference is that local variables are local and affect only a business rule unlike the global variables, which can be used in multiple rules.

Let us straight away get into the creation of a new business rule with two local variables in the following steps:

1. Log in to the EAS console as admin. In **Enterprise View**, go to **Business Rules | Repository View | Rules**. Right-click on **Rules** and select **New Rule** to create a new one.

2. The very first thing before we start adding calculations and create variables, we need to associate the rule with an outline. Select the **SRGD Planning** outline.

3. We intend to create two local variables for the Entity and Client dimensions, which will be used in the business rule. Hence, go to the **Variables** tab to create local variables.

4. In the **Variables** tab, there are two sub sections—**Local Variables** and **Run-Time Prompts**. We first create local variables and then use them for run-time prompts. First things first, got to the **Local Variables** sub-section and select **Add** as highlighted in the following screenshot to create our first local variable:

5. This leads to a new window which is again very familiar to us. We have to provide information for fields similar to what we had done for global variable creation, as shown in the following screenshot:

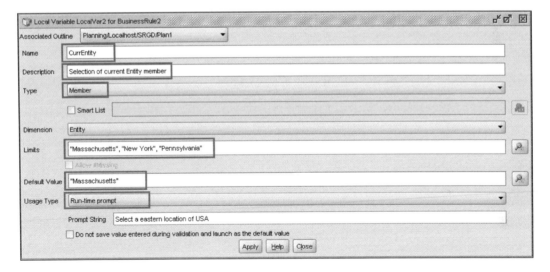

- ° **Associated Outline**: The outline of SRGD planning has already been selected.

- ° **Name** and **Description**: Provide an appropriate name and description for the variable. We will name it CurrEntity, as shown in the screenshot.

- ° **Type**: Select **Member** for type.

- ° In our case, as per our requirement, we want planner to select eastern location of USA, which is Massachusetts, New York, or Pennsylvania. Hence, we select the variable type as **Member**. If the requirement is to select both Massachusetts and New York, or New York and Pennsylvania, then we would have selected **Members**.

- ° **Limits**: We'll now select **Usage Type** as **Run-time Prompt**. As we select this usage type, immediately we can see the **Limit** option enabled and we'll select three Eastern locations as shown in the previous screenshot.

6. Save and apply the settings. As we select **Apply**, a new pop-up window appears as shown in the following screenshot:

7. Select **OK** to conclude the creation of our first local variable — `CurrEntity` — as shown in the next screenshot:

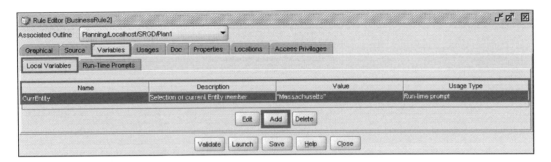

Now, we'll create one more local variable for the **Client** dimension member by the name `CurrClient`. We know that the clients for Massachusetts, New York, and Pennsylvania are Global Entertainment Ltd, Global Teleco Ltd, and Global Motors Ltd respectively. Select **Add** as shown in the previous screenshot to create one more local variable.

Hence, we'll create the local variable with type **Member** again and select the clients in **Limits** as shown in the next screenshot.

Provide information for **Name**, **Description**, **Type**, **Dimension**, and **Limits** as shown:

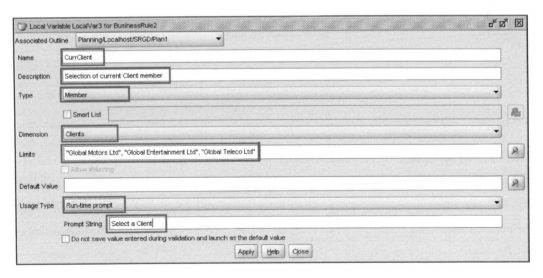

8. We had selected three members for **Limits** as shown. Now click on the 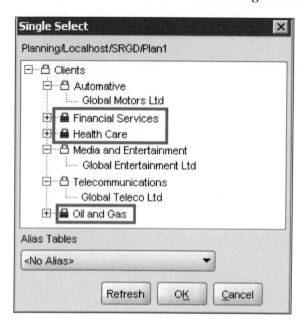 button next to **Default Value** to select a member. This opens a new member selection window which we can see in the following screenshot:

Paying closer attention, we see that **Financial Services**, **Health Care**, and **Oil and Gas** are locked. They are locked and we cannot select the members in the locked hierarchies. The simple reason being, we set the limit of the variable by selecting Global Motors Ltd, Global Teleco Ltd, and Global Entertainment Ltd, and the default value can be the member which has to be out of the limited set of three. We can observe that all the members are locked, but the only difference is that for the members—Automotive, Media, as well as Entertainment and Telecommunication, the lock color is different, highlighting that we need to select their children.

Select **Global Entertainment Ltd** as default. Save and apply your changes.

9. We have named the two local variables as CurrEntity and CurrClient. If you're wondering why there is no space between the two words 'current' and 'entity', then the answer is that name of a variables cannot have spaces in between and if we try to name so, then we would get the following error message:

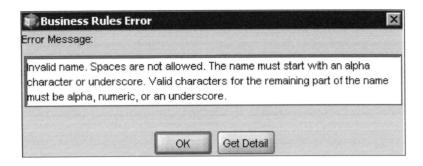

10. Therefore, we created two local variables, as you can see in the following screenshot:

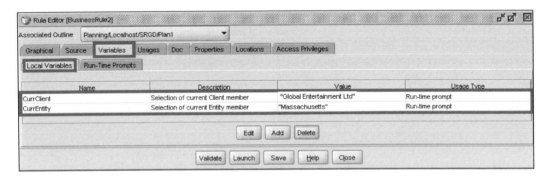

11. Remember that we had created one global variable that is `CurrPeriod`. Now, we'll add global variable `CurrPeriod` to the business rule. In the same **Variable** tab we see another sub-section **Run-Time Prompts** as shown in the next screenshot. Select **Run-Time Prompts** as shown.

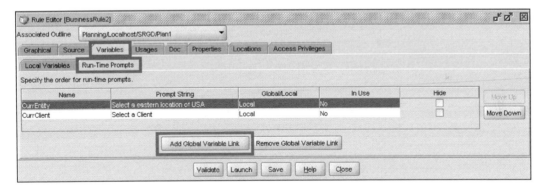

12. We see that in run-time prompts the 2 local variables are present and we see the highlighted information of **No** for **In Use** indicating that the run-time prompt variable is not currently in use in any of the business rules. The option will turn to **Yes** as soon as the variable is used in a business rule. That's exactly the reason, we see separate entries for each of the variable showing whether it is in use in the business rule or not.

We can change the order in which run-time prompts would appear to the planner with the help of the **Move Down** and **Move Up** options shown in the previous screenshot.

Now, select **Add Global Variable Link**, it will open a new window as shown in the following screenshot:

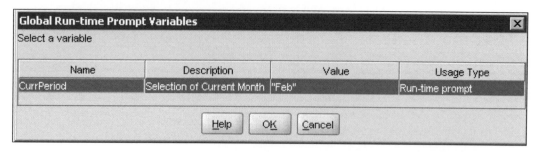

We can see the already created global variable `CurrPeriod`. Select it to add it to the rule. After the addition of the global variable, it would appear as follows:

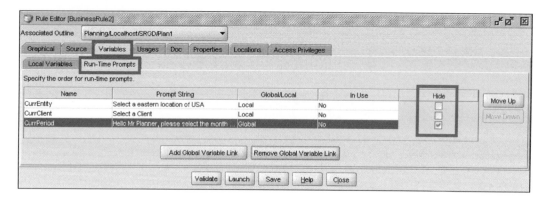

The right-most column **Hide** hides the variables from being prompted during run-time. Hence, we need to ensure that none of the variables are ticked under the **Hide** column. It is extremely important to unhide all the variables.

13. So far, we have only created local variables and added a global variable. We are still left with some more work on this business rule before we can use it in a data form. Go to the **Graphical** tab and select **BR language**.

Drag and drop **Amount = Units X Rates** as shown in the next screenshot.

Select **Destination** from the **Formula** tab and select the **Account** dimension as **Salaries** as shown in the following screenshot:

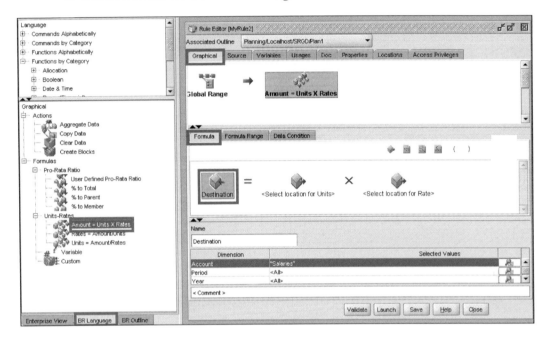

Likewise, select the following options:

  ○ Select **Headcount** from the **Account** dimension for **Select locations for Units**

  ○ Select **Average Sal** from the **Account** dimension for **Select location for Rate** from the **Formula** tab

14. Go to formula range. Here, we are going to select the variables which we had created so far. We created two local variables for the **Entity** and **Client** dimensions, and one global variable to assume the member of **Period** dimension.

First, we'll select the variables for **Period**, **Entity**, and **Clients**.

Let us start with the **Period** dimension. Click on the ![button] button, as highlighted in the following screenshot:

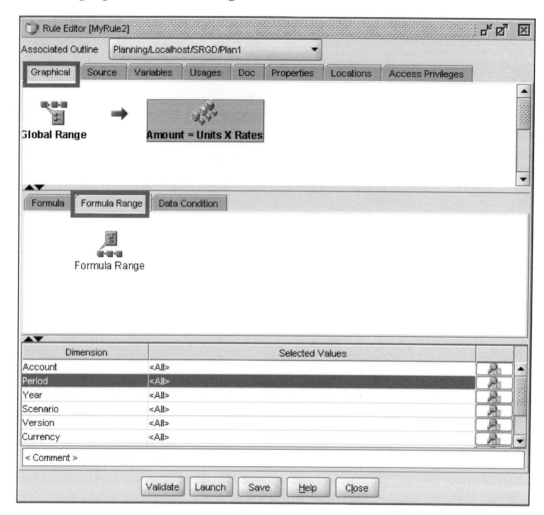

It will lead to a new member selection window.

15. In the **Period** dimension member selection window, we see that there are three tabs that we have not paid attention to so far. As we created a global variable to assume the **Period** dimension member, we shall not select any member in the **Member** tab; rather we'll select **Global Variables** as shown in the next screenshot.

In **Global Variables**, we see the variable **CurrPeriod**, which we had created earlier. Select the variable **CurrPeriod**.

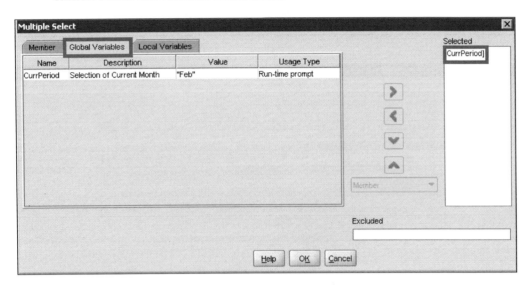

16. On similar lines, we have to select local variables for the **Entity** and **Client** dimensions. Click on the ⬛ button against the dimension **Entity** which will lead to a window in which we select the **Local Variable** tab and we can see the variable **CurrEntiy** which we had created earlier of the type **Member** and associated to **Entity** dimension. Hence, we could see the variable as it had already been associated with the dimension. Now, select the variable.

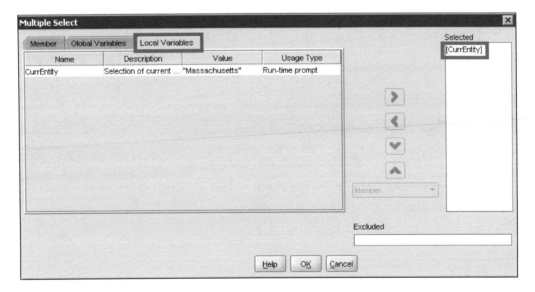

We can only see the **CurrEntity** local variable over here because it's of the type **Member** and was associated with the **Entity** dimension. However, the other local variable was associated with the **Client** dimension.

The Rule Development environment is intelligent enough to filter out non-applicable variables.

Similarly, select **CurrClient** for **Client** dimension.

After the selection of two local variables—CurrClient and CurrEntity, and one global variable—CurrPeriod, the editor screen should appear as follows:

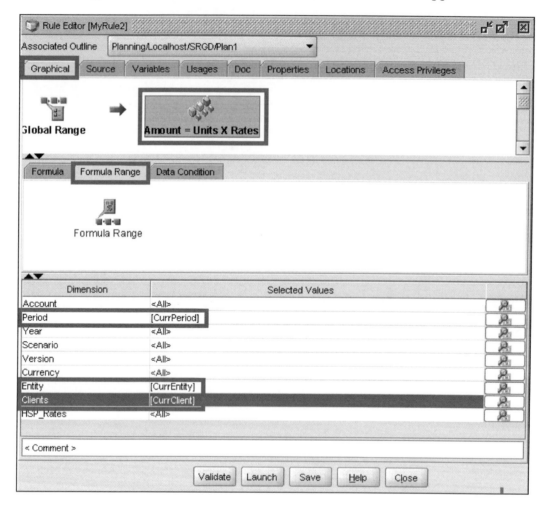

17. We are not yet done as far as **Formula Range** is concerned.

    We need to select the following members:

    - ° Select the member V1 for Version dimension
    - ° Select the member Plan for Scenario dimension.
    - ° Select the member FT10 for Year dimensions.

    We need to recall that these members are selected as per the member selection of **Page** in our data form.

    At the end of variable and member selections, your rule editor screen would appear as follows:

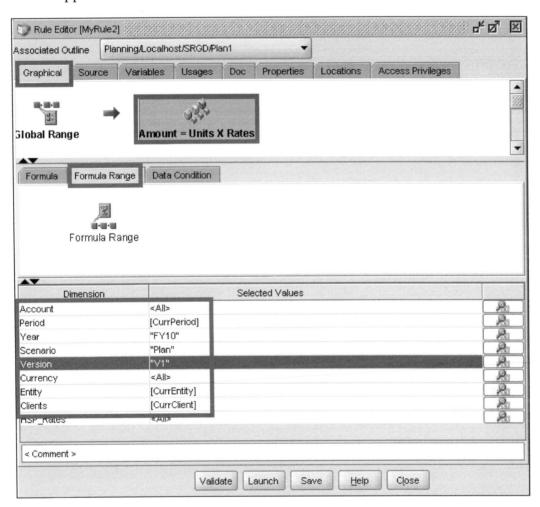

We can also add an **Aggregate Data** function in this rule, just as we had done in the previous chapter when we created our first rule.

18. We had already explored and worked in the **Variable** tab. Go to the **Properties** tab where we will name the business rule as MyRule2 and won't disturb the other fields of the **Properties** tab.

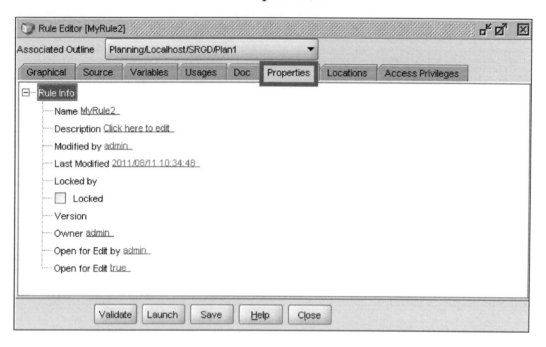

19. Go to the **Locations** tab. We would fist see it as empty; select the outline of **Plan1** of the SRGD Planning application by using the **Add** button as shown in the following screenshot:

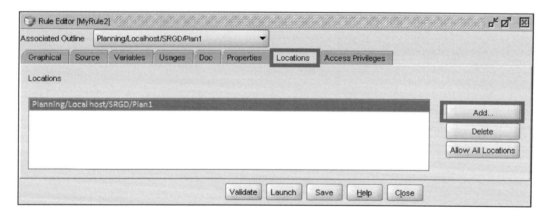

As far as `MyRule2` is concerned, we are dealing with the **Entity** dimension members of Massachusetts, New York, and Pennsylvania, while we have **Client** dimension members for Global Motors Ltd, Global Entertainment Ltd, and Global Teleco Ltd. We need to recall that these were the members that we had limited as far as our variables—`CurrEntity` and `CurrClients` are concerned.

Coming to the users, we need to refer to *Chapter 12*, *Budget Process Management* in the section *Creation of planning unit hierarchy*.

We can see that the following planners have the responsibility of filling in data for their respective **Client** and **Entity**:

Client	Entity	Planner
Global Motors Ltd	Pennsylvania	Ford_owner
Global Entertainment Ltd	Massachusetts	Walt_owner
Global Teleco Ltd	New York	Tele_owner

Hence, we will provide privilege of **Validate or launch** to the users— `Ford_owner`, `Walt_owner`, and `Tele_owner`, while we will give privileges of **Validate or Launch** and **Modify rule repository objects** to the user **admin**, as shown in the following screenshot:

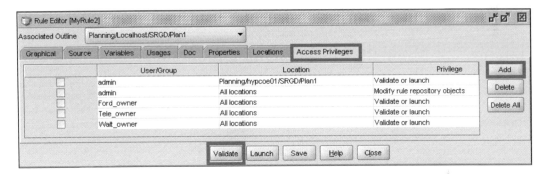

Save the form. We will validate it in the next step.

20. Select **Validate** to validate, as shown in the previous screenshot and it will pop up a window where we need to validate against the defined location.

It should be validating against all the run-time prompts (variables) including the global variable for **Period** unless any of the variables are hidden.

If all the variables (local and global) do not appear, we need to check if any of the variables are hidden.

Hence, we see three run-time prompts (variables) as shown in the following screenshot:

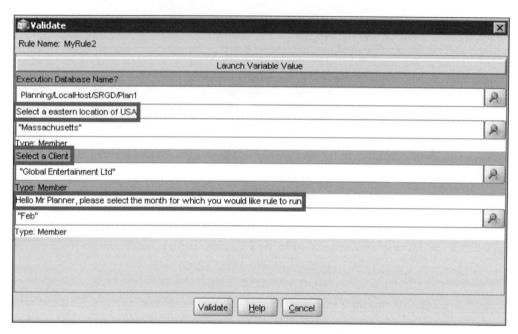

Upon selecting **Validate**, it will validate and give us a message that there are no errors, as follows:

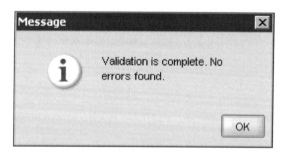

21. Save the rule.

Business Rule and Data Form

In this section, we'll associate the newly created business rule `MyRule2` to the data form—`Rule Form 2`, which we created earlier.

Login into the SRGD Planning application and go to **Administration | Manage | Data form and Ad hoc grids**.

Here, select the data form **Rule Form 2** and select **Edit** to add the newly created business rule to it.

The last tab of the form is **Business Rules**. Go to this tab and add the rule **My Rule 2** as shown:

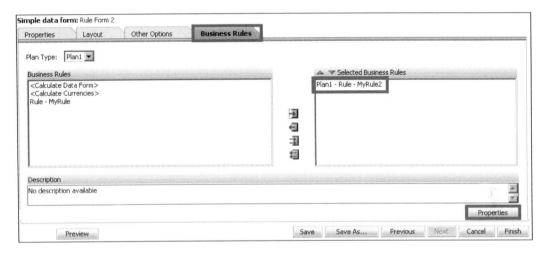

Select the rule and set its properties by selecting the highlighted **Properties** button as shown in the previous screenshot.

Check the **Run on Save** option. Also select the **Use Members on Data Form** option. Using this option will enable propagation of the members selected on the form in POV or page to the business rule run-time prompt automatically. This is an extremely important option.

Save the newly made changes to the form.

Runtime prompts

Now open the data form **Rule Form 2.** We see that **FY10, Plan,** and **V1** are in the data form that we had fixed in our business rule.

We can also see that the data for Global Entertainment Ltd for the months of Jan, Fen and March for Massachusetts are already present. We need to remember that these numbers were entered in the previous chapter.

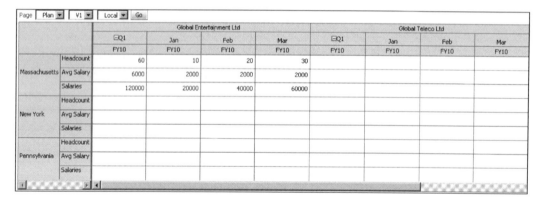

Now, we will enter data for the month of **Jan** and **Feb** for the location **New York**, and clients for its client Global Teleco Ltd for the months of Jan and Feb as shown in the next screenshot:

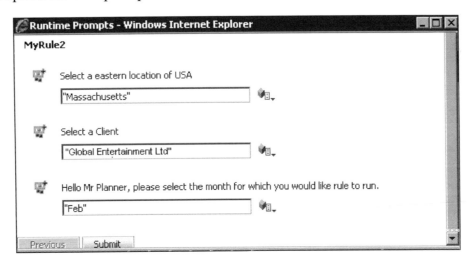

Page	Plan ▾	V1 ▾	Local ▾	Go							
		Global Entertainment Ltd				Global Teleco Ltd			
		⊟Q1	Jan	Feb	Mar	⊟Q1	Jan	Feb	Mar
		FY10	FY10	FY10	FY10	FY10	FY10	FY10	FY10
Massachusetts	Headcount	60	10	20	30				
	Avg Salary	6000	2000	2000	2000				
	Salaries	120000	20000	40000	60000				
New York	Headcount					90	40	50	
	Avg Salary					11000	5000	6000	
	Salaries								
Pennsylvania	Headcount								
	Avg Salary								
	Salaries								

We will enter data for both the months of Jan and Feb. But we will run the rule only for the month of Jan and see the result.

After entering data values, save it by clicking on the 🖫 button or click on **Go**. It will open a run time prompt window:

Now, we need to recall that the default selection of members such as Massachusetts, Global Entertainment Ltd and Feb is by the virtue of **Default Value** of the variables that we created at the beginning of this chapter.

Now, it is important to change the selection of **Entity, Client**, and **Period**, as we had entered values for New York, Global Teleco Ltd, and Jan. We are deliberately missing out Feb as we intend to check if the rule runs only for Jan in this case. Hence we do the selection of members as shown in the next screenshot and select **Submit**.

The business rule is set in a manner that it's supposed to be run on save. Hence, upon saving the form, it opens a new window, where it prompts the user with three variables and a clear message to select the Eastern location, client, month for entity, and period dimension respectively.

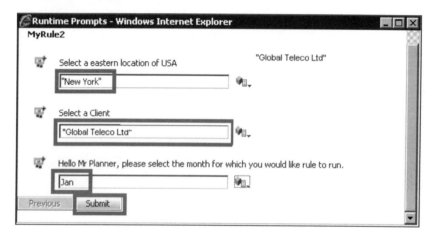

The data form will now take few seconds and return the following results:

		Global Entertainment Ltd				Global Teleco Ltd			
		⊟Q1 FY10	Jan FY10	Feb FY10	Mar FY10	⊟Q1 FY10	Jan FY10	Feb FY10	Mar FY10
Massachusetts	Headcount	60	10	20	30				
	Avg Salary	6000	2000	2000	2000				
	Salaries	120000	20000	40000	60000				
New York	Headcount					90	40	50	
	Avg Salary					11000	5000	6000	
	Salaries						200000		
Pennsylvania	Headcount								
	Avg Salary								
	Salaries								

The data has been saved.
Rule was run successfully

Page   Plan ▼   V1 ▼   Local ▼   Go

Our first observation is that the rule is run and data is saved, as clearly shown in the previous screenshot.

The most important observation is that the **Salaries** value is only computed for the month of **Jan** as **200000**, while it is not run for **Feb**, because we deliberately selected the month of **Jan** to run the rule.

Likewise, we can login into the SRGD Planning application as `Walt_owner`, `Ford_owner`, or `Tele_owner` and provide only the appropriate data for their location and client, and run the rule.

We can repeat the same by entering data for another location, entity, and period, and then run the rule.

These run time prompts are very handy as it gives a planner flexibility of running a rule of the location or period or so, which he wishes to run.

Summary

In this chapter, the second installment of *Business Rules*, we started by learning the concept of variables and we learned about two kinds of variables—Global and Local.

After assuming requirement, we had created data form to suite to our requirement and we had created a global variable for the **Period** dimension and two local variables for the **Entity** and **Client** dimensions. We have seen all the steps involved in variable creation.

We created a new rule, added the variables to it, and finally associated the rule with the earlier created data form, and finally we had demonstrated the run time prompt feature.

This is it!

Finally, we have come to the end of the road and I would like to thank the readers, who have given me company in my journey, right from creation of a sample Planning application to running complex business rules.

During this journey, we have created multiple Planning application and have explored all the subjects and objects of Hyperion Planning.

We started the book with the very basic understanding of the architecture of Oracle Hyperion Planning and then explored the basics of Planning, Budgeting, and Forecasting. We have also spent time in terms of understanding the very basics of financial terms like P&L, Balance sheet, and so on. It is because; these concepts will make us more fluent in terms of designing a Planning application and understanding a business requirement.

We then learned some shortcomings, as far as budgeting with spread sheets are concerned. Later, we introduced the necessity of a software product like Oracle Hyperion Planning.

From then onwards, we dove deep into the product by understanding its skeleton with the help of Planning dimensions. Initially, we tried our hands on a 'Sample Planning Application' and later we dared to create our own Planning application assuming requirements close to real life scenarios. We explored all the objects of Planning like Data forms, Task lists, Workflows, and Business rules. All of these objects and concepts were explored strictly from functional and technical aspects of budgeting.

I thank the readers again for buying and reading the book. I wish you all a great Hyperion career ahead.

Index

J

Java Application Server
and WebServer 16
JVM 271

L

layout, data forms
about 251, 252
Validation Rules 252
Layout tab 251
library job console, EPMA modules 141
local variables
used, for creating business rules 570-584
location, business role 552, 553

M

Make Data Form read-only property 254
mass allocate, miscellaneous options 307-309
member formulas
used, for calculation in planning application 524, 525
member name 340
members
about 341
HSP_RATES dimension 87
scenario dimension 82, 84
version dimension 84
metadata
about 218, 219
process 142
metadata load
about 225, 226
flat file 225, 227
outline load utility 225, 226
outline load utility, location 226
metadata process 142
miscallaneous options, data spread
about 304, 305
mass allocate 308
miscellaneous options, data spread
grid spread 305-307
mass allocate 307, 309
modes
about 479

advanced mode 481
basic mode 479, 480
multicurrency planning application
about 78
and single currency planning application, differences 78

N

not signed off state, free-form budgeting
approve action 430
promote action 430
reject action 430
sign off action 430
not started state, free-form budgeting
start action 428

O

object security
about 350, 371
data form, access 374, 375
data form, creating 372
data form, security access 372, 374
user access, to members 375-378
offline 19
online 19
operational planning 7
Oracle Business Intelligence (OBI)
about 17, 22, 24
and Hyperion Reporting Products 24
Oracle Data Integrator (ODI)
about 22
Financial Data Quality Management (FDQM) 23, 24
Oracle E-Delivery 38, 39
Oracle Enterprise Performance Management (EPM) 25, 26
Oracle EPM
about 10
architecture 28
configuration 48
configuring, in single machine 50
deployment 30-33
installation files, setting up 35
installation media, preparing 39
installation, on multi-machine deployment 48

usages tab, global variables 568
user authentication
  about 350, 357
  user, creating 358
  user creating, steps 359, 360
  user provisioning 360, 361
user-defined dimension 80
user groups
  need for 351
user provisioning 360-363
users and tasks
  about 350, 363, 364
  roles, planning 365-367
users import access
  about 384
  East_owner 385-387
  US_owner 384, 385
US_owner 384, 385

V

validate, business role 555, 556
validation rules
  actions 329
  and conditions 332
  condition 328
  creating 325-330
  data form, creating 322-325
  implementing 321, 322
  need for 320, 321
  operator 328
  process 329
  source type 328
  source value 328
  target type 329
  target value 329
  testing 331, 332
variables
  about 561, 562
  gloabal variables 563
  local variables 563
variable tab, global variables 565-568
version dimension
  about 201, 202, 240
  standard bottom-up 201

standard target 201
structure 240
version dimension, data entry
  about 282, 283
  case 1 283
  case 2 284
  case 3 284
version dimension, hyperion planning
    dimension
  about 84
  standard bottom up, member 84
  standard target, member 84
  view, in EAS console 86
  view, in planning application 86

W

Web and WebApp tier 28
WebAppSserver preparation 34
web browser preparation 34
WebServer
  and Java Application Server 16
web server preparation 33
workflow process
  about 400
  export, file based 418
  flat file, creating 418-422
  import, file based 418
  Planning Unit Hierarchy, creating 402
  requisites 400-402
  scenario and version assignment 417
  setting up, steps 400

Y

year and period dimension, hyperion
    planning dimension
  about 81
  view, in EAS console 82
  view, in planning application 82
year dimension 206
yes_boss 465

Z

zero foot print 18

Thank you for buying
Getting Started with Oracle Hyperion Planning 11

About Packt Publishing

Packt, pronounced 'packed', published its first book "Mastering phpMyAdmin for Effective MySQL Management" in April 2004 and subsequently continued to specialize in publishing highly focused books on specific technologies and solutions.

Our books and publications share the experiences of your fellow IT professionals in adapting and customizing today's systems, applications, and frameworks. Our solution based books give you the knowledge and power to customize the software and technologies you're using to get the job done. Packt books are more specific and less general than the IT books you have seen in the past. Our unique business model allows us to bring you more focused information, giving you more of what you need to know, and less of what you don't.

Packt is a modern, yet unique publishing company, which focuses on producing quality, cutting-edge books for communities of developers, administrators, and newbies alike. For more information, please visit our website: www.packtpub.com.

About Packt Enterprise

In 2010, Packt launched two new brands, Packt Enterprise and Packt Open Source, in order to continue its focus on specialization. This book is part of the Packt Enterprise brand, home to books published on enterprise software – software created by major vendors, including (but not limited to) IBM, Microsoft and Oracle, often for use in other corporations. Its titles will offer information relevant to a range of users of this software, including administrators, developers, architects, and end users.

Writing for Packt

We welcome all inquiries from people who are interested in authoring. Book proposals should be sent to author@packtpub.com. If your book idea is still at an early stage and you would like to discuss it first before writing a formal book proposal, contact us; one of our commissioning editors will get in touch with you.

We're not just looking for published authors; if you have strong technical skills but no writing experience, our experienced editors can help you develop a writing career, or simply get some additional reward for your expertise.

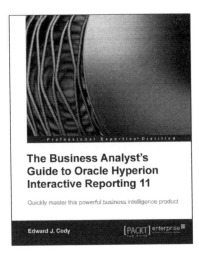

The Business Analyst's Guide to Oracle Hyperion Interactive Reporting 11

ISBN: 978-1-849680-36-3   Paperback: 232 pages

Quickly master the extremely robust and powerful Oracle Hyperion Interactive Reporting 11 tool

1. Get to grips with the most important, frequently used, and advanced features of Oracle Hyperion Interactive Reporting 11

2. A step-by-step Oracle Hyperion training guide packed with screenshots and clear explanations

3. Explore the features of Hyperion dashboards, reports, pivots, and charts

Oracle Essbase 9 Implementation Guide

ISBN: 978-1-847196-86-6   Paperback: 444 pages

Develop high-performance multidimensional analytic OLAP solutions with Oracle Essbase 9

1. Build multidimensional Essbase database cubes and develop analytical Essbase applications

2. Step-by-step instructions with expert tips from installation to implementation

3. Can be used to learn any version of Essbase starting from 4.x to 11.x

4. For beginners as well as experienced professionals; no Essbase experience required

Please check **www.PacktPub.com** for information on our titles

1949300R00330

Printed in Great Britain
by Amazon.co.uk, Ltd.,
Marston Gate.